Cognition, Creativity, and Behavior

Cognition, Creativity, and Behavior

Selected Essays

Robert Epstein

Foreword by Carl D. Cheney

Westport, Connecticut
London

Library of Congress Cataloging-in-Publication Data

Epstein, Robert.
  Cognition, creativity and behavior : selected essays / Robert
Epstein ; foreword by Carl D. Cheney.
      p.   cm.
  Includes bibliographical references and index.
  ISBN 0-275-94452-2 (alk. paper)
  1. Behaviorism (Psychology) 2. Cognition. 3. Creative ability.
  4. Skinner, B. F. (Burrhus Frederic), 1904–   . I. Title.
  BF199.E67   1996
  150.19'434—dc20   95-30657

British Library Cataloguing in Publication Data is available.

Copyright © 1996 by Robert Epstein

All rights reserved. No portion of this book may be
reproduced, by any process or technique, without the
express written consent of the publisher.

Library of Congress Catalog Card Number: 95-30657
ISBN: 0-275-94452-2

First published in 1996

Praeger Publishers, 88 Post Road West, Westport, CT 06881
An imprint of Greenwood Publishing Group, Inc.

Printed in the United States of America

The paper used in this book complies with the
Permanent Paper Standard issued by the National
Information Standards Organization (Z39.48–1984).

10 9 8 7 6 5 4 3 2

Copyright Acknowledgments

The author and publisher gratefully acknowledge permission to reprint the following material.

An expanded and edited version of Robert Epstein's "Generativity Theory and Creativity" in M. A. Runco & R. S. Albert (Eds.), *Theories of Creativity.* Newbury Park, CA: Sage Publications, 1990.

An edited version of Robert Epstein's "Bringing Cognition and Creativity into the Behavioral Laboratory" in T. J. Knapp & L. Robertson (Eds.). *Approaches to Cognition: Contrasts and Controversies.* Hillsdale, NJ: Lawrence Erlbaum Associates, 1986.

An expanded version of Robert Epstein's "How to Get a Great Idea." Reprinted with permission from the December 1992 *Reader's Digest.*

Robert Epstein, Robert P. Lanza, and B. F. Skinner (1980). "Symbolic Communication Between Two Pigeons (*Columba livia domestica*)," *Science, 207,* 543–545. Copyright 1980 by the American Association for the Advancement of Science.

Robert Epstein, Robert P. Lanza, and B. F. Skinner (1981). "'Self-Awareness' in the Pigeon." *Science, 212,* 695–696. Copyright 1981 by the American Association for the Advancement of Science.

Robert Epstein and B. F. Skinner (1981). "The Spontaneous Use of Memoranda by Pigeons." *Behaviour Analysis Letters, 1,* 241–246.

Robert Epstein and Samuel D. Medalie (1983). "The Spontaneous Use of a Tool by a Pigeon." *Behaviour Analysis Letters, 3,* 241–247.

Robert Epstein, C. E. Kirshnit, R. P. Lanza, and L. C. Rubin's "'Insight' in the Pigeon: Antecedents and Determinants of an Intelligent Performance." Reprinted by permission from *Nature,* vol. 308, pp. 61–62. Copyright © 1984 Macmillan Magazines Ltd.

Robert Epstein (1985). "The Spontaneous Interconnection of Three Repertoires." *The Psychological Record, 35,* 131–141.

Robert Epstein (1987). "The Spontaneous Interconnection of Four Repertoires of Behavior in a Pigeon (*Columba livia*)." *Journal of Comparative Psychology, 101,* no. 2, 197–201. Copyright 1987 by the American Psychological Association. Reprinted by permission of the publisher.

An edited version of Robert Epstein's "Simulation Research in the Analysis of Behavior" in A. Poling & R.W. Fuqua (Eds.), *Research Methods in Applied Behavior Analysis.* New York: Plenum Press, 1986.

Robert Epstein (1983). "Resurgence of Previously Reinforced Behavior During Extinction." *Behaviour Analysis Letters, 3,* 391–397.

Robert Epstein (1985). "Extinction-Induced Resurgence: Preliminary Investigations and Possible Applications." *The Psychological Record, 35,* 143–153.

Robert Epstein (1984). "Spontaneous and Deferred Imitation in the Pigeon." *Behavioural Processes, 9,* 347–354.

Reprinted from *Journal of Behavior Therapy and Experimental Psychiatry, 15,* Robert Epstein, "An Effect of Immediate Reinforcement and Delayed Punishment, with Possible Implications for Self-Control," 291–298. Copyright 1984, with the kind permission from Elsevier Science Ltd, The Boulevard, Langford Lane, Kidlington OX 5 1GB, UK.

Robert Epstein (1984). "The Case for Praxics." *The Behavior Analyst, 7,* 101–119.

Robert Epstein (1985). "Further Comments on Praxics: Why the Devotion to Behaviorism?" *The Behavior Analyst, 8,* 269–271.

Robert Epstein (1987). "The Debate about Praxics: Some Comments Meant Especially for Students." *The Behavior Analyst, 10,* 127–131.

M.J. Willard and Robert Epstein (1980). "Our Most Unforgettable Character." *The Behavior Analyst, 3,* 35–39.

Edited version of Robert Epstein (1991). "Skinner, Creativity, and the Problem of Spontaneous Behavior." *Psychological Science, 2,* no. 6, 362–370.

Robert Epstein (1986). "In the Yellow Wood" in S. Modgil & C. Modgil (Eds.), *B. F. Skinner: Consensus and Controversy.* Sussex, England: Falmer Press.

Robert Epstein (1982). "A Note on the Mythological Character of Categorization Research in Psychology." *The Journal of Mind and Behavior, 3,* no. 2, 161–169.

Robert Epstein (1984). "The Principle of Parsimony and Some Applications in Psychology." *The Journal of Mind and Behavior, 5,* no. 2, 119–130.

Edited version of Robert Epstein (1985). "The Positive Side Effects of Reinforcement: A Commentary on Balsam and Bondy (1983)." *Journal of Applied Behavior Analysis, 18,* no. 1, 73–78.

An expanded version of Robert Epstein's "Get Your Child to Say Yes." Reprinted with permission from the January 1992 *Reader's Digest.*

Robert Epstein (1992). "The Quest for the Thinking Computer." *AI Magazine, 13,* no. 2, 81–95. Copyright © 1992, American Association for Artificial Intelligence.

Edited and expanded version of Robert Epstein and Jon Koerner (1986). "The Self-Concept and Other Daemons." in J. Suls & A. Greenwald (Eds.), *Psychological Perspectives on the Self.* Vol. 3. Hillsdale, NJ: Erlbaum.

Robert Epstein (1981). "Growing Older, or What Else I Learned in Graduate School." *Harvard Magazine, 83,* no. 6, 5–6.

Robert Epstein (1985). "Why the Cognitivists Hate the Behaviorists: The Pecker-Envy Hypothesis." *The Journal of Irreproducible Results, 30.* no. 4, 31.

Every reasonable effort has been made to trace the owners of copyright materials in this book, but in some instances this has proven impossible. The author and publisher will be glad to receive information leading to more complete acknowledgments in subsequent printings of the book, and in the meantime extend their apologies for any omissions.

To Bill Mace,
scholar, role model, friend.

CONTENTS

Foreword		xi
Introduction		xiii
Part I	GENERATIVITY AND CREATIVITY	
1	Just How Predictable Is Human Behavior?	3
2	Generativity Theory and Creativity	13
3	Bringing Cognition and Creativity into the Behavioral Laboratory	37
4	How to Get a Great Idea	51
Part II	THE COLUMBAN SIMULATIONS	
5	Symbolic Communication Between Two Pigeons *(Columba livia domestica)*	63
6	"Self-Awareness" in the Pigeon	69
7	The Spontaneous Use of Memoranda by Pigeons	73
8	The Spontaneous Use of a Tool by a Pigeon	77
9	"Insight" in the Pigeon: Antecedents and Determinants of an Intelligent Performance	83
10	The Spontaneous Interconnection of Three Repertoires	89
11	The Spontaneous Interconnection of Four Repertoires	99
12	Simulation Research in the Analysis of Behavior	107
Part III	RESURGENCE, IMITATION, AND SELF-CONTROL	
13	Resurgence of Responding after the Cessation of Response-Independent Reinforcement	125

14	Resurgence of Previously Reinforced Behavior During Extinction	131
15	Extinction-Induced Resurgence: Preliminary Investigations and Possible Applications	137
16	Spontaneous and Deferred Imitation in the Pigeon	147
17	An Effect of Immediate Reinforcement and Delayed Punishment, with Possible Implications for Self-Control	153

Part IV BEYOND BEHAVIORISM: THE CASE FOR A SCIENCE OF BEHAVIOR

18	The Case for Praxics	165
19	Why the Devotion to Behaviorism?	189
20	Final Comments on Praxics	193

Part V B. F. SKINNER

21	Our Most Unforgettable Character	201
22	Behaviorist at Fifty	207
23	Skinner, Creativity, and the Problem of Spontaneous Behavior	209
24	In the Yellow Wood	223

Part VI COGITATIONS

25	The Myth of Categorization	229
26	The Principle of Parsimony and Some Applications in Psychology	237
27	The Positive Side Effects of Reinforcement	247
28	Should You Punish Your Child?	255
29	The Quest for the Thinking Computer	267
30	The Self-Concept and Other Daemons	279

Part VII GROWING OLDER

31	Growing Older, or What Else I Learned in Graduate School	303
32	Another Breakthrough in Data Interpretation at Harvard	307
33	Why the Cognitivists Hate the Behaviorists: The Pecker-Envy Hypothesis	309
34	A Day of Peace on Earth	313

References	315
Index	345

FOREWORD

The natural science known as the experimental analysis of behavior is sometimes accused of failing to deal with real-life issues or with complex cognitive aspects of human behavior. Some consider the field to be relevant only to rats pressing levers or pigeons pecking disks. But what of such phenomena as language, creativity, self-control, self-awareness, and problem solving? These are said to be the important issues with which we should be most concerned—the tough problems of modern psychological science. Can a rigorous, laboratory-based science of behavior tackle such phenomena?

The present volume helps meet the challenge. It demonstrates that many areas of complex human behavior can be treated in an objective way and, in so doing, shows how the experimental analysis of behavior can shed light on virtually any human behavior. In its rigor, it replaces mystery with understanding and wonder with technique—with methods for helping children, for enhancing creativity, for generating solutions to problems, and for investigating a wide range of everyday human endeavors. Because problems in our world are often due to excessive, inappropriate, or deficient human behavior, behavior should be investigated by the best means our culture can produce. This book is a step in the right direction. In my view, it includes some of the most original and important work to have appeared in many decades in the behavioral sciences.

Epstein's concept of generativity is an especially significant contribution, and his extension of Generativity Theory to the moment-to-moment analysis of the creative process is persuasive. The theory and the research pertaining to these issues by themselves justify the book. This work has far-reaching implications with regard to unraveling the continuous, probabilistic flow of the behavioral stream. Expansion of this topic by further research is waiting. It is curious how many aspects of the work reported in these papers await further elaboration by the behavioral sciences community; the breadth of Epstein's explorations has left us all with a great deal to do.

Robert Epstein is an energetic, always original scientist. He may not be able to do everything, but it seems he can do anything. His work and his writings, as the examples reported here demonstrate, range across many topics and contribute significantly to our understanding and appreciation of what a science of behavior is all about.

>Carl D. Cheney
>Professor of Psychology
>Utah State University

INTRODUCTION

Cognition, Creativity, and Behavior is a collection of papers about that formidable triumvirate. Here is where I stand on each topic:

Cognition. As a graduate student, I had the following bastardized quotation taped at eye level to the exterior of my office door:

> *Prayer of the Devout*
> *Cognitive Scientist*
>
> "Oh, Mind, if I have one,
> please reveal to me today
> the proper set of Rules—
> if there are any."
>
> —after Voltaire

Voltaire was actually more concerned with God and Soul,[1] but what the heck. I didn't think much of the study of mind, even if it had been dressed up with a nine-letter word ("cognition"). I was an adherent of the school of thinking called "behaviorism," about which I am occasionally critical in this volume. My mentor and friend, B. F. Skinner, was one of the principal authors of this school, and I disagreed with him about very little.

By 1983, about two years after I had completed my graduate training, my views began to evolve, in large part because of some historical research I was doing on the history of behaviorism (see Part IV) and, to some extent, because of the increasingly complex behavioral phenomena I was studying in the laboratory (Parts I, II, and III). My historical research convinced me that behaviorism, as such, was the unfortunate outcome of a turf battle in early psychology departments. Some early psychologists, especially those who studied animals, were interested in studying behavior for its own sake. Psychology as a distinct scientific discipline, however, had its roots in the German practice of "introspection," a tool for studying the mental world. The word "psychology" means the study of *mind*, and that's what the field was about.

Those concerned with behavior per se fought "battles" (see Chapter 20) for meager resources in fledgling departments, and they almost always lost. They responded, in part, by attacking the subject matter—the *sine qua non*—of their adversaries. Hence the constant attacks by Skinner and others on the study of mind.

I concluded, reluctantly, that the turf battle, which has been waged from about 1913 to the present day, was and still is a tragic mistake. Behavior is a legitimate subject matter for science, and so is mind, for those who are mindful of it.

I include "cognition" in the title also because of the behavioral phenomena I have studied. I have been concerned with complex performances by both humans and nonhumans—especially novel and problem-solving performances—the kinds that inspire theories of cognition. Unlike my mentor, I respect both the theories and the theoreticians who build them, and they in turn have taken interest in some of the interpretations I have offered. That's the way science should be. An "ism" and "battle lines" should never have been part of the picture. Behaviorism is baggage.

Ironically, it was Fred (the "F" stands for "Frederic") Skinner who pushed me over the brink of understanding. In 1983 he asked me to edit a manuscript of his entitled "Cognitive Science and Behaviorism" (Skinner, 1984), and it bothered me that after half a century he was still wasting his time bashing cognitivists. Why not just get on with the study of behavior and learn as much as we can from our colleagues in psychology and other fields? I made editorial changes in the manuscript, and I also sent him a ten-page proposal for creating a new, independent, biologically-based science of behavior.

To my delight, Fred sent me an encouraging note, which read in part:

> I agree with most of your paper on praxics. I have always thought it was the best Greek root but did not like those who used it....
>
> As I have said many times, behaviorism is the philosophy of a science of behavior, not that science.... I agree that the practicing scientist should not be called a behaviorist and that he or she suffers when so called in many ways. Nevertheless, behaviorism is well established in the field of philosophy as a philosophy, and I see no reason for abandoning it there.
>
> Praxics as the name of a special field reminds me of ethology, which certainly gains by using that word to distinguish a special branch of biology, but I believe ethologists remained in departments of biology.
>
> Certainly money is available for sciences, not for philosophies, and praxics may be better than the experimental analysis of behavior for that reason. I am not sure that praxicist is any better than behavior analyst, although I never like behavior used as an adjective.
>
> At the last meeting of ABA [Association for Behavior Analysis], three people came to me proposing some kind of superstructure to bring Division 25 [of the American Psychological Association], the Association for Behavior Analysis, and some of the behavior therapy and behavior education people under one roof. Possibly your Praxics Society could do that.[2]

Alas, the world needs more Skinners and not more "Skinnerians."

Creativity. Creativity is still considered by many to be mysterious, and only a small elite are said to possess it. I read claims of the sort almost daily, both in the popular press and in the literatures of mental health, education, and the behavioral sciences. The claims puzzle me. The laboratory phenomena I've observed over the years, in studies with both animals and people, have convinced me that creativity is both orderly and predictable—even the dramatic cases of creativity we label "insightful."

All behavior is "generative"—continuous, probabilistic, and novel—and generative processes are lawful (Part I). Moreover, no one has a lock on such processes. The people we label creative just have special skills, and anyone can acquire or augment such skills. This is, potentially, good news for our children, for our ailing businesses and industries, for the sciences, and for the leaders and experts struggling to deal with the world's many problems—if what has been learned in the laboratory can be transformed into viable technologies, and if such technologies are ever marketed and applied. Alas, scientific knowledge often travels in small circles, and the vast majority of the inventions listed in the U. S. Patent Office have never been produced. Myths about creativity and mismanagement of our creative resources might persist for a long time to come.

Behavior. Behavior is a legitimate subject matter for scientific inquiry, and it is, in my opinion, the most important subject matter in all the sciences. Few would challenge the first assertion, and I make the latter claim for two reasons. First, virtually all progress made by human beings—the invention of agriculture, the creation of law and government, advances in art and architecture—and virtually all problems suffered by human beings—the spread of AIDS, world hunger, the destruction of the environment—are essentially behavioral. People behave well or misbehave, with persuasive consequences.

Second, the practice of science itself is behavioral. Advances in molecular biology, quantum physics, materials science, and so on, depend on people behaving in certain ways: choosing careers in the sciences, appropriating funds, studying, challenging prevailing theories, improving methodologies, and so on. Advances in the scientific understanding of behavior should, in theory, be able to improve the practice of all science.

This volume includes about half of the papers I have published to date, and I've added a new paper, Chapter 1, to try to set the stage. I excluded papers that seemed wholly irrelevant to anything current, out of place in this volume, or overly technical—such as the study that demonstrates that standard laboratory pigeon feeders dispense food at "a monotonically increasing, negatively accelerated function of magazine-cycle duration" (based on the title, an editor at a commercial magazine thought the article had something to do with marketing strategies). My goals are (a) to present some relatively interesting papers that can stand alone and (b) to organize and edit them so that sections have some integrity and so that the overall volume paints a fairly consistent picture of my evolving views on cognition, creativity, and behavior.

Parts I and II focus on generativity research and theory and on some "Columban" (pigeon) simulations of human behavior, and Part III includes some related laboratory studies. As I have noted above, Part IV is concerned with efforts to create a comprehensive science of behavior, and Part V includes essays about Skinner, one of the principal architects of behaviorism. Part VI includes forays into artificial intelligence, child rearing, categorization research, and other topics, and Part VII takes the volume as far afield as I know how to travel at this point: to some uncertain reflections on growing older and to a modest proposal for a day of world peace.

One must make compromises in a collection of this sort. Papers on a particular topic tend to overlap; one can say the same thing in only so many ways. I have eliminated a few glaring redundancies, but that has meant nontrivial alterations in papers that have appeared previously; so much for the historical record. I have allowed other redundancies to remain for the sake of continuity within particular essays, and I have also expanded several of the articles. Popular magazines sometimes alter manuscripts dramatically for reasons of taste or space. Where articles have appeared in edited form in the popular press, I have chosen to include my original manuscripts rather than the magazine versions. The latter might prove to be more readable for introductory courses; complete references are given in the frontmatter of this volume.

Some of the research described in this collection was supported with funds from the National Science Foundation, the National Institute of Health, and Sigma Xi. Additional funds were provided by Aubrey Daniels and Associates and by a Presidential Award from National University. The Center for Behavioral Epidemiology of the School of Public Health at San Diego State University has provided valuable resources; my special thanks to Dr. Melbourne F. Hovell, Director of the Center. Dennis S. Thompson of Naturally Intelligent Software did much of the computer programming that has helped to propel my recent research.

I am grateful to Becky Brooks, a former student of mine at the University of California San Diego, for the many hours she devoted to helping me prepare this manuscript. My editor at Praeger, Liz Murphy, was patient and understanding to a fault, and for that I am grateful indeed. I also thank Shelly Bailey, my assistant at National University, for many comments and corrections, and Justin Epstein and Andi Shibata for editorial assistance. Finally, my heartfelt thanks to the many students and colleagues who helped me conduct all aspects of the research reported herein, as well as to the colleagues who have commented on the chapters as I composed them over the past fifteen years.

NOTES

1. According to Voltaire, the prayer of a certain Swiss captain before battle was:

   "Oh, God, if there is one, take
   pity on my soul—if I have one."

2. Letter from B. F. Skinner to Robert Epstein, May 14, 1984. Reprinted by permission of the B. F. Skinner Foundation.

PART I

GENERATIVITY AND CREATIVITY

1

JUST HOW PREDICTABLE IS HUMAN BEHAVIOR?

Summary. Human behavior appears to be orderly—perhaps even predictable moment-to-moment in time under laboratory conditions—but that should not be considered a threat to "free will." Determinism, the doctrine that all events have causes, is an unprovable assumption, held as a matter of faith by some scientists but not necessary to the scientific endeavor. Even if human behavior proves to be highly predictable under controlled conditions, it will always be difficult to predict outside the laboratory. Moreover, individuals will always *feel* free, if only because of the computational complexities required to make predictions.

We were sitting on the lawn in front of the Life Science Center, about ten of us. It was the first mild day of the spring of 1972, and we had successfully badgered our professor into holding the class outside. My hair was much longer then. Almost everyone's was long then, male and female.

We were discussing conformity and freedom, and I, the only avowed Skinnerian at Trinity College, was causing a ruckus. I insisted, echoing Skinner, that human behavior was orderly and predictable—even "determined," I hazarded, although I did not understand what that meant. These, of course, were fighting words to a group like this. "Prove it!" I was told. "*Prove* that our behavior is predictable!"

"Well, for one thing," I said, "your reactions to my assertions are quite predictable." (Ugly response.) "And, for another, even a total stranger would predict that you will behave very much like students in this situation. You will orient frequently toward the professor, signal him when you want to talk, take notes, and so on. Someone who knows you well as individuals could make more precise predictions. We all know, for example, that Radical Randy will talk the most and shout the loudest." (Evil eye from Randy.)

"This may not sound like much, but think of the hundreds of thousands of things you will *not* do in this situation. I predict, for example, that not one of you will dance a jig on this lawn while this class is meeting." (Not one of them had the good sense to jump up and dance, probably because they didn't know what a jig was.) "You will not make love out here, probably ever," (giggles) "you will not play with toys here, and you will not pull the hairs out of Dr. Mace's beard."

"Ahh, Epstein," (this from Randy, predictably), "but we are only here in the first place because we *want* to be. We are only following the rules because we *want* to. Everyone here—except *you*, maybe—is *free*." (Cheers from the others, also predictable.)

Poor Randy. I knew the answer to this one, too. I had read Skinner's *Beyond Freedom and Dignity*, which was a best-seller at the time.

I paused, dramatically. "You only *want* to be here because of prior events in your life, over which you had no control. You had no control over the parents or genes you got, over the neighborhood in which you were raised, over the schools you went to, over the teachers you were assigned, over the colleges that were foolish enough to admit you [this, to Randy], over the classes that were listed in the catalog, and over the topic that was assigned to us for this week. Unless I am mistaken, you also had no control over the weather today. Your sense of freedom, in other words, is an illusion. It's just a product of your ignorance." (I had been trained in a rather brutal debating style in high school.)

Well, after arguing dexterously along these lines for a while, I was pretty sure I had things wrapped up. Had I not *proven* that free will was an illusion?

To my amazement, no one was convinced. In fact, to my knowledge, I never convinced any of my fellow students that human behavior is predictable. All I ever really accomplished, I think, was to teach them not to discuss such matters in my presence.

I did not set out, years ago, to devise a more convincing proof. But my laboratory research seems, over the past dozen years, to have supplied me with the seeds of just such a proof.

DETERMINISM

Ism-words, with few exceptions, refer to ideas or concepts in which people "believe" or "have faith," often without question. Lutheranism, Communism, and Judaism, for example, entail concepts of this sort. If you believe in the Holy Trinity, no argument should be able to dissuade you. If you believe in Creationism, you will find a biblical rationale for the fossil record.

Psychology has had its share of isms. Those who subscribe to "nativism," for example, believe that human behavior is largely hereditary—that intelligence and other characteristics are inherited from one's parents. "Environmentalists," on the other hand, believe that experience makes us what we are. Those who believe in "behaviorism" assert, among other things, that mind, the traditional subject matter of psychology, is not worth studying.

Determinism is the doctrine that all events have causes. When applied to behavior, this means that everything we do, think, and say, is caused, fully, by prior events and current circumstances. Getting up in the morning is *caused* (by the diminution of sleep deprivation, by the sunrise, and by our alarm clocks); deciding to have toast instead of cereal is *caused* (by the freshness of the bread and sogginess of the cereal); and even indecision is *caused* (by the sogginess of the bread and sogginess of the cereal). Stated in its extreme form, determinism is the belief that all human action is *compelled*. It is the doctrine that we have no choice, that free will is an illusion. It is, in short, the doctrine I was espousing back in 1972 (though I didn't know it).

B. F. Skinner, who died in 1990, was a strict determinist. He believed that our behavior is determined fully by our genes, our environmental histories, and current circumstances. He could not prove this and never claimed to. It is not a hypothesis that he tested in the laboratory. He just *believed* it. He accepted it as a necessary working assumption of science: After all, why bother to look for order if you don't believe it's there in the first place?

Although Skinner became widely known for this deterministic stand, many other distinguished scientists and nonscientists have subscribed to this view. William James, an eminent philosopher of the last century who wrote America's first psychology textbook, was a determinist, as was the father of psychoanalysis, Sigmund Freud.

Even Mark Twain was a believer. He made a powerful case for determinism in a wonderful essay called "The Turning Point of My Life." Asked by an editor to pinpoint that critical point, at first Twain thought it might have been when, as a boy, an epidemic of measles swept through his town. His mother tried to confine him to his room, but he kept slipping out through his window to visit friends. To punish him, she apprenticed him to a printer, which is how he got interested in writing.

But no, he realized, that point was just a link in a long chain, no better than any other link. If his parents hadn't moved to that town when they did, he never would have gotten sick. And his parents would never have existed if his grandparents hadn't run across each other. Twain decides that the turning point in his life was when Caesar crossed the Rubicon. "Circumstance," Twain wrote, "is man's master—and when Circumstance commands, he must obey; he may argue the matter—that is his privilege, just as it is the honorable privilege of a falling body to argue with the attraction of gravitation—but it won't do any good, he must *obey*."

Twain made determinism sound appealing, but most philosophers and theologians reject it, in part because it seems to remove from our shoulders the responsibility for immoral behavior. The determinists argue, in turn, that even though people are not responsible for what they do, we can continue to punish immoral behavior simply for practical reasons.

Such issues are not decided by facts, because facts do not decide isms. Matters of faith are decided by role models, early rearing, traumatic experiences, and prevailing cultural values. In our culture, it is fashionable at the moment to believe that people have free will, so indeterminism generally rules the day.

Indeterminism has also emerged triumphant in modern physics. Early in the century, most physicists who cared about the matter used determinism as a working assumption, as Skinner always did. Quantum mechanics, which suggested that the movements of subatomic particles were probabilistic—that, as a result of some event, a particle *might* end up here or *might* end up there and that no more could be said—seemed, to some, to contradict determinism. In 1928, in his book *The Nature of the Physical World*, Eddington, following other prominent physicists of the day, argued that our understanding of the world could be advanced without determinism, and that view prevails today.

Science can never actually decide the matter of determinism. Experiments can never prove that all events are caused; neither can they show that an event is not caused. Science can't prove determinism, it can't disprove determinism, and, most important of all, it doesn't *need* determinism.

You are free to believe in it or not, as you please.

PREDICTABILITY

Although it can't shed any definitive light on determinism (or most other isms), science can tell us to what extent some phenomenon is *predictable*. We could argue 'til Armageddon about whether people have free will, or we could just pose a simpler question: How well can human behavior be predicted?

The social, behavioral, and biological sciences all suggest that the answer is "pretty well," at least in some situations. An economist will tell you that when a precious commodity is in short supply, the demand for it will increase. A social psychologist will predict an increase in aggression under crowded conditions. An ethologist will note the similarity in facial expressions from one culture to another. A physiologist concerned with cigarette smoking might predict that people who turn to low nicotine cigarettes will take deep drags and hold their breath longer than usual, thereby maintaining their usual nicotine levels. Developmental psychologists have shown that children begin to recognize themselves in mirrors at about eighteen months of age.

A list of all of the regularities various sciences have discovered in human behavior would be quite long. Clearly, human behavior is far from disorderly. Children walk before they run. Adults stop on red and go on green.

That doesn't settle the matter, however. Radical Randy would, I predict, be unimpressed with such a list. "Oh, yeah?" he would say. "Let's see you predict what I am going to say next." He would pause, and I would be in trouble.

For the most part, you see, science cannot make accurate predictions about individuals. Instead, it usually makes *actuarial* predictions. It makes predictions about what *many* or *most* people will do, or, in some cases, about what the "typical" person will do—even though the typical person might not even exist! For example, the consensus right now is that violent movies or television programs do not induce violent acts in young viewers. *In general*, a viewer will not turn violent after watching a violent act. Yet a number of gruesome exceptions to this rule have been documented. Do your children fit the rule or the exception? Unfortunately, no one can tell you for sure.

Something that may be true about a group may not be true about most of its members. For example, say that the average IQ in your town is 100 (it probably is). If you guess that the next person you see has an IQ of 100, you will probably be wrong. Even though the average is truly 100, you will find that very few people—less than 10 percent—will have that particular IQ. The vast majority will have higher or lower IQs. Wherever there is variability, it's difficult to make precise predictions.

Actuarial prediction has many practical applications; I don't mean to demean its importance. But the ultimate challenge has always been the prediction of the behavior of the individual. After all, if you can predict what every individual will do, it's a small matter to be able to predict what the group will do.

Randy would still not be satisfied, however. "You're just trying to get off easy, Bob." (I hated being called Bob; he would say it now just to irritate me.) "We all know that an individual's behavior is predictable over a long period of time. True, I brush my teeth every morning, eat three meals a day, and go to school every fall, but I'd like to see you predict what my right hand is going to do in the next ten seconds."

If human behavior is predictable, we should be able to do just that. We should be able, with reasonable success, to predict the behavior of an individual moment-to-moment in time. And I will go yet a step further—further, I predict, than even Randy would go. We should be able to make such a prediction even if we have placed our subject in a situation that he or she has never seen before. We should be able to predict *new* behavior in *new* situations moment-to-moment in time.

That, I think, would wrap it up.

GENERATIVITY THEORY

I have been at work for several years on a formal theory, called Generativity Theory, that makes predictions of this sort. It predicts ongoing behavior in new situations, continuously in time. The theory is mathematical, but the basic ideas behind it can be described in words.

You learn to do many things in your life—to tie your shoes, to find your way home, to open doors, to sing, to dance, to use a knife and fork, to drive a car, to ride a bicycle, to dress, to make a bed, to bake cakes, and so on. Nature provides you with many other abilities, some trivial and some not. You attack or run away when threatened; you blink when a speck of dust blows in your eye; you sneeze when your nasal passages are irritated.

You also learn the appropriate occasions for engaging in these behaviors. You don't open doors that say "Employees Only" unless you're an employee. You change your clothes in private, not on the subway. You don't tell jokes at funerals.

You learn such things in many ways, ways that behavioral scientists have been studying for nearly a century. You learn by observing others (your father puts the barbecue grill close to the fire, and the hamburgers are burning), by instructions (your mother tells you to move the grill up), by reinforcement and punishment (you touch the grill without a glove on and are burned), and by exposure to paired stimulus events (you hear a buzzing beside you, and a bee stings your arm). (What a lousy picnic!)

The behavior provided by your genetic endowment is also available, and it turns up frequently (you pull your hand away instantly from the hot grill, for example, and you shout and crouch after you are stung).

Note, however, that you are always going beyond the behavior you learned or were endowed with by evolution. Left to their own devices, organisms do new things constantly. Virtually every sentence one speaks or writes is new. A child quickly stacks building blocks into patterns he or she has never seen. Artists, composers, writers, and inventors do dramatically new things for a living.

In other words, as some linguists and Gestalt psychologists have put it, behavior is *productive* or *generative*. It is ever-changing and ever-novel. Even responses that appear to be the same are always different in some small way.

Generativity Theory suggests that new behavior is generated from old behavior, or, more precisely, that previously established behavior—established by any means—is constantly transformed into new behavior. The theory specifies a set of rules or laws, called *transformation functions*, which say how transformation comes about.

At the moment, the transformation functions are a set of four equations, each of which describes some simple behavioral phenomenon that has been studied in the laboratory.

The first equation describes a process often called "extinction": If some behavior is ineffective, you will eventually stop engaging in it. If you keep trying to catch the eye of someone to whom you are attracted, and he never responds, you will eventually stop trying.

The second equation describes a process called "reinforcement": If behavior is effective, the probability that you will engage in it again increases. If you manage to catch this fellow's eye, and he smiles, the probability that you will approach him greatly increases.

The third and fourth equations describe phenomena called "resurgence" and "automatic chaining," respectively. Resurgence is a very useful effect of extinction: When behavior that has recently been effective is no longer effective, other behavior that used to be effective under similar conditions tends to recur. Thus, when you turn the knob on your office door and, for some reason, the knob won't move, other behaviors that have gotten you through doors in the past rapidly increase in probability. You turn harder, you lift the knob up or push it down, you lean against the door or kick it, you shout for help. What you do depends on your history with doors.

The resurgence principle says that if one behavior *decreases* in probability, other behaviors will *increase* in probability. Automatic chaining says the opposite: If one behavior *increases* in probability, other behaviors will also *increase* in probability. It is often the case that something you do changes your environment in some way, and the change in your environment often makes it more likely that you will do something else. For example, you open a drawer to get a pen, and you spot a letter you meant to mail two weeks ago; the likelihood of retrieving and mailing the letter increases dramatically. Even turning your head can have profound effects, because it changes your visual field; if you look behind you and spot a mugger approaching, you will run.

Generativity Theory asserts that all of these processes (and undoubtedly others) act simultaneously. Moreover, they all act on all of the behaviors that can occur in the situation. The ever-changing, ever-novel character of behavior is, according to the theory, the inevitable result of the simultaneous actions of many processes acting on many behaviors.

The transformation functions generate a "probability profile": a graph that contains overlapping probability curves for any number of different behaviors. The probability curves show, at every point in time, the different probabilities of occurrence of each of the behaviors.

It is difficult to do justice to the transformation process in words. Thousands of computer operations are required to compute the changing probabilities of even a few behaviors. But you may find it helpful to think of the process as an *interconnection of repertoires*.

You have, by various means, learned thousands of different things. And, under most conditions, you are inclined to do more than one thing at the same time, either because multiple behaviors are resurging, or because you are exposed to stimuli that control many different behaviors. These separate behaviors constantly become interconnected in new ways: They come together in new sequences; for example, old words and phrases come together to produce new sentences. They sometimes merge into new forms: Different brush strokes blend into intermediate strokes; the words "huge" and "gigantic" become "gi-huge-ic."

Many creative people describe a process of this sort when they recall creative moments. Albert Einstein, for example, and the French mathematician Poincaré, each attributed their creative thoughts to interconnections that had somehow come about between radically different ideas. Rothenberg, a psychiatrist, said that creativity is the result of "Janusian" thinking; Janus was the god with two faces. The writer Arthur Koestler attributed creativity to "bisociation," which, he said, is "any mental occurrence simultaneously associated with two habitually incompatible contexts."

A variety of research with both animals and people has, in recent years, demonstrated the efficacy of Generativity Theory. As a number of chapters in this volume will show, a variety of complex behavior—even the behavior we call "creative"—is both orderly and predictable.

FREE WILL

Over lunch the other day, a friend told me that she was frightened by the possibility that human behavior—and, presumably, *her* behavior—was predictable. If our behavior is predictable, won't dictators have their way with us? Won't corporations charge us for the air we breathe? Is life even worth living?

Even a perfect Generativity Theory would not, in my opinion, pose the slightest threat. Dictators of one sort or another are always trying to have their way with us, and corporations are already trying to charge us for the air we breathe. People who seek to control others manage, by sheer determination, to stumble onto effective methods all the time, methods that scientists often even haven't considered. When it comes to the management of human behavior, practice is usually way ahead of theory.

If human behavior is predictable, then isn't free will an illusion, like I told my fellow students long ago? I've changed my mind about this (and perhaps I will again someday); I no longer try to convince people that they lack free will. Determinism, after all, can't be proven. And even with a theory of human predictability, we will still be free in some very real ways.

First of all, human behavior, like other phenomena in the physical world, seems to be probabilistic, which means, loosely speaking, that it is in the nature of behavior to vary. One can't hold one's hand still in midair for even a fraction of a second, and it's easy enough in the laboratory to arrange conditions under which two behaviors will compete with each other indefinitely. Generativity Theory predicts the *probability* of behavior, and it is possible that, in principle, we can do no better.

Second, predicting behavior is hard work. To do a good job, you need to know a great deal about your subject, and you need to do a great many computations. You can't do computations like that in your head. This means, for one thing, that you will always *feel* free; what you do, moment-to-moment, will always seem somewhat whimsical and mysterious. Similarly, the people around you will probably always seem unfathomable, just as they seem now.

Finally—and this is the key point—scientists will be justified in saying that human behavior is predictable when an effective set of principles has proved itself *under controlled conditions in the laboratory*. But even armed with such principles, *outside the laboratory scientists will be able to make only the most trivial predictions*. With very few exceptions, the real world is just too complicated for any serious predicting. The principles guiding the fall of a leaf are well understood, but predicting the path of any particular leaf would be extremely difficult; for all practical purposes, such a feat would be impossible.

No doubt some will feel that I have paid only lip service to free will. They will want to know *for certain* that they are free. But indeterminism, like determinism, cannot be proven. I can offer no more than I have.

Perhaps some will be disturbed by the mere prospect of a theory of human predictability, even if people are free in the ways I have described. But ignorance, too, is disturbing. And the facts, if they are there to be found, are bound to be found by someone. If human behavior proves now to be predictable, then, presumably, it always has been, and it always will be. Our finding out about it won't change the facts.

Having discovered the facts, it is the obligation of the scientific community to keep the public informed. An informed and educated public is always the best protection against abuse.

The public will probably benefit from Generativity Theory, as it has from many other scientific theories. The theory may help us to devise more effective problem-solving programs for computers, and it may also help us to improve ways to make ourselves and our children more creative. It suggests, for example, that since new behaviors occur when old ones combine, we will be more creative if we have diverse experiences. It also implies that people are more likely to do new and interesting things in enriched and challenging environments, designed to stimulate the occurrence of multiple repertoires.

As it stands now, Generativity Theory could be put to a curious test. Picture this: A man is sitting at a keyboard, occasionally pressing buttons. Lights flash intermittently. The transformation functions are continuously generating probability curves that predict what the subject will do during the next few seconds. You are watching these curves on a screen, occasionally glancing over at the subject to see what he actually does. The computer records the subject's responses as they occur, and it alters its subsequent predictions accordingly.

The computer could conceivably stay ahead of the subject by several seconds in this situation, with reasonable success. With the parameters better tailored to the individual, it could, presumably, do better. With a more powerful set of equations, it could, presumably, do better still. We could, in this very simple situation, predict the behavior of an individual moment-to-moment in time.

So, Randy—no longer very Radical, I suspect—what do you have to say now? (No, don't even bother. I think I know....)

2

GENERATIVITY THEORY AND CREATIVITY

Summary. Creative behavior is orderly and predictable. Previously established behavior manifests itself in orderly ways in new situations to produce new behavior, which in certain contexts is labeled "creative." The manner in which novel behavior emerges is describable by a set of transformation functions, each of which operates on the probability of every behavior that can occur in the situation. The functions predict continuous and probabilistic changes in behavior, which one might then label post hoc as interconnections. This concept, called Generativity Theory, has proved useful both in predicting and engineering increasingly complex, novel performances in nonhuman animals. It has also led to the development of an effective problem-solving algorithm derived from empirically-based principles of behavior, and it has allowed us to predict, with reasonable success, ongoing, novel performances in human subjects.

Novel human performances have recently been predicted with some success by equations and a computer algorithm, instances of a theory called Generativity Theory (Epstein, 1985a). The theory asserts that ongoing behavior is generated as the probabilities of a large number of behaviors are subjected continuously to a number of simple transformation functions, which are presumed to have physical reality in the nervous system. It treats behavior as novel, fluid, and probabilistic, rather than as stereotypic and repetitious, and hence the theory is a departure from many conventional, learning-type theories of behavior. Generativity Theory grew out of a series of studies in which novel, complex performances were constructed with pigeons.

THE COLUMBAN SIMULATIONS

In 1978 at Harvard University, B. F. Skinner and I began a project called the Columban Simulation Project, after *Columba livia*, the taxonomic name for pigeon. We set about trying to get pigeons to do some of the complex and mysterious things that people do, and we were successful in several instances. The simulations are significant in the present context in how they differ from most previous research on animal behavior. Previous research was concerned largely with training or conditioning—with procedures that brought about the *acquisition*, or, in some cases, the *maintenance* of behavior.

Pavlov's dogs, for example, acquired a new way of responding to a bell, and Thorndike's cats learned, rather clumsily, to escape from a box; they acquired, through reinforcement, the behavior they needed to open a door. In the extensive research on schedules of reinforcement that was systematized by Ferster and Skinner in 1957, we learned how behavior is maintained by the pace at which reinforcement is delivered. Particular patterns and rates of reinforcement, it was determined, produce particular patterns and rates of responding, and many researchers are still concerned with these relationships.

The first of the simulations was in this vein. Two pigeons were taught to engage in an exchange that suggested "symbolic communication." With the birds on either side of a clear partition, one "informed" the other about a hidden color, the latter "thanked" the informer, and so on (see Chapter 5). The birds engaged in the exchange repeatedly, and they did fairly little that had not been taught (Epstein, Lanza, & Skinner, 1980).

A second simulation, a follow-up of the first, was more illuminating. In the previous study one bird had learned to peck the color corresponding to each of three letters, and the other pigeon had learned to peck the letter corresponding to each of three colors. We switched the positions of the birds and trained each in the other's role; now each knew both sequences. Then, without providing further training, we removed the partition and gave a single bird access to both of the response panels at once.

Over a period of 15 minutes or so—without our intervention—the two sequences came together to produce a new one. The bird pecked behind a curtain at a hidden color, then pecked and thus illuminated a corresponding letter, and finally, pecked the corresponding color on the second response panel; by successfully matching the hidden color, the bird received food, and thus it repeated the sequence many times (Chapter 7). It appeared that the bird was pecking the letter key "in order to help it remember" the color it had seen behind the curtain. The same sequence emerged when we tested the other bird, and control procedures suggested that the birds were indeed using the letter keys as memoranda.

We had witnessed the spontaneous interconnection of two separate repertoires of behavior. We had this opportunity because—for a few minutes, anyway—we were not concerned with teaching the bird anything; rather, we allowed the bird to do something on its own. We were concerned, not with acquisition or maintenance, but with what some linguists and Gestalt psychologists call "production" or "generation."

A third study also resulted in significant behavior that was not trained. A bird that had been taught (a) to use a mirror to locate spots on the walls and floor of its chamber, and (b) to peck blue spots on visible parts of its body, proved able, without further training, to use a mirror to locate spots on its body which it could see only in a mirror (Chapter 6). Some psychologists claim that the ability to use a mirror in this fashion is a sign of "self-awareness" (for further discussion, see Chapters 3 and 30).

Questions began to take shape: On those occasions when behavior appeared that had not been trained, where had it come from? And did tools exist with which one could predict it? The answers were discouraging. Still, the Harvard studies led to others, conducted at Simmons College, the Foundation for Research on the Nervous System in Boston, and elsewhere, in which more dramatic cases of novel behavior were generated and, finally, to tools for analyzing, predicting, and constructing such performances in both humans and nonhumans.

ANALYZING NOVEL BEHAVIOR

The analysis of novel, ongoing behavior involves two separate tasks. First, one must assess the contribution made by an organism's history (cf. Birch, 1945; Köhler, 1925; Schiller, 1952; Shurcliff, Brown, & Stollnitz, 1971). What an organism will do, moment-to-moment in time, either in an old situation or a new one, depends on what has happened to it in the past. Ideally, we should try to assess the contribution of both ontogenic and phylogenic histories.

The contribution of previous learning may be studied easily enough, at least with laboratory animals. One simply provides or fails to provide certain experiences and then places the animal in the situation of interest. By systematically varying histories in this fashion, one can assess the contributions that they make to the performances that emerge in that situation.

But the behavior that appears will, almost certainly, be different than the behavior that has already been established. Even in old situations, organisms do new things. With the same teeth and the same toothbrush, one never brushes one's teeth the same way twice. And even in familiar situations, every sentence one speaks or writes is new in some way. In new situations, especially ones in which old behavior is ineffective, dramatic new behavior can occur, behavior people sometimes label "creative" or "insightful."

Old situation or new, a second, more difficult task is suggested. We must discover a set of principles that will allow us to predict how previously established behavior is transformed into new behavior in given situations—a set of "transformation functions" (cf. Bingham, 1929; Chomsky, 1965; Hull, 1935; Maier & Schneirla, 1935; Sternberg, 1988; Wertheimer, 1945).

I will elaborate these tasks by exploring three classic cases of complex behavior. The first two involve novel performances in pigeons, and the third, problem-solving behavior in humans.

"INSIGHT"

In 1917 the German psychologist Wolfgang Köhler showed that chimpanzees could solve a variety of mechanical problems in a remarkably human-like way. A wide range of performances was reported. As is the case with humans, the animals failed most of the time, and most of the successful performances were haphazard and clumsy. But, occasionally, something remarkable happened. An animal looked thoughtful for a while and then, quite suddenly, solved the problem rapidly and completely. It did everything but shout "Eureka." Köhler (1925) called this kind of performance "insightful," and its occurrence was said to show that the mechanistic analysis of behavior was inadequate.

Perhaps Köhler's most famous case of "insight" involved the box-and-banana problem: Six chimpanzees were placed in a large room in which a banana was suspended out of reach. A wooden box was available on the floor. After a number of fruitless attempts to get at the banana by jumping, most of the chimps lost interest. But one, Sultan, looked pensive. He looked back and forth from the box to the banana, and then, after about 5 minutes, suddenly moved the box less than a meter away from the position on the floor beneath the banana and, wrote Köhler, "springing upwards with all his force, tore down the banana" (Köhler, 1925, p. 38).

In a study published in 1984, my colleagues and I showed that pigeons could solve the box-and-banana problem in an equally dramatic fashion the first time they were presented with it (see Chapter 9). Each pigeon was confronted with the following situation: A small facsimile of a banana was suspended out of the pigeon's reach in a position selected by a random number, and a box was placed elsewhere in the chamber. The pigeon had received food in the past for pecking the banana, and it had also learned that making contact with the banana by jumping and flying did not bring food.

Each of three pigeons that had acquired relevant skills before the test—skills that chimpanzees and children acquire when they are very young—solved the problem in about 1 minute: At first the pigeon looked confused. It stretched toward the banana, looked back and forth from the banana to the box, and so on. Then, quite suddenly, it began to push the box toward the banana, sighting the banana as it pushed. Each pigeon stopped pushing when the box was beneath the banana and then immediately climbed and pecked.

To try to understand this performance, we first investigated the role that previous experience played in its emergence. The three birds who were successful had learned the following:

1) *Directional pushing*. The pigeons had received food for pushing the small box toward a green spot placed at random positions along the base of the chamber. It takes weeks or months to train a pigeon to push toward targets in this way, and many steps are involved. At first the pigeon earns food simply by pushing, then by pecking the green spot, then by orienting toward the spot and pushing toward it slightly, and so on (Chapter 10).

2) *Climbing and pecking*. The pigeon received food for stepping onto a series of progressively taller boxes. Then a box was fixed in position on the floor, and the banana was suspended over it. The pigeon received food for climbing onto the box and pecking the banana. The position of the box and banana was varied.

3) *Extinction of jumping and flying*. The banana was suspended out of reach of the bird, no box was available, and no food was presented. The bird was left in this situation until jumping and flying toward the banana disappeared.

Different training histories produced systematically different outcomes. With one bird we established both the climbing and pushing repertoires, but we did not extinguish jumping and flying. Like Sultan, this bird jumped (and, unlike Sultan, it also flew) toward the banana when given the test. After about 5 minutes, jumping and flying disappeared, and the bird solved the problem within the following 2 minutes.

We gave two other birds food for pecking the banana when it was within reach, but we did not teach climbing. When the banana was suspended over the box, each bird stretched repeatedly toward the banana, but neither successfully climbed and pecked. Apparently, without a history of climbing, a pigeon will have trouble with the box-and-banana problem.

With two other birds we taught climbing and pecking, and we also extinguished jumping and flying, but we did not teach pushing. Neither bird pushed the box when given the test.

We taught two birds simply to push the box for long periods of time. We never taught them to push toward a target. We also established climbing and pecking and extinguished jumping and flying. When given the test, each bird pushed the box aimlessly for long periods of time. Each looked up only rarely. One bird, after 14 minutes of pushing, looked up when the box was beneath the banana; it immediately climbed and pecked. In contrast, the three birds that had learned directional pushing pushed smoothly toward the banana.

It seems that novel performances vary systematically with training history, but that only raises more difficult questions. How, moment-to-moment in time, do previously established repertoires become interconnected? Where, in short, did the new performances come from?

For convenience, I will divide the performance into four parts, although these divisions are somewhat arbitrary and the analysis of the performance will be oversimplified because of them. I will consider (1) the period of apparent confusion, (2) the first push, (3) the pushes that bring the box to the banana, and (4) the cessation of pushing.

Apparent confusion. The first, apparently chaotic, responses we see can be understood in terms of a phenomenon called *stimulus matching*. The bird's training has made two stimulus configurations meaningful: banana-over-box, which is the occasion upon which pecking the banana has paid off, and box-with-spot, which is the occasion upon which pushing has paid off.

These two stimuli can be considered ends of a continuum of stimuli in which the test configuration is an intermediate case (Figure 2.1). In other words, the test situation contains elements of two stimuli that control two different behaviors. It contains what might be called "multiple controlling stimuli." When an organism is first confronted with more than one controlling stimulus, each of the responses controlled by the separate stimuli tends to occur. For example, a new driver who is approaching a stoplight on which both red and green are illuminated will feel confused and will tend to stop *and* go—literally to move the right foot back and forth between the accelerator and brake pedals. The competition is unstable; at the intersection, other factors come into play, and the driver eventually proceeds.

In the laboratory, the effects of multiple controlling stimuli or intermediate stimuli can be studied in an experiment of this sort: A pigeon is placed in an enclosed chamber in which are located a standard automatic feeder and two standard plastic keys. Over the two keys is a row of 12 small lights. When light 1 is illuminated, the pigeon receives food for pecking the left key; when light 12 is illuminated, the pigeon receives food for pecking the right key. Soon, the pigeon reliably pecks left or right, according to which of the two small lights is illuminated. Light 1 now "controls" left key pecks, and light 2 now "controls" right key pecks (Figure 2.2).

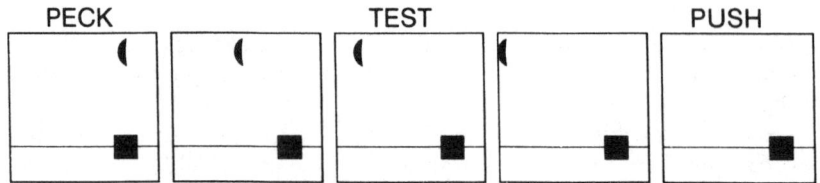

Figure 2.1. A continuum of stimuli. The bird has seen the configuration in the left panel many times during training: Banana-over-box is the occasion upon which climbing and pecking has produced food. The bird has also seen approximations of the panel on the right: Box-alone has been the occasion upon which pushing has produced food (see Chapter 10 in this volume for details). The test situation (center) can be considered an intermediate, combining elements of both training conditions and thus prompting "confusion" and a competition of repertoires.

When light 6 is illuminated, the pigeon pecks *both* keys, and the pecks distribute themselves roughly equally across the two keys. Lights 2 or 11, on the other hand, produce pecks almost exclusively on the left or right keys, respectively. In other words, the distribution of pecks roughly matches the position of the illuminated light (Figure 2.3).

In the box-and-banana test, then, we should at first expect our subject to show signs of confusion: to behave with respect to both the banana and the box, to stretch toward one, turn, orient toward the other, and so on, which is indeed what we observe.

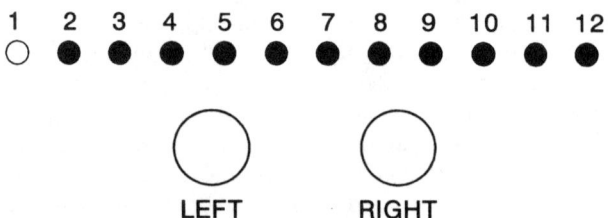

Figure 2.2. Response panel for an experiment on stimulus matching. The bird learns to peck the left key when light 1 is illuminated and the right key when light 12 is illuminated. When intermediate lights are illuminated, the bird pecks both the left and right keys.

First push. As was true with our driver, this competition should be unstable; it should change over time. Recall that, before the test, the bird had seen the banana alone and out of reach; jumping and flying had been extinguished in this situation. Thus, in the competition between the two behaviors, behavior with respect to the box should quickly triumph. (It follows that if jumping and flying have not been extinguished, we should predict a great deal of behavior with respect to the banana before the other repertoire wins out. As noted above, we achieved such a result.)

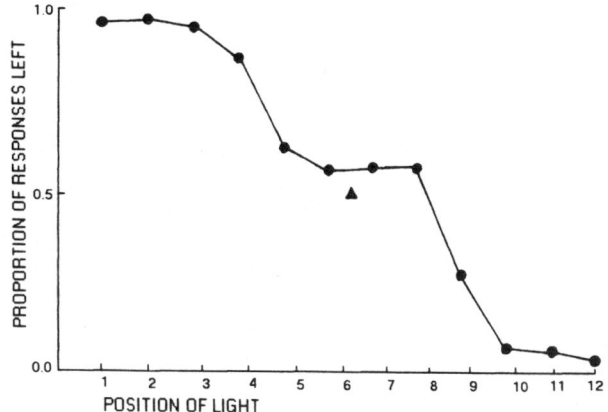

Figure 2.3. Results of an experiment on stimulus matching. Shown are the proportion of pecks left as a function of the position of the illuminated light (see Figure 2.2). When lights 1, 2, or 3 are illuminated, the birds tend to peck the left key exclusively. When lights 10, 11, or 12 are illuminated, the birds tend to peck the right key exclusively. Pecks are distributed on both keys when lights 4 through 9 are illuminated. The triangle shows the proportion of pecks left when lights 1 and 12 are illuminated simultaneously. The results are averaged across three subjects.

In the dynamic interplay between the behaviors, the bird should come to face the box more and more directly. It thus comes to face a close approximation to the stimulus that controls pushing (Figure 2.1, right panel), and hence, it begins to push.

Pushes toward banana. Why the bird pushes toward the banana is a more complicated matter. We cannot yet give a definitive account of this behavior, although we can offer various suggestions.

One possibility, which we will reject, is that, to the pigeon, the banana, raised 41 cm in the air, looks like the round green spot at ground level. If so, we would have a case of what is called "stimulus generalization"—a spread of effect from one stimulus to another because of common physical characteristics. The particular characteristics of the stimuli (which, after all, don't seem very similar) might not even be important in this instance. Perhaps the bird treats the banana like the green spot because, during the test, the banana is the only conspicuous stimulus in the chamber (the spot is absent). Perhaps the bird has learned, not to push toward the spot, but to push toward a conspicuous stimulus.

We tested this possibility by training two birds who had never seen the banana to push toward the green spot. Then the box was placed in the center of a cylindrical chamber, and the banana was suspended at an edge of the chamber at a position determined by a random number. Neither bird confronted with this situation appeared even to orient toward the banana, and neither bird pushed the box beneath the banana during three two-minutes trials (Figure 2.4).

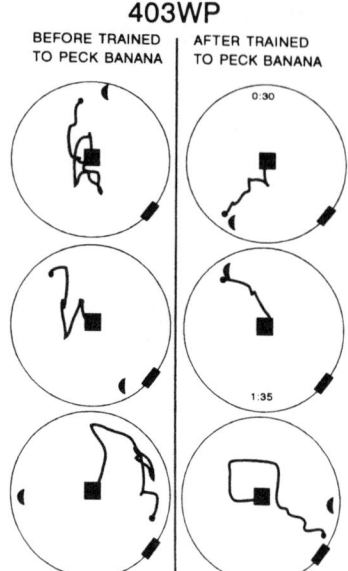

Figure 2.4. A bird that has been trained to push toward a green spot at ground level but that has never seen the facsimile of the banana does not push toward the banana when given the opportunity (left panel). After pecks to the banana have been reinforced with food, however, the pigeon pushes a box fairly directly toward the banana, although it has never been taught to do so (right panel). Shown are two-minutes trials with one bird. No food was presented during these trials.

But then, with the box absent from the chamber, we lowered the banana and taught each bird to peck it. Now, confronted with the test situation, each bird oriented toward the banana repeatedly, and each pushed the box beneath the banana on two of three test trials (Figure 2.4). (Since climbing had not been trained, neither bird then climbed onto the box.)

Thus, stimulus generalization seems not to be involved in successful performances. The birds push toward the banana, it seems, only when pecking the banana has been reinforced. This is encouraging, for we can now say that the bird is pushing toward the banana for roughly the same reasons that an intelligent child might do so: because it has learned to push toward things, and, loosely speaking, because it thinks the banana is important.

Pushing toward the banana suggests another kind of generalization that has been called "functional generalization" (Bruner, Goodnow, & Austin, 1956). We often treat two things alike, not because they have common physical characteristics, but because they have common functions (for example, "things to sit on") or because we have common histories with respect to them (for example, "things that burn"). Consider a child faced with a variant of the box-and-banana problem: A cookie jar is out of reach on a kitchen shelf. After some reaching, the child clumsily moves a chair beneath the shelf, climbs, and brings down the jar. Will she do the same to retrieve a roll of toilet paper that resembles the cookie jar? Probably not. But she will probably retrieve a small toy, even though the latter looks nothing like the jar. Again, stimuli that have little resemblance can produce similar behaviors.[1]

Various accounts may be given of the directional pushes as they occur moment-to-moment in time. N. E. Miller (personal communication) has suggested that directional pushes win out over other ones because the bird is inclined both to push *and* to orient toward the banana. The pushes that triumph are the sum of these two responses. M. Branch (personal communication) has suggested that, because of the bird's history of pecking the banana, the banana is a conditioned reinforcer. Animals will work to clarify stimuli of this sort. By pushing the box toward the banana, the pigeon brings the banana closer and thus clarifies it.

Cessation of pushing. The bird stops pushing in the correct place because of a simple but important phenomenon called "automatic chaining." In the laboratory, we make responses occur in sequence by using the stimulus that controls one response as the reinforcer for another response. Because we usually establish the last response first, the second-to-the-last response second, and so on, this procedure is often called "backward chaining."

But, in the real world, an organism often generates its own chains of behavior, because its own behavior often produces a stimulus that controls other behavior. In other words, an organism's behavior changes its environment, and a changed environment, in turn, changes behavior. A movement as simple as turning one's head can have a profound effect. You turn your head toward your calendar and are reminded of an important appointment. You open your bedroom shade and see someone stealing your car. Indeed, one can hardly do anything at all without changing the probability of subsequent behavior.

As the pigeon pushes, it arranges for itself closer and closer approximations to a stimulus that it has seen before: box-under-banana, the stimulus that controls climbing and pecking. Thus it reaches the banana, climbs, and pecks.

In summary: The period of apparent confusion can be understood as an effect of multiple controlling stimuli. The bird starts to push because of the dynamics of the competition between behavior with respect to the banana and behavior with respect to the box. The bird pushes toward the banana because of its history of directional pushing and its history of pecking the banana (how these histories manifest themselves moment-to-moment in time is not yet clear). And the bird stops pushing because of automatic chaining: Its own behavior produces a stimulus that controls other behavior.

TOOL USE

Epstein and Medalie (1983) presented a pigeon with another classic problem—variously called the "marble-under-the-couch" problem, or the "stick" or "rake" problem (Hobhouse, 1901; Köhler, 1925; Shurcliff et al., 1971). A young boy is playing with a marble, which rolls under a couch, just out of his reach. He stretches repeatedly toward the marble, to no avail. Emotional behavior appears; the child whines, and he strikes the couch with his fist. After a minute or two, both the reaching and the emotional behavior subside. The child's eyes fall on a magazine on the floor beside him. He clutches the magazine and clumsily thrusts it under the couch. He strikes the marble, which, unfortunately, moves the wrong way.

Even though he was not entirely successful, the child has done something remarkable: He has used an object as a tool to extend his reach. How can we account for such behavior?

A disclaimer is necessary. Usually, the first time children do such things, they do so for relatively trivial reasons, or for many reasons, some of which are relatively trivial (cf. Chapter 3). For example, they have almost certainly seen cartoon characters or siblings or parents solve such problems before. If so, the behavior is imitated, or imitation may at least contribute to its occurrence.

If the children can follow instructions, then, almost certainly, language, too, plays a role. A babysitter or parent says, "If you want to get the marble, hit it with the magazine." Current or past instructions of this sort probably always contribute to the emergence of novel behavior in humans. After all, most of the new dishes one prepares originate with recipes. But a question remains: What determines novel behavior that is not controlled by models or instructions? How might we account for a child's success in the marble-under-the-couch problem in the unlikely event that the child has never seen anyone solve such a problem and has never been told how to solve such a problem?

Some experiments with pigeons are suggestive (Chapter 8). Medalie and I first provided a pigeon with a skill it would need to solve a certain problem: The pigeon was trained to push a flat hexagonal box toward green spots placed at random positions around the base of a cylindrical chamber. Then a marble of sorts—a target—was created: A Plexiglas partition was added to the pigeon's chamber, which had a 6-cm gap along its base. In the center of this gap we placed a small, square metal plate, and, with the hexagonal box absent from the chamber, the bird received food for pecking this plate. Each depression of the plate produced a brief, high-pitched tone, but the feeder was operated only occasionally after a tone.

Over a period of days, the plate was gradually moved to a position 10 cm behind the Plexiglas wall, so the bird had to stretch its neck beneath the wall to peck the plate. Then the hexagonal box was placed in the center of the chamber on the bird's side of the Plexiglas wall, and pushing the box was extinguished while pecking the plate continued to be reinforced. In other words, with the wall and plate in the chamber, the bird was taught not to push the box.

A small change in the situation turned it into a problem for the bird: We moved the metal plate to a point 16.5 cm behind the wall, so that the plate was just beyond the bird's reach. We now had a situation similar to the marble-under-the-couch problem. The bird had a potential tool (the box) available to it which it knew how to use. And it had a target (the plate) which, presumably, it "wanted to reach." With the box, the bird could presumably reach the plate. Note, however, that the bird had never learned to push the box under anything and that it had never learned to push the box toward the plate.

At first the pigeon stretched repeatedly and forcefully toward the plate. It also behaved "emotionally": It turned, raised it wings, and scraped its feet on the floor. As behavior with respect to the plate weakened, behavior with respect to the box began to appear. At 30 seconds into the session, the bird pecked weakly at the box but did not move it. At 92 seconds into the session, the bird suddenly began to push the box directly toward the wall. When the box crossed beneath the wall, the bird pushed it back and forth erratically several times. Then it stretched again toward the plate and quickly pushed the box against it, thus producing the high-pitched tone. The bird began now to peck the box repeatedly and thus maintained the tone continuously.

A simple principle, called the *principle of resurgence*, sheds light on the appearance of the bird's pushes and perhaps on the appearance of comparable human behavior: When, in a given situation, behavior that was recently successful is no longer successful, behavior that was previously successful in similar situations tends to recur (Part III, this volume; cf. Enkema, Slavin, Spaeth, & Neuringer, 1972; Epstein & Skinner, 1980; Estes, 1955; Lindblom & Jenkins, 1981; Mowrer, 1940; O'Kelley, 1940a; Sears, 1941).

The dynamics of resurgence can be demonstrated experimentally. A pigeon is placed in a standard three-key chamber, and, at first, pecks on the right key are occasionally reinforced with food. The pigeon pecks this key exclusively. Then reinforcement is shifted to the center key: Many thousands of pecks occur on the right key over a period of weeks, but they eventually disappear, and the bird comes to peck the center key exclusively. Finally, all reinforcement is withheld.

Resurgence is typically evident during the first hour in which reinforcement is withheld (see Chapter 15). For one bird, for example, nearly 2,000 pecks occurred on the center key during the hour, and the rate of pecking this key fell off dramatically during the last 20 minutes. Responding on the left key, where the bird had no history of reinforcement, was negligible. But responding on the right key reappeared. The bird did not peck it at all for 40 minutes, but pecking reappeared on this key just as the rate of pecking the center key began to decline. The bird pecked the right key nearly 900 times during the last 20 minutes.

The recurrence of previously reinforced behavior is a common phenomenon, reports of which have appeared many times in both the experimental and clinical literatures of psychology. If you are turning a doorknob that has always turned easily, for example, and it fails to turn, any and perhaps all of the behaviors that have ever gotten you through doors are likely to appear: You may turn harder, pull up on the knob, kick the door, shout for help, and so on. Freud's concept of regression could be considered a special case of resurgence in which the behavior that recurs is infantile.

It would seem that our tool-using pigeon becomes increasingly interested in the box because its behavior with respect to the plate is unsuccessful. As behavior with respect to the box weakens, behavior with respect to the box should appear. Why the bird pushes toward the plate is another matter, which was discussed earlier.

Note that in the latter experiment, multiple repertoires of behavior were made available by multiple controlling stimuli, whereas in the tool use experiment, multiple repertoires were made available by resurgence.

EXTRAPOLATING TO HUMAN BEHAVIOR

There are two ways in which we might demonstrate a relationship between nonhuman animal behavior and human behavior. First, we might use a nonhuman animal to simulate the human case. Rather than providing the animal with an arbitrary set of experiences, as a circus trainer might do, we might first study human subjects to try to identify the experiences they have had that allowed them to emit some interesting behavior in a new situation. Then we would provide the animal with comparable experiences. If it subsequently emitted human-like behavior in the new situation, we will have taken a step toward showing the importance of those experiences in the emergence of the behavior; moreover, our conjecture that those experiences were responsible for comparable human behavior will have received some support. With laboratory animals, we might then demonstrate that these experiences are necessary for the emission of the behavior; with humans, unfortunately, our conjecture will likely remain a conjecture.

For example, in the insight experiment, pigeons that had learned (a) to push directionally and (b) to climb and reach, solved the problem in a human-like fashion. Did humans and chimpanzees learn these things before they solved comparable problems? The answer seems to be yes, although controlled experiments with children probably cannot be performed. In the 1940s, however, Birch showed that laboratory-reared chimpanzees who had never been allowed to handle sticks could not solve Köhler-type stick problems. After the chimps were given the opportunity to handle sticks, they solved the problems readily.

The second way to show a relationship between nonhuman animal behavior and human behavior is also indirect. One can cast the transformation principles that one has developed with nonhuman animals into formal terms—into equations or a computer algorithm—and then see how well the formal apparatus can predict human behavior.

Note that neither of these methods tells you what you really want to know. Neither the experiences nor the principles you have uncovered with nonhuman animal subjects are necessarily responsible for human behavior—even if they successfully predict it. Unfortunately, as is true in neurology, astronomy, meteorology, evolutionary biology, and other disciplines, we must rely on indirect methods to further our understanding of the subject matter. To carry out a rigorous analysis with human subjects would require experimentation that is unethical (Chapter 12).

GENERATIVITY THEORY AND THE TWO-STRING PROBLEM

In the 1920s N. R. F. Maier devised what has become a classic and frequently studied problem, called the "two-string" or "pendulum" problem (Maier, 1931a). Maier presented adult human subjects with the following situation: Two long strings were suspended from a high ceiling, and various objects were placed on a table near the strings. A subject was told, "Your task is to tie the ends of these

Generativity Theory and Creativity

strings together. If necessary, you may use one of these objects to help you." In one variation of the experiment, the critical object was a pliers.

Almost invariably, the first thing subjects do is to pull one string toward the other, only to find that the second string is too far away to reach (Figure 2.5). Having failed with the first string, and geometry notwithstanding, many subjects then try to pull the second string toward the first. Eventually, a subject picks up the available objects. With a pliers, many subjects try repeatedly to reach the second string by holding the first string in one hand and the pliers in the other; the pliers extends the reach a few inches, but not nearly enough to reach the other string.

Figure 2.5. When faced with Maier's two-string problem, subjects usually begin by pulling one string toward the other. After they find that they cannot reach the second string, they often pull the second string toward the first.

The solution is to use the pliers (or some other heavy object) to construct a pendulum. One ties the object to the end of one string, sets the string in motion, brings the first string to the center position, and catches the second string when it swings to the center. Many subjects have trouble with this problem. Verbal or nonverbal hints often help. A particularly effective hint, Maier found, was to set one string in motion slightly by brushing against it. According to our current understanding, such an act would work for two reasons: First, by setting the string in motion, the experimenter has modeled some the behavior the subject must emit to solve the problem. Second, the moving string itself is a "discriminative stimulus" for behavior with respect to pendula; that is, it makes such behavior more likely.

I presented 30 college students, divided into two groups of 15, with the two-string problem to determine whether the principles I have described earlier could be used to predict human performances in this situation. Two observers monitored nine behaviors continuously during each session. Observers recorded every instance that they saw of behaviors such as: "pulls one string toward the other," "picks up object," "ties object to string," "reaches with object," "sets string in motion from below shoulder line," "sets string in motion from above shoulder line," and so on. The behaviors were defined precisely and in such a way as to make them easily discriminable. While they recorded their observations, the observers listened, through earphones connected to a common tape recorder, to instructions that allowed them to synchronize their observations in successive 15-second intervals.

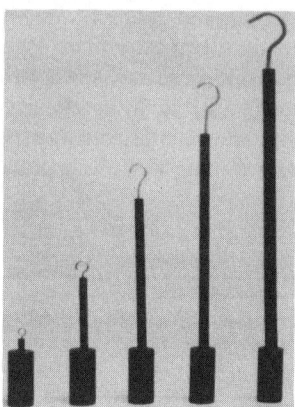

Figure 2.6. The set of objects used in the present version of the two-string problem. One group of subjects had access to Object 1 (at left), and the other group had access to Object 5 (at right). Each object can be used to construct an equally good pendulum, but subjects tended to try to use Object 5 to extend their reach. Note that the objects are part of a series in which the rods grow progressively longer and thicker and in which the hooks and hook openings grow larger.

The instructions and setup were identical for each group, but the first group had access to a short object (Figure 2.6, object on left) and the second to a long object (Figure 2.6, object on right). Note that these objects are topological distortions of each other: They are members of a series of objects in which the rod gets increasingly longer and thicker, the hook gets increasingly larger, and the hook opening gets increasingly larger. We conjectured that the short object would produce rapid solutions to the problem, because it might strengthen behavior with respect to weights and pendula, and that the long object might interfere with a solution, because it might induce subjects to try to extend their reach, as many subjects had done with Maier's pliers. The long object was not long enough to allow the subject to solve the problem by reaching.

In a baseline study with 148 students, none of whom was a subject in the experiment, our supposition that the short object would produce more rapid solutions was reinforced. Students were shown one object or the other and asked, "What would you do with this object?" Eighty percent of the students who were shown the short object indicated that they would use it as some sort of weight ("use it as a paperweight," "make a pendulum," "a weight," "a weight on a balance," and so on). No one indicated that it might be used to extend one's reach.

In contrast, more than 80 percent of the students who were shown the long object indicated that they would use it to extend their reach ("pull down shade," "fish hook," "open high window," "ice hook," and so on), and not one of these subjects indicated that the object might be used as a weight.

Generativity Theory and Creativity

Simulation and predictions. A computer simulation of the two-string problem was constructed as follows: Four linear equations were used to represent some of the phenomena I discussed earlier. In each equation, the probability of some behavior during one cycle of the program was determined by the probability of that behavior on the previous cycle, minus some fraction of the latter probability or plus some fraction of 1 minus the latter probability (Figure 2.7). Thus, the probabilities always fell between 0 and 1. In each cycle of the program, each of the equations operated on each of the behaviors for which an initial probability was specified. Seven behaviors were specified in the case that will be described.

(1) *Extinction:* $y_{n+1} = y_n - y_n * \varepsilon$

(2) *Reinforcement:* $y_{n+1} = y_n + (1 - y_n) * \alpha$

(3) *Resurgence:* for $\lambda_{yy'} < 0$ and $y'_n - y'_{n-1} < 0$,

$y_{n+1} = y_n + (1 - y_n) * (-\lambda_{yy'}) * y'_n$

(4) *Automatic Chaining:* for $\lambda_{yy'} > 0$ and $y'_n - y'_{n-1} > 0$,

$y_{n+1} = y_n + (1 - y_n) * \lambda_{yy'} * y'_n$

Figure 2.7. *Equations used to generate the probability profile shown in Figure 2.8. y_n is the probability of behavior y at cycle n of the algorithm, y'_n is the probability of behavior y' at cycle n of the algorithm, ε is a constant for extinction (it determines the rate at which the probability of behavior y decreases over cycles of the algorithm), α is a constant for reinforcement (it determines the rate at which the probability of behavior y increases over cycles of the algorithm as a result of certain environmental events), and $\lambda_{yy'}$ is the constant of interaction between behaviors y and y'.*

The first two equations represented extinction and reinforcement, respectively. For the two-string problem, it was assumed that no reinforcers were available, and therefore alpha was set at 0. Thus, every time the program cycled, every behavior was assumed to decrease in probability according to equation 1. The continual and gradual weakening of all possible responses would seem to characterize all problem situations, since, by definition, reinforcement is unavailable in such situations.

Equations 3 and 4 represented the phenomena we have labeled resurgence and automatic chaining, respectively. They each made use of a matrix of values which specified the manner in which every possible behavior was assumed to interact with every other possible behavior in the situation. Negative values specified the resurgence relation: As one behavior decreased in probability, another behavior increased in probability. Positive values specified the automatic chaining relation: As one behavior increased in probability, the environment was changed in such a way that another behavior increased in probability. Thus, a -0.2 relating "pulls string" to "picks up object" suggests that when pulling the string is unsuccessful, picking up the object will become somewhat more likely. A 0.4 relating "picks up object" to "ties object to string" suggests that after one picks up the object, one is then more likely to tie the object to the string.

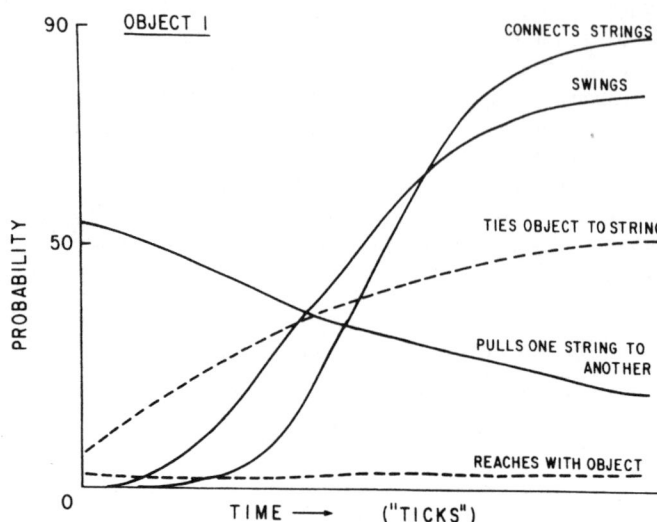

Figure 2.8. *A probability profile generated by the transformation functions described in the text, shown for five behaviors relevant to Maier's (1931a) two-string problem. The abscissa is labeled "ticks," which are cycles of the computer algorithm. The profile was generated with parameters for the short object (Object 1), which produced rapid solutions to the problem and no irrelevant reaching. Note that pulling one string to the other decreases steadily in probability and that other behaviors increase in probability in an orderly sequence. Tying the object to the string makes swinging more likely, which, in turn, makes connecting the strings more likely.*

The interaction matrix is, in effect, a numerical summary of that part of the organism's history which is pertinent to the problem, including the instructions that may have been given to a human subject. For example, if the subject had never learned to tie, 0s would appear at every position in the "tie" row and "tie" column of the matrix, and, presumably, a solution would not appear. If the task were simply "to select one string and pull it as hard as possible," the behavior "connect the two strings" would probably not appear in the matrix.

The matrix also specifies relationships that are possible between the behaviors in the problem situation. Picking up an object has no obvious relationship to pulling one string toward another, but it does directly change the environment in a way that should make tying more likely.

In future applications of this model, all of the free parameters could, in theory, be obtained in baseline studies. In the present application, only the initial probabilities were obtained from data, and other parameters were estimated. The choice of values was not especially critical in this case. It appears that, as is the case in catastrophe theory, the outcome of the simulation depends little on the value of any one parameter or small subset of parameters. The solution "explodes" over a wide range of values.

The model produces probability profiles of the behaviors that have been specified in it—overlapping curves showing the manner in which the probabilities of the various behaviors change over time (Figure 2.8). With just three linear equations (1, 3, and 4) that describe behavioral phenomena that are known to occur in organisms, the model generated a solution to the two-string problem. The dynamics of the behaviors seemed reasonable.

Although verbal descriptions in terms of the principles we discussed earlier oversimplify these dynamics (as they did in our discussion of earlier problems), we offer some interpretations: The probability of "pulling one string to the other" started out high because of the subject's instructions, but, because the behavior was not successful (it produced neither a solution nor stimuli that occasioned other behavior), its probability decreased over time. The extinction of pulling led to the resurgence of other possible behaviors, including "picking up the object" (not shown), which, in turn, increased the probability of "tying object to string." That, in turn, increased the probability of setting the string in motion, which increased the probability of "catching swinging object" (not shown). As the probability of catching increased, the probability of connecting the strings quickly exploded, driven by the long progression of related behaviors. With the long object, the solution still appeared, but it was impeded by the appearance of reaching, which occurred early in the session and then gradually disappeared.

This approach could, in principle, be used to predict the dynamic interactions of any number of behaviors in any situation. To extend the model to other situations, one would estimate the equation constants, the initial probabilities of each of the behaviors, and the interaction values. The success of the prediction would depend on the accuracy of one's estimates, the applicability of the equations to that organism, and the stability of the situation.

Note that the probabilities generated in a probability profile do not necessarily sum to 1 at any given point in time. Far from being illogical, this is a fundamental requirement of the model. The nervous system can presumably support many behaviors simultaneously, far more than the behaving individual may be aware at any point in time. When the system is highly active, so that several incompatible behaviors are each highly probable, the individual presumably feels confused and stressed. The system may also be relatively inactive and behavior weak across the board. In any case, the generative dynamics presumably do not stop and may be identical even at very different levels of activity.

How probability curves sum at a given point in time—or, more generally, how one decides what behavior one will actually see—requires yet another level of analysis, beyond the scope of the current discussion.

Results. In a unique, novel performance, the probability of a particular response cannot be computed by observing a single subject, just as the heritability of a trait cannot be estimated by looking at a single phenotype.[2] Therefore, even though the computer model could be used to estimate the probability of ongoing behavior in an individual, it cannot be validated on an individual. Hence, we pooled our data across subjects in each of the two groups.

As we predicted on several grounds, subjects solved the problem faster and more easily with the short object. All of the subjects who had the short object solved the problem within the allotted 15 minutes, and the average solution time was 2.75 minutes. Only 11 of the 15 subjects who had the long object solved the problem within 15 minutes. If we grant the four unsuccessful subjects 15-minute solution times, the average solution time for the long object proves to be 7.25 minutes.

We also examined transitional probabilities, or, more precisely, the proportion of cases in which one behavior followed another within the same 15-second observation interval or during the next 15-second observation interval. In some cases these proportions were revealing. For example, the probability of tying within an interval of picking up the object was high for each object: 0.59 for Object 1 and 0.48 for Object 5. But the probability of reaching with the object within an interval of having picked it up or tied it to a string was 0.00 for the short object and 0.21 for the long object (Table 2.1).

Both transitional probabilities and an analysis of films revealed cases of what appears to be automatic chaining. With the short object, for example, the probability of setting the string in motion from above the shoulders (which suggests a deliberate swing) within an interval of having set it in motion from below the shoulders (which suggests simply putting the object down or letting it go) was extremely high: 0.47.

When Maier (1931a) set the string in motion for his subjects, they solved the problem easily. And, indeed, when one looks closely at successful performances, one often finds that a subject has "accidentally" set the string and weight in motion just before a successful swing. In one case the long object swung back and forth in front a subject's face while she tied it to the string; she swung it almost immediately after it was secured. In several cases, with the object tied to the string, subjects dropped the object or let it go in a way that suggested that they had "given up." But a heavy object at the end of a long string invariably swings. The sight of a swinging string soon led to a solution for most subjects.

In order to assess the value of the probability profiles that had been generated by the computer, we constructed frequency profiles for each group. We tallied the number of times each behavior had been observed during each tenth of a session (Figure 2.9). The dynamics of the interactions between the behaviors (treating the group as a single subject) looked similar to the dynamics predicted by the simulation. As predicted, in each group the frequency with which pulling was observed started out high and gradually decreased over the session. For the group that had the long object, reaching appeared early in the session and then gradually disappeared. The frequency with which swinging was observed increased toward the end of the session in each group, and, of course, the curve for connecting the strings rose rapidly at the end of the session.

Thus, the equations accomplished two things: They generated a solution to the two-string problem, and they predicted some of the dynamics of real solutions.

FOUR REPERTOIRES

The approach I have outlined has proved fruitful in allowing us to construct complex, novel performances in laboratory animals. For example, we recently achieved the spontaneous interconnection of four repertoires of behavior in a pigeon (Chapter 11). The pigeon had learned: (a) to open a Plexiglas door, (b) to move a box toward targets, (c) to climb (but not to peck anything overhead), (d) to peck the banana when the bird was on the floor and the banana was within reach above it, and (e) not to jump or fly when the banana was out of reach. The bird never saw any two of the training objects (box, banana, or portable doorway) together at the same time.

Table 2.1. Two-string problem: results and transitional probabilities.

	Object 1	Object 5
Number of subjects	15	15
Number of solutions	15 (100%)	11 (73%)
Avg. time to solution (min.)	2.75	7.25*
P (pulling with object / start of session)	0.33 (10/30)	0.30 (9/30)
P (tying / picking up object)	0.59 (30/51)	0.48 (20/42)
P (reaching with object / picking up object)	0.00 (0/51)	0.12 (5/42)
P (starting pendulum motion from above or below waist / tying)	0.43 (27/63)	0.22 (15/68)
P (reaching with object / tying)	0.00 (0/63)	0.09 (6/68)
P (reaching with object / picking up object or tying)	0.00	0.21
P (starting pend. motion from above shoulders / starting pend. motion from below shoulders)	0.47 (8/17)	0.13 (6/48)
Number of pulls with object	21	35
Number of reaches with object	0	15

*Assumes 15-minute solution times for each of the four subjects who failed to solve the problem. For the eleven successful subjects, the average solution time was 4.43 minutes.

It was then presented with the following problem: The banana was placed out the bird's reach, and the box was placed behind the door. In just under 4 minutes, the bird managed to retrieve the box from behind the door, push it to the right place, climb, and peck the banana. A formal analysis of this performance predicts many aspects of it, including the floor path along which the bird pushed the box. For example, it was predicted that pushes should extinguish in a damped oscillatory pattern around the position on the floor beneath the banana, and that is a reasonable description of what occurred.

THEORETICAL ISSUES

The stimulus problem. One of the most bothersome problems in the histories of philosophy, psychology, and praxics is the problem of similarity. Experience with one stimulus automatically makes other stimuli have certain effects, but, at this point in time and with very few exceptions, it is difficult to predict what those stimuli will be and what effects they will have. I have therefore omitted stimuli from the model I described above. The box is always the box, from all angles and under all variations in lighting. And what the bird would do with a slightly different box is not specified. (Presumably, it would not do as well.) The new situations I have introduced are new only in that they contain new arrangements of items the organism has seen before (with the exception of the weight in the two-string problem).

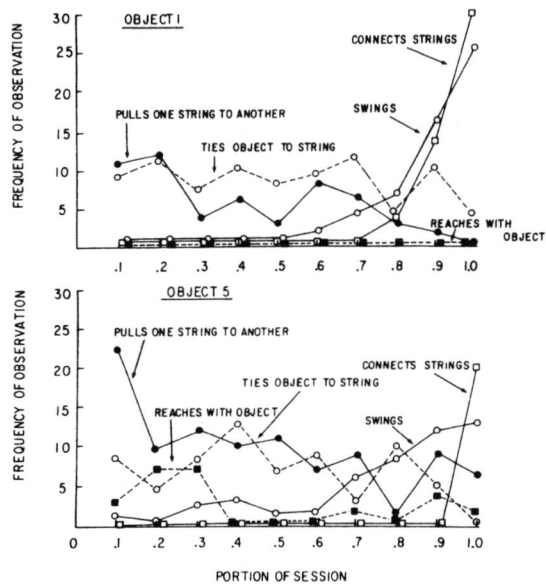

Figure 2.9. The frequency with which two observers recorded the appearance of five of the behaviors that were monitored in the experiment described in the text. Plotted are the sums of their observations during each tenth of a session. The top panel shows the results with 15 subjects who were given access to the short object (Object 1), and the bottom panel shows the results with 15 subjects who were given access to the long object (Object 5). Note the similarity of these curves to those generated by the transformation functions (Figure 2.8). In general, pulling one string toward the other decreases steadily in frequency. Tying the object to the string appears at a low frequency throughout the session. Swinging increases in frequency toward the end of the session, which, in turn, allows the subjects to connect the strings. Also note the appearance of reaching early in the sessions recorded in the lower panel.

It is difficult to imagine a stimulus that is truly new to an adult organism; the colors, shape, size, and so on, have all been seen before, and, presumably, they all control certain behaviors. But until the stimulus problem is solved, it will be difficult to say what these behaviors are.

Moreover, the situation in which the model makes predictions is assumed to be more or less stable. If the organism or some other factor changed the situation appreciably, presumably some of the parameters in the model would have to be changed. Ideally, the parameters would be updated in real time, as they are in simulations of weather or space flight. At the moment, however, they are fixed.

Time. At present the model does not deal directly with time, although it would be a small matter to extend it in this way. The model simply cycles. By fitting group or individual data to the predicted curves, a duration could be assigned to each cycle. Ideally, one of the parameters in the model would be the cycle resolution, which would correspond to the speed with which an individual or group emits a particular sequence.

Interpreting the profile. What do the overlapping curves of the probability profile mean in terms of the behavior of an individual? When five behaviors all have certain probabilities at some point it time, does this mean they are literally competing with each other in the organism? Should we expect to see the organism alternating among them, as the pigeon alternates between the banana and the box when first confronted with the box-and-banana problem? Or should we simply read off the most probable behaviors at every point in time and expect to see those behaviors occur in sequence?

Behavior is surely probabilistic, and it is hard to imagine an adequate treatment of behavior that does not make probabilistic predictions, but the notion that several behaviors exist in the organism at the same time goes beyond the facts. One sees sequences, or, as William James put it, a "stream," even when two behaviors are alternating with each other. Hull's "habit family hierarchy" implied that many behaviors were stacked up in the organism, each waiting to appear at the right moment. But until such a hierarchy is shown to have some basis in physiology, I suggest that the probability profile be interpreted literally. To say that several behaviors have various probabilities of occurring at some point in time is to say just that and nothing more. The profile tells you how to place your bets. When the time comes, the organism will, in all likelihood, be engaged in just one of those behaviors.

Thinking. Occasionally, having just been escorted into the room, a subject looked at the two strings, looked at the object, and, then, like Sultan, *waited a few moments* and then suddenly and completely solved the problem. What happened here, and is the approach we have outlined useful?

The phenomena I have already described may be responsible for the solution. I cannot prove this conjecture, but neither can one disprove it. In the two-string problem in particular, perceptual behavior probably always plays a role in a successful performance. The subject *sees herself* pulling one string to the other and failing to reach it (the behavior is extinguished), *sees herself* picking up the object (resurgence) and tying it to the object (automatic chaining), *sees herself* swinging the object (automatic chaining), catching (automatic chaining), and connecting the strings (automatic chaining).

She may even envision only a subset of these steps or the last few. She may envision the sequence suddenly, extremely rapidly, or "as a whole."

This sounds somewhat disturbing and even somewhat miraculous until one admits the obvious: *Perceptual and other covert behavior of this sort often fails.* You think something through, rapidly or painstakingly, and then find that the behavior doesn't work. The string is too stiff to knot. The hook pulls out of the weight. Pulling one string toward the other works just fine, after all.

In short, it would be difficult and perhaps impossible to rule out the possibility that covert behavior and overt behavior are describable by the same laws.

On a practical note, the phenomena being modeled here at the behavioral level could also be modeled at other levels of analysis: cognitive, neurophysiological, and so on. The computational approach I described could prove just as powerful at other levels of analysis. Ideally, the resultant probability curves would look the same.

Goals. What has happened to the "goal"? I ascribed one neither to the pigeons nor to our human subjects. If, by a goal, one means some future event, then goal has no place in a scientific account of behavior; future events do not control present ones. A more conservative tactic has been to move the goal into the organism: The future event is not moving the organism; the organism's image of that event is doing it.

This matter is strictly empirical. Perceptual activity is behavior. If an organism perceives the target while it is behaving in other, more obvious, ways, the perceptual activity itself, like the rest of its behavior, is presumably determined by transformation phenomena and the organism's genetic and environmental histories. This does not mean that covert behavior of this sort is epiphenomenal. Automatic chaining is a very real and powerful phenomenon, which means that an organism's own behavior—even its perceptual behavior—can set the occasion for other behavior. If models of behavior that take into account only overt activity prove somewhat inadequate, then one potentially productive solution might be to expand them to take into account the role that covert activity probably plays in many situations. As we noted above, the same set of principles may prove useful in each domain.

GENERATIVITY AND CREATIVITY

Previously established behavior manifests itself in new situations in orderly ways. New sequences, new topographies, or behaviors that have new functions may appear. The manner in which such behavior emerges is describable by a set of transformation functions, each of which operates on every possible behavior that can occur in the situation. The functions predict continuous and probabilistic changes in behavior.

This approach to understanding the emergence of ongoing, novel behavior has proved useful in the prediction and engineering of increasingly complex, intelligent performances in nonhuman animals. It has also led to the development of an effective problem-solving algorithm derived from empirically-based principles of behavior, and it has allowed us to predict, with reasonable success, ongoing, novel, intelligent performances in human subjects, most recently in studies with retarded children (Epstein, 1988).

I have avoided using the language of creativity in discussing generative phenomena. Such language is heavily value laden (see Csikszentmihályi, 1990), and hence it may obscure an understanding of the generative phenomena upon which it depends. Behavior called "creative" by one group might be harshly judged by another. Moreover, the language of creativity is often reserved for the *product* of behavior, not for the behavior itself. The product is of necessity a poor index of the creative process. The product is continuously edited and often rejected by the behaving individual as he or she, having been creative one minute, steps back during the next and *judges* the product—acting, in effect, as an agent for a larger cultural entity. Action is generative, but *re*action is often corrective and inhibiting. The language of creativity obscures these distinctions and hence should be used with caution in an analysis of generative phenomena.

NOTES

1. The term "functional generalization" is troublesome for two reasons: First, it implies an explanation, although at best it simply *describes* a spread of effect between stimuli which is not based on common physical characterstics. I *explain* the bird's behavior by referring to its history (both pecking the banana and pushing toward the spot have been reinforced) and the current circumstances. Why such a history affects the bird in this way is a matter for the physiologist. The term has also been defined more narrowly than I have used it. Consider Bruner, Goodnow, and Austin (1956): "The problems of specifying the properties of objects that mediate a common categorizing response become less arduous when the category is a functional or utilitarian one. Rather than an internal state rendering a group of things equivalent, now equivalence is based on an external function. *The objects of a functional category fulfill a concrete and specific task requirement*—'thingslarge enough and strong enough to plug this hole in the dike'" (p. 5, italics added).

2. Curiously, the frequency profile, which can be generated now for individual subjects, creates smooth curves that resemble probability curves (Epstein, 1993). Thus, frequency profiles and probability profiles can be compared, and both can be generated in real-time for individual subjects. A manuscript describing this methodology in detail is in preparation.

3

BRINGING COGNITION AND CREATIVITY INTO THE BEHAVIORAL LABORATORY

Summary. Praxics has made little contact with the complex behavioral phenomena that lead people to speak of cognition and creativity, but advances are possible. At least four sources of novel behavior are readily accessible to laboratory study—imitation, instructions, variation, and the spontaneous interconnection of repertoires. The latter process is especially dramatic: Behaviors that have been established separately can, in new situations, come together to produce blends, new sequences, or behaviors that have new functions.

Four categories of complex behavior have traditionally given praxists[1] trouble and, not surprisingly, have stimulated theories about cognition and creativity.

Novel behavior. The most perplexing has been novel behavior. Humans and other organisms do things they have never done before and, occasionally, things no member of their species has ever done before. The mystery of novelty underlies most theories of creativity and has spurred such concepts as "generativity" in language production (Chomsky, 1965) and "productivity" in problem solving (Wertheimer, 1945).

Delays. Second, behavior often appears to be under the control of events that occurred in the remote past. Köhler (1925) notes a case in which some food was buried outside of a chimpanzee's cage in full view of the chimpanzee. When the animal was released the next morning, it immediately unearthed the food. Few people would be content to speak of action at a distance in this situation, in part because we know that intervening events can change the outcome. Clearly, environmental events change organisms, and the changes often manifest themselves in subsequent behavior, even after long intervals of time have elapsed. We know very little about what those changes are. Meanwhile, control of behavior by temporally remote stimuli spurs theories of "memory."

Covert activity. Third, thoughts, feelings, and so on, are accessible only to oneself, and as long as that remains the case, speculative theories about their nature and significance will flourish.

Complex, distinctively human behavior. And finally, complex human behavior, such as language, or the behavior attributed to a self-concept, is often difficult to account for. When an environmental or biological account of distinctively human behavior is not apparent, people often appeal to a construct. Only humans sing "The Star-Spangled Banner," but since one is taught in a conspicuous way to do so as a child, we don't bother with a construct. In contrast, many would insist that Francis Scott Key's composition, which is not easily traceable to either biological or environmental factors, was a product of creativity and various cognitive processes.

CREATIVITY

Creativity is a natural category, and as such, is probably not worth trying to define (Epstein, 1980b).[2] It is, moreover, a particularly elusive one. It is a judgment pronounced by a community on behavior or a product of behavior, and like all such judgments (for example, of "morality" or "beauty"), it differs from one community to the next and changes from time to time. A cubist painting would not have been judged creative in fifteenth century Europe; it would have been burned. Western music critics wouldn't presume to be able to judge the creativeness of a traditional Japanese composition without special training in the criteria the Japanese use to make such a judgment.

The judgment also depends on who did what first. If Einstein had emerged from the patent office only to find that others had already proposed the theory of relativity, Wertheimer (1945) would not have bothered to determine what was so productive about his thought processes. Deviance alone is not sufficient for the judgment of creativity; it must be deviance that is valuable to other people.

The elusive judgment, furthermore, once made, can be retracted. A current popular song was no doubt judged a creation of the composer until he lost a plagiarism suit. The scientific works of a young academician were no doubt judged creative before it was discovered that he had stolen some of them from fellow scientists. Computer-generated poetry is never judged to be creative once its origins are revealed. The more we know about the sources of behavior, the less inclined we are to speak of creativity, or, to paraphrase Samuel Butler, creativity is only a word for man's ignorance of the gods.

Such a concept does not seem suitable for the laboratory. What is worth studying, however, is novelty. Novel behavior has to occur before a community can select some of it and call it "creative." Why it selects some and rejects others is no mystery; novelty itself is the mystery.

SOURCES OF NOVELTY

At least four sources of novelty are readily accessible to laboratory study. Two—imitation and instructions—are social phenomena that involve conspicuous controlling stimuli; the others—variation and the spontaneous interconnection of repertoires—are individual phenomena that seem to be responsible for novelty's air of mystery. A discussion of these phenomena must be preceded by at least a few words about a rather troublesome problem: how do we *measure* novelty?

Measurement. If we look only at behavior, our determination will be constrained by our level of observation. If we look at behavior too closely, we will judge all behavior to be novel, for we never do exactly the same thing twice. A rat sometimes presses the lever with one paw and sometimes with the other, and presses constantly vary in force and duration. We often seem to be repeating something we have done before, but that is only because we are so insensitive to detail (Epstein, 1982a). The same word, spoken twice, leaves easily distinguishable records on a spectrogram. Even an identical repetition could still be judged novel, since it is both unique in time and the product of a changed organism; as William James (1890) noted, we don't call two ticks of a clock the "same" tick.

On the other hand, if we overlook too much detail or summarize over too long a period of time, we will judge very little behavior to be novel. We would take no notice, for example, when Mozart sat down to write a symphony if he had already written one before. This is the problem addressed by Skinner in his "Generic Nature" paper in 1935, but his solution, unfortunately, is not applicable here, for we are not interested in a recurring unit of behavior but simply in one special instance.

Topography, in general, might mislead us, no matter what our level of analysis. A painter's hand may have moved (more or less) in every possible way it could have moved before he (or she) began work on the canvas before him. What will make this work unique is a new sequence of strokes. Perhaps, in our determination of novelty, our focus should be on new combinations of old behaviors.

Still other complications present themselves when we look exclusively at behavior: Is smoother or more forceful motor performance "novel"? How should we treat apparently "random" changes in behavior? One alternative is to look at the product of behavior, which is what researchers have tended to do (e.g., Goetz & Baer, 1973). We can in so doing establish fairly objective criteria for novelty suited to our domain of interest. We can look for uncommon words in a composition, for example, or block structures greater than a certain height, or new color combinations in a drawing. Although response product is a convenient measure, objective measures of behavior itself will be helpful in cases in which the relevant behavior is observable and in which observations are made at an appropriate level (e.g., Maltzman, 1960; Schwartz, 1980).

Imitation. One important source of novelty is a social process—imitation. If you can do something you have never done before just because you see someone else doing it, you are capable of infinitely more behavior than you would be otherwise. Most of the novel behavior a child exhibits is imitated: blowing on hot food, playing "patty cake," turning door knobs, and so on. And as any linguist will attest, in the early years most words are acquired through imitation. Imitation can be either innate or learned; it can be specific to certain behaviors or generalizable to many; and it can occur either soon after a model has behaved or after a substantial delay.

Both innate and learned imitation have been studied as part of the Columban Simulation Project (Baxley, 1982; Epstein, 1981a, 1984e).[3] An experiment on learned imitation revealed that pigeons imitate each other to some extent even without training (Epstein, 1984b).[4] Several experiments have been conducted in which a naive pigeon on one side of a clear partition watches a pigeon on the other side peck a ping pong ball, pull a rope, or peck a key for food reinforcement. Given access to similar operanda, the naive pigeon will imitate the leader at a low rate day after day without any reinforcement. Moreover, it will subsequently continue to peck or pull for several sessions without a leader present.

Instructional control. A second source of novelty in human behavior, also a social process, is instructions. The first time we drive a car or play the piano or bake a cake, we are usually following instructions. We could simulate the effect of instructions in producing new behavior by bringing several different responses under the control of different discriminative stimuli and then presenting the stimuli in new orders or by bringing the force of a response under the control of the size of some stimulus and then making the stimulus smaller or larger than it ever was before (cf. Catania, 1980). Human language will be considerably more powerful in this capacity than anything we can simulate with pigeons.

Variation. A third and in many respects the most fundamental source of novelty is variation, nature's own source of novelty, both at the ontogenic and phylogenic levels. We speak of classes of responses, just as taxonomists speak of classes of organisms, because—although it is true that the same response never occurs twice—related responses covary. Like Darwin, we depend on variation to account for novelty, at least in some instances, and again, like Darwin, we know nothing about the underlying mechanism. We also depend on variation to produce novel behavior: We are able to "shape" behavior only because there is always a distribution of responses from which to make a selection. As long as the response we reinforce is not near the mode of the distribution, a new distribution will appear from which we can make another selection. By continuing to strengthen infrequent responses, we can eventually produce behavior that has never occurred before, as when we gradually increase the force requirement for a lever press in a classroom demonstration until a rat presses with a force equal to its own weight. Relatively little research has been done on variation per se; it is simply a fact about behavior which we make use of daily but which is otherwise quite mysterious.

Interconnection. A fourth source of novelty is a phenomenon we might call "the spontaneous interconnection of repertoires" (cf. Hull, 1935). Separate repertoires of behavior can come together in new situations to produce blends, new sequences of behavior, or—by bringing an organism into contact with new contingencies—behaviors that have new functions. This is in many respects the most dramatic and mysterious source of novelty and is probably responsible for much of the behavior people call creative in science and the arts, as well as certain productive aspects of language (Place, 1981).

Several popular and highly speculative theories of creativity describe a similar process: Writer Arthur Koestler (1964), for example, attributed creativity to something he calls "bisociation," which is "any mental occurrence simultaneously associated with two habitually incompatible contexts." Rothenberg (1971), a psychiatrist, said that creativity is based on what he calls "Janusian thinking" (from Janus, the god with two faces), which is the ability "to conceive and utilize two or more opposite or contradictory ideas, concepts, or images simultaneously." Norman Maier (1929), a Gestalt psychologist, defined "reasoning," which was to him a creative process, as "the combination of isolated experiences." The mathematician Poincaré (1946) spoke of the collision of ideas, rising into consciousness "in crowds" "until pairs interlocked" in accounting for some of his achievements.

The combinatorial process described above is less speculative than the latter four, but if it works in covert behavior the way it works in overt behavior, it may be just the process about which Koestler and others were speaking. The spontaneous interconnection of repertoires is actually surprisingly accessible to laboratory study. It has occurred in a number of the Columban Simulations. One was called "The Spontaneous Use of Memoranda" (Epstein & Skinner, 1981), which was a follow-up of the symbolic communication demonstration we did with Jack and Jill (Epstein, Lanza, & Skinner, 1980). After we established the original exchange, we changed the positions of the birds until each had acquired both the "speaker" and "listener" repertoires. Among other things, each subject had now learned to pair colors (red, green, and yellow) with letters (R, G, and Y) and letters with colors. When the partition that had separated Jack and Jill was removed and one bird was given access to both response panels at once, a new sequence emerged without our intervention: Those parts of the speaker and listener repertoires which were successful in this new situation became interconnected to form a new chain. A bird would peck a color hidden behind a curtain, peck (and thus illuminate) the corresponding black-on-white letter, cross to the other side of the chamber, *look back* at the illuminated letter, and, finally, peck the corresponding color key.

The repertoires that had been established prior to the test not only provided the makings of the new sequence, they also brought the pigeon into contact with new contingencies, according to which a peck at a letter key now served a new function—that of mediating the delay between a peck at the hidden color and a peck at a corresponding color on the other panel. Without providing any additional training, we conducted a series of tests over a 5-month period which indicated that these pecks were indeed functioning as memoranda. When the task was made easier, for example, the pigeons stopped pecking the letter keys; when the task was made more difficult, they began pecking them appropriately once more. When Jack was distracted by a loud noise before a peck at a color key, he would start and then *look back* at the illuminated letter key before pecking the corresponding color key.

An even more striking example of the spontaneous interconnection of repertoires occurred in our experiment on "insight" (Epstein, 1981a; Epstein, Kirshnit, Lanza, & Rubin, 1984). A pigeon was trained both to push a box toward a target and to climb onto a stationary box and peck a small toy banana. When the banana was placed out of reach and the box placed elsewhere on the floor of the chamber—a situation very much like the one with which Köhler (1925) confronted his chimpanzees—the two repertoires occurred one after the other, and hence the pigeon "solved the problem." We have conducted this experiment now many times and have varied the training histories to determine the contributions of a number of different experiences. For example, if brute force attempts to get at the banana by flying and jumping are extinguished before the test, the solution may occur rather quickly (in about a minute, for several birds). If such behavior is not extinguished, the pigeon will first attempt to reach the banana by brute force, as did Köhler's chimpanzees.

On the basis of various controls we have completed so far, we can give a tentative, moment-to-moment account of a successful performance. The test situation is a new one for the bird, so at first there may be very little behavior and then what appears to be competition between the climbing and pushing repertoires (stimuli are present which control both repertoires).[5] The bird manages to look "puzzled": It looks back and forth from banana to box, stretches toward the banana, motions toward the box, and so on. At some point the bird starts to push the box. If it had been previously trained to push the box toward a small green spot at the base of the chamber—one training scenario—it very clearly starts to push to box *toward* the banana. This, it now appears, is a matter of generalization, although not based on physical similarity but rather on the fact that behavior with respect to both the green spot and the banana had been reinforced. A bird trained to push the box toward the green spot but not to peck the banana or climb on the box did not push the box toward the banana when the banana was placed out of reach in the chamber.[6]

Once the bird has pushed the box in the neighborhood of the banana, it has arranged for itself a new stimulus—box under banana—which is the occasion upon which the second repertoire, climbing onto the box and pecking the banana, had been reinforced. We call this process "automatic chaining," since the bird has automatically arranged the discriminate stimulus for the second link of a two-component chain.

Reinforcement. I have mentioned four sources of novelty but have managed to omit reinforcement. Psychologists have been using reinforcement to promote novelty for decades (e.g., Goetz & Baer, 1973; Maltzman, 1960); isn't it a source of novelty? Reinforcement, I submit, is probably not a source of novelty per se but rather: 1) It may stimulate activity and in so doing increase the amount of variation we see in behavior. But almost any stimulus will do that; it needn't be a reinforcer. 2) By strengthening one response over another from the distribution of available responses, it can produce a new distribution in which, because behavior varies, new behavior occurs. Variation is the actual source of novelty in this case (cf. Fenner, 1980; Staddon & Simmelhag, 1971). 3) It can serve to establish a discrimination between what is new and not new. Given reinforcement, for example, for building novel block structures, a child would come to preserve structures that he (or she) hasn't seen before and destroy or alter structures like those he had already built. Similarly, if income and recognition are contingent on originality, an artist might push aside or alter a design that resembles that of another artist or another of his or her own works. Schwartz's (1980) finding that pigeons cannot learn to emit novel sequences of pecks indicates only that he could not establish the discrimination between old and new sequences, not that pigeons are incapable of significant novel behavior (cf. Pryor, Haag, & O'Reilly, 1969).

"Promoting Creativity." Arieti (1976), Guilford (1950), Koestler (1964), Maltzman (1960), Osborn (1953), Skinner (1970, 1981b), Torrance (1962, 1963),

and many others have offered techniques for "promoting creativity." Many techniques, such as brainstorming, free association, spending time alone, daydreaming, "free thinking," and inactivity, provide circumstances under which behavior is free to vary or old behaviors are likely to come together in new ways.

MEASURES OF MIND

In their influential text on theories of learning, Bower and Hilgard (1981) ask, "Do behaviorists confuse the subject matter of [psychology—which is to say, cognition] with the evidence available for drawing inferences about the subject matter?" (p. 211). A sentence or two earlier they query, "Is physics the science of physical things, or the science of meter readings?" The rhetoric is misleading.

Let us assume that physics is indeed the science of physical things.[7] Praxics would seem to have a lot in common with it, for analysts of behavior use meters (videotape recorders, computers, cumulative recorders, event recorders, and so on) to measure physical things—events in behavior and the environment.

Bower and Hilgard overlook the fact that physicists use measuring devices, not to make inferences about physical things, but to measure them. The things they measure presumably exist. Praxists do the same. It is the cognitivists who are doing something unique—that is, using measuring devices to measure events in behavior and the environment, and then using the obtained measurements to speculate about a domain that can never be directly measured and whose very existence is uncertain. ("Cognition," after all, is just a nine-letter substitute for a four-letter word. What they're really interested in is Mind.)

Reaction time. The problem of measurement is not a trivial one for cognitivists, for there must always be some doubt about whether their measurements are making contact with the mental phenomenon in which they are interested. The problem is exemplified in the use of reaction time to make inferences about mental processes.

Oswald Külpe, a student of Wundt's, struck a near-fatal blow against the use of reaction time in his *Outlines of Psychology* in 1893. Donder's subtraction procedure, he argued, is valid only if complicated tasks, such as discrimination or choice, preserve the simpler components of which the complicated task is supposedly composed. There is no way to know a priori that this is the case, since direct measurement of the processes is impossible. As Woodworth (1936) later put it, "Since we cannot break up the reaction time into successive acts and obtain the time of each act, of what use is the reaction time?" (p. 309). Külpe and contemporaries were also disturbed by contradictory and unreliable results. With the emergence of functional and behavioristic psychologies in the first two decades of this century, the use of reaction time as a means of inference about cognition lost its popularity.

With the rise of cognitive psychology in the 1950s and 1960s, however, reaction time has come into use again and in fact may now be psychology's most popular measure of behavior. But the old problems have not gone away. Since the object of study can never be measured directly, the same data are always subject to more than one interpretation. Consider the debate that has been raging since the 1950s about whether perception works by template matching (Selfridge & Neisser, 1960; Uhr, 1963) or feature detection (Selfridge, 1959), or the recent debate about whether the facts from which mental imagery is inferred require functional mental images (Kosslyn & Pomerantz, 1977) or a set of propositions (Pylyshyn, 1973), or the controversy over whether retrieval from short-term memory is a serial or a parallel process (Corcoran, 1971; Donahoe & Wessells, 1980; Sternberg, 1969, 1975). Data cannot resolve such debates because components of the various models (rehearsal buffers, storage bins, executive processors, tree structures, and so on) are not constrained by direct observations (of neural structures, for example), and hence, as Anderson (1978) has noted, the models can almost always be modified to take descrepant data into account.

Kosslyn and other "cognitive scientists" are not, for all the trappings, studying cognition; they are studying the effects of extremely complex histories, stimulus materials, and instructions on reaction times and other measures of behavior—and then showing how information processing systems might behave in such ways. This enterprise can shed light on people only if people are information processors, a debatable assertion (Epstein, 1981a, 1982b, 1984a).

Skinner and I conducted a modest program of research with a pigeon using reaction time. We first arranged contingencies to produce good waiting behavior and fast key pecks. An auditory ready signal of varying length preceded the onset of a keylight. If a peck occurred within a certain period of time, a feeder operated. The requirement was changed until we reached what appeared to be an asymptotically fast reaction, which was in the range of human simple reaction time (about 200 msec). We then added a discrimination: a peck produced food if the key became transilluminated with green and had no consequence if it became transilluminated with white. With the discrimination well established, the average reaction time to green increased over the simple reaction time. According to Donder's method, the difference in the two times should give us the time for "pure discrimination."

Using similar procedures with humans, Hick (1952) estimated this time to be about 110 msec, and Hyman (1953) found a difference of about 100 msec. The average difference for our pigeon was about the same—120 msec. This tells us that similar requirements produce similar changes in reaction time for humans and at least one pigeon. We add nothing to this fact by claiming that we have measured the time of "pure discrimination" in the pigeon. No doubt there are other correspondences between changes in reaction times in humans and pigeons (cf. Blough, 1977; Hollard & Delius, 1982). But why this is so—or not so—is a matter for the physiologist. Models of the mind can neither account for nor in any way shed light on such a coincidence.

SELF-CONCEPT

The concept of a self-concept exemplifies the dilemma of cognitive psychology and has provided an opportunity for demonstrating some advantages of a behavioral approach.[8] The behavior from which it is inferred fits into the fourth category of troublesome phenomena I outlined earlier: It is complex, distinctively human, and not easily traceable to environmental or biological factors. Like language, the behavior that comes under the rubric of "self" is acquired haphazardly over a period of years; in many cases the controlling stimuli are not observable by others.

Like "creativity," "self-concept" is a natural category and hence difficult to define. A wide variety of behavior is said to provide evidence for its existence: body-directed behavior in front of a mirror, pointing to one's picture, gazing at one's picture longer than at another person's picture (for young children, anyway—perhaps, under some circumstances, adults would do the opposite), imitating a videotape of oneself more than a videotape of someone else, and so on. At least these are the measures used by psychologists who study the self-concept (e.g., Amsterdam, 1972; Gallup, 1970; Lewis & Brooks-Gunn, 1979). The verbal behavior said to show "self-knowledge"—describing one's thoughts, feelings, aches and pains, actions, and so on—would also seem to contribute to various notions of "self"; Skinner (e.g., 1945b, 1957, 1963, 1974) has offered an account of verbal behavior of this type.

"Self-concept" is one of many psychological terms which is often reified. It is said not only to exist but to grow, in embryonic fashion (Lewis & Brooks-Gunn, 1979). It is, furthermore, mistakenly used to explain behavior that, at best, it only characterizes. Gallup (1979), for example, attributes a lack of behavior said to show self-awareness to a lack of "a sense of identity" and "a sufficiently well-integrated self-concept." That kind of explanation is no explanation at all. Since we can never test for the existence of self-concept independently of the existence of the behaviors said to show it, we can never test the explanation. And no explanation is given for why the self-concept itself may be lacking.

Such a concept obscures the search for more concrete determinants of the behavior. Since it functions grammatically as an explanation, no further explanation is sought. Yet more concrete explanations are usually available.

The rubric of self also mistakenly implies that all of the various "self" behaviors have the *same* cause or causes—in the worst case, the cause is said to be the self itself. But, parsimony notwithstanding, it is absurd to think that mirror-directed behavior has the same determinants as an answer to the question "Where does it hurt?" or that a child comes to respond to photographs of its face differently than to photographs of other faces for still the same reasons. Each of the various behaviors said to show the existence of a self-concept demands its own investigation and analysis. A child has many thousands of learning experiences during his or her first few years of life, and physical maturation has profound effects. A child not only rapidly acquires a wide variety of self-controlled behaviors but many other complex behaviors, as well—verbal and other social behaviors, complex motor skills, and so on. That many "self" behaviors seem to be acquired more or less in unison (Kagan, 1981) is not surprising—after all, *many other* complex behaviors are also acquired during the same period. The first few years of life are a period of rapid acquisition; covariance is—indeed, it *must be*—the rule.

And what of parsimony? A different set of determinants for each of a dozen different "self" behaviors is hardly appealing. The parsimonious solution may prove to lie with a general set of principles of behavior change—one set of functions describing such phenomena as reinforcement, extinction, resurgence, automatic chaining, maturational factors, and so on—that cut across many different "self" behaviors, and, of course, many other behaviors, as well. When a child selects his or her photograph from among a group of photographs, the child's behavior has the same functional characteristics as the behavior of a pigeon in a "delayed matching-to-sample" task. Similar principles might adequately describe both performances, and, in fact, it would be difficult at this point to rule out the possibility that similar neurophysiological processes underlie each performance. Automatic chaining must operate across many species and across many behaviors, verbal and non-verbal, self and non-self: An organism's own behavior changes its environment in such a way that the probability of subsequent behavior is changed. A student draws an arc on a geometry exam and, in so doing, creates new intersections where the point of the compass can rest. A pigeon pushes a box for the first time toward a suspended banana and, in so doing, sets up box-under-banana, the stimulus in whose presence climbing and pecking the banana had been reinforced in the past; the pigeon stops pushing, climbs, and pecks (see Epstein et al., 1984).

These matters aside, the behaviors that come under the rubric of "self" do seem to have one functional characteristic in common: They all seem to be controlled either by one's own body or by one's own behavior. I use "controlled" here in a technical sense: One's behavior or body is the setting for the "self" behavior; it is the stimulus to which one responds. One responds to one's mirror image—a reflection of one's body—in a special way. One answers the question "Where does it hurt?" by pointing to a location on one's body and the question "How do you feel?" by describing a state of one's body. One answers the question "What did you do last night?" by describing one's behavior.

So "self" behaviors are indeed self behaviors in some sense—they are "self"-controlled. But that does not justify the reification of the "self-concept"; nor does it tell us where these behaviors come from.

Mirrors. When first confronted with a mirror, virtually all birds and mammals, including both human children and adults, react either with indifference or as if they are seeing another organism of their species (Dixon, 1957; Gallup, 1968, 1970; Lewis & Brooks-Gunn, 1979; von Senden, 1960; Wolff, 1943). A variety of fish, birds, and mammals engage in social or aggressive displays or attack their mirror images (Boutan, 1913; Gallup, 1968; Köhler, 1925; Lissman, 1932; Lopez, 1979; Ritter & Benson, 1934; Tinbergen, 1951). Unlike other animals, humans and chimpanzees, after sufficient exposure to a mirror, come to react to their mirror images as images of their own bodies (Gallup, 1979; Lewis & Brooks-Gunn, 1979), although there is at least one contradictory report with chimpanzees (I. S. Russell, 1978). This phenomenon—often labeled "self-recognition"—has been studied for at least a century (consider Darwin, 1877).

The modern literature on the topic begins with a paper by Dixon (1957). Human children, according to Dixon, are said to progress through four stages of behavior with respect to their mirror images. In the first few months of life, there is little reaction. Soon the child begins to react to the image as if it were another child, by smiling, playing, touching, vocalizing, and so on. The third stage is one of "testing" or "discovery," characterized by "repetitive activity while observing the mirror image intently, e.g., alternately observing a hand or foot and its mirror image, opening and closing the mouth with deliberation or rising up and down slowly while keeping [the] eyes fixed on the mirror image" (p. 253). Finally, when the child is between 18 and 24 months old, it begins to react to the image as a reflection of its own body.

In the late 1960s Amsterdam (1968, 1972) devised an objective test to determine whether a child had reached the final stage. A mother would smear some rouge on her child's nose and then encourage the child to look at a mirror. If the child touched his or her nose, the child was said to be able to recognize his or her "self." By age 2, most children would do this. Using a mirror to locate a mark on one's body that one cannot see directly is now said to be "the most compelling example of self-directed behavior" (Lewis & Brooks-Gunn, 1979, p. 212).

Gallup (1970) showed that the same effect could be obtained with chimpanzees. Four chimpanzees were exposed to a large mirror for a total of 80 hours over a 10-day period. Social behavior was observed to decline over this period and self-directed behavior (such as grooming) to increase. Then the animals were anesthetized and a red dye was painted over an eyebrow bridge and on the top half of an ear. When the animals recovered, they were observed for 30 minutes in the absence of a mirror and for 30 minutes in the presence of a mirror. There were substantially more movements judged to be "mark-directed" in the presence of the mirror (virtually none without the mirror, and an average of 6 per animal with the mirror). Similar tests Gallup that arranged with nonhuman primates other than chimpanzees produced negative results. Since he attributed the behavior to a self-concept, he concluded that only man and the great apes (chimpanzees, at least) have this cognitive capacity.

"Self-awareness" in the pigeon. Epstein, Lanza, and Skinner (1981) provided an alternative account of mark-directed behavior in the mirror test by showing that, after some rather simple training over a period of less than 15 hours, a pigeon, too, could use a mirror to locate a spot on its body which it could not see directly. We first trained the pigeon to peck at blue stick-on dots placed on different parts of its body. Then we added a mirror to the pigeon's chamber and reinforced pecks at blue dots placed on the walls and floor. Finally, we briefly flashed blue dots on the walls or floor when the pigeon could see them only in the mirror. It received food if it turned and pecked the position where a blue dot had been flashed. We then conducted the following test: A blue stick-on dot was placed on the pigeon's breast and a bib placed around its neck in such a way that it prevented the bird from seeing the dot. The pigeon was observed first for 3 minutes in the absence of a mirror and then for 3 minutes in the presence of a mirror. Three subjects were tested. Independent observers scored videotapes for "dot-directed" responses. None were observed when the mirror was absent, and an average of 10 per bird were observed when it was present—greater than

10 times the rate of mark-directed responses that Gallup (1970) observed (Epstein, 1985f).

One might conclude from this experiment either that: (1) pigeons have a self-concept (few psychologists are likely to go to that extreme), (2) the mirror test is a bad test of self-concept (many will put their money here), or (3) as has already been asserted on other grounds, the self-concept is simply a superfluous scientific category.

These issues aside, we may also have in hand an account of the emergence of such behavior in chimpanzees and children, for there is ample evidence that both chimpanzees and children who pass the mirror test have already acquired both of the repertoires we established in our pigeons: They presumably have touched themselves many times in the places they must touch during the test, and they have had ample opportunities to come under the control of the contingencies of reinforcement which govern mirror use.

Contingencies. Normally, moving toward an object brings it closer and ultimately produces contact with it; one must move in a special way—which most of us never learn perfectly—to produce contact with an object whose reflection we see in a mirror. A mirror thus provides a new set of relationships between one's movements and their consequences—a new set of "contingencies."

These contingencies are rather weak, which is to say that under most circumstances: (1) the reinforcement they provide comes with less effort and more immediately if one simply faces an object directly, and (2) there is no penalty for *not* coming under their control. One would expect, therefore, that only special circumstances would bring an organism's behavior under their control and that the more sensitive the organism's behavior is to its consequences, the more readily the control will be established.

A pigeon, needless to say, would not normally come under the control of these contingencies. We had to supplement them. Attending to an object in the mirror and then finding it in real space not only produced the natural consequence—contact with the object—it also produced food, a powerful, effective reinforcer for a hungry pigeon. The food only supplemented the natural contingency; it did not obliterate or override it. The pigeon's behavior had to be under the control of the correspondence between mirrored and real space in order for food to be delivered.

"Discovery." The period of "testing" or "discovery" that Dixon (1957) described is undoubtedly the period during which a child's behavior comes under the control of the contingencies of reinforcement which govern mirror use. The child slowly learns the correspondence between the locations of parts of his or her body (and, presumably, of other objects) in real and mirrored space. Unlike the pigeon, the child needs no trainer, but this means only that a child's behavior is so sensitive to its consequences that even occasional exposure to weak contingencies is sufficient for control to be established. Because the contingencies are weak, however, and because the exposure is occasional, it often takes months for control to be established. Presumably, given systematic training, a child or monkey could learn the task even faster than our pigeons.

The same two repertoires probably account for a pigeon's, a chimpanzee's, and a person's success in the mirror test—and hence for some of the behavior often explained by the mythical "self-concept." The only impressive thing about chimpanzees and children is that they can acquire the second repertoire—albeit quite slowly—without explicit training. This is a matter of sensitivity to contingencies. *That* is how man and the great apes differ from other organisms, which should surprise no one.

CONCLUSIONS

Praxists have never really met the cognitivists' challenge because in restricting our research to simple behaviors and simple stimuli, we have ignored most of the complex phenomena that they investigate daily. Cognitivists and developmentalists have not found useful answers because they have not asked the right questions. There is little value in trying to determine what a mental structure looks like or how it grows. We achieve a more effective understanding by discovering how the behavior of an organism, both inside and out, is determined by environmental histories and genetic endowments, and ultimately, how changes in behavior are mediated by the body. A model of problem solving is no substitute for a determination of how genes and the environment produce effective behavior. A specification of deep structure or rules of transformation can't tell us where these things come from or how to put them into someone when they seem to be lacking. Attributing insightful behavior to insight is uninformative. Attributing behavior said to show self-awareness to a self-concept tells us nothing.

The time has come for praxists to answer the challenge by bringing complex behavior into the laboratory—in a sense, by giving the freely-moving organism a little more freedom to move.

NOTES

1. "Praxics"—a blend of "physics" and "praxis," the Greek for "to behave"—is a term I and others now use for the study of behavior. "Behaviorism," properly speaking, is the name of a school of philosophy. For a fuller discussion of this terminology, see Chapter 18, this volume.
2. Catania (1979) justifiably makes the same point about the word "learning."
3. The rationale for using pigeons in such experiments is given at length elsewhere (e.g., Chapter 12, this volume). Carefully constructed simulations of complex human behavior with nonhuman subjects can provide "plausibility proofs" of the role that certain environmental histories play in the emergence of the behavior. In some cases more definitive research cannot be conducted, usually for ethical reasons. The plausibility of such simulations rests on five factors: the topography of the behavior, the function of the behavior, the structure of the organism, the generality of the behavioral processes invoked, and evidence that humans have had the relevant histories. Not all of the studies referred to in the present paper meet these criteria.
4. There is a previous report of spontaneous imitation in pigeons (Zentall & Hogan, 1976). In that report, however, the observing animals were technically not "naive," since they had been hopper-trained, and the observed effect was small. There are perhaps

hundreds of other investigations of both innate and learned imitation in both animals and humans (e.g., see Flanders, 1968; Miller & Dollard, 1941; Porter, 1910; Thorpe, 1963).

5. Multiple repertoires can be made available in several ways. The first, which seems to apply in the version of the box-and-banana experiment described above, is multiple controlling stimuli: Compound, ambiguous, and novel stimuli should increase the likelihood of all of the behaviors controlled by their constituents. There is some evidence that this is an orderly, quantifiable process (Cumming & Eckerman, 1965; Migler, 1964). A second phenomenon is the resurgence of previously reinforced behavior during extinction (Epstein, 1983a, 1985a; Epstein & Medalie, 1983; cf. Epstein & Skinner, 1980; Hull, 1934; Leitenberg, Rawson, & Bath, 1970; Maltzman, 1955; Staddon & Simmelhag, 1971). Resurgence during extinction may be one of the most important determinants of behavior that is often mistakenly labeled—even by me—"spontaneous" (e.g., Epstein & Medalie, 1983; Epstein & Skinner, 1981).

6. I have tested this interpretation by repeating the test with two other birds who have had such training and then testing them again after they have been trained to peck the banana. The pigeons pushed more directly toward the banana in the second test. Similarly, a child who has spotted a cookie jar on a table and then retrieved it by pushing a chair toward the table and climbing on the chair will more likely do so the next day to retrieve a toy car than to retrieve a roll of toilet paper, although the latter more closely resembles the cookie jar. Such behavior suggests a process akin to what some describe as "functional" categorization (e.g., Bruner, Goodnow, & Austin, 1956).

7. Some physicists would debate the matter. According to Wheeler (1981), for example, quantum mechanics has taught us that "No elementary phenomenon is a phenomenon until it is a registered (observed) phenomenon"; that is, "until is has been brought to a close by an irreversible act of amplification" (pp. 24–25). Different registering devices, furthermore, provide different answers to the same question. According to this view, physics might be construed to be the science of meter readings.

8. A more detailed analysis of this topic appears in Chapter 30, this volume.

4

HOW TO GET A GREAT IDEA

Summary. Everyone has enormous creative potential. The people we tend to label "creative" have special skills, which anyone can master. Generativity Theory suggests four categories of skills that appear to be of special value in enhancing creativity.

The guests had arrived, and the wine, as usual, was warm. I had forgotten, once again, to put it in the refrigerator. The last time this happened, I put the bottle in the freezer when dinner began and promptly forgot about it until the next day. The result? A cracked bottle of 1982 Château Veyrac.

But this time a friend said, "Don't worry. If I can use your kitchen for a few minutes, I'll chill the wine for you right away."

Five minutes later she emerged from the kitchen with the same bottle of wine, now perfectly chilled. She was reluctant at first to reveal how she had accomplished this bit of wizardry, but when we threatened to report her for witchcraft, she relented.

"It was easy," she said. "I filled a large bowl with water and ice. Then I poured out the wine into a plastic bag and dipped the bag into the ice water. A few swishes and the wine was cold. The hard part was getting the wine back into the bottle, because I couldn't find a funnel. So I made a cone with wax paper and poured the wine through that. Instantly chilled wine and nothing to wash!"

My guests and I applauded warmly.

"What a remarkably creative person you are!" said another guest to the woman. "I wish *I* could be that clever."

"Yes," said another, "how wonderful it would be if we all could be like that."

The murmurs of assent around the room clinched her point: Most people think that originality is valuable, but very rare.

A decade of research on creativity has convinced me that my guests were wrong. I now believe that *everyone* is creative—and perhaps equally so. Everyone has the creative capacity of Shakespeare or Thomas Edison or Picasso.

It's just that most people never tap that capacity, or, to be more precise, they don't act on creative impulses when these impulses occur.

It's true that some people do more creative things than other people do. I think I know why that's true, and I think I know how to correct the situation—that is, how to unlock the creative potential that exists in every person.

Unlocking that potential could have real benefits for all of us, both as individuals and as members of society. In our daily lives we're always striving for new ideas: better ways to handle our kids and partners, better ways to run our businesses or impress our bosses —even new ways to have more fun.

American corporations, meanwhile, are desperate for new ideas because of fierce competition from foreign companies. The National Academy of Sciences reported recently that in 1977 34 percent of U. S. patents went to foreign firms; by 1987 that number had increased to 47 percent. And *Fortune* magazine reports that in the last few years Japan has gained patent shares and the U. S. has lost patent shares in 38 of 48 product categories. According to James Clark, head of Silicon Graphics, one of the most innovative high-tech companies in the world today, "We're losing our creative edge. American industry is on the decline because U. S. managers are too concerned about protecting short term earnings to innovate."

What's going on, and how can we address the problem?

Driven by industry's need, creativity products now abound in the marketplace. Self-help books and computer programs are promising a more creative you. You can buy creativity games, creativity headphones, and creativity audio and videotapes. For a reasonable sum, you can even spend an hour in a "creativity tank."

What *is* creativity, anyway, and what can you do to enhance it?

To answer that question, start by looking around you. The first thing you'll notice is that you and everyone around you are doing creative things all the time. They may be *small*, but they are creative nonetheless.

Your three-year-old daughter is trying to retrieve a toy from under the sofa. She stretches and stretches, but she can't quite reach the toy. Then she looks around, grabs a magazine that was lying on the floor, and uses the magazine to push the toy out from under the sofa. For a toddler, that's quite an accomplishment.

You're locked out of your house. You check under the mat for the spare key. You push and pull on the doorknob in new ways. You circle the house looking for open windows. You grab a ladder from the garage and climb to a window that looks ajar. You call your spouse from a neighbor's phone and ask for help. In an emergency, you might break a window or pry a door open. Although none of these ideas is elegant, they are also far from routine.

All around you people in every walk of life are generating new ideas, important and unimportant. You drive down the road and see men puzzling over how to remove a truck from a muddy ditch. An hour later you drive by again, and the truck is gone. Somehow, the men have done the job. A business associate is struggling with a new computer printer. The next day, the printer is running smoothly. Somehow, the right buttons got pushed. Your neighbor is using a rake to try to retrieve a kite from a tree, but the rake won't reach. When you look out the window again, the kite is gone. Somehow, your neighbor solved the problem.

If you examine your behavior closely enough, you will find that everything you do is *new*. It may not be *important*—that's another matter—but it's definitely *new*, if only in small ways.

Every sentence that you speak or write is new in some way. The sentence I just wrote, for example, is a sentence I have *never* written before (and so is *this* one!). When you say "Good morning" to your boss or spouse, you say it a little differently each time. The differences are noticeable enough so that someone who knows you well can usually discern your mood from those two simple words.

Even the child who has to write "I won't throw chalk at the teacher" fifty times writes it a *little differently* each time. The last ten sentences are usually pretty hard to read.

Using an instrument called a spectrograph, researchers find that spoken words vary dramatically in their acoustical characteristics from one repetition to another and from one person to another. That's why we're still having trouble building computers that can understand human speech.

All human behavior—thinking, speaking, writing, playing, and tooth brushing—is variable. Everything we do is genuinely *novel*, and in that sense, every one of us is creative all the time.

But isn't there a difference between everyday creativity and the dramatic cases of creativity we attribute to writers, composers, artists, inventors, and scientists?

Generativity Theory, the theory that has grown out of my research, suggests that the answer to this question is no. The theory suggests that the same simple processes are responsible both for everyday problem solving and the most remarkable examples of composing or painting. You have a great deal in common with Einstein and Mozart, even though you may not yet have achieved your full potential.

Even pigeons can do remarkably creative things under the right conditions. In a series of experiments I conducted a few years ago, I showed that pigeons that have had relevant experiences can solve a classic problem—the "box-and-banana problem"—in a human-like fashion. I first rewarded the pigeons with food for climbing onto a box and pecking a small facsimile of a banana suspended above their heads. I also taught them to push a box toward targets at ground level. Finally, I confronted each pigeon with a problem—a situation the pigeon has never seen before: The toy banana was suspended out of reach, and the box was on the floor about eighteen inches from the position directly beneath the banana. Would the pigeon push the box beneath the banana to reach it by climbing onto the box?

A pigeon in this situation behaves very much like we do in comparable situations: At first it looks confused. It walks back and forth and stretches repeatedly toward the toy banana. It may jump and fly toward the banana, but no food is given. Finally, after just a minute or two, the pigeon starts to push the box directly toward the banana, sighting the banana as it pushes. Then it stops pushing in just the right spot, climbs, and pecks the banana.

If a pigeon can do that, just think of the possibilities for the rest of us!

Different training histories produce different, but predictable, outcomes. Pigeons that have never been trained to push the box stretch toward the banana and look confused, but they can't solve the problem. Pigeons that have never been trained to climb push the box to the right place, but they are unable to climb and peck. (One ambitious bird leaned against the box so hard that it tripped over the box and fell.)

Clearly, different experiences make a big difference in creative performances, but there's more to creativity than experience. What you have learned in the past *unravels* and *develops* and becomes *transformed* in new situations. New performances emerge as *different behaviors*—like climbing and pushing—compete with each other simultaneously. *The blending and alternation of multiple behaviors is the stuff of creativity.* New behaviors emerge as old ones emerge and compete.

These and many other experiments with both pigeons and people led to the development of Generativity Theory, a scientific theory of creativity. Through equations and a computer model, the theory has been successful in predicting and engineering creative performances in people, and it also suggests concrete ways of enhancing creativity in all of us.

We can see old ideas blending to form new ones everyday, in every walk of life. A friend told me that, as a child, she longed for a swimming pool and finally invented her own. She had helped place leaves into large plastic bags, and she knew how to run the water hose. Why not put water into the bag? Her pool-for-one worked well, and she was proud of her invention.

When replacing light bulbs, I've occasionally dropped one onto the floor. The result is a grenade-like explosion. "If only the floor were softer," I thought after one such frustrating incident. Now I place a soft pillow on the floor before I start. I unscrew the old bulb and drop it onto the pillow, freeing both hands to install the new bulb. This is especially efficient when the old bulb is hot.

Ideas are competing and blending whenever we use common objects in new and unconventional ways for the first time. One of my students told me that when he lacked a screwdriver one day, he resorted to using the metal tab on his pants zipper. (To spare him further embarrassment, I didn't ask for the details.) We've all used screwdrivers or rocks in place of hammers, and some of us have even used padlocks, hairbrushes, and shoes. The edge of a magazine can serve as a reasonably good straight-edge, but I know someone who, needing a perfectly rigid edge, took apart a picture frame and used the pane of glass.

The blending of ideas has helped some of the world's greatest geniuses in much the same way that it helps us each day. For example, the eminent mathematician Henri Poincaré made his most important discovery one restless evening after having drunk too much coffee. Wrote Poincaré, "Ideas rose in crowds; I felt them collide until pairs interlocked, so to speak, making a stable combination." The great American writer, Thomas Wolfe, attributed his progress

How to Get a Great Idea 55

to "a whirling vortex and a creative chaos ... of infinite confusion." Albert Einstein spoke of "combinatory play" in explaining his own creative ability. Rothenberg, an American psychiatrist, attributes creativity to "Janusian thinking"; Janus was the god of *two* faces. And the great English poet and playwright, John Dryden, spoke of "a confus'd mass of Thoughts, tumbling over one another in the Dark" as essential to his own creative efforts.

The next time you feel confused, remember that you're in good company. Confusion is a sign that important ideas are in stiff competition, and competition between ideas is the starting point of new ones.

Some of the greatest inventions in history came about as a result of this process. Edwin Land, one of America's most prolific inventors, credited his 3-year-old daughter with setting ideas in motion that led to the invention of the Polaroid camera. On a visit to Santa Fe in 1943, she asked him why she couldn't see the picture he had just taken? During the next hour, as Land walked around Santa Fe, all that he had learned about chemistry came together, with amazing results. Said Land, "All that we at Polaroid had learned about making polarizers and plastics, and the properties of viscous liquids, and the preparation of microscopic crystals ... was preparation for that day in which I suddenly knew how to make a one-step photographic process."

Velcro was the creation of the Swiss engineer, Georges de Mestral. Returning from a hunting trip, he became intrigued with the way thistle blossoms clung to his clothing. Again, a confusion of ideas—hooks, cloth, and thistles—led to a remarkable invention. Even the word "Velcro" is a blend of these ideas: *velours* for cloth, and *crochet* for hook.

You can take advantage of what scientists know about creativity to discover the new ideas that are already in you every day and to enhance your own ability to generate new, useful ones. Here are four easy methods for discovering and generating your own new ideas:

1. Capture the Fleeting. We all have novel ideas all the time, and at least *a few* of them *are* interesting and worth pursuing. The problem is to *seize* the interesting ones before they slip away.

How many times have you learned of a new invention or technique, a new gadget or a prize-winning slogan, and thought, "I could have come up with that" or even "I thought of that last year!" Indeed, you might have done just that, but you probably let the idea come and go without acting on it.

A little girl once told me that a good idea is like a rabbit. It runs by *very* fast, and sometimes you can only see its ears or its tail. To capture a rabbit, you've got to be *ready* for it. People we call "creative" are always poised for the capture, and that may be the only difference between "creative" people and the rest of the world. Artists, for example, carry sketchpads, and writers carry notebooks with them everywhere or keep tape recorders by their beds. *You* can do similar things.

The American poet Amy Lowell wrote of the urgency with which she captured new ideas for a poem. "I never deny poems when they come," she wrote. "Whatever I am doing, whatever I am writing, I lay it aside and attend to the arriving poem." Like many writers, Lowell sought paper and pencil when she saw a good idea coming; these days a pocket tape recorder can also do the trick. I enter new ideas into a pocket computer; when it's not handy, a scrap of paper will do.

Good ideas really do come and go quickly, and sometimes the very greatest ideas have been lost when the creator has failed to capture them. For example, from his bed in the middle of the night, the biologist Otto Loewi once hastily scribbled some notes about a solution to a critical problem he was encountering in his research on the chemical activity of brain cells. The next morning, to his utter dismay, he found that he could not read his notes! He had written them in almost total darkness, and they were indecipherable. Fortunately, late the next night the same idea occurred to him. This time, he took no chances. He slipped on his clothes, went straight to his laboratory, and put his new ideas to work. This research earned him a Nobel prize and greatly augmented our understanding of the nervous system.

In a letter to a friend written in 1821, Ludwig von Beethoven recounts how he thought of a beautiful canon while dozing in a carriage. "But scarcely did I awake when away flew the canon," he wrote, "and I could not recall any part of it." Fortunately—for Beethoven and for us—the next day in the same carriage, the canon came back to him, and *this* time he captured it by writing it down.

The other day I reorganized some files on research I'm conducting now on humor. In one was a tattered napkin, complete with food stains. It was on this napkin, back in 1985, that I first captured a new idea about how humor works, and I've been following up ever since.

When a good idea comes to you, grab it! Jot it down on a tablecloth, or write in on your arm if necessary! *It may never come back again, so act quickly.*

To catch a rabbit, you also need to be in the right place at the right time. To capture your best ideas, you need to find the times and places that work for you. You will probably find that peace and quiet are key. For many, the "three b's of creativity" are helpful— *the bed, the bath, and the bus*— since these are occasions when you are alone with your thoughts.

Great artists and composers don't take such matters for granted, and neither should the rest of us if we want to discover our very *best* ideas. For example, Mozart once wrote, "When I am, as it were, completely myself, entirely alone, and of good cheer—say, travelling in a carriage, or walking after a good meal, or during the night when I cannot sleep; it is on such occasions that my ideas flow best and most abundantly. *Whence* and *how* they come I know not; nor can I force them."

We all have fantasies and dreams, but very few of us take advantage of the new ideas they contain. Albert Einstein once wrote, "When I examine myself and my methods of thought, I come to the conclusion that the gift of fantasy has meant more to me than my talent for absorbing knowledge." Einstein fantasized about riding trains and elevators and even beams of light. Most of us probably have even richer fantasies than Einstein's.

The surrealist painter Salvador Dali tapped his creative potential by lying on a sofa with his hand grasping a spoon, which he balanced on a edge of a glass on the floor. Just as he would drift off to sleep, while in a semi-sleep state called the "hypnogogic" state, Dali would drop the spoon into the glass. The sound of spoon against glass would awaken him, and he would immediately sketch the images he had been envisioning while in the very fertile semi-sleep state.

Everyone experiences this strange hypnogogic state, not just wild-eyed artists, and everyone can take advantage of it. I've jumped out of bed twice in just the last week with new ideas flowing from this state—one for a cartoon and the other for a lecture demonstration.

Not every idea you capture will have value, of course. But the point is to *capture first and evaluate later.*

Find the best places and times for your new ideas to emerge, and then listen carefully. And *always be ready*—for a new invention, a new story, a new recipe, or a new approach to a problem in your life—no matter when and where such ideas occur. Then *capture* your idea in any way you can. You can follow up later at your leisure.

2. Seek Challenges. Failure is a great spur to creativity because it makes many behaviors occur simultaneously, which results in rapid and new combinations.

When you're stuck behind a locked door, every behavior that's ever gotten you through a door turns up quickly: You may push or pull on the doorknob, bang the door, or even shout for your mother. Scientists call the recurrence of old behaviors in a challenging situation *resurgence*. The more behaviors that resurge, the greater the number of possible interconnections and combinations, and the greater the number of possible new ideas.

If you sit at home unchallenged all day, your new ideas may all be pretty mundane (but they're still there!). The process is enhanced if you take some risks and fail sometimes.

Failure is widely recognized by scientists, inventors, writers, and artists as a great spur to creativity. The writer Henry Miller traces the agony of learning to write in this way: "I imitated every style in the hope of finding the clue to the gnawing secret of how to write. Finally I came to a dead end, to a despair and desperation which few men have known, because there was no divorce between myself as writer and myself as man.... I realized that I was nothing—less than nothing—a minus quantity. It was at this point, in the midst of the dead Sargasso Sea, so to speak, that I really began to write. I began from scratch, throwing everything overboard, even those whom I loved. Immediately I heard my own voice [and] I was enchanted."

Sometimes you need great courage to be creative. To act on a new idea means taking a risk. But without risk, there can be no progress, either in your own life or in the world at large. In 1869 the great Russian chemist, Dmitri Mendeleev, published a "periodic table" of the elements of matter, especially remarkable in that it was incomplete. Where there were holes in the chart—that is, where elements were missing—he predicted that they would eventually be discovered. His colleagues laughed—until indeed they were. Galileo was humiliated and banished for challenging the earth-centered view of the universe, but even under duress, he is said to have murmured to his inquisitors "Yet the world does move."

In an article entitled "I'd Pick More Daisies," Nadine Stair, an 87-year-old woman from Kentucky, stated the case, ever so gently, for taking risks in life. The article began, "If I had my life to live over, I'd try to make more mistakes next time. I would relax. I would limber up. I would be sillier than I have been this trip." One happy result of making more mistakes is the generation of new and interesting ideas.

3. Surround Yourself with New Combinations of Objects, People, and Situations. Exposure to *multiple stimuli* works a little like challenges. It makes many behaviors strong simultaneously, again enhancing the number and rate of possible combinations.

Sometimes new combinations of stimuli can make you feel confused. Have you ever approached a stoplight on which *green* and *red* were illuminated at the same time? I have, and it made my head spin. But remember that you're in the company of some very distinguished people when you're feeling confused, and you may be just on the verge of some great new ideas.

The modern theory of electron spin was invented when a young physicist, pondering over the strange behavior of electrons, saw a paper plate spin into the air at a restaurant. A spot of sauce on the plate made a peculiar pattern as the plate spun, and that pattern reminded the scientist of a phenomenon he had observed in the laboratory. From that, a new theory was born.

Closer to home, your microwave oven owes its existence to a chance combination of stimuli at the Raytheon laboratories in Massachusetts, back in 1946. Percy Spencer, one of the scientists investigating microwave radiation there, happened to have a piece of candy in his pocket during a laboratory session. Exposed briefly to the radiation, the candy grew warm. Undoubtedly, Spencer felt considerable confusion at that moment, but he followed up on this chance event, and ultimately microwaves were developed for use in cooking.

You can make yourself think in interesting new ways by deliberately surrounding yourself with new combinations of people, items, and situations. Invite a new combination of friends or business associates to a meeting or party, or bring people of two or even three generations together at the same time. Have you ever brought your friends and your parents together in the same room? It can be awkward, but it definitely gets you thinking in new ways about both your friends *and* your parents. Remember that it was Land's 3-year-old who got him thinking about instant photography. Anyone can jog your thinking in interesting ways, and the more diverse the company, the more interesting the jogs.

Put new and crazy items—like your kids' toys—on your desk. Keep clay or Silly Putty in your top drawer, and play with it when you're working on a sticky problem. Turn pictures upside down or sideways. Stand on your desk. These suggestions may sound odd, but they're precisely the kinds of things that creativity consultants and creativity products encourage you to do.

Remember, the more diverse the stimulation, the more interesting the ideas. You can *make* your world diverse and stimulating through very simple actions.

4. Learn Something New—Anything Will Do. The more you have learned, and the more *diverse* your training, the greater the number and range of behaviors that can become interconnected. Many breakthroughs in science, engineering, manufacturing, and other fields come from a blending of ideas culled from two *different* fields.

One of the problems I've studied is called "The Two-String Problem." Two long strings are hanging from a ceiling, far apart from each other, and you are asked to tie the ends of the strings together. You quickly find, however, that you can't reach both strings at once. What can you do?
The experimenter usually provides an object, such as a pliers, and you are told that you may use it to help solve the problem. But the pliers isn't long enough to help you reach both strings at once. Now what?
People often have trouble solving this simple problem, even after ten or fifteen minutes. (Has the solution occurred to you yet?) But one college student found the solution almost immediately: He tied the pliers to one of strings and set it in motion like a pendulum. As it swung back and forth, he walked quickly to the other string and drew it as far as it would go toward the swinging string. He caught the swinging string when it swung near him and promptly tied the two strings together.
I asked him how he had managed to solve the problem so quickly, and he explained that he had just come from a physics class on pendulum motion. *What he had learned in one context transferred quickly to a completely different one.* Would someone who had recently fixed a grandfather clock have also solved the problem readily? Probably so.
A friend told me how she gets her two boys to divide a cupcake or cookie exactly in half. "I tell them that one will do the cutting and the other will select whichever half he wants. The child doing the cutting always cuts straight down the middle so he won't get cheated."
I asked her how she came up with this wonderful idea.
"Easy," she said. "I saw a TV program on international negotiation!"
Rubbermaid recently expanded its product line to include office furniture manufactured by using the same blowmolding techniques the company uses to produce small plastic items for the home. Bud Hellman, an executive there, came up with the idea while touring a Rubbermaid plant where picnic coolers were being manufactured. According to Hellman, "If top management hadn't encouraged us to look at processes and technologies elsewhere in the company, none of this would have ever happened."
To enhance your creativity, learn some new things. And don't take the same old type of course or read the same old type of book. Learn something entirely different! If you're a banker, take up tap dancing. If you're a nurse, try a course in mythology. The new will interconnect with the old in novel and potentially fascinating ways.

Why does it seem sometimes that we have lost our creativity? After all, the generative processes never stop. So why do we have so few good ideas?

Our educational system is a big part of the problem. The creative process would be greatly augmented if our children were taught to master a large number of diverse subject areas, but our schools struggle these days just to teach the three R's.

What's more, our teachers don't have the time or resources to teach skills that enhance the creative process other than in very narrow contexts. If anything, our children are taught to *ignore* the constant flow of novel ideas that pass through their heads. During much of our youth, we are *criticized* or *punished* for acting on or even expressing our new ideas. One of the worst things a child can do in school is to daydream, even though the daydream, like the hypnogogic state, is one of our deepest wells of creativity.

Even though we may have been ignored or punished, the new ideas still keep flowing. You just can't shut off the generative processes. So becoming more creative is really a matter of learning to *pay attention* once again to the endless flow of novelty, and of learning to *capture, express, and act upon* the new that's within you.

PART II

THE COLUMBAN SIMULATIONS

5

SYMBOLIC COMMUNICATION BETWEEN TWO PIGEONS (*COLUMBA LIVIA DOMESTICA*)

Summary. Through the use of learned symbols, a pigeon accurately communicated information about hidden colors to another pigeon. Each verbal exchange was initiated with a spontaneous request for information. The two pigeons engaged in a sustained and natural conversation without human intervention.

In a recent report, Savage-Rumbaugh, Rumbaugh, and Boysen (1978) described the first successful demonstration of symbolic communication between two nonhuman primates. They showed that chimpanzees' nonverbal communication ability could be enhanced through learning. Specifically, the chimpanzees exchanged information about food through the use of geometric symbols. They were first taught to name a number of foods by pressing buttons on which corresponding symbols were marked. Then they were taught to request hidden food by using its symbolic name. Finally, in a test of how well information about a given food could be transmitted from one chimpanzee to another, one chimpanzee watched while some food was hidden and, in the presence of the second chimpanzee, was asked by the experimenter to indicate the symbolic name for that food. If the second chimpanzee then correctly asked for that food by using its symbolic name, both subjects were rewarded with the food. Also briefly described was a situation in which the chimpanzees spontaneously used symbols to request food from each other. Evidently, communication through the use of symbols is not an activity that is necessarily unique to man. The question naturally arises as to whether it is unique to primates.

This report presents, to our knowledge, the first instance of such symbolic communication between non-primates—two White Carneaux pigeons (*Columba livia domestica*). Pigeons are known to communicate under natural conditions by using coos, short grunts, and wing claps (Levi, 1957). We present here data showing that their natural inclination to communicate can be enhanced through learning and, in particular, that they are able to transmit information to one another by using symbols.

The communication system was similar to that of Savage-Rumbaugh et al. (1978). The pigeons expressed words or short phrases by depressing keys embossed with English letters or letters arranged to form words. Depressing a key illuminated it, affording both birds a clear view of the chosen symbol. The keys were arranged on adjoining keyboards (Figure 5.1) in a two-bird chamber 49 cm wide by 30 cm deep by 29 cm high. The front, top, and sides of the chamber were Plexiglas, and a Plexiglas partition in the center gave each bird a clear view of the other bird and its keyboard. Electromechanical feeders at the base of each of the side walls could be operated separately to give each bird access to mixed grain. A white noise source in one corner of the chamber partially masked extraneous sounds, but no other precautions were taken to shield the subjects from the visual and auditory distractions of the laboratory room. Events in the experiment were controlled and recorded by electromechanical equipment.

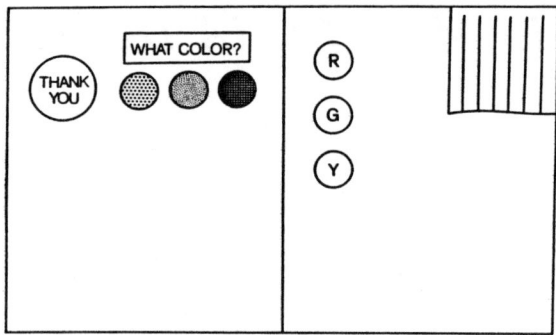

Figure 5.1. Adjoining keyboards for the two pigeons. Jack's is on the left and Jill's is on the right. Jack needs information about the color recessed 5 cm behind the curtain in the upper right-hand corner of Jill's keyboard. The R, G, and Y on Jill's keyboard are black on white. The three keys below the WHAT COLOR? key on Jack's keyboard are yellow, red, and green from left to right.

The subjects were two moderately hungry pigeons named Jack and Jill.[1] Each had had previous experience as a laboratory subject, but neither had been used before in procedures related to language or communication. Jack was the observer throughout the study, and Jill the informer. Each was trained separately for 5 weeks in daily sessions 1 to 3 hours in length before their communication ability was tested.

The animals were first taught to relate symbolic names to colors. Jill was taught to name three colors in response to the keyboard-imposed question "What color?" Jack was taught, conversely, to select the color corresponding to a designated name. When the pigeons were correct, they were rewarded with grain; when incorrect, all chamber lights were extinguished for several seconds. Both subjects learned to relate the colors and symbolic names with greater than 90 percent accuracy during the first 3 weeks of training.

After Jill, the informer, had reached this level of accuracy, she was taught to search for a color that was hidden from view. This was accomplished first by moving the colored lights progressively deeper into a recess in the upper right-hand corner of her keyboard (Figure 5.1) until they were 5 cm behind the surface. Jill learned to look at a color by inserting her head into the recess. The recess was then gradually covered by a curtain of gray, opaque vinyl until the colors were entirely hidden. (These precautions were taken to prevent Jack, the observer, from seeing the colors.) Jill learned to thrust her head through slits in the curtain to look at the hidden colors. She continued to name the colors with nearly 100 percent accuracy during this period.

After Jack had demonstrated his competence in decoding symbols into colors, he was taught to ask for symbols by depressing the WHAT COLOR? key. Finally, he was taught that after having been given a symbol, he should reward the informer with food before attempting to decode the symbol. He accomplished this by depressing the THANK YOU key, thus illuminating the key and operating Jill's feeder. Decoding accuracy declined during this period but reached better than 90 percent in 5 days of training. The subjects practiced their individual assignments for several sessions before the first interanimal test.

During the first interanimal test, greater-than-chance symbolic communication was achieved.[2] However, since neither bird had ever worked with the other before, each was somewhat distracted by the other's presence. To remedy this, we housed the subjects together continuously in the experimental chamber. After 5 days, both pigeons were responding accurately and efficiently on more than 90 percent of the trials.

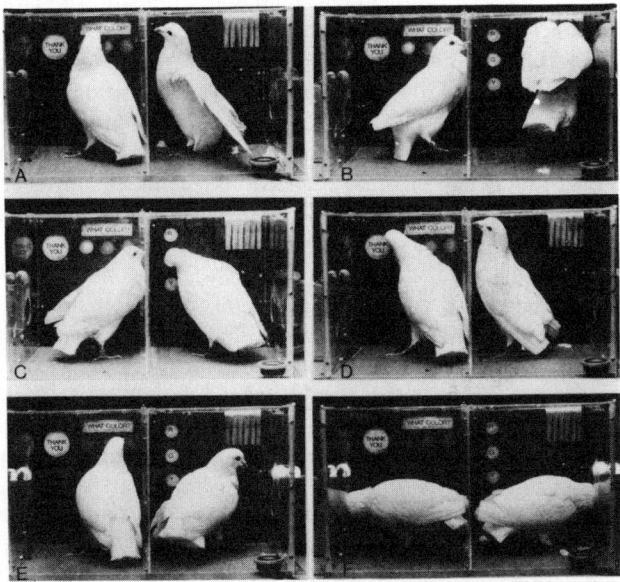

Figure 5.2. Typical communication sequence. (A) Jack (left) asks Jill (right) for a color name by depressing the WHAT COLOR? key. (B) Jill looks through the curtain at the hidden color. (C) Jill selects the symbolic name for the color while Jack watches. (D) Jack rewards Jill with food by depressing the THANK YOU key. (E) Jack selects the correct color as Jill moves toward her reward. (F) Jack is rewarded with food.

The final performance was a sustained and natural conversation (Figure 5.2). Jack initiated it by asking Jill for information about the hidden color. In response, Jill looked at the color behind the curtain and then depressed the key with the symbolic name for that color, illuminating the symbol. Having seen Jill accomplish this, Jack depressed the THANK YOU key, rewarding Jill with food. Then Jack looked closely at the illuminated symbol, decoded it, and selected the appropriate color on his panel, after which the equipment automatically rewarded him with food. Typically without hesitation, Jack than requested another color name.[3] Errors were infrequent, and both subjects were highly attentive and cooperative. If one delayed in depressing a key, the other often vigorously pecked at the restraining partition in an attempt to hasten performance.

To guarantee that the communication depended on the symbols, a control session was conducted in which the symbol keys on Jill's keyboard were covered. She proved unable to convey to Jack information about the hidden colors through any gestures or sounds. Jack's accuracy in selecting colors dropped to 30 percent for the 135 trials in this session.

There are a number of procedural differences between this study and that of Savage-Rumbaugh et al. (1978). First, taking into account the fact that the brain of the pigeon is smaller than that of the chimpanzee, and not wishing to tax the relatively limited information-processing capacity of our subjects, we used 3 rather than 11 stimulus objects. Second, we did not attempt to reverse the informer and observer roles. (We believe that this can be done but is not essential to the demonstration of interanimal communication.) Third, we used colors rather than foods as the stimulus objects to avoid the possibility that our subjects would fail to "distinguish between the use of a food name as its name and use of that name as a request for food" (Savage-Rumbaugh et al., 1978). Fourth, events in all interanimal test sessions in our experiment were controlled by electromechanical equipment, eliminating possible experimenter cuing effects and the need for "experimenter-blind" conditions. Fifth, our observer could not simply duplicate the symbol provided by the informer but instead had to decode the symbol into its referent. Sixth, we did not vary the position of our symbols. (Position was no doubt significant to our subjects, just as the position of letters and figures in mathematical notion is significant to mathematicians.) Seventh, every conversation in our experiment was initiated by the observer's spontaneous request for information. Finally, the observer sustained the informer's cooperation by thanking her with a food reward for supplying information.

We have thus demonstrated that pigeons can learn to engage in a sustained and natural conversation without human intervention, and that one pigeon can transmit information to another entirely through the use of symbols.

It has not escaped our notice that an alternative account of this exchange may be given in terms of the prevailing contingencies of reinforcement. Jack "initiated the conversation" by pecking the WHAT COLOR? key because a peck at that key had illuminated it and because this illumination had been reliably followed by the illumination of one of the symbol keys. This was, in turn, the occasion upon which a peck at the THANK YOU key, followed by a peck at a corresponding color key, had produced reinforcement. Jill responded to Jack's "request for information" because the illumination of the WHAT COLOR? key was the occasion upon which looking at the hidden color and then pecking a corresponding symbol key had been reinforced. The performances were established through standard fading, shaping, chaining, and discrimination procedures (Catania, 1979; Honig, 1966; Skinner, 1938, 1953). A similar account may be given of the Rumbaugh procedure,[4] as well as of comparable human language (Skinner, 1957).

Postscript. *This article, which appeared in* **Science** *in 1980, prompted media coverage around the world. The* **New York Times** *reported that Noam Chomsky compared the pigeons' performance to a circus act.* **TIME** *magazine reported the study as a serious advance, entitling their article "Pigeon Talk" (and thus missing out on the pun "Pigeon English"). The* **Fiji Times**—*"the first newspaper published in the world today"—gave it prominent billing, and the* **National Enquirer** *sought photos. The article, of course, was a satire—the only one* **Science** *had ever published, to our knowledge. The opening of the last paragraph was a take-off on the conclusion to Watson and Crick's famous paper on the structure of DNA, published in* **Nature** *in the 1950s.*

NOTES

1. The pigeons were both male, but we named them Jack and Jill in tribute to Leonard Bloomfield, who in *Language* (1933) represented communication behaviorally by describing an episode in which Jill asked Jack to get her an apple.
2. If the birds had responded at random to the symbol and color keys, they would have been correct on only about 11 percent of the trials. They responded correctly on more than 50 percent of the trials of the first interanimal test.
3. The hidden colors were changed in a pseudo-random sequence from trial to trial throughout the experiment.
4. Similar accounts may also be given of other recent work with nonhuman primates. See, for example, critiques by Rachlin (1978) and Terrace (1979). Other achievements with nonprimates are also relevant; consider, for example, Straub, Seidenberg, Bever, & Terrace (1979).

6

"SELF-AWARENESS" IN THE PIGEON

Summary. Each of three pigeons used a mirror to locate a spot on its body which it could not see directly. Although similar behavior in primates has been attributed to a self-concept or other cognitive process, the present example suggests an account in terms of environmental events.

The chimpanzee has been said to show signs of "self-recognition," "self-awareness," and a "self-concept" because it can use a mirror to locate an object on its body which it cannot see directly (Gallup, 1970, 1979). According to Gallup (1970), four chimpanzees showed a variety of self-directed behavior after having been exposed to a large mirror for several days.

After 10 days of exposure (approximately 80 hours), "self-awareness" was tested as follows: A chimpanzee was anesthetized and a red odorless dye was painted onto the top of an eyebrow ridge and the upper half of an ear. After recovering from the anesthesia, the animal was observed in the absence of a mirror for 30 minutes and in its presence for 30 minutes. There were few "mark-directed responses" during the first period and between four and ten such responses during the second.

After hundreds of hours of exposure to mirrors, primates other than man and the great apes have shown no such self-directed behavior. This has been said to indicate a "qualitative psychological difference among primates" (Gallup, 1970). Monkeys fail the task reportedly because they "lack a cognitive category that is essential for processing mirrored information about themselves." More specifically, they are said to lack "a sense of identity" and "a sufficiently well-integrated self-concept" (Gallup, 1979).

We have found that a pigeon (*Columba livia domestica*) is also capable of using a mirror to locate an object on its body which it cannot see directly and offer a nonmentalistic account of this behavior. The subjects were three adult male White Carneaux pigeons, each of which had had a variety of laboratory experience but no previous exposure to mirrors. The pigeons were maintained at about 80 percent of the weight they achieve when feeding without restriction. Sessions up to 2 hours in length were conducted daily in a small (32 by 36 by 42 cm) chamber. A mirror (34 by 21 cm) was positioned about 4 cm behind the right-hand wall, which was made of clear Plexiglas. Blue dots could be presented from behind three openings in the left-hand wall, which was painted white. A dot could also be presented from behind one opening in the rear wall, which was painted gray and white. The pigeon could be given access to mixed grain through an opening in the center of the left-hand wall. The Plexiglas front allowed us to see the bird at all times. We could also insert a clear rod, at the end of which was a blue dot, through a gap at the base of the front of the chamber. We used the rod to present dots at various positions on the left wall and floor of the chamber.

Two repertoires were established over a 10-day period. First, with the mirror concealed, we placed small (1-cm diameter) blue stick-on dots one at a time on the wings, breast, neck, and abdomen of the bird. We shaped movements of the head toward the dots and then reinforced pecks at them on a rich variable-ratio schedule (between one and five pecks had to occur before food was presented). Having pecked at dots placed in a number of different positions, the pigeon would readily scan its body, locate a dot, and peck it.

Second, with the mirror exposed, we reinforced pecks to blue dots presented one at time on the left and rear walls and the floor of the chamber. After a few minutes of such training, we presented a dot only briefly and reinforced pecks at the spot where it had been. Finally, a dot was flashed only when the pigeon could see it in the mirror. Food was presented if it then turned and pecked the place where a dot had been flashed. The pigeon now readily faced the mirror and responded appropriately to certain visual stimuli that appeared in it by turning and pecking the corresponding position in real space. Dots were never placed on its body during this condition.

The two repertoires were established in only 3 or 4 hours. The animals were exposed to the mirror for less than 15 hours over the 10-day training period.

We then conducted the following test. A blue dot was placed on the pigeon's breast and a white bib (note that the birds were white) placed around its neck in such a way that, with the pigeon standing fully upright, we could just see the dot. The bib made it impossible for the bird to see the dot directly. If it lowered its head even slightly, the bib covered it (Figure 6.1, A and B). In a control condition (3 minutes for one subject and 5 minutes for the others), the pigeon was placed in the chamber with the mirror covered. If the pigeon could see the dot or locate it using tactile cues, it presumably would peck it at this point. None of the subjects did so. When we uncovered the mirror, each pigeon approached it and, within a few seconds, began repeatedly moving its head downward toward the position on the bib that corresponded to the dot (Figure 6.1, C and D). The second bird we tested continued to bob and peck in this fashion for more than 6 minutes (approximately 23 dot-directed responses occurred over this period). The number of dot-directed responses occurring during the last 3 minutes of the control period and the first 3 minutes of the experimental period were scored by three independent observers from video tapes (Table 6.1).[1]

To control for the possibility that movements toward the bib were produced simply by the uncovering of the mirror, before beginning the test described above, we placed the third subject into the chamber wearing the bib but without

"Self-Awareness" in the Pigeon

the dot on its breast. The mirror remained covered for 5 minutes and was then exposed for 5 minutes. During neither period did the bird bob or peck at the bib. It is therefore likely that the movements toward the bib that occurred during the subsequent test were indeed under the control of the dot.

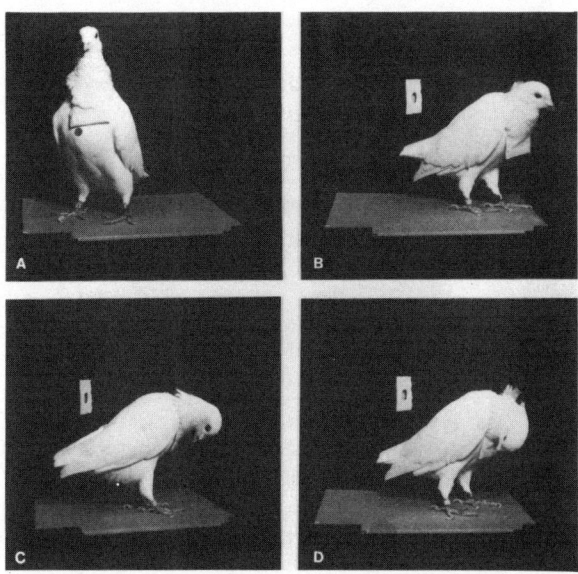

Figure 6.1. A pigeon uses a mirror to locate a spot on its body which it cannot see directly. (A) With the bird standing fully upright, the spot is just visible below the edge of the bib around its neck. (B) The pigeon faces the mirror (not shown) at right. Note that the bib covers the spot when the bird leans forward. (C and D) The pigeon bobs and pecks toward the position on the bib that corresponds to the hidden spot.

Note that no food was presented during the tests and that before this time the birds had never had dots on their bodies when exposed to a mirror.

We have demonstrated that a pigeon can use a mirror to locate an object on its body which it cannot see directly. We should not attribute this, however, to a pigeon's "self-awareness" or claim that a pigeon has a "self-concept." We believe that such constructs impede the search for the controlling variables of the behavior they are said to produce. We suggest that, before they were tested, Gallup's chimpanzees had already acquired repertoires similar to those of our pigeons. They had presumably touched their ears and the upper parts of their eyebrow ridges many times, and over the 80 hours of exposure to a mirror before the test, they should have had many opportunities to discover the contingencies that govern mirror use. A chimpanzee with no prior exposure to a mirror does not make self-directed movements in the mirror test (Gallup, 1970).

The fact remains that other primate species, such as macaques and rhesus monkeys, have not shown signs of "self-awareness" in the mirror test. For example, Gallup (1979) reported a negative result with a crab-eating macaque even after 2,400 hours of exposure. It may be that the more mobile macaque had fewer opportunities to come under the control of the contingencies governing mirror use. In any case, mere exposure presents an animal with only a small subset of possible contingencies. If the contingencies governing mirror use are made more explicit, a macaque or other primate should come under their control, as did our pigeons.

Table 6.1. Number of dot-directed responses in the control and experimental conditions (median scores).

Subject	Mirror Covered	Mirror Exposed
162 WP	0	9
110 YP	0	16
293 WP	0	4

We have shown how at least one instance of behavior attributed to "self-awareness" can be accounted for in terms of an environmental history. We submit that other instances, including those exhibited by humans, can be dealt with in a similar way.[2]

NOTES

1. The observers were twice shown a videotape of the six intervals in random order. The second time they pressed a telegraph key whenever they saw what they judged to be a dot-directed response.

2. There is a considerable amount of research on "self-awareness" in humans, some of which makes use of the mirror test. Consider Lewis and Brooks-Gunn (1979), Amsterdam (1972), Dixon (1957), and Mans, Cicchetti, and Sroufe (1978). Before children are successful, they are said to go through a phase of "testing" or "discovery" during which, among other things, they engage in repetitive activity while closely observing their mirror image. The contingencies of reinforcement that govern mirror use probably take hold during this period.

7

THE SPONTANEOUS USE OF MEMORANDA BY PIGEONS

Summary. Two pigeons were trained to engage in an exchange in which each could function as either "speaker" or "listener." When, without subsequent training, each was placed alone in a situation in which it could play both roles, the two repertoires became interconnected. Behavior emerged which can reasonably be called memorandum-making.

We recently described "the first instance of symbolic communication between...two pigeons" (Epstein, Lanza, & Skinner, 1980) and here report additional language-like accomplishments. In the original exchange, the pigeons, named Jack and Jill, could observe each other through a Plexiglas partition and peck (and thus illuminate) keys embossed with colors or letters.

Jack's task was to peck a color matching one to which only Jill had access. He invoked Jill's help by illuminating a key labeled WHAT COLOR? Jill then thrust her head through a curtain and pecked a plate on which one of three colors (red, green, or yellow) could be seen. She then pecked (and illuminated) a corresponding black-on-white letter (R, G, or Y). Having observed this, Jack pecked a key marked THANK YOU, thus operating a feeder for a few seconds on Jill's side of the partition. Finally, Jack pecked the corresponding color, and a correct selection operated his feeder. He invariably then pecked WHAT COLOR? again. (Hidden colors appeared in a pseudo-random sequence.) The birds engaged in this exchange for sustained periods during which both were correct on 90 percent of the trials. Had they been responding at random, accuracy would have been about 11 percent.

The simulation was prompted by recent investigations with chimpanzees (Savage-Rumbaugh, Rumbaugh, & Boysen, 1978) and was accomplished through standard techniques of operant conditioning. It was designed to call attention to the possible contribution of an environmental history in the acquisition of certain language-like behavior and was offered as an alternative to current mentalistic and purposive accounts.

In the original procedure, each bird was trained in only one role. Jill was, in a sense, a "speaker"; she "said something about" a hidden color. Jack was a "listener"; he waited for and made use of a symbol provided by Jill. In the present experiment we trained each pigeon to play both roles and then conducted a test in which the repertoires became interconnected without our intervention, to produce new behavior. The behavior was studied over a 5-month period and, we believe, can reasonably be called memorandum-making.

The new repertoires were established using standard fading, shaping, chaining, and discrimination-training procedures (Catania, 1979; Skinner, 1938) in the same manner as the original performances. We were not able to omit any steps in training nor to reduce the necessary training time in establishing the new roles—in other words, we found no evidence that a bird had benefitted from being a listener in becoming a speaker or vice versa.

When each bird had mastered both roles, we conducted the following test: The partition was removed and one bird placed alone in the chamber with access to both panels at once. All keys were active, as they had been in the two-bird situation, although the contingencies were changed slightly as follows: Pecks at the THANK YOU or WHAT COLOR? keys illuminated them as always, but pecks were no longer required, since no exchange was possible. For the same reason, a peck at the THANK YOU key did not operate the right-hand feeder. A peck at the hidden color, followed by a peck at a corresponding letter illuminated the letter, as in the two-bird situation, although a peck at the letter was not necessary. A peck at the hidden color, followed by a peck at the corresponding color on the left-hand panel would operate the left-hand feeder.

A half-hour session was conducted with each bird under these conditions. At first, Jack played the role occasioned by the nearest panel. Facing the left panel, he pecked WHAT COLOR? and then THANK YOU and the color keys, as he had done in the listener role. After a few minutes he moved to the right, checked the hidden color, and then pecked the corresponding letter, as he had done in the role of speaker. He walked from one position to the other, pecking keys in this fashion until, midway through the session, a sequence occurred that produced food: He checked the hidden color, pecked the corresponding letter, and then crossed the chamber and pecked the corresponding color. During the remaining 15 minutes, this sequence occurred 20 times and stabilized in a manner suggesting that he was using the symbol keys as memoranda. He would check the hidden color, peck the corresponding symbol key, cross the chamber, and then, before pecking the appropriate color, *look back* (sometimes, several times) at the illuminated letter (Figure 7.1). The social responses (WHAT COLOR? and THANK YOU) disappeared entirely. Jill's performance was remarkably similar. The sequence emerged in much the same manner and occurred 21 times during a half-hour session. The performances grew more stable and accurate in subsequent sessions. Color-to-color sequences did not occur.

We found ample evidence in subsequent tests to support our supposition that pecks at the symbol keys were functioning as memoranda. We first noted that these pecks could have been mediating the delay that necessarily occurred between a peck at the hidden color and a peck at a matching color key. Delays can interfere with accurate matching (Cumming & Berryman, 1965; Spear, 1978) and have been known to produce mediating behavior (e.g., Blough, 1959). With a sufficiently short delay, a memorandum should not be necessary; at long delays, it should be critical.

We reduced the delay by removing the curtain from in front of the hidden color. Within three weeks, the responses to the symbol keys disappeared. (Their disappearance was gradual. The pigeons often pecked weakly at or in the direction of a letter as they crossed the chamber. These "glancing" pecks became weaker and less frequent over a period of days.) When we reintroduced the curtain, Jack reverted to the use of memoranda almost immediately. Jill did not.

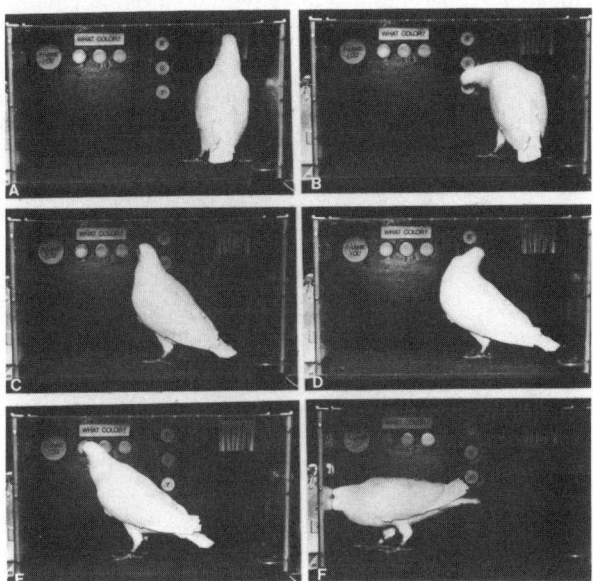

Figure 7.1. Although it was never explicitly trained and although it is not required, Jack uses a symbol key as a memorandum as he crosses the chamber from right to left. (A) Jack looks behind the curtain at the hidden color. (B) He pecks the letter corresponding to the color (in this case, Y for yellow), which is then illuminated. (C) He walks to the color keys (yellow, red, and green, from left to right). (D) He looks back at the illuminated letter. (E) He pecks the yellow key. (F) The feeder is operated and he eats. If the task is made easier, steps B and D disappear; if it is then made more difficult, they reappear. If he is distracted as he is about to peck the color (E), he looks back again at the letter before completing the sequence.

After Jack had continued to make memoranda for 11 sessions, we looked at the effect of a distraction on his performance. He would peck the hidden color, peck the corresponding symbol key, and walk across the chamber to the color keys. As he was about to peck, we would operate a loud buzzer, placed in the right-hand feeder opening. Jack would start, *look back* at the illuminated symbol, and, finally, peck the color key.

After 17 sessions, we removed the curtain once again. One color-to-color match occurred within the first session, and the use of memoranda disappeared almost entirely within five sessions.

Although the curtain had been restored for 25 sessions, Jill did not revert to pecking the symbol keys. To make the task still more difficult for her, we introduced a delay between the peck at the hidden color and the illumination of the color keys. The delay was brief at first (0.75 sec) and was increased very gradually (and occasionally decreased as necessary) over 10 sessions to shape good waiting behavior in front of the color keys. With the delay at 1.75 seconds, Jill still matched colors with greater than 60 percent accuracy.

Finally, the delay was increased during a half-hour period to 5 seconds. Jill's performance was seriously disrupted. She would peck the hidden color, extinguishing the color key lights, and then, finding the color keys dark, typically peck the hidden color again, thus resetting the delay. On the fifteenth trial she rechecked the hidden color (red) 13 times, then pecked the corresponding symbol key (R) repeatedly during the delay, and, finally, pecked the matching color. She bridged the delay intervals in this fashion on 16 of the remaining 24 trials and pecked an inappropriate symbol key only once. She had not pecked the symbol keys for 67 days before this session.

That the pigeons were using the symbol keys as memoranda is indicated in several ways. First, before pecking a color key, they commonly looked back at the symbol key they had illuminated. Second, they relied less on the symbols when the task was easier and more when it was more difficult. Third, when distracted before pecking a color key, Jack would look back at the symbol he had illuminated.

We emphasize that after establishing the "speaker" and "listener" repertoires we did not intervene in any way to promote their interconnection. The use of a memorandum emerged when previously established behavior brought the pigeons into contact with new contingencies. A similar phenomenon may be responsible for a variety of novel behaviors in animals and humans.

8

THE SPONTANEOUS USE OF A TOOL BY A PIGEON

Summary. A pigeon was trained to push a flat, hexagonal box toward a target placed at random positions around the edge of large chamber. It was subsequently trained to peck a small metal plate, which was positioned at the base of a clear Plexiglas wall. When the plate was moved out of reach behind the wall, the bird stretched repeatedly toward it for more than a minute-and-a-half, then pushed the box toward the plate, thrust it beneath the wall, and, with the box in contact with the plate, pecked repeatedly at the box. The performance was genuinely novel and in several respects resembled the behavior of chimpanzees or children in similar situations. Based on other experiments, a tentative, moment-to-moment account of the performance can be given in objective terms.

Problem solving has been studied extensively by comparative (e.g., Schiller, 1952), Gestalt (e.g., Duncker, 1945; Ellen, 1982; Köhler, 1925; Maier, 1931a), and, more recently, cognitive psychologists (e.g., Weisberg & Alba, 1981), as well as by behavioral biologists (e.g., Beck, 1980), but has been relatively neglected by analysts of behavior (cf. Skinner, 1966). A behavior-analytical approach to problem solving could shed light on (a) the role that certain environmental histories play in the emergence of problem-solving behavior (cf. Birch, 1945), and (b) principles that allow moment-to-moment prediction of problem-solving behavior as a function of species, environmental history, current stimuli, and other variables. As such factors come to be better understood, we should be able to produce genuinely novel, increasingly complex instances of problem-solving behavior in organisms that would not normally exhibit such behavior.

Described is a "Columban simulation" (Baxley, 1982; Epstein, 1981a) in which our current understanding of such factors is put to use to produce behavior that can reasonably be called "spontaneous tool use" in a pigeon.

METHOD

Subject and Apparatus

One male, adult White Carneaux pigeon (282 WP) served as the subject. It had had a variety of laboratory experience prior to the experiment and was maintained at approximately 80 percent of its free-feeding weight. Sessions were conducted in a cylindrical wire-mesh chamber, 50 cm high and 70 cm in diameter. A standard feeder was attached to the base at the position shown in Figure 8.1. A removable clear Plexiglas wall was placed at the position shown in the figure during some conditions. There was a gap of 6.3 cm at the base of the wall. A hexagonal cardboard box, 15 cm wide and 2.5 cm high, was employed during some conditions, as was an aluminum plate, 3-cm square, positioned so that its plane was parallel to the plane of the Plexiglas wall. The lower edge of the plate was 1 cm from the floor. The plate was attached to a microswitch. Each peck at the plate produced feedback in the form of a brief high-pitched tone.

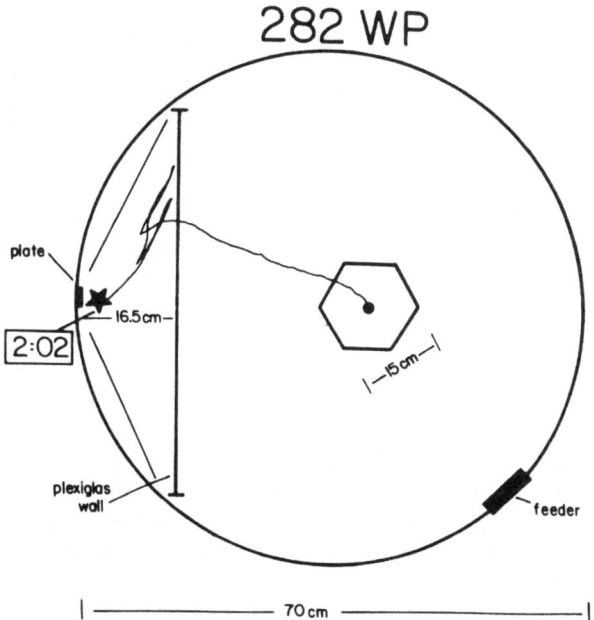

Figure 8.1. Floor diagram of the cylindrical chamber. The vertical line marks the position of a clear Plexiglas wall, positioned 6.3 cm above the floor. After stretching repeatedly toward the metal plate at left for 92 seconds, the bird suddenly pushed the box toward it. When its head reached the wall, it pushed the box back and forth several times; then it stretched again toward the plate and, finally, at about 2 minutes into the session, pushed the box solidly against the plate and pecked the near side of the box repeatedly, thus activating a high-pitched tone.

The Spontaneous Use of a Tool by a Pigeon

Procedure

Two repertoires were established—directional pushing and pecking the metal plate. First, over a 6-month period a total of about 60 hours was spent establishing a repertoire of directional pushing. The basic steps were as follows:

Pushing was established during the first hour through shaping, and then, over the next several hours, the frequency of reinforcement was reduced until the bird pushed for long periods without food. Reinforcement was contingent upon covering as much of the floor space as possible. (The bird had had almost identical training with a larger box in a previous experiment [Epstein, Kirshnit, Lanza, & Rubin, 1984].) Then pecks at a small (4-cm diameter) circular green spot, placed at random positions along the base of the chamber, were reinforced on a rich variable-ratio (VR) schedule.

The box was suspended on a thin wire mounted horizontally and attached to both sides of the chamber so that the box could move along it only in a straight line. The spot was placed at one end of the wire and "sight and push" behavior was established; an obvious head movement in the direction of the spot followed by one or more pushes from behind the box which pushed the box toward the spot were reinforced. The requirement was increased until food was presented only when the box was pushed all the way to the spot. The spot was moved from one end of the wire to the other and the position of the wire changed in the chamber until the bird reliably pushed toward the spot no matter what its position. The wire was removed, the box was placed a few centimeters from the spot, and sight-and-push behavior was reinforced as before. Over a period of months, as the bird became increasingly successful at pushing the box directly toward the spot, the distance from the box to the spot was gradually increased until the bird could push in reasonably straight lines toward the spot, no matter what its position and no matter what its distance from the box. To improve control by the spot, pushing in its absence was extinguished. Pushes were never reinforced in the absence of the spot for at least the last 5 months of training.

The second repertoire was established during the last month of training. The Plexiglas wall was placed in the chamber for about 15 minutes each day. The box and spot were never present when the wall was in place. The metal plate was positioned at the midpoint of the base of the wall, and pecking it was reinforced on a rich VR schedule. Over 10 sessions, the plate was gradually moved to a position 10 cm behind the wall, so that the bird had to stretch beneath the wall to peck it. With the plate and the wall removed and the box and the spot restored, directional pushing was also reinforced for short periods each day.

With the two repertoires now well established, the last phase of the experiment began. The box was placed in the chamber as shown in Figure 8.1. The spot was not present. With the plate still 10 cm behind the wall, pecking the plate was reinforced and behavior with respect to the box was extinguished until it was neither pecked nor pushed for five consecutive, daily 30-minute sessions. (The bird pecked the box a few times in only the first of six such sessions.) As was the case above, directional pushing was also reinforced for a short period each day (5 to 10 minutes) in the absence of the wall and plate.

A test was then arranged as follows: The plate was placed in a position known to be just out of reach of the bird—16.5 cm behind the wall. The box was placed in the chamber as shown in Figure 8.1. The spot was not present. No reinforcers were delivered, and the session was videotaped.

RESULTS

With the plate out of reach, the bird stretched repeatedly toward it. Behavior that might be called "emotional" appeared: wing raising, turning, and scraping the feet on the floor. As the frequency of stretching decreased, behavior with respect to the box emerged; the bird oriented toward it and pecked it weakly several times. At 92 seconds into the session, the bird pushed the box rapidly toward the metal plate. When its head reached the wall, it pushed the box back and forth rapidly several times. Then it stretched again once toward the plate and pushed the box against it, thus activating the high-pitched tone (Figure 8.1). It pecked the near side of the box repeatedly, producing a steady tone for more than 5 seconds until the session was terminated. The first tone sounded at a little over 2 minutes into the session.

DISCUSSION

Though, in our opinion, a subjective evaluation of the bird's behavior does not in any way contribute to an understanding of it, we offer one for comparison purposes. People viewing the videotape of this performance often reported feeling increasingly tense or excited over the course of the session; they often marked the bird's "frustration" or "confusion" and the obvious "intentionality" of the pushing. In short, we may have in hand a genuine instance of what many call "problem solving." The suddenness and directness of the pushing also appear to satisfy Köhler's (1925) criteria for "genuine" or "insightful" solutions (cf. Epstein et al., 1984; Koffka, 1924). The course of the performance—from unsuccessful "brute-force" behavior to a period of "confusion" or "pensiveness" to a sudden successful sequence—also resembles progressions reported when both chimpanzees and humans have solved a variety of problems (e.g., Duncker, 1945; Köhler, 1925; Maier, 1931a).

Because the bird had not touched the box in the presence of the wall and plate for more than five sessions and because pushing had never produced reinforcement under such circumstances, pushing the box in the test situation would appear to be "spontaneous." In lay terms, the bird pushed the box only when it "needed to." And because the bird used the box as an extension of its own beak, it could be said that we had observed a legitimate instance of "tool use."

A tentative, moment-to-moment account of the behavior can be given in terms of objective principles. The behavior one might attribute to "need" can be accounted for by a simple principle called "experimental regression" or "resurgence": When, in a given situation, some response is extinguished, other responses that were reinforced under similar circumstances tend to recur (Epstein, 1985b; cf. Epstein & Skinner, 1980; Estes, 1955; Leitenberg, Rawson, & Bath, 1970; Lindblom & Jenkins, 1981; Masserman, 1943; Mowrer, 1940; O'Kelley, 1940a; Sears, 1941; Staddon & Simmelhag, 1971). Thus, when the plate is placed out of reach, pecking it is quickly extinguished and other behavior—box pushing—increases in strength. The behavior we interpret as "confusion" is probably produced, at least in part, by competition between the repertoires as they vary in strength. Why the bird pushes toward the plate is still under investigation. It appears at the moment to be a matter of what is often called "functional" generalization, as opposed to generalization based on common physical characteristics. In other words, based on other experiments and work in progress (cf. Epstein et al., 1984), we conjecture that a bird that had been trained only in directional pushing but never to peck the plate would not push toward the plate in the test situation. We believe the bird pushes toward the plate because of a history of directional pushing *and* because of the history of reinforcement with respect to the plate.

We emphasize that we never trained the bird to push the box toward the plate; that, over the last 5 months of training, behavior with respect to the box had never been reinforced in the absence of the green spot and that such behavior had been deliberately extinguished; that behavior with respect to the box had never been reinforced in the presence of the wall and plate and that such behavior had been deliberately extinguished; that the bird had never been trained to push the box under anything; and that the spot was absent during the test. The bird's performance must consequently be regarded as genuinely novel. Although it can safely be said that previous training was critical to the bird's success (cf. Epstein et al., 1984), the performance may be regarded as exemplary of a general principle of novelty in behavior: Previously established behavior manifests itself in new situations to produce new, yet predictable behavior.

9

"INSIGHT" IN THE PIGEON: ANTECEDENTS AND DETERMINANTS OF AN INTELLIGENT PERFORMANCE

Summary. In 1917 Wolfgang Köhler observed some rather extraordinary instances of problem solving by a number of chimpanzees (Köhler, 1925), and his observations have been the subject of controversy ever since (Chance, 1960; Weisberg & Alba, 1981). The period of quiescence that sometimes preceded the solution, its sudden onset, and its smooth, continuous emergence were proffered as evidence that (a) contrary to suggestions of learning theorists of the day, problem solving was not necessarily a trial-and-error process, and (b) constructs such as "insight" were necessary for an adequate account (Duncker, 1945; Ellen, 1982; Köhler, 1925; Maier, 1931a). In an attempt to shed further light on these issues, we replicated with pigeons a classic problem with which Köhler confronted his chimpanzees. Pigeons who had acquired relevant skills solved the problem in a remarkably chimpanzee-like (and, perforce, human-like) fashion. The possible contributions of different experiences were determined by varying the training histories of different birds. We offer a tentative moment-to-moment account of a successful performance.

Köhler placed a banana out of reach in one corner of a room and a small wooden crate about 2.5 m from the position on the floor beneath it. After a number of fruitless attempts by all six chimpanzees in the room to jump for the banana, one of them paced for several minutes, then suddenly moved the box half a meter from the position of the banana "and springing upwards with all his force, tore down the banana" (Köhler, 1925). Both research (Birch, 1945) and theory (Hull, 1935) suggest that chimpanzees will not solve problems of this sort if they have not first had certain experiences. We speculated that two behaviors had to have been acquired: pushing objects toward targets and climbing on objects to reach other objects. Since a pigeon normally does neither, it seemed an ideal candidate to test the contribution that previous learning might make to success in this problem.

Eleven adult male pigeons served as subjects. Each was maintained at about 80 percent of the weight it would achieve given free access to food. Most had had a variety of laboratory experience, but none had ever been used in a problem-solving experiment. Birds 269WP and 270WP were racing Homers; the others were White Carneaux. All sessions were conducted in a cylindrical wire-mesh chamber 69 cm in diameter, except those of birds 110YP, 233WP, and

274WP, which were conducted in smaller rectangular chambers. A cardboard box, 8-cm high with a base 10-cm square, was employed in some conditions, as was a small facsimile of a banana, 7 cm in length. A standard grain dispenser was attached to the base of each chamber.

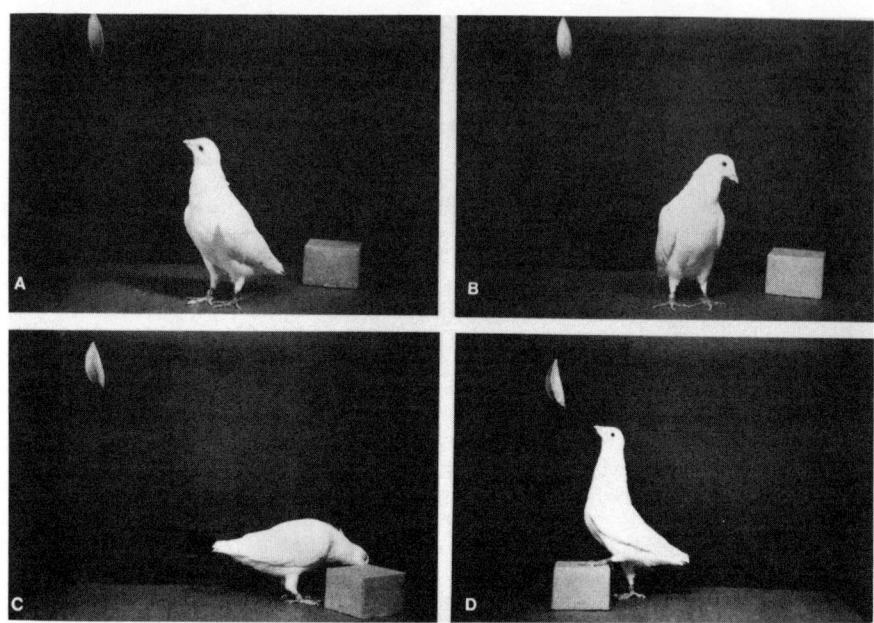

Figure 9.1. "Insight" in the pigeon. *(A,B) The bird looks back and forth from banana to box. (C) It pushes the box toward the banana. (D) It climbs and pecks.*

The following history yielded successful performances with all of the birds we tested: 1) A repertoire of "directional pushing" was established. Each bird was trained to push the box toward a green spot, 4 cm in diameter, which was placed at random positions along the base of the chamber wall(s). Pushing was extinguished in the absence of the green spot. Major training steps included (a) reinforcing aimless pushes, (b) reinforcing pecks to the spot, (c) reinforcing sighting the spot and pushing the box toward it, with the movement of the box constrained by a thin wire, (d) reinforcing sight-and-push behavior with the wire removed and the box close to the spot, and (e) gradually increasing the distance between the box and the spot (Epstein & Medalie, 1983). Proficient performances were established in 8, 1, and 4 weeks, respectively, for the subjects whose performances are shown in Figure 9.1c. The banana was never present during this training. 2) Concurrently, each bird was trained to climb onto the box and peck the banana, which was suspended overhead. The box was fixed in place during this condition, and pecking it was never reinforced. The position of box and banana was changed repeatedly. In the presence of box and banana, the bird would reliably climb onto the box and peck the banana. In the absence of the banana and in the presence of the spot, the bird would push the box

"Insight" in the Pigeon

toward the spot. 3) Each bird was occasionally placed alone with the banana until the bird neither flew nor jumped toward it.

The following test situation was arranged: The banana was suspended out of reach (41 cm from the floor) at a point (determined by a random number) near an edge of the chamber, and the box was placed elsewhere in the chamber. All test sessions for these and all other subjects were filmed or videotaped.

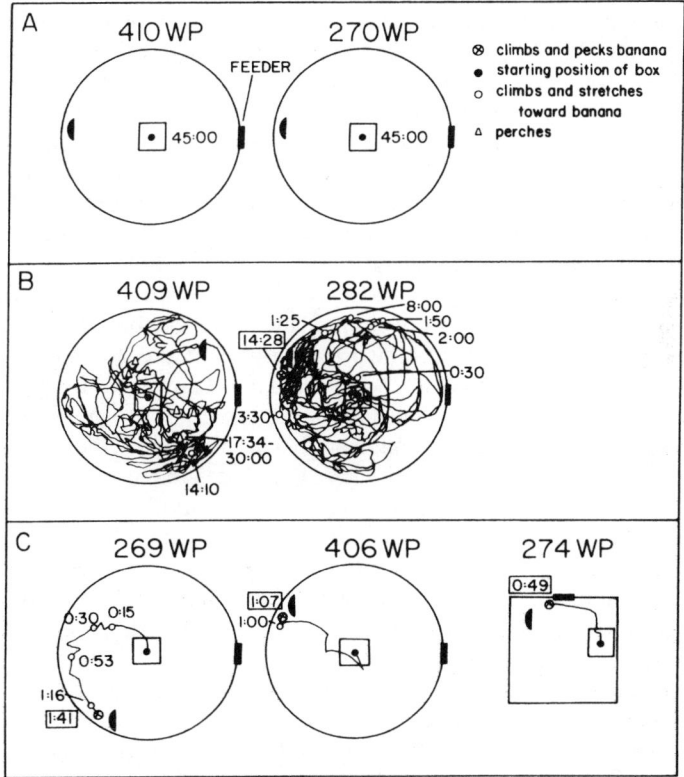

Figure 9.2. Birds that had been trained to climb and peck but never to push did not push the box in the test situation (Panel A). Birds that had been trained (a) to climb and peck and (b) to push the box aimlessly for long periods of time pushed the box over much of the floor space of the chamber. The birds rarely looked up while pushing. One of the birds stopped pushing in the appropriate place and climbed and pecked the banana after having pushed for more than 14 minutes (Panel B). Birds that had been trained (a) to climb and peck and (b) to push the box toward a green spot placed at random positions along the base of the chamber solved the problem efficiently and in a manner suggestive of human problem-solving behavior (Panel C). Other controls are described in the text. The times given are in minutes and seconds. A boxed time is the time to solution.

The performances for the first three subjects were remarkably similar (Figure 9.1). At first each pigeon appeared to be "confused"; it stretched and turned beneath the banana, looked back and forth from banana to box, and so on. Then each subject began rather suddenly to push the box in what was clearly the direction of the banana. Each subject sighted the banana as it pushed and readjusted the box as necessary to move it toward the banana. Each subject stopped pushing in the appropriate place, climbed, and pecked the banana (Figure 9.2c).

A fourth bird (233WP) solved the problem after 24 minutes. The performance was disrupted by 1,000 watts of lighting which had been added to facilitate filming. When, after 20 minutes, the lighting was reduced, the bird solved the problem in just under 4 minutes.

We conducted four variations on this training with other pigeons. Two birds (294WP and 273WP) were trained to peck the banana but not to climb. Jumping and flying were extinguished, and the birds were placed alone with the box until they showed no signs of discomfort in its presence. Then the banana was suspended out of reach above it. Each bird stretched repeatedly toward the banana at first. Subject 273WP stumbled onto the box and then fell off. After the first few minutes of each session, attempts to reach the banana ceased. We terminated each session after 10 minutes. We concluded that the establishment of climbing was probably critical to the solution.

Two birds (270WP and 410WP) were trained to climb and peck but not to push. Jumping and flying were extinguished. Neither bird pushed the box when given the test (Figure 9.2a). Two birds (409WP and 282WP) were trained to climb and peck and to push the box around the chamber for long periods of time. They were never trained to push toward a target, nor to push in straight lines. Jumping and flying were extinguished. The birds pushed apparently aimlessly when given the test (Figure 9.2b). We concluded that a repertoire of directional pushing was probably critical to an efficient solution.

With one bird (110YP) we established directional pushing and climbing-and-pecking but did not extinguish brute force attempts to reach the banana. Like Köhler's chimpanzee, the bird jumped and flew repeatedly toward the banana for several minutes, then pushed the box toward the banana, climbed, and pecked. The solution appeared after about 7 minutes.

Based on these and other experiments, a tentative, moment-to-moment account of a successful performance can be given. At first stimuli were present which controlled both behavior with respect to the banana and behavior with respect to the box. The behavior we interpreted as a sign of perplexity was probably the result of competition between these behaviors. Behavior with respect to the banana quickly disappeared very likely because of the recent history of extinction of jumping and flying when the banana was out of reach (compare the performance of bird 110YP). The birds may have begun to push because, as behavior with respect to the box increased in relative frequency, the birds faced the box more directly, which was very nearly the stimulus in the presence of which pushing had been reinforced (the green spot was absent). Why the animals pushed toward the banana is a more mysterious matter, still under investigation. A process akin to what some call "functional generalization" (Bruner, Goodnow, & Austin, 1956) (as opposed to generalization based solely on common physical characteristics) seems to be involved: Birds that were trained to push toward the spot but not to peck the banana did not push toward the banana in the test situation but did push toward the banana when subsequently trained to peck it. In other words, the birds pushed toward the banana apparently for the "right reasons"—because they had learned directional pushing and because some history of reinforcement had made the banana "important." Directional performances may also have been produced by a summation of prevailing responses: Banana-directed pecks may have strengthened banana-directed pushes (N. E. Miller, personal communication). The birds stopped pushing in the right place because of a phenomenon called "automatic chaining": In the course of pushing toward the banana, they set up for themselves a stimulus (box-under-banana) that controlled other behavior (climbing and pecking).

We appear to have in hand an instance of "insightful" problem solving. The suddenness, directness, and continuousness of the performances satisfy Köhler's criteria for "genuine" or "insightful" solutions (Köhler, 1925; Koffka, 1924), and people viewing the tapes have liberally attributed a wide range of human emotions and thoughts to the pigeons. A surprisingly common comment was, "Did the pigeon really do that?" We may also have in hand an account of similar performances in chimpanzees and children, for the experiences we provided are ones that they have likely had before they are successful in similar situations, and the behavioral processes we have invoked are fairly general in the animal kingdom (Epstein, 1981a).

We emphasize that we did not train the birds to push the box toward the banana; that, except during very early stages of training, behavior with respect to the box was never reinforced in the absence of the green spot and that such behavior was deliberately extinguished; that pushing the box was never reinforced in the presence of the banana and that such behavior was deliberately extinguished; and that the spot was absent during the test. The successful performances must consequently be regarded as genuinely novel.

10

THE SPONTANEOUS INTERCONNECTION OF THREE REPERTOIRES

Summary. A previous study (Epstein, Kirshnit, Lanza, & Rubin, 1984) showed that pigeons that had acquired two relevant behaviors (pushing a box toward targets, and climbing onto a box and then pecking a small facsimile of a banana) could solve the classic box-and-banana problem. A human-like solution emerged as a result of the manner in which the two repertoires became interconnected moment-to-moment in time (Epstein et al., 1984; Epstein & Medalie, 1983). In the current experiment, a pigeon acquired three separate behaviors: (1) climbing, (2) pushing toward targets, and (3) pecking the banana. When the pigeon was confronted with the problem, a swift but erratic and not especially "insightful" solution emerged. Some simple principles shed light on the differences between the performances generated by the interconnection of two repertoires and the interconnection of three repertoires in this situation.

The emergence of novel behavior has long been a subject of speculation and debate, but, for the most part, it has defied rigorous scientific analysis. Several sources of novel behavior are amenable to such analysis (see Chapter 3). One, the spontaneous interconnection of repertoires, is probably responsible for the rather dramatic instances of novel behavior which lead people to speak of insight, creativity, reasoning, and so on. People are often unaware of the precise sequence of events which culminates in a "new idea," but when such sequences are observed, interconnection seems to be at work and the process seems to be orderly.
Psychologists have long recognized interconnection as a possible source of novelty, but accounts have been speculative. For example, Maier (1929, 1932) arranged situations in which separately established behaviors in rats combined to produce simple novel performances. In one situation, a rat was trained to climb a pathway to reach food and, in the absence of the pathway, given the opportunity to explore the floor area in a room. When the pathway was placed in the room, the rat approached it readily and climbed. Rats were able to do this in the dark, and rats that had not been given the opportunity to explore failed the task. Simple accounts of these results were offered by Dashiell (1930), but Maier (e.g., 1931b) insisted that the "integration of past experiences" was a higher-order *Gestalt* phenomenon that is not reducible to simpler ones. The

assertion has been echoed repeatedly since then, primarily by Gestalt psychologists (e.g., Duncker, 1945; Ellen, 1982). According to Maier (1931b), integrations were produced by a "field of strain" set up by current stimulus conditions and the organism's motivational state.

Hull (1935, 1952) objected to Maier's analysis on the grounds that it was tautological. To explain sudden integrations of previously established behaviors in terms of unanalyzable Gestalts is, according to Hull, "merely [to] re-assert the fact of problem solution in a new terminology without in any sense deducing the outcome from any principles whatever" (1935, p. 227). Hull suggested that current principles of learning and motivation could account for the problem-solving performances of Maier's (1929, 1932) rats and Köhler's (1925) chimpanzees. Unfortunately, his accounts were nearly as speculative as those offered by the Gestaltists. He did not offer new data, and his explanations depended heavily on speculations about internal motivational states, internal stimuli, "action tendencies," and "anticipatory goal reactions," none of which had been documented in the reports he was analyzing.

Epstein and Medalie (1983) and Epstein et al. (1984) have identified some simple, empirically-validated phenomena that reliably produce a variety of novel performances (also see Epstein, 1983a, 1984e). These phenomena can be observed and studied directly, and their role in the emergence of problem-solving or other novel performances can be tested in detail.[1]

The approach may be summarized as follows: Interconnection is likely when multiple behaviors are made available, either through resurgence of previous reinforced behaviors during extinction (Epstein, 1983a, 1985d) or by multiple controlling stimuli (Cumming & Eckerman, 1965; Migler, 1964; cf. Epstein et al., 1984). Multiple behaviors may combine to produce new sequences (Epstein & Skinner, 1981), behaviors that have new functions (Epstein & Skinner, 1981), or behaviors that have new topographies. Interconnections come about moment-to-moment in time through a variety of processes, any and all of which may be operating simultaneously. One important process is automatic chaining: One behavior changes the environment or the orientation of the organism and hence produces stimuli that make other behaviors more or less likely. When topographies are compatible, blends may appear, as one sees in verbal behavior or painting. The dynamics can be extremely complicated as behaviors are simultaneously waxing or waning in strength, resurging, producing new stimuli, and so on.

Epstein et al. (1984) reported that pigeons that had acquired relevant behaviors could solve one of the box-and-banana problems with which Köhler (1925) had confronted his chimpanzees.[2] The solutions were rapid and remarkably human-like. An account of their emergence was offered in the terms described herein. By varying the training histories of different animals, the authors also were able to offer reasonable guesses about the contributions that several different histories make to success in the problem.

"Insightful," human-like performances were produced when pigeons had acquired two repertoires: First, in the absence of the banana, they were trained to push a small box toward a green spot placed at random positions around the base of a chamber. Second, in the absence of the spot and with the box fixed in position beneath the banana, they were trained to climb onto the box and peck the banana. Finally, in the absence of both the box and the spot, the banana was placed out of reach, and jumping and flying toward it were extinguished.

In the test situation, the banana was placed out of reach near an edge of the chamber at a position determined by a random number, and the box was placed in the center of the chamber. Each pigeon was thus confronted with a stimulus configuration it had never seen before, one which was identical to the one with which Köhler (1925) had confronted his chimpanzees. Each of three pigeons that had had all of the training herein described behaved in a similar fashion. At first, the bird appeared to be "confused": It stretched toward the banana, turned back and forth from the banana to the box, and so on. Then, rather suddenly, it began to push the box toward the banana, sighting the banana and readjusting the path of the box as it pushed. Finally, it stopped pushing when the box was near the banana, climbed onto the box, and pecked the banana. The performances lasted 49, 67, and 101 seconds, respectively.

The problem would be more difficult if a bird were trained separately (a) to peck the banana when it was within reach and (b) to climb onto the box (that is, to climb but not to peck anything overhead). Would a solution still emerge if the climbing and pecking repertoires were separated? The question has theoretical significance, since the moment-to-moment account of the performance reported by Epstein et al. (1984) would apply only partially to this case. The principles they invoked predict the period of confusion and pushes toward the banana, but at that point the account breaks down. These issues will be discussed later. At the moment, an empirical question is posed: Can a solution to the box-and-banana problem emerge from the interconnection of the three separate repertoires?

METHOD

Subject and Apparatus

One adult male White Carneaux pigeon (159WP) served as the subject. He had previously been used in a variety of experiments but had never been used in a problem-solving experiment.[3] He was maintained at roughly 90 percent of his free feeding weight. All sessions were conducted in a cylindrical wire-mesh chamber 76 cm in diameter. A small cardboard box, 8 cm high and 10 cm square, was employed in some conditions, as was a facsimile of a banana, 7 cm in length and made of yellow cloth mounted on a wire frame. A round piece of cardboard, which was 4 cm in diameter and painted fluorescent green, served as the target during training.

Training Procedure

Thirty-nine training sessions were conducted over an 11-week period. The total training time was 28 hours. The three repertoires were established using methods similar to those described by Epstein and Medalie (1983) and Epstein et al. (1984):

Session 1. Adaptation.
Session 2. Hopper training.
Sessions 2 to 5. Pushing the box was shaped and maintained on a rich variable-ratio schedule of access to grain. The feeder was operated by hand, and each reinforcement lasted approximately 3 seconds. The schedule was gradually thinned, and reinforcement was make contingent on sequences of pushes which covered a large area of the floor. Not all pushes were reinforced. Since head-on thrusts allow poor control, they were never reinforced. Appropriate pushes hook the box at one of its corners near an upper edge and thus rotate it slightly. The bird's head must be tilted to one side or the other while pushing in this manner (Figure 10.1).

Session 6. Pecking the green spot was shaped and maintained on a rich variable-ratio schedule. The spot was moved to different locations along the base of the chamber wall.

Sessions 6 to 20. The box was mounted on a wire that was stretched taut from one side of the chamber to the other. The wire allowed the box to move freely in a straight line. The spot was placed at one end and the box was placed near it. A two-response sequence was established: The feeder was operated when the bird pecked the spot and then moved its head behind the box and pushed the box toward the spot. The sequence was altered as rapidly as possible in a number of ways: First, we replaced the peck with mere head movement in the direction of the spot—a conspicuous observing response. Second, the distance between the box and spot was gradually increased, and food was gradually made contingent on multiple pushes toward the spot. In all sessions, the spot was repeated moved from one end of the wire to the other, and the wire was repeatedly repositioned.

Sessions 20 to 21. Pecking the box was extinguished in the absence of the green spot.

Sessions 21 to 25. During the first part of each session, the training was continued with the box mounted on the wire, as previously. Then, for only a few minutes at first and for increasingly longer periods thereafter, the training was continued with the wire removed. The box was placed close to the spot at first and gradually moved farther away. The wire was reintroduced and the box was moved closer to the spot from time to time when the performance deteriorated. To correct a tendency to peck from only one side (that is, leaning left), the wire was suspended close to the wall in a way that forced the bird to peck from the other side.

Sessions 26 to 29. The training was continued without the wire. The position of the spot was moved repeatedly, and the distance between the spot and the box was varied until the bird could reliably sight the spot and push the box from the center of the chamber to the spot in a continuous series of pushes. The feeder was operated when the box made contact with the spot. By Session 29, the pigeon performed this task reliably.

Sessions 30 to 31. The banana was suspended from the ceiling of the chamber within reach of the bird. Pecking the banana was shaped and maintained on a rich variable-ratio schedule. The position of the banana was changed repeatedly. In the absence of the banana and in the presence of the spot, we continued to reinforce directional pushes for a few minutes each day, as described previously.

Sessions 32 to 39. In the absence of both the banana and the spot, a small box, roughly 3 cm high and 4 cm square at its base, was fixed into position on the floor of the chamber, and stepping onto it and standing was reinforced. Taller boxes were immediately substituted until the bird reliably climbed onto the test box, which was 8 cm high. Pecking the boxes was extinguished. For a few minutes each day, with the box removed and the banana within reach, pecking the banana was reinforced as described. With the banana removed and the box and spot present, directional training also proceed as described. The positions of the box, spot, and banana were changed repeatedly.

Sessions 38 to 39. For a few minutes each day, in the absence of the box and spot, the banana was suspended out of reach, 41 cm from the floor, and reinforcement was withheld. The purpose of this procedure was to extinguish jumping and flying toward the banana, but we observed little jumping and no flying. The position of the banana was changed repeatedly.

During the thirty-ninth session: (a) In the absence of the spot and the banana, the pigeon repeatedly climbed onto the box. (b) In the absence of the spot and the box and with the banana suspended within reach, the pigeon pecked the banana readily. (c) In the absence of the banana, the pigeon pushed the box rapidly and in reasonably straight lines from the center of the chamber to various locations in which the spot was placed around the base of the chamber of wall. (d) In the absence of the spot and the box and with the banana suspended out of reach, the pigeon stretched toward the banana but neither jumped nor flew toward it.

Test

The box was placed in the center of the chamber, and the banana was suspended out of the bird's reach, 41 cm from the floor, at a location about 3.5 cm from the edge of the chamber on a radius selected by a random number (84 degrees clockwise from the feeder). The trainer placed the bird in the chamber and then sat in a chair beside it, as she had during training. The performance was videotaped.

RESULTS AND ANALYSIS

The bird's performance during the test is shown in Figure 10.1 in frames from the videotape. The overall performance was similar to successful performances reported by Epstein et al. (1984). A period of apparent confusion was evident, during which the bird stretched toward the banana and looked back and forth repeatedly from the box to the banana (frames 2.0 sec to 20.0 sec). Then the bird pushed the box in a manner that brought the box to rest beneath the banana (frames 22.0 sec to 48.0 sec). It began to climb at 50.0 seconds and finally pecked the banana at 59.5 sec (Figure 10.2).

This performance is unlike those reported by Epstein et al. (1984) in two critical respects. First, in the earlier study the pigeons sighted the banana repeatedly as they pushed, especially when the box was near the banana. The pushes were not only directional; they appeared to be "directed." In the current performance, there was little evidence of sighting, even when the box was beneath the banana. Second, in the earlier study the birds climbed as soon as the box reached the banana; indeed, two of them climbed and stretched toward the banana even before the box reached it. In the current study the box was brought near the banana at about 34 seconds, at which point the bird pecked it back and forth weakly for nearly 18 seconds before climbing. Finally, in the previous study all three of the birds pecked the banana immediately after climbing. In the current performance, nearly 10 seconds elapsed between the time the bird began to mount the box (50.0 sec) and the time it pecked the banana (59.5 sec).

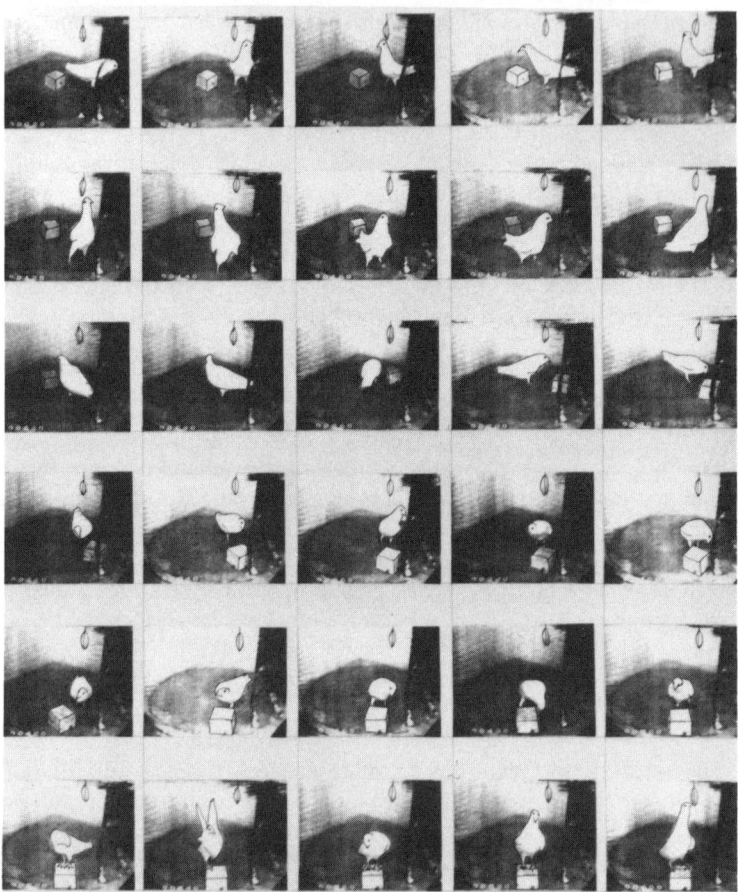

Figure 10.1. Videotape frames showing the bird's performance during the test at 2-second intervals, from 2.0 seconds to 60.0 seconds. Thus each row of the figure shows 10-second intervals of the performance. The figure was constructed as follows: A dub of the original tape was made, onto which a digital timer added running time to the lower left of the picture, with a 0.1-second resolution. Then a Tektronix raster-scan printer was used to print frames at the intervals shown. The bird, box, and banana were outlined in black ink to make them easier to identify. A period of "confusion" is evident during the first 20 seconds. The bird pushes the box and brings it to rest near the banana during the next 30 seconds. It begins to climb at 50.0 seconds and ultimately pecks the banana about 10 seconds later. A white triangle in the first frame marks the spot on the floor beneath the banana (the triangle was added to the photograph; there was no such mark on the chamber floor). See the text for a detailed analysis of the emergence of the performance.

All in all, the performance did not seem to be especially "insightful," which is to say that it did not fulfill one of Köhler's requirements for genuine insight, namely that once the performance begins, it occurs in a smooth, continuous fashion until it is complete. In this case, the pushing, climbing, and pecking were somewhat disjointed from each other; they appeared to be three "unrelated" acts, as opposed to a single response unit. The final peck seemed to be "accidental" (Figure 10.2).

The differences between the performances can be understood in terms of some simple principles. For convenience, the performance will be divided into six parts:

Period of apparent confusion. In the previous study, the behavior that suggested confusion appeared to be the result of competition between behaviors set up by the new arrangement of the box and the banana. Because of the bird's training, banana-over-box controlled behavior with respect to the banana, and box-with-spot controlled behavior with respect to the box. In the test, the bird was faced with a stimulus that was approximately intermediate between these two: The banana was shifted away from the box, and the spot was shifted outside the field of vision. Hence, one would expect behavior with respect to each stimulus to occur (consider Cumming & Eckerman, 1965; Migler, 1964).

In the current study, four controlling stimuli were established—box-alone, box-and-spot, banana-within-reach, and banana-out-of-reach. The test configuration was not a clear intermediate; rather, it was a compound whose elements were similar or identical to three of the training stimuli. The compound produced multiple, incompatible behaviors with respect to both the banana and the box.

Starting to push. In both studies, the competition that was set up initially was unstable, since reinforcement was withheld. Behavior with respect to the banana weakened rapidly relative to behavior with respect to the box because of the recent history of extinction of jumping and flying when the banana was suspended out of reach (compare the performance of bird 110YP in Epstein et al. [1984]). In the previous study, as behavior with respect to the box increased in relative frequency, the bird faced it more directly; it thus faced a close approximation to the stimulus that controlled pushing, and, indeed, it began to push.

In the current study, as the bird came to face the box more directly, it should have been inclined to push *and* to climb, since box-and-spot controlled pushing and box-alone controlled climbing. No climbing occurred, but we would expect to see climbing in replications of this experiment. Note that climbing would rapidly extinguish, and we would then expect to see a resurgence of pushing (Epstein, 1983a, 1985d),[4] at which point the performance should continue more or less as it does below (with the possible exception that the bird might fail to climb again when the box reached the banana).

Pushing toward the banana. Why the birds pushed toward the banana is still under investigation. Epstein et al. (1984) described a pilot study which is suggestive: Two birds, trained to push toward the spot but never to peck the banana, did not push toward the banana in the test situation. Subsequent to this test, pecking the banana was reinforced, and then the test was repeated. Now each bird sighted the banana and pushed the box toward it (each test consisted of three 2-minute extinction trials with the banana in three different locations). Each bird stopped pushing near the banana and neither climbed. This suggests that the spread of effect between the target spot and the banana does not occur because of common physical characteristics ("stimulus generalization") but rather because of a common reinforcement history ("functional generalization") (Epstein, 1984e; Epstein et al., 1984). In other words, in both the current and the previous performances, the birds push toward the banana apparently because of (a) a history of reinforcement for pushing toward the spot and (b) a history of reinforcement for pecking the banana.

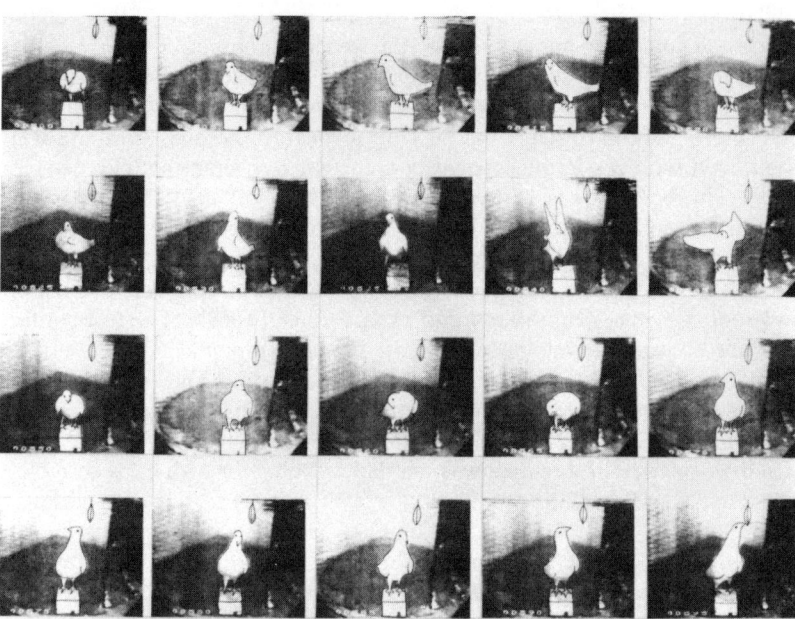

Figure 10.2. Videotape frames showing the bird's performance during the final 10 seconds of the test, from 50.0 seconds to 59.5 seconds, in 0.5-second intervals. See the text for an analysis of the performance.

Stopping. From this point on, the previous performances and the current one differ considerably. In the previous study, we attributed the cessation of pushing to "automatic chaining": As the bird pushed, it set up increasingly closer approximations to a stimulus that controlled other behavior—box-under-banana, which controlled climbing and pecking. The tendency to stop should have increased as the box approached the banana.

But in the current study, *the pigeon had never seen box-under-banana.* The bird should have been no more inclined to stop pushing when the box was beneath the banana than when the box was far away. Indeed, the bird did not stop pushing when the box reached the banana (Figure 10.1, frame 36.0 sec); it pushed somewhat beyond (frames 36.0 sec to 48.0 sec). How did the bird manage to keep the box in the right area so long, and why did it eventually stop pushing? As the pilot study described, the banana seemed to have acquired some of the controlled characteristics of the green spot. Thus when the bird pushed the box beyond the banana, it should then have tended to push the box back toward the banana again, in a damped oscillatory pattern. Since reinforcement was withheld, pushing should have tended to disappear with the box still near the banana, and indeed that is what occurred.

Climbing. The principle of resurgence seems useful again at this point: With pushing and reaching toward the banana reasonably well extinguished, other previously reinforced behaviors, such as climbing, should have appeared. Thus, finally, the bird climbed.

Pecking the banana. The last 10 seconds of the performance are shown in 0.5-second intervals in Figure 10.2. Perched on the box, the bird at first faced away from the banana (that is, faced left in the figure), made a preening movement (52.0 sec), stumbled briefly and flapped its wings (53.5 sec to 54.5 sec), faced down (56.5 sec), faced slightly left (57.5 sec), faced forward (58.0 sec), faced right (59.0 sec), and finally pecked the banana (59.5 sec). Automatic chaining should seem to be responsible for the peck: The bird's own behavior (orienting to the right) produced a visual stimulus (banana within reach) that controlled other behavior (pecking). Because this process is orderly, it would be inaccurate to call the peck "accidental," but the bird clearly did not climb onto the box "in order to" peck; which is to say, it did not climb because climbing had previously produced an opportunity to peck. Climbing and pecking were indeed disjointed.

Various behaviors have been described herein as if they were discrete, but in fact they are probably best described by smooth, continuous curves. The behaviors may appear to be discrete only because at any one moment we see only the most probable one, but at that same moment another behavior might be highly probable, a third less probable, and so on. The behaviors and their interactions may prove to be describable by continuous functions.

CONCLUSIONS

The present performance was not especially "insightful," but neither was it "trial and error." These terms have occasionally been used as if they encompassed all problem-solving performances, but in fact they describe only rather extreme cases, each of which is relatively rare. "Insightful" performances are characterized by periods of confusion or inactivity followed by the sudden and continuous emergence of the solution (Koffka, 1924; Köhler, 1925; Yerkes & Yerkes, 1929). "Trial and error" solutions are characterized by the appearance of a great deal of behavior that is irrelevant to the problem; they are clumsy and slow. But virtually none of Köhler's (1925) chimpanzees performed in either fashion on any occasion, and the same may be said for human subjects (consider Duncker, 1945).

A more effective way to understand problem-solving performances and indeed all novel behavior is to identify the principles according to which new behavior is continuously generated under new circumstances. The same set of functions should presumably predict a wide range of possible performances in a problem-solving situation, including non-solutions, absurd and awkward solutions, insightful solutions, and so on. Indeed, all behavior—no matter what post hoc labels we may apply—should be predictable according to such principles. The principles should predict *different* performances as a function of relevant parameters: the genes and ontogenic history of the individual, current stimuli and the manner in which such stimuli are changed over time as a result of the organism's behavior, and so on. If one knows the transformation functions and the relevant parameters, one should be able to predict where in this range the performance will fall and to provide a detailed probability profile of the succession of behaviors that will appear.

NOTES

1. They can also be represented formally. The author has recently presented equations and a computer model which predict the emergence of novel performances moment-to-moment in time. The model has been validated with human subjects.

2. A preliminary report appeared in Epstein (1981a).

3. This was in fact "Jack" in Epstein, Lanza, & Skinner (1980) and Epstein & Skinner (1981).

4. The principle of resurgence may be stated as follows: When, under given stimulus conditions, a response that was recently reinforced is no longer reinforced, behavior that was reinforced in the past under similar stimulus conditions tends to recur. The principle has, in various guises, enjoyed a long and distinguished history in both clinical and experimental psychology. For further discussion and a review of empirical support for this principle, see Chapter 15.

11

THE SPONTANEOUS INTERCONNECTION OF FOUR REPERTOIRES

Summary. A pigeon was trained (a) to peck a small facsimile of a banana placed within its reach, (b) to climb onto a box, c) to open a door, and (d) to push a box toward targets. When confronted with a new situation—the banana was placed out of reach, and the box was placed behind the door—the four repertoires came together rapidly to produce a human-like solution to the problem. A tentative account of the performance is offered in terms of empirically validated principles.

Epstein, Kirshnit, Lanza, and Rubin (1984) reported that pigeons with appropriate training histories can solve the classic box-and-banana problem in an insightful, human-like fashion. The contributions of different experiences were assessed by varying the training histories of different birds. All three of the birds that had learned (a) to push a box toward a small green spot placed at random positions around the base of a large cylindrical chamber, (b) to climb onto a box and peck a small facsimile of a banana suspended overhead, and (c) not to jump or fly toward the banana when it was suspended out of reach in the absence of the box, solved the problem in what has traditionally been called an "insightful" manner (Koffka, 1924; Köhler, 1925; Yerkes & Yerkes, 1929): Each bird first appeared to be confused; it stretched toward the banana, motioned toward the box, looked back at the banana, and so on. Then, in a continuous series of movements, it pushed the box toward the banana, sighting the banana and realigning the box as it pushed, stopped pushing when the box was near the banana, climbed, and pecked. The performances lasted roughly 1 to 2 minutes.

Birds that had learned to peck but not to climb did not successfully climb when the banana was suspended above the box. Birds that had learned to climb and peck but not to push did not push in the test situation. Birds that had learned to push but never to push toward targets pushed aimlessly during the test; one bird managed to solve the problem after 14 minutes in a manner one might call "trial and error." Another procedure produced behavior suggestive of the classic performance of Sultan, one of Köhler's (1925) chimpanzees: A bird whose jumping and flying had not been eliminated jumped and flew toward the banana for several minutes and then, after a total of about 7 minutes, solved the problem in the insightful manner described earlier.

Epstein et al. (1984) also offered a running account of the successful performances in terms of relatively simple principles. The solution can be understood as the interconnection of two repertoires of behavior which had been established separately and which were controlled by separate stimuli. The two repertoires were made to occur in close temporal proximity by the new arrangement of box and banana, which contained approximations of the stimuli that controlled each of the repertoires separately. The period of apparent confusion was probably the result of the competition between these repertoires (Cumming & Eckerman, 1965; Epstein, 1985b; Epstein et al., 1984; Migler, 1964). The sequence that emerged seems to have been determined by several processes, one of which is automatic chaining: As the bird pushed the box closer to the banana, it arranged for itself an increasingly close approximation of the stimulus—box under banana—that controlled climbing and pecking; hence it stopped pushing, climbed, and pecked.

Other studies have also identified *resurgence* as a phenomenon that makes multiple repertoires available in problem-solving situations (Epstein & Medalie, 1983; Epstein, 1985d): When, in a given situation, recently successful behavior is no longer successful, other behaviors that were successful under similar conditions in the past tend to recur (Barker, Dembo, & Lewin, 1941; Epstein, 1983a; Epstein & Skinner, 1980; Estes, 1955; Freud, 1920; Hull, 1934, 1952; Leitenberg, Rawson, & Bath, 1970; Maltzman, 1955; Masserman, 1943; Mowrer, 1940; Notterman, 1970; Pryor, Haag, & O'Reilly, 1969; Sears, 1943; Staddon & Simmelhag, 1971; Yates, 1970). Resurgence seems to be the principle phenomenon that allowed pigeons to solve a problem by using a box as a tool to extend their reach (Epstein & Medalie, 1983), and it also seems to have been involved in a more complicated performance in which a rapid, although not especially insightful, solution to the box-and-banana problem was generated by the spontaneous interconnection of three repertoires (Epstein, 1985b).

In the present experiment, a pigeon was provided with four separate repertoires appropriate to the solution of a still more complicated problem.

METHOD

Subject and Apparatus

The subject was an adult, male, White Carneaux pigeon (289WP) that had been previously used in a variety of laboratory experiments, including a problem-solving experiment in which it had been trained in directional pushing (see below). It was maintained at roughly 80 percent of the weight it would normally attain given free access to food. Training sessions were conducted daily in a cylindrical, wire-mesh chamber, 76 cm in diameter. A cardboard box, 8 cm high and with a base 10 cm square, was employed in some conditions, as was a small, yellow, cloth-covered facsimile of a banana, 7 cm in length. A portable enclosure, shaped like half a cylinder, was placed in the chamber under some conditions. The enclosure was 12 cm deep at its center, and it had a wire-mesh back and a door in front which could be opened. The door itself was made of clear Plexiglas and measured 18 cm high by 27 cm wide; its outer edge was covered with opaque black tape. It did not swing freely; its movement rotated a metal gear, the teeth of which caught a piece of metal that was fixed to the door frame. Moving the door thus produced audible clicks. A standard grain dispenser was attached to the base of the chamber as shown in Figure 11.2.

Procedure

There were five parts to the training, which was accomplished in 24 sessions over a period of 9 weeks. The bird received a total of about 16 hours of training during this period and had previously received about 12 hours of training in directional pushing.[1] The major steps in establishing directional pushing were as follows: At first aimless pushes were reinforced (with 3-second operations of the grain dispenser); then pecks to the green spot were reinforced; then the box was mounted on a thin wire that constrained its movement, the spot was placed at one end, and sighting the spot and pushing the box toward it was reinforced; the wire was removed, the box was placed close to the spot, and the sight-and-push sequence was reinforced; the distance between the spot and the box was gradually increased.

With directional pushing well established, a few minutes were spent each day on one or more of each of the four other aspects of training: In the absence of the box, banana, and spot, opening the enclosure door was shaped and maintained with intermittent food presentations. In the absence of the enclosure, box, and spot, the banana was placed within reach of the bird, and pecking it was shaped and maintained with intermittent food presentations. In the absence of the banana, enclosure, and spot, the box was fixed in place on the floor of the chamber, and stepping onto it and standing in place was shaped (using a series of increasingly taller boxes) and maintained with intermittent food presentations. Finally, in the absence of the other objects, the banana was placed out of the bird's reach, and the bird was placed alone with it until the bird neither flew nor jumped toward it. All of the objects were moved repeatedly to different positions in the chamber during all phases of training.

The following test situation was arranged: The banana was suspended out of the pigeon's reach (41 cm from the floor) at a point (determined by a random number) 5 cm from an edge of the chamber. The portable enclosure was placed opposite this point at the other side of the chamber, the box was placed in the center rear of the enclosure, and the enclosure door was closed. A video camera recorded the test session from a position about 1.5 m from the chamber. The pigeon was placed in the chamber, and the chamber door was immediately closed. The session was timed from the moment the chamber door was closed.

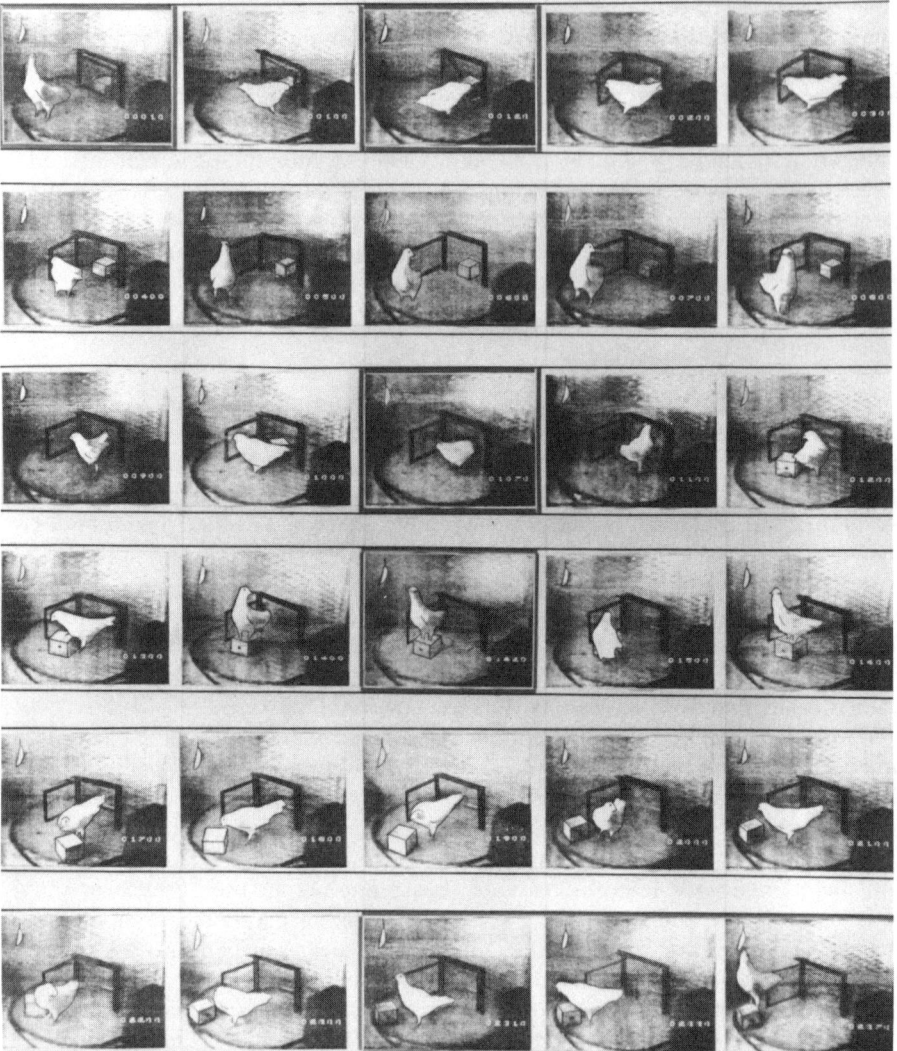

Figure 11.1. Videotape frames showing the bird's performance at 10-second intervals. Photos outlined in gray show the performance at other times. The figure was constructed as follows: A dub of the original videotape was made, onto which a digital timer added running time to the lower right of the picture, with a 0.1-second resolution. Then a Tektronix 4632 raster-scan printer was used to print frames at the intervals shown. The bird, box, banana, and enclosure door were outlined in black to make them easier to identify. During the first few seconds of the performance, the bird stretched toward the banana. At about 10 seconds into the performance (00100 in the figure), the bird began to open the enclosure door. After it approached the banana again and pecked again at the open door, the bird pecked weakly at the box (88 sec, not shown), stretched again toward the banana, and then began to push the box out of the enclosure (107 sec). It climbed and stretched toward the banana at 142 seconds and did so again at 160 seconds. Finally, it brought the box to rest near the banana, began to climb (233 sec), and pecked the banana (237 sec).

RESULTS

The results are shown in Figure 11.1. At first the bird stretched toward the banana, then it oriented toward the enclosure door and box. After about 10 seconds, it approached the enclosure door and pecked it open. Pecks on the door persisted even after it was fully open. From 50 to 100 seconds into the session, the bird oriented and stretched toward the banana several times, pecked the box briefly at 88 seconds (not shown), and again pecked the open enclosure door. Finally, at 107 seconds, it began to push the box out of the enclosure. It sighted the banana several times as it pushed, stopped pushing about halfway across the chamber, climbed, and stretched toward the banana (142 sec). Then it dismounted, pecked weakly at the enclosure door (150 sec), climbed onto the box again and stretched again toward the banana (160 sec), after which it dismounted and pushed the box along the path indicated in Figure 11.2 (164 sec to 230 sec). It oriented toward the banana at 221 seconds (not shown) and again at 231 seconds, after which it immediately climbed and pecked the banana (237 sec).

The obvious competition of repertoires that occurred throughout this session can be understood as the result of multiple controlling stimuli or "stimulus matching" (Cumming & Eckerman, 1965; Epstein, 1985b; Epstein et al., 1984; Migler, 1964). The bird was exposed to simultaneously-presented approximations of stimuli that controlled four separate repertoires, and hence each of the behaviors appeared. The sequence of their appearance and reappearance was constrained by the changing arrangement of stimuli, the bird's training history, and behavioral processes such as automatic chaining and resurgence: The bird's first stretches toward the banana disappeared rapidly, both because they were not reinforced and because of the bird's history of nonreinforcement when the banana was alone and out of reach. Unsuccessful stretches should have produced, among other things, a resurgence of other behaviors that had been successful in the chamber; thus the bird oriented toward and then approached the enclosure door and box, but the physical setup at this point prevented contact with the box. The bird pecked the enclosure door open, and this behavior, too, went unreinforced, increasing the probability of alternative behaviors. For nearly 1 minute pecking the enclosure door alternated with stretching toward the banana, until, finally, the bird approached and pushed the box. With the box halfway across the chamber, other behavior interfered (note that the spot—the usual target—was absent and that pushing was also unreinforced): The bird climbed, faced the banana, and immediately stretched toward it (the banana was now more nearly in the orientation that had allowed the bird to peck it during training sessions), but food was still withheld, so the bird dismounted, again pecked weakly at the enclosure door, which was immediately in front of the bird, and then pushed the box closer to the banana. Previous experiments (Epstein, 1985b; Epstein & Medalie, 1983; Epstein et al., 1984) have shown that pigeons that have learned both to push a box toward the training target and to peck the banana will push the box toward the banana, a phenomenon suggestive of what some call "functional generalization" (Bruner, Goodnow, & Austin,

1956; Stemmer, 1972). Since the bird had never seen box-under-banana (cf. Epstein et al., 1984), it pushed somewhat beyond the banana, but then, since the banana was still the target, pushed back toward the banana, and so on, until pushing extinguished in roughly a damped oscillatory pattern of pushes in the area of the banana (Figure 11.2). With pushing and pecking the enclosure door greatly weakened, the bird climbed and, orienting toward the banana, immediately pecked.

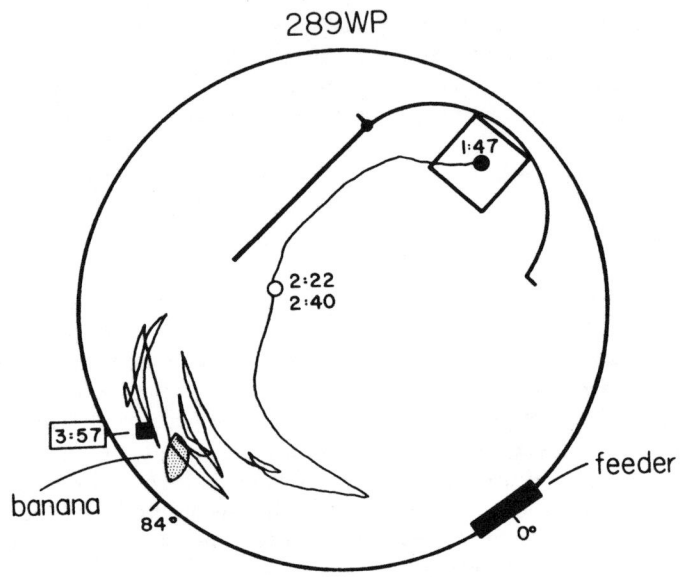

Figure 11.2. Floor diagram of the chamber. The bird pushed the box fairly directly toward the banana but did not stop pushing when the box first approached the banana. Rather, it pushed somewhat beyond, pushed back toward the banana and then somewhat beyond, and so on, in roughly a damped oscillatory pattern. In so doing the bird kept the box within a few cm from the position on the floor beneath the banana for more than 50 seconds before it finally climbed. The open circle marks the position at which the bird twice climbed and stretched toward the banana before bringing the box to rest near the banana. Times are shown in minutes and seconds.

DISCUSSION

This test was my first and only attempt at obtaining the interconnection of four repertoires of behavior in a pigeon, and I believe that a positive result is significant even if attempts with other pigeons fail. If my analysis of the performance is correct, however, additional attempts will succeed, subject to individual differences among subjects, which should affect both the rapidity and smoothness of the process of interconnection. As noted above, when another pigeon was confronted with a simpler problem, three repertoires came together to produce a solution in less than 1 minute (Epstein, 1985b).

A large number of repertoires can undoubtedly be made to compete with each other in a novel situation, but that does not guarantee that they will combine successfully to produce adaptive behavior. Trivial factors can have profound effects: A turn of the head radically changes the visual field and hence may increase the probability of inappropriate behaviors; critical behaviors that persist too early in the performance may weaken to such an extent that they are unavailable at appropriate points later in the performance; the problem may be structured so that a slight variant of an appropriate behavior leads to a cul-de-sac (the box could easily have become trapped behind the open door of the enclosure, for example).

I have described elsewhere a general approach to understanding and predicting ongoing, novel performances in both human and non-human animals (Epstein, 1985a, 1986a).[2] Previously established behavior manifests itself in new situations in orderly ways as a function of the genes and ontogenic history of the individual, as well as of the current stimuli and the manner in which they are changed over time by the organism or other agents. Our understanding of ongoing behavior will be enhanced by varying species and individuals, by varying training histories, and by the further elaboration of the principles that predict the transformation of previously established behavior under new circumstances.

This approach to understanding ongoing behavior has been helpful in two ways: It has allowed us to engineer increasingly complex, novel performances in relatively simple organisms (Epstein, 1985b; Epstein & Medalie, 1983; Epstein & Skinner, 1981; Epstein, Lanza, & Skinner, 1981; Epstein et al., 1984), and it has led to the development of a formal theory, called Generativity Theory, which has proved useful in predicting ongoing behavior in human subjects under laboratory conditions (Epstein, 1985a). The approach might also prove helpful in the design of problem-solving software for artificial intelligence systems.

NOTES

1. The bird had previously been a subject in a replication of the "tool use" experiment (Epstein & Medalie, 1983), for which it was trained to push two types of boxes toward the green spot. It had had no experience with the enclosure door or the banana in this experiment and had not been taught to climb.

2. The interconnection of repertoires has often been suggested as a source of novelty in behavior. Consider Hull (1935), Koestler (1964), Maier (1929), Maier and Schneirla (1935), Poincaré (1946), and Rothenberg (1971).

12

SIMULATION RESEARCH IN THE ANALYSIS OF BEHAVIOR

Summary. The simulation is a useful tool in science and engineering when the subject matter cannot easily be manipulated directly—often the case in astronomy or evolutionary biology, for example. A simulation is plausible to the extent that it accurately represents the object or process it is meant to simulate. The Columban Simulations of complex human behavior are plausible to varying degrees. Computer simulations of cognitive processes are highly implausible, particularly those that depend on the assumption that humans are information processors.

The more interesting some instance of human behavior, the more difficult it is to analyze (perhaps that's why we call it interesting). And where objective analysis is difficult, fictions turn up. Consider the following cases:

At age one most children react to their mirror images as if they are seeing other children; by age two, most children react as if they are seeing themselves. How can we account for the change? Does it help to say that the child has developed a "self-concept"?

Virtually all human beings acquire language and, by age five, have fairly rich vocabularies. They also seem capable of emitting an infinite number of different sentences. How can we explain this? Does it help to say that we are born with "language organs" or that a set of "cognitive rules" is guiding us?

A two-year-old girl is faced with the proverbial "marble-under-the-couch" problem: She stretches toward the marble but cannot reach it. After repeated attempts, she looks around the room and reaches suddenly for a nearby magazine. She casts about with it until she knocks the marble out from under the couch. Do we shed light on this behavior by attributing it to "insight" or "reasoning"? If not, what contribution, if any, can we make?

An audience of cognitive psychologists has listened with adoration to a prominent colleague. A member of the audience, known for his wit, raises his hand, stands, and deadpans, "But how is this relevant to *pigeons*?" There is a swell of laughter and some applause. Could we predict who would laugh? Does it help to say that someone has a "sense of humor"? (Did *you* laugh?)

These and many other instances of complex behavior in people are difficult to analyze for several reasons. First, they are all multiply determined at the time they occur. Sofa, marble, magazine, toys, television, and so on, strengthen many behaviors, and the child's own behavior changes the environment and hence changes the probability of subsequent behavior. Second, they are the result of complex environmental histories and, presumably, biological factors. Language is acquired haphazardly over a period of years, and although it may not be systematically trained, speaking and speaking grammatically are more effective than not speaking or speaking ungrammatically; in other words, children are exposed from birth to subtle and complex "contingencies of reinforcement" which support speaking and speaking grammatically. Modeling, instructions, and physical maturation also undoubtedly make important contributions. Third, they are all typically human phenomena; problem solving, language, wit, the behaviors that come under the rubric of "self-awareness," and so on, are all relatively rare in nature; the study of non-human organisms is not as informative as it is for simpler behavioral phenomena. And finally, because the histories are complicated and the phenomena relatively unique to humans, it is difficult, if not impossible, to explore them through experimentation.

Similar problems are faced in many domains of scientific inquiry. Complexity (say, in meteorology), the importance of events in the remote past (say, in evolutionary biology), inaccessibility (say, in astronomy), or ethical considerations (say, in neurology) often prevent direct study. Fortunately, methods have evolved which allow at least some tentative analyses. This paper concerns one of the most powerful of such methods—the simulation—and its application in the analysis of complex human behavior.

ONE HUNDRED BABIES

B. F. Skinner once told me that an Indian (of the Asian variety) tried to induce him to move to India by offering him a hundred babies with which to do research. As appalling as the offer may sound, without those babies some of the most interesting questions in the analysis of behavior can never be answered definitively.

Let's say, for example, that you are interested in the origins of language. If you took an extreme nativist position, you might assert that spoken language would emerge even if a child were never exposed to it—as, presumably, would walking. How would you test such an assertion? You might wait for a naked child to appear at the edge of the woods, but you would have a long wait and could never be certain of the child's history. The handful of feral children that have turned up have not shed light on the issue; the so-called "wild boy of Burundi," for example, was indeed mute but turned out to be brain damaged, autistic, and profoundly retarded (Lane & Pillard, 1978).

More definitive answers could come only from carefully conducted deprivation studies. One would have to raise some children from birth without exposing them to language (taking care, somehow, to deprive them of nothing else). A positive result would be extremely informative: If the children came to make sounds that had characteristics of known languages, your hypothesis will have been supported. Perhaps non-linguistic sounds of certain frequencies were responsible; we could control for that possibility with still other children. A negative result would be less informative: Perhaps we inadvertently deprived the children of something besides the sound of language.

According to Salimbene, a medieval historian, in the thirteenth century the Roman emperor Frederick II conducted such an experiment:

> His...folly was that he wanted to find out what kind of speech and what manner of speech children would have when they grew up, if they spoke to no one beforehand. So he bade foster mothers and nurses to suckle the children, to bathe and wash them, but in no way to prattle with them or to speak to them, for he wanted to learn whether they would speak the Hebrew language, which was the oldest, or Greek, or Latin, or Arabic, or perhaps the language of their parents.... But he laboured in vain, because the children all died. For they could not live without the petting and the joyful faces and loving words of their foster mothers. (quoted in Ross & McLaughlin, 1949, p. 366)

We are better off, some people say, not knowing the answers to certain questions. This issue aside, we can *only* know the answers to certain questions in the analysis of behavior by employing extreme and entirely unacceptable methods of the sort Frederick (the one with the "K"!) was said to employ. For all practical purposes, then, we can never develop definitive accounts of certain complex human behaviors (though it is a useful exercise to devise the necessary methods).

This sad pronouncement applies to all of the examples of complex behavior I gave above, as well as to countless others. You may suspect, for example, that a child can not efficiently solve the marble-under-the-couch problem unless he or she has already learned—perhaps through shaping, modeling, instructions, or some combination of these—both to grasp objects and to make contact with objects using other objects. Again, how would you test such a hypothesis? Simply testing a child who lacks such skills before and after you have established those skills would *not* be adequate, for you would still somehow have to control for prior learning.

It is a truism that all scientific pronouncements are tentative. But some are far more tentative than others. If we could carefully control and monitor all of the conditions that we believed to be relevant to the emergence of some behavior—genes, learning experiences, nutrition, and so on—we could establish with greater confidence the contributions of each. In cases in which we cannot, for some reason, experiment directly, we must resort to indirect methods. Which brings us to the laboratory simulation.

SIMULATIONS IN THE SCIENCES

As is the case in the analysis of behavior, the most interesting questions in the natural sciences are the most difficult to analyze. The origin of the universe, of life, and of species is still attributed by many to a deity, and not only is it impossible to disprove such a theory, it is equally impossible to prove an alternative. Scientists bring diverse methods and information from many fields to bear on such questions. One helpful method is the simulation. Consider some examples:

In the 1950s the biologists S. L. Miller and H. C. Urey tested a theory of the origin of life by simulating some of the conditions believed to be typical of primitive earth. The "soup" they prepared contained no organic materials at first but soon yielded both amino and hydroxy acids, important precursors of life as we know it (Miller & Orgel, 1973). They did not *prove* that the theory was correct; they merely *proved* its *plausibility*. In recent years, new geological and other data have revised our conception of earth's primitive atmosphere. New theories of the origin of life are tested in laboratory simulations like Miller and Urey's (e.g., Pinto, Gladstone, & Yung, 1980). As is true in any domain of science, the dominant theory at any point in time will usually be the one that accounts for more data—in this case, a steady accumulation of data in several fields.

Recently evidence was presented which supports a rather fantastic explanation for the mass extinction of dinosaurs and other organisms which occurred on earth 65 million years ago. Some now believe that a large asteroid struck the earth and kicked up enough dust to darken the skies for several months, thus destroying vital food chains (Alvarez, Kauffman, Surlyk, Alvarez, Asaro, & Michel, 1984). Critical evidence comes from laboratory simulations of large-body impacts (Kerr, 1981). Again, such simulations don't prove the theory, but, in conjunction with the fossil record and other geological data, they lend credence to it.

The computer has become one of the most powerful tools of simulation research. If the variables controlling some phenomenon are sufficiently understood so that it can be described in formal terms—so that "laws" in the form of equations or algorithms can be stated—the computer can be used to plot the course of extremely complex systems that involve many such phenomena. With accurate equations and parameters, the behavior of such systems can be predicted. Such is the basis of long-term prediction in meteorology, astronomy, and other sciences. In recent years, computers have been used successfully to predict the course of chemical reactions by utilizing laws of chemical and physical processes (Edelson, 1981). Computer simulations have also been used for many years in the social sciences—in economics, cognitive psychology, game theory, political science, and so on—but, as the introduction to a book on the subject points out, "the researcher must know a great deal about the real system before he can presume to simulate it" (Dawson, 1962, p. 14); where basic principles are still under investigation and formal statements are crude and simplistic, computer simulations are probably premature. It's true that you can, by accelerating processes or varying parameters, use computer simulations to discover things you didn't know, but your results will be no better than the equations with which you started.

Most of the simulations I have mentioned have been attempts at faithful reproductions of certain phenomena in all their complexity—"causality-based descriptions combining the underlying fundamentals of the many components of ... highly complex system" (Edelson, 1981, p. 981). But as Edelson points out, the language of simulation and modeling is used in diverse ways. Some simulations mimic phenomena in relatively arbitrary ways. At one extreme are "models" which look or behave like something but whose resemblance is superficial and which have no predictive value. The circus animal that wears glasses and turns the pages of a book appears to be a "reader" but does not do these things for the same reasons a person does and is not affected by the words on each page as a person is.

The language of simulation is usually reserved for models that are at least predictive. Even predictive models, however, may have varying degrees of similarity to the object. An engineering text (Murphy, 1950) makes some useful distinctions, adapted somewhat for this discussion: A *true simulation* faithfully reproduces all significant characteristics of some phenomenon; Miller and Urey attempted a true simulation. An *adequate simulation* reproduces only some significant characteristics. A *dissimilar simulation* bears no apparent resemblance to the object but is still predictive. An electrical circuit, for example, can simulate characteristics of a vibrating mechanical system. Virtually all computer simulations fall in this category.

The computer simulation requires its own analysis, for although it bears no apparent resemblance to its object, it can represent formally any number of the object's characteristics. If it faithfully represents all significant characteristics—say, in the case of the marble problem, critical experiences, current stimuli, relevant principles of behavior, and so on—we might call it a *true computer simulation*. Edelson's (1981) simulations of chemical reactions fall in this category. If it behaves appropriately and is predictive but uses algorithms which may be unrelated to those which characterize the object—say, it produces various solutions to the marble problem simply by calling them up from memory—we might call it a *dissimilar computer simulation*, and so on.[1]

What follows is an example of what was intended as a true simulation of an instance of complex human behavior.

"SELF-AWARENESS" IN THE PIGEON

A variety of behavior is said to indicate that a person has a "self," "self-awareness," "self-knowledge," or a "self-concept." People tell you what they're thinking and where it hurts; at some point children recognize photographs of themselves and their reflections in a mirror; children will apparently imitate videotapes of themselves longer than videotapes of others; and so on (Gallup, 1968; Kagan, 1981; Lewis & Brooks-Gunn, 1979). Little progress has been made in accounting for such behavior. Kagan (1981) suggests that physical maturation is the key. Lewis and Brooks-Gunn (1979) and Gallup (e.g., 1979) attribute it to the development of a cognitive entity called the "self-concept."

Behavior with respect to one's mirror image is said to be a "compelling" example of the development of self. Such behavior is said to progress through a series of four stages, first noted by Dixon (1957). At first a child shows little or no reaction. When a few months old it begins to react as if it's seeing another child—by laughing, touching, and so on. The third stage, which Dixon (1957) called a period of "testing" or "discovery," is critical: Children often stare at their reflections while they make slow, repetitious movements of the mouth, hand, leg, and so on. Finally, by about age two, most children react as if they are seeing themselves, at which point they are said to be "self-aware" (Amsterdam, 1972; Lewis & Brooks-Gunn, 1979). Amsterdam (1968, 1972) devised an objective test of such behavior: A child had to use a mirror to locate some rouge that had been smeared on its nose (which, presumably, it could not see directly). Chimpanzees, after extensive exposure to mirrors, also come to exhibit such behavior, although monkeys apparently do not, and it is claimed that only humans and the great apes are capable of it (cf. Epstein & Koerner, 1986). How can one account for the change?

This is another one of those "origins" problems. Without the 100 babies, one can use only indirect methods to determine the possible role of experience, physical maturation, and so on. The Miller and Urey approach could be used as follows: Suppose that success in the mirror test is due to some rather simple learning experiences, ones which chimps and children actually have before they are successful in the test (Gallup, 1970; Lewis & Brooks-Gunn, 1979). Perhaps they must acquire two behaviors—touching themselves where they must touch during the test, and locating objects in real space given only mirror images. One could test such a theory by establishing such behaviors in organisms that would normally be incapable of success in the mirror test and seeing whether they were then successful.

Epstein, Lanza, and Skinner (1981) did so with pigeons. Pigeons were taught over a period of a few days (a) to scan their bodies for blue stick-on dots and peck them and (b) to peck certain positions on the wall and floor of their chamber given only the brief flash of a blue dot in a mirror. A blue dot was then placed on each pigeon's breast and a bib placed around its neck in a way that made the dot invisible to the pigeon but visible to others when the bird stood fully erect. Each of three birds was observed for 3 minutes in the absence of a mirror and 3 minutes in its presence. Independent observers judged few or no "dot-directed" pecks during the first period and an average of 10 per bird in its presence. Even though no reinforcers were delivered during the test and though the birds had never before worn blue dots when exposed to the mirror, it seemed that each pigeon was now able to use a mirror to locate a spot on its body which it could not see directly. We thus proved the plausibility of our hypothesis, just as Miller and Urey had proved the plausiblity of one theory of the origin of life.[2]

THE COLUMBAN SIMULATIONS

There are at least four classes of behaviors that have resisted analysis—covert behaviors ("thoughts," "feelings," "images"); complex, typically human behaviors that are difficult to trace either to environmental or biological factors (language, the behavior that comes under the rubric of "self," problem-solving behavior); behavior controlled by temporally remote stimuli (which leads some people to speak of "memory"); and novel behavior ("creativity," "productive thinking") (Epstein, 1986a). As I noted above, complexity, inaccessibility, the importance of events in the distant past, ethical considerations, or some combination of these factors make it difficult to study such phenomena directly.

The "self-awareness" experiment was one of several simulations I have conducted with B. F. Skinner and others to try to investigate such recalcitrant behaviors; the project came to be called the "Columban [from *Columba livia*, the taxonomic name for pigeon] Simulation Project" (Baxley, 1982; Epstein, 1981a).

Rationale. The rationale, briefly stated, for this work is as follows: If you have reason to believe, based on principles of behavior established in the laboratory and information about a person's past, that certain experiences were responsible for the emergence of some mysterious behavior, you provide support for this conjecture if, after providing an animal which does not normally exhibit such behavior with these experiences, the animal exhibits similar behavior (Epstein, 1981a). You can thus use animals to shed light on the possible contributions of certain environmental histories in the emergence of certain mysterious behaviors in humans. If your simulation is successful, you have not *proved* that the conjecture was correct—that the environmental history you identified is responsible for the emergence of the behavior in humans; rather, you have provided a "plausible account" of the behavior—what some philosophers call a "plausibility proof."

Plausibility. The plausibility of a simulation—that is, how "true" it is—depends on a number of factors which tend to be unique to the domain of the simulation. The plausibility of the Columban simulations rests on five criteria, not all of which are met by all of the simulations.

First, if one makes use of certain techniques of conditioning or appeals to certain principles of behavior, the applicability of these techniques and principles to people must be shown. The greatest strength of the Columban simulations lies in the demonstrated generality of behavioral phenomena such as chaining, discrimination, generalization, extinction, and so on, to scores of species, including *Homo sapiens*.

Second, the topography of the behavior in the simulation should resemble the topography of the simulated behavior; that is, the result should look right. In the "self-awareness" experiment, the pigeon's beak clearly moves toward a mark on its body which it cannot see directly; limbs aside, the behavior looks much like that of a chimp or child being subjected to the same test.

Third, the function of the behavior in the simulation should resemble the function of the simulated behavior; that is, the behaviors should occur for roughly the same reasons. Say we could get a pigeon to make a pecking movement toward the center of its breast simply by tugging on a tail feather. If we learned that during the mirror tests the tail feathers of our birds were being tugged, we would dismiss the results as uninformative. In fact, the birds pecked at their breasts because they had been taught to scan their bodies for blue dots and peck them and, as the various control conditions showed, because they spotted a blue dot in the corresponding position in the mirror. They did not peck simply because a mirror had been uncovered (uncovering the mirror while a bird wore a bib but no dot did not result in breast-directed behavior). And they did not peck simply because they felt the dot or saw it directly (dot-directed pecks did not occur in the absence of the mirror).

Fourth, the more structurally similar the organism is to a human, the more plausible the simulation. The more dissimilar the organism, the greater the likelihood that the result is due to an interaction between the conditioning you have provided and peculiarities of that organism. Ideally, of course, one would test humans themselves. Chimpanzees would probably be the next best candidates. Pigeons are hardly ideal, but one can do much worse. Pigeons are used, not because of significant structural overlap with humans, but for other reasons, to be discussed in the final section of this chapter.

Fifth, and most important, it is critical that humans have had the experiences you have identified; the more evidence you have that this is so, the more plausible your simulation. The "self-awareness" simulation is strong here in one respect and weak in another. As noted above, there is considerable evidence that chimps and children have acquired both of the repertoires we identified before they are successful in the mirror test; chimps and children are unique in that they can learn to use mirrors through mere exposure to the contingencies of reinforcement which govern mirror use (Epstein, 1986a; Epstein & Koerner, 1986).

COMPUTER SIMULATIONS OF COGNITIVE PROCESSES

Psychologists don't generally do the kind of simulation described above (also see other chapters in Part III of this volume). More common is the computer simulation—and not of behavior or of physiology, but of "mental processes" (e.g., Kosslyn & Schwartz, 1977; Newell & Simon, 1972; Simon, 1981). For example, Winograd's (1972) robot SHRDLU uses a sophisticated model of language processing to decipher the commands it is given. Anderson's (1972) FRAN is based on a model of human associative memory and can replicate some standard results of verbal learning experiments. Newell and Simon's (1972) General Problem Solver solves a limited class of logical problems (for example, in chess and mathematics). How do the Columban and computer simulations compare?

Plausibility. Computer simulations of cognition are implausible in several respects. They live up best to the second criterion described above. The "topography" of the behavior of a computer is presumably its output; in a successful simulation the computer presumably produces output (protocols, diagrams, latencies, and so on) which resembles either some property of human behavior (e.g., latency) or some product of human behavior (e.g., a protocol). The "function," however, of the behavior of a computer would seem to have little in common with that of human behavior. A computer's behavior is almost always "rule-governed"; that is, it is controlled by instructions. The behavior of organisms, on the other hand, is often multiply determined and, in particular, is often "contingency-shaped" (Skinner, 1966); that is, it is determined by the consequences of past behavior. A CRT that simulates a "mental image" (e.g., Kosslyn & Schwartz, 1977) does so because of a set of instructions that someone entered into the computer; whereas a college sophomore responds in certain ways in a "mental imagery" experiment because she has learned to speak English, because she has been given certain instructions and been asked certain questions, because she has been shown certain stimuli, and so on.

Computers and people would seem also to have little common structure. The anatomy and physiology of a pigeon are certainly closer to the anatomy and physiology of a person than are those of a computer. As Edelman (1982), a biologist, put it, "We are not clockwork machines, and we certainly are not possessed of brains that are like digital computers. We are part of that seamy web of natural selection which has itself evolved a selection machinery called our brain" (p. 48). Since they are also products of evolution, presumably the same could be said of pigeons.

Finally, the history which one identifies in a Columban simulation—the origins of the behavior—is one which might indeed be possible for a human. No one would claim, however, that computer simulations of mental processes uncover anything about the origins of human behavior; it would be absurd to assert that a man behaves in certain ways because someone input a program into him.[3]

Computer simulations of cognition, in short, may be plausible in the way they mimic human behavior but are plausible on no other grounds.

Other problems. There are other reasons for objecting to computer simulations of cognition as tools for understanding human behavior or brain function (cf. Epstein, 1981a). Even prominent cognitive psychologists have found reasons to object (e.g., Miller, 1981; Neisser, 1976).

Computer models of cognition are, almost without exception, unconstrained by physiological data. They are not models of the brain (though such models have been developed—consider Edelman & Reeke, 1982). Some cognitivists defend this merely on the grounds that little is known about the nervous system; others go so far as to assert that physiological data are irrelevant to the study of cognition. You can, they say, discover the "software" that runs the brain—the "rules," the "instructions," the "organization"—without knowing anything about the hardware (consider Fodor, 1981; Simon, 1969). This assertion has several flaws:

First, it rests on a faulty characterization of software. Some cognitivists would have us believe that computer software does not actually exist in the computer—that it is the mental world of the machine.[4] But computer software has physical status—it is in no sense "mental," "metaphysical," or even particularly abstract. It usually exists as a magnetic array or a pattern of high and low voltages in a physical device. With the proper equipment and a translation table, one could literally read off one's software directly from the device. How a given pattern controls the operation of the machine and eventually produces certain output could in principle be established by running the machine very slowly—by "single stepping" it. In this sense, one might call the DNA of living cells "software"—highly compact, *physical* information which is critical in certain controlling operations. The "software" of the brain—perhaps a superfluous concept—can be found *in* the brain.[5]

Second, as any programmer can tell you, one can write a large number of different programs to do the same job (consider Moore, 1959). The issue has been brought to the attention of cognitive psychologists by Anderson (1978), who argues that pictorial and propositional accounts of mental imagery and indeed "wide classes of different representations" can be made to yield identical behavioral predictions and therefore that we can never decide between such models on the basis of behavioral data alone. The argument has been made in a different way in Quine's (1969a) classic essay, "Ontological Relativity," in which he shows that an infinite number of mutually incompatible theories—not translatable one into the other—can be generated to account for the same data. Computer models of cognition will, in other words, most likely be "dissimilar" computer models.

Third, even granting that we could somehow deduce the existence of one and only one program by studying merely the behavior of our machine, the program would tell us nothing about the hardware—what it is made of, how to repair it, how to improve it, whether it uses Jacobson junctions or some other sort of gates; we would still have to start from scratch to learn where and how the program exists in the machine and how the machine works. In other words, Anderson's (1978) argument applies as well to hardware as it does to software. Even if it were possible to discover *the* program in cognition, it would tell us nothing about the brain.

Fourth, wanting to discover the program when you are working with a computer—although perhaps a thankless task—is not an unreasonable means for understanding its behavior, since a program is what you use to control a computer; it makes no sense to ask about its phylogenic or ontogenic histories. But we can control organisms only by manipulating the environment, genes, or the body; as I have indicated above, we will never be able to change line 455 in an instruction set in the mind. In that sense, computer models of mind can provide only the most trivial and ineffectual understanding of behavior, for they yield no means to control it.

Fifth, existing computer models encompass fairly narrow domains of human behavior, and there is little overlap between models. Models of attention, memory, imagery, language, perception, and so on, often have little in common, and Boden (1977, p. 444) has argued that more comprehensive simulations are in principle unattainable. Ironically, in the seventeenth century Descartes proposed a model of human functioning that was far more comprehensive than any existing computer model; he used his famous hydraulic metaphor to try to account for the emotions, thought, perception, sensation, and skeletal movements. His model was entirely hypothetical, of course, which made his task somewhat easier than that faced by today's computer modelers.

Sixth, as I have noted previously, rules may be entirely the wrong approach for representing human functioning. The behavior of a computer is truly rule-governed. Its every action is governed by an instruction (LOAD, JUMP, POP, IF A THEN B), and the instructions are stored in some form in the machine. Human behavior, too, can be governed by instructions: Someone tells us where to turn ("Turn at the next corner"), or we read a recipe from a cookbook ("Add three eggs"), or we recite a rule that we have memorized as an aid to better performance ("Slow and steady wins the race"). But it's easy enough to envision intelligent systems that make no use whatsoever of rules, and no rules whatsoever need be *stored* in us—even the rules we recite aloud—for us to behave as we do.

Must an organism be equipped with a library of words, images, instructions, maps, and so on, to behave effectively in the world? Absolutely not. But clearly an organism is changed by its exposure to such things—changed in such a way that subsequent behavior will be different. An undergraduate exposed to a photograph in an imagery experiment on Monday will behave differently to similar photographs on Tuesday. How might we account for such a change without resorting to the representation and storage metaphors? What is the minimum picture we might paint?

Say that when some neuron (or group of neurons, or synapse, or group of synapses, or circuit, etc.) in a frog's (or undergraduate's) brain is in a certain state—call it the active state—the frog tends to flex its leg when exposed to the flash of a red light. And say further that this cell is normally inactive but that we can make it active simply by pairing the flash of a red light with the application of a shock to the frog's leg. *Voilà*. We can, by this operation, change the frog so that, in the future, when it is exposed to the flash of a red light, it will flex. Note that when the frog is so changed, it contains no rule about the new relationship that has been established between an environmental event and an event in its behavior. True, we could describe the relationship with a rule: "When you see a red flash, flex." But the cell is not such a rule; nor does it contain one. The active cell is in no sense analogous to the computer instruction; at best, it is analogous to a "flag" in a computer memory. But a flag is a far cry from an instruction. And the cell is not the red light, either, nor an encoding of it. It is simply the simplest possible manifestation of *change* in an organism that can effect subsequent behavior in meaningful ways.

As Epstein (1981a) has noted, the stimulus that produces a change in us need not in any fashion produce a change that corresponds to the stimulus, for *to produce a change* is not necessarily *to produce a correspondence*. The change sometimes manifests itself, of course, in behavior that in some sense corresponds to the stimulus, but the nature of the change is simply not yet known.

Information processors. The major problem lies with the assertion—which somehow always remains unanalyzed—that humans are "information processors"; that the human brain (or mind?) is an instruction-driven symbol system; that, in short, we work like computers. An *American Scientist* article is flagged, "*When considered as a physical symbol system*, the human brain can be fruitfully studied by computer simulation of its processes" (italics added). Newell and Simon (1972) assert, "programmed computer and human problem solver are both species belonging to the genus IPS [Information Processing System]" (p. 870). It is true that programs can be written that get computers to behave in some (usually trivial) respects like people do. But one commits an error of logic in asserting from that fact and in the absence of other evidence that computer simulations of "cognitive processes" shed light either on the brain or on human behavior.

The major flaw in modern cognitive science can be reduced to a single syllogism, one that pervades the literature in this field. From premises (i) and (ii) below, the invalid inference (iii) is drawn:

(i) *Premise 1:* All computers are entities that are capable of behaving intelligently.

(ii) *Premise 2:* All computers are information processors.
(iii) *Conclusion:* All entities that are capable of behaving intelligently are information processors.

In other words, all A (computers) are in the set B (entities that are capable of behaving intelligently); all A are in the set C (information processors); therefore, B is contained in C; or:

$$[(A \supset B) \cap (A \supset C)] \supset (B \supset C).$$

Sometimes a more modest assertion, implied by the expression above, is made: Since all D (human beings) are in B, all D must be in C (Figure 12.1); or *Homo sapiens* is a "species belonging to the genus IPS"; or:

$$[(A \supset B) \cap (A \supset C) \cap (D \supset B)] \supset (D \supset C).$$

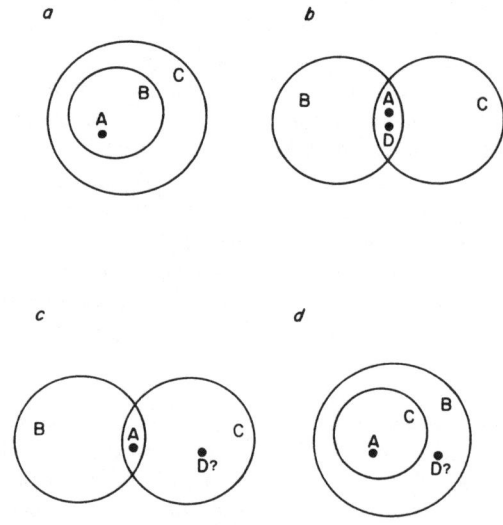

Figure 12.1. A Venn diagram that represents the syllogism described in the text. B is the set of all entities that are capable of behaving intelligently. C is the set of all information processors (for our purposes, the set of all entities whose behavior is governed by an instruction-driven symbol system). And D is the set of all human beings. An assertion that pervades the literature in cognitive science is that B is contained in C (panel a). A more modest assertion, implied by the first, is that D, the set of all people, necessarily lies in the intersection between B and C (panel b). Neither assertion is supported by evidence, however, and there is ample reason to be skeptical of both assertions. Although A is contained in both B and C, and although D is contained in B, the membership of D in C is uncertain (panel c). One could also argue that all Cs are contained in B (that all information processors are capable of behaving intelligently), but D might still lie outside of C (panel d).

Note that although these expressions are false and the conclusions invalid, the conclusions may still be "true." Symbol manipulation may be the basis of all intelligent behavior (B ⊃ C) or at least all human behavior (D ⊃ C). But, as things stand, there is no evidence to support these conclusions; in other words, they are drawn (incorrectly) entirely from the premises. There is ample reason, on the other hand, to be skeptical about a characterization of people in terms of programs and symbols.

As long as the primary assertion of cognitive science remains unsupported by independent evidence, computer models of mind will tell us only the obvious—how we can get information-processing systems to behave like people.

PIGEONS

Why pigeons? As in most laboratory sciences, one starts one's investigations with the materials at hand. Pigeons have been used for many years in behavioral psychology because they are inexpensive, highly resistant to disease, and easy to handle; because they often live 15 or even 20 years in captivity; because their visual sensitivity is similar to that of humans; and because many of the behavioral processes that have been identified in pigeons have been shown to be applicable to humans and other animals. Pigeons, unexpectedly, proved to be good candidates for the Columban simulations precisely because they are so different from people. Since there is little physical resemblance and since the history and current conditions controlling a pigeon's behavior are apparent or at least accessible, one is less tempted to anthropomorphize than one might be with more human-like animals. The tendency to anthropomorphize in work with chimpanzees has been costly. It has, on the one hand, led to many instances of overinterpretation to which ethologists, linguists, and psychologists alike have objected (e.g., Chomsky & Premack, 1979; Epstein, 1982b; Epstein, Lanza, & Skinner, 1980; Sebeok & Umiker-Sebeok, 1980; Terrace, Pettito, Sanders, & Bever, 1979) and, more importantly, has obscured an account of the conditions that actually produce complex behavior in chimpanzees.

A point mentioned briefly above is worth emphasizing. It would be fatuous to assert that human behavior and pigeon behavior necessarily have the same causes. A history of conditioning which leads to the emergence of novel, interesting, human-like behavior in pigeons is not necessarily responsible for comparable human behavior; conditioning may not even be necessary for the human's achievement. The account becomes increasingly plausible, however, as one establishes the generality of behavioral principles, as one demonstrates that humans have indeed had certain experiences, and so on. Although pigeons are a good starting point for the investigation of certain complex human behaviors, one should hardly limit one's investigations to pigeons.[6]

CONCLUSIONS

Frederick II was a competent scientist, although irresponsible by current standards. We who are less bold can still shed light on the emergence of some otherwise mysterious human behaviors. Where a direct attack is impossible, we can construct plausible accounts of the emergence of certain complex human behaviors through careful simulations. Such simulations have so far revealed the possible role that certain complex histories of conditioning play in the emergence of novel behavior and have called attention to several behavioral processes that have received relatively little attention in laboratory praxics.[7]

NOTES

1. I have heard such programs called, respectively, "simulation-mode" and "performance-mode." Weizenbaum's (1966) famous ELIZA program, which simulates a therapist, would be an example of the latter. Although it engages in fairly natural exchanges, no one would claim that it does so because it incorporates "true" models of language or therapy.

2. Normal children and chimpanzees seem to be unique in that mere exposure to the contingencies of reinforcement which govern mirror use is sufficient to establish appropriate behavior (cf. Mans, Cicchetti, & Sroufe, 1978). Why the same does not occur with monkeys is a matter for further research.

3. A related argument is often made, but I think it's incorrect. Occasionally a program is equated with a kind of inner agent. Writes Edelman (1982), "In recent times, the brain has been looked at as a kind of computer. The difficulty with that view has to do not so much with the theory of computation as with the famous ghost that haunts all considerations of the brain, namely, the homunculus. Who, in fact, is telling whom what to do? Who is writing the program?" (p. 22). According to Skinner (1969b), "There is a homunculus in any machine built and instructed by men..." (p. 61). But a program is a far cry from a little man inside the head; it is, as I discuss below, simply part of the structure of the computer which is critical to certain controlling operations—analogous, perhaps, to synaptic states in the brain. Cognitivists are not so naive as to think that there are homunculi in the head; the very attraction of the computer as a model of human "intelligence" is that the computer, once programmed, needs no helping hand to behave intelligently. The fact that the programmer is human is irrelevant to their position. An unprogrammed computer might be limited in its behavior, but so is the feral child; they were each produced and programmed by outside agents—mainly, people. An inner agent is no more necessary to the analysis of one than it is to the analysis of the other. The cognitivist is concerned only with whether or not the program is a good representation of the mental world, not with the origin of the representation.

4. Simon (e.g., 1969) and others would have us believe that cognition stands in relation to the brain as molecular physics does to quantum mechanics—that is, that it is at a "higher level" of analysis. But unlike the "levels" at which we observe physical phenomena in biology, chemistry, physics, and their various subdivisions, cognition is rather difficult to locate. Just where and what is it? The word "level" is hardly a solution to the mind-body problem; nor should it justify scientific inquiry into the metaphysical. As I have noted previously, the prayer of a cognitive scientist as he sits down before his computer terminal must go something like this: "Oh, Mind, if I have one, please reveal to me today the proper set of Rules—if there are any."

5. Where software ends and hardware begins is not always clear. "ROM"s, for example, are storage devices from which one can only read. They are preset with instructions or data during manufacture. Is a ROM hardware or software? Hardware that contains software? More important, the instructions need not be represented in a magnetic array; they could literally be "hard wired": The modern equivalent of wires, relays, resistors, capacitors, and diodes, properly connected, could fulfill the same function that the program fulfills. One can have either a software or hardware "spooler," a hardware or software "latch," a hardware or software "timer," and so on. In general, there is a hardware equivalent for every software function and vice versa.

6. Hake (1982) and others have noted, as I did early in the chapter, that some domains of human behavior seem to be so uniquely human that animal studies can shed little light on them. Where, however, such behavior is derivable from simpler behaviors or general processes, animal studies can still be useful. Studies that employ animals to explore complex, typically-human behavior are growing in both number and scope; animals studies have been proposed to study even subtle verbal processes (consider Catania, 1980). I don't think we yet fully appreciate what animals can tell us about complex behavioral phenomena.

7. This chapter is dedicated to the memory of Don F. Hake, a pioneer in the study of cooperative behavior with human subjects (e.g., Hake, 1982; Hake & Olvera, 1978; Hake & Vukelich, 1972, 1973), who died in 1982.

PART III

RESURGENCE, IMITATION, AND SELF-CONTROL

13

RESURGENCE OF RESPONDING AFTER THE CESSATION OF RESPONSE-INDEPENDENT REINFORCEMENT

Summary. In an autoshaping experiment, food-deprived pigeons pecked rapidly at a moving dot that preceded the delivery of food. When the moving dot and food were no longer correlated, the rate of pecking dropped nearly to zero. When, subsequently, no food was given, pecking reappeared at a high rate (nearly 200 pecks per minute for each subject), the rate dropping again in subsequent sessions. In two other experiments, designed to clarify relevant variables, the effect was replicated. The data suggest that although response-independent reinforcement produces a decrement in responding, it does not reduce a tendency to respond under other conditions.

In an experiment on what has come to be called autoshaping (Brown & Jenkins, 1968), conducted in 1946, a pigeon appeared to drive a spot of light across a wall when the excursion of the spot had frequently preceded the delivery of food (Skinner, 1971b). Recent experiments with rats and pigeons (to be reported elsewhere) only partially replicated the earlier observation and did not confirm that interpretation. The pigeons were probably following the dot rather than driving it. A surprising result in the last experiment in this series in the subject of this paper.

EXPERIMENT I

Method. Two male, adult, Racing Homer pigeons were subjects. Neither had served in laboratory experiments. The chamber was equipped with a feeder and dim houselight. On one wall to one side of, and several inches above the level of, the feeder opening, a 0.9-cm dot of white light was projected from behind the wall on a clear plastic panel 12 cm long and 2 cm high (Figure 13.1). The dot moved either to the right or left at various speeds. After adaptation and hopper training, food was given whenever the spot reached the end of its excursion. A trial consisted of (i) the appearance, excursion, and disappearance of the dot, followed at once by (ii) 4-second access to food, followed by (iii) a blackout averaging about 1 minute 20 seconds. There were about 40 trials each day during 1-hour sessions. Events were controlled by electromechanical equipment and a PDP-8 computer.

Figure 13.1. A pigeon pecks a small (0.9 cm) dot of white light moving away from the feeder recess (lower left) at the rate of 1.7 cm/sec. During the actual experiment, the chamber was almost completely dark.

Results. The subjects began pecking the dot in an unusually short time—subject 1 (272 WP) on the sixth pairing and subject 2 (273 WP) on the twenty-third. Rate of responding stabilized after four sessions. During subsequent pairing conditions the rates were approximately 250 and 450 pecks per minute for each bird, respectively. The speed and direction of the dot were occasionally changed, but the result was irrelevant to the resurgence phenomenon and hence will not be reported here. Dot and food were paired for 52 sessions, during the last 10 of which the dot moved from left to right, away from the food hopper, at a rate of 3 cm/second.

In order to ensure that pairing was responsible for maintaining the pecking, we presented the dot and food independently of each other, at the same average rate as before (about 40 times per session). Extinction was virtually complete after a few sessions, although between 5 and 15 responses per minute still occurred, presumably as the result of occasional adventitious pairings of food and dot.

When, to test this explanation, we presented the dot as usual but gave no food during the session, rapid responding was resumed after about 15 minutes. Figure 13.2 shows cumulative record segments for the two birds from three consecutive daily 1-hour sessions. The segments on the left, for the last extinction session, show little responding. The middle segments are from the first session in which only the dot was presented. Each bird waited about 15 minutes without responding and then began to peck at a rate typical of that under the paired conditions. The segments on the right are from the next session, in which, again, only the dot was presented. Pecking still occurred at a high rate, although extinction had begun.

Averages for the last five sessions under paired conditions are shown at the left in Figure 13.3. Extinction was virtually complete after seven sessions for 272

WP and after two sessions for 273 WP. The birds pecked between 5 and 15 times per minute for the remaining six sessions for the first subject and nine for the second. The resurgence in rate after food presentations were discontinued is shown in the graph on the right in Figure 13.3. The session averages were 158 responses per minute and 188 responses per minute, respectively. Extinction then followed during the dot-only condition. Thus, a high rate of responding was restored by the cessation of free food.

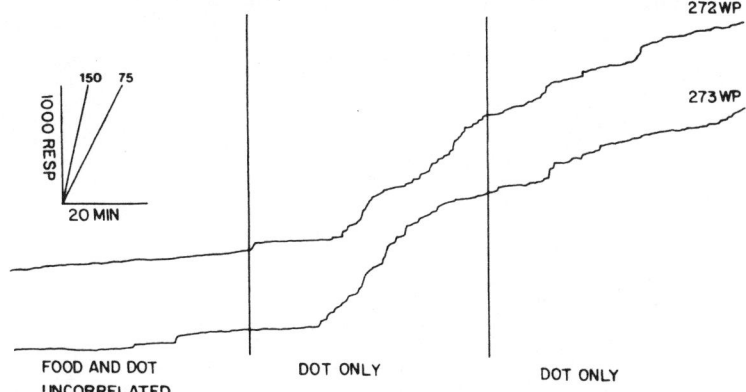

Figure 13.2. Cumulative record segments for the two subjects in Experiment I. The segments in the left panel are from the last 1-hour session in which in which the food and dot presentations were uncorrelated and show virtually no responding. Segments in the center panel are from the next session, in which only dot presentations occurred. The subjects paused for between 10 and 15 minutes and then began to peck at high rates. Segments in the right panel are from the next session, in which a second extinction has begun.

EXPERIMENT II

Given the histories of the birds in Experiment I, the resurgence of pecking could have been due to several possible sequences of conditions: (i) response-independent reinforcement, followed by cessation of response-independent reinforcement and presentation of a salient stimulus, (ii) uncorrelated presentations of the stimulus reinforcer, followed by the cessation of reinforcement and continuing presentations of the stimulus, or (iii) stimulus-reinforcer pairings, followed by uncorrelated presentations of the stimulus and reinforcer, followed by the cessation of reinforcement and continuing presentations of the stimulus (as in the first experiment).

In a further experiment, using three naive Silver King pigeons with no previous history in the chamber, only a dim houselight was illuminated for 17 consecutive daily 1-hour sessions. Then the moving dot was presented for three sessions (moving from left to right at a rate of 1.7 cm/second). The pigeons did not peck the spot.

The birds were then hopper trained, and food was presented in a response-independent manner for 15 sessions (4-second hopper operations about 40 times per hour). Then, once again, the moving dot was presented for three sessions (at the same speed and direction as above) with no presentation of food. If the resurgence effect were a "frustration" phenomenon (Amsel, 1958) or a species-specific reinforcer-withdrawal effect such as polydipsia (Falk, 1971), we should expect pecking at this point. None occurred.

In a third condition the dot and food were presented independently for 15 sessions, followed, once again, by three sessions in which only the dot presentations occurred. No pecking occurred during this test.

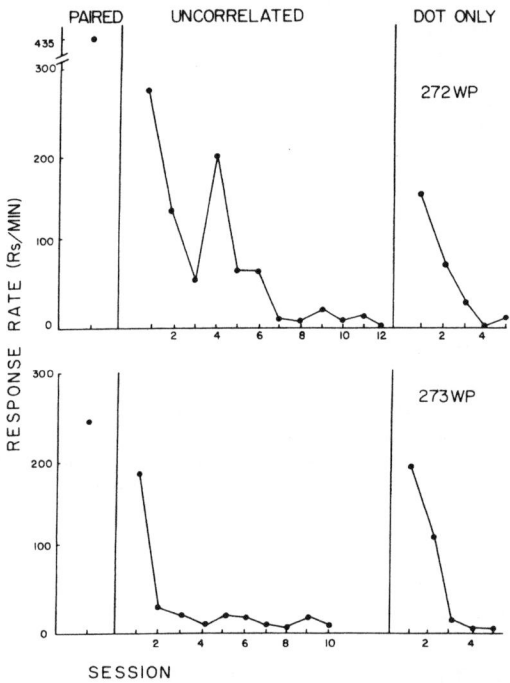

Figure 13.3. Average rates of responding for the three conditions of Experiment I. The average rate of responding over the least five sessions in which the dot and food were paired is shown in the left-most portion of each graph. There was a decrement in responding when the dot and food were presented independently. The right portions of the graphs show a subsequent resurgence in responding when response-independent food was discontinued, followed by a second extinction.

Finally, all three of the elements in Experiment I were restored. The moving dot was paired with food (the dot moved from left to right, away from the food hopper at a rate of 1.7 cm/second) until each subject had spent from 20 to 25 sessions pecking the dot (half the number of sessions of Experiment I). Then we extinguished pecking by presenting the food and dot independently of each other, and, after pecking was extinguished, we discontinued presentations of free food.

The results are shown in Figure 13.4. Resurgence is indicated for subject 1 (278 WP) and possibly for subject 2 (279 WP) but not for subject 3 (280 WP). Either the large effect we observed in Experiment I was anomalous, perhaps

Resurgence of Responding

restricted to the breed we had used (Racing Homer), or, and this seems more likely, prior exposure to the dot alone minimized the effect in Experiment II. This may explain why no pecking occurred during the second and third conditions of the experiment. In other words, we have not eliminated the possibility that resurgence is a frustration or adjunctive phenomenon.

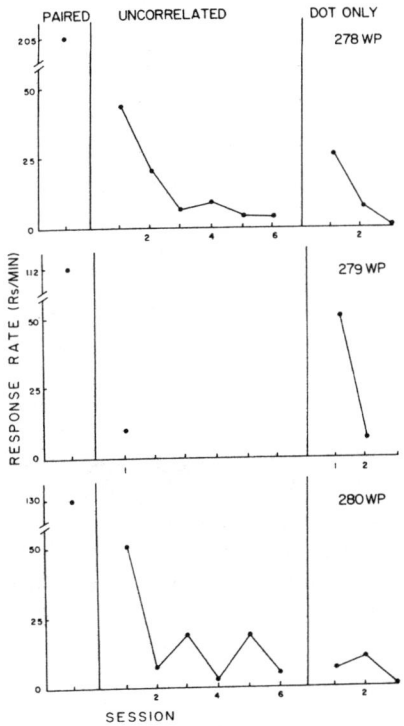

Figure 13.4. Average rates of responding for the three subjects in the fourth condition of Experiment II. Resurgence is indicated for the first and possibly the second subjects.

EXPERIMENT III

To check the possibility that the large effect in Experiment I was not replicable with pigeons other than Racing Homers, we repeated the experiment with three naive White Carneaux pigeons (292 WP, 293 WP, and 294 WP). We used the fewest conditions that seemed necessary to produce the effect, namely: (i) pairing, followed by (ii) uncorrelated presentations, followed by (iii) presentations of the dot alone. The dot moved from left to right at a rate of 1.7 cm/second in all conditions. Two of the three subjects showed the same effect as in Experiment I. Some resurgence was evident in the third subject. During pairing, the average rate of responding was between 200 and 275 per minute for all subjects. Between four and nine sessions of uncorrelated presentations were then conducted, which reduced the rate of responding to between 5 and 15 responses per minute. Given the dot alone, subjects 292 WP and 293 WP did not peck for between 8 and 20 minutes and then began pecking at high rates throughout the remainder of the session. The average session rates for these subjects were 98.3 and 85.5 per minute, respectively. A second extinction was complete within four sessions.

DISCUSSION

We conclude that:

(i) The resurgence effect is replicable.

(ii) It is not easily accounted for by current knowledge about either operant or respondent behavior. Current formal theories of response strength would not predict resurgence (Mackintosh, 1975; Rescorla & Wagner, 1972).

(iii) It does not necessarily originate through Pavlovian contingencies. It may follow a history of response-dependent reinforcement.

(iv) It may be related to a history of adventitious reinforcement, which necessarily occurs in automaintenance.

(v) It may be a frustration or adjunctive phenomenon, but if so, it requires a history of pecking the conditioned stimulus.

(vi) It may be due to a restoration of conditions present during conditioning, as in spontaneous recovery (Skinner, 1950), although it is difficult to specify the details or to suggest relevant tests at this point.

(vii) The data suggest that response-independent reinforcement does not "extinguish" responding in the usual sense, although it produces a substantial decrement. Apparently the tendency to respond under other conditions remains.

14

RESURGENCE OF PREVIOUSLY REINFORCED BEHAVIOR DURING EXTINCTION

Summary. Pigeons' pecks on one of two keys were reinforced with food and then extinguished over one or more sessions. In a test session, an alternative response was reinforced 20 times and then all reinforcement was withheld. After delays ranging from 21 to 195 seconds, during which the frequency of the alternative response could be observed to decrease, pecking reappeared at relatively high rates on the key correlated with a history of reinforcement. The data provide support for a widely applicable principle: When recently reinforced behavior is no longer effective, previously reinforced behavior recurs.

A simple principle of potentially wide application may be stated as follows: When, in a given situation, recently reinforced behavior is no longer reinforced, behaviors that were previously reinforced under similar circumstances tend to recur. The principle has been stated in various ways for more than fifty years (Barker, Dembo, & Lewin, 1941; Estes, 1955; Freud, 1920; Hull, 1952; Maltzman, 1955; Masserman, 1943; Mowrer, 1940; Notterman, 1970; Sears, 1943; Yates, 1970), although no systematic investigations have been made. Recent statements of the principle often cite no references (e.g., Notterman, 1970; Yates, 1970; cf. Staddon & Simmelhag, 1971).

Previous studies, inspired by Freudian theory, typically used punishment rather than extinction to induce earlier forms (Everall, 1935; Hamilton & Krechevsky, 1933; O'Kelley, 1940a, 1940b; Martin, 1940; Mowrer, 1940; Sanders, 1937). Reports of extinction-induced resurgence have been incidental to other observations and concerns (consider Barker et al., 1941; Leitenberg, Rawson, & Bath, 1970; Miller & Miles, 1936; Pryor, Haag, & O'Reilly, 1969); consequently, critical controls have not been conducted. Previous observations (e.g., Barker et al., 1941; Leitenberg et al., 1970) have not distinguished the resurgence effect from frustration effects (Amsel, 1958) or the variability in behavior which is typically induced in extinction (Antonitis, 1951). Previously reinforced behavior may have recurred in some studies because reinforcement of an alternative behavior had prevented the extinction of the previously reinforced behavior (Leitenberg et al., 1970; Rawson, Leitenberg, Mulick, & Lefebvre, 1977). Resurgence has not been demonstrated when the previously reinforced response has itself been extinguished. In spite of occasional restatements in the modern psychological literature, the principle is not generally invoked, even when it would be useful in interpreting effects that otherwise appear anomalous (e.g., Enkema, Slavin, Spaeth, & Neuringer, 1972; Epstein & Skinner, 1980; Lindblom & Jenkins, 1981).

The following experiment provides support for a general principle of resurgence as stated above.

METHOD

Six male, adult Racing Homer pigeons served as subjects. None had served in laboratory experiments prior to this one. Each was maintained at approximately 80 percent of its free-feeding weight. A standard Skinner box was employed, on one wall of which were two standard keys, 12 cm apart, and a feeder recess where grain could be presented. Three-second presentations of food served as reinforcers. A peck on either key produced a brief high-pitched tone as feedback. The chamber was illuminated by an overhead white light. Extraneous sounds were masked by a ventilation fan and white noise. A video camera with a wide-angle lens was mounted to a side wall of the chamber and afforded a clear view of the bird and front panel. A TRS-80 microcomputer scheduled reinforcers during the first phase of the experiment and recorded the number of pecks during all phases. Pecking was also recorded continuously on two cumulative recorders during all phases. One-hour sessions were conducted daily. All test sessions were videotaped.

The experiment had three phases. In the first, pecking either the left key (subjects 26Y, 28Y, and 38Y) or the right key (subjects 17Y, 21Y, and 39Y) was reinforced intermittently with food. Pecking was reinforced on a variable-interval 1-minute schedule until a moderate, steady rate of responding was established. Then reinforcement was withheld for one or more sessions (Table 14.1); the number of sessions was determined by random number (the upper limit was set at 15). All sessions were 1 hour in length. Finally, a test session was conducted as follows: Reinforcement was withheld for at least 30 minutes and until no peck had occurred for at least 10 minutes (in most cases, more than 20 minutes). Then some alternative response, incompatible with key pecking, was reinforced 20 times (Table 14.1). The bird was observed on a video monitor and the feeder was operated with a hand switch. After 20 reinforcements of the alternative response, all reinforcement was subsequently withheld.

RESULTS AND DISCUSSION

Results from the test sessions are shown in Figure 14.1. Relatively few key pecks occurred before reinforcement. The responses of subjects 17Y, 26Y, and 28Y were concentrated in the first few minutes of the session, a phenonemon called "spontaneous recovery" (subject 17Y pecked only once). After reinforcement of the alternative behavior ceased, pecking resumed on the key correlated with a history of reinforcement. Few pecks occurred on the control key either before or after the alternative behavior was reinforced (Table 14.1), which indicates that the resumption of pecking on the other key was not simply a frustration effect (Amsel, 1958) or a result of the increase in variability in behavior which is often observed during extinction (Antonitis, 1951).

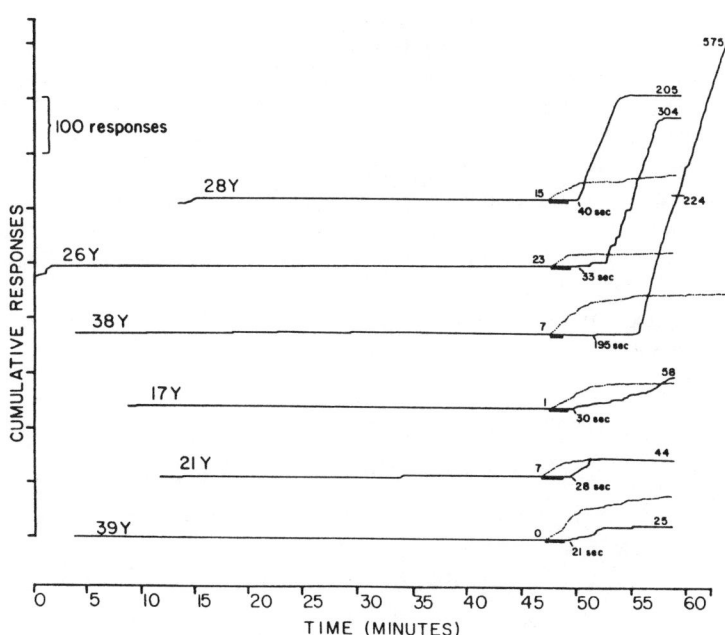

Figure 14.1. Cumulative records of responding on the key correlated with a history of reinforcement, shown for the entire test session of each of the six subjects. The left-hand portions of each curve show few or no responses. The dark areas below the curves at right mark the period during which some alternative response (Table 14.1) was reinforced 20 times. Following the termination of the last reinforcer, pecking resumed after a delay, the duration of which is marked below each record. Sessions were terminated 10 minutes after the termination of the last reinforcer, except for bird 38Y. The small numbers above each curve indicate the total number of responses at that point in the session; thus, bird 28Y pecked 15 times during the first few minutes of the session and an additional 190 times during the 10 minutes following the last reinforcer. The dotted lines show occurrences of the alternative response (Footnote 1).

A consistent feature of all of the cumulative records is the interval of time which occurs between the last reinforcer and the first key peck. The dotted traces show clearly that the interval was produced by repeated occurrences of the alternative response.[1] In general, the higher the rate of the alternative response, the longer the interval (compare, for example, the records for birds 38Y and 17Y). Moreover, the resumption of key pecking was generally correlated with a decrement in the rate of the alternative response.

The current study includes three features which were lacking in previous work: First, a second key was included so that the resurgence effect could be distinguished from other extinction effects. Second, key pecking was extinguished for between 1 and 12 sessions before an alternative response was reinforced (Table 14.1); thus, the possibility was minimized that the previously reinforced behavior recurred simply because reinforcement of an alternative behavior had prevented its extinction. Third, large effects were shown for individual organisms in a single session (cf. Hull, 1934).

Free reinforcers during extinction are known to have discriminative properties and may reinstate responding (Hollis, 1968; Reid, 1958; Spradlin, Girardeau, & Hom, 1966).[2] Reinforcement of the alternative response in the present experiment may have reinstated key pecking because, in the past, the operation of the feeder was the occasion upon which subsequent key pecks had been reinforced. Thus the reinforcers may have had two opposing effects. First, as discriminative stimuli, they may have reinstated a tendency to peck the key, and second, as reinforcers, they may have strengthened incompatible behavior that prevented key pecking. When reinforcement ceased, the onset of key pecking may have been prevented until the incompatible behavior was sufficiently weak (cf. Staddon, 1977).

Table 14.1. Training histories for each of the subjects.

Bird	Number of Sessions, VI Reinforcement	Number of Extinction Sessions	Control Key Alternative Response	Pecks Before Reinft	Pecks After Reinft
17Y	31	11	head back	0	0
21Y	36	5	quarter turn right	0	0
26Y	49	2	wing raise	1	0
28Y	42	1	head down	0	0
38Y	11	6	head down	0	1
39Y	15	12	head turn right	0	0

Although this explanation cannot be ruled out in the present instance, resurgence has appeared in procedures that do seem to rule out the discriminative role of the reinforcer. When the alternative response is reinforced intermittently and for a long period of time, thousands of responses may appear before the rate declines in extinction, and it may be hours before previously reinforced behavior appears (Epstein, 1983b; cf. Leitenberg et al., 1970). It is also possible that the reinstatement of responding which is produced by a free reinforcer may in part be extinction-induced: The reinforcer may strengthen an alternative response, which is then quickly extinguished (cf. Henton & Iversen, 1978; Skinner, 1938).

Resurgence is undoubtedly affected by many variables—the schedules according to which both the old and new behaviors are reinforced, the type and magnitude of the reinforcers (will the old response resurge if the old and new responses are established with different reinforcers?), the period of time over which the responses are reinforced, the time that elapses after the old response is last reinforced, the overlap in the stimulus conditions under which the responses are reinforced, and so on. Matters are complicated when many responses are available to resurge, as is probably the rule in the natural environment: What variables determine the order of resurgence and the distribution of responses? The degree of extinction of the previously reinforced response is undoubtedly an important factor. It is likely that the more complete the extinction, the less the resurgence (Rawson et al., 1977). The data for birds 17Y and 39Y show, however, that resurgence can occur even when extinction has been extensive and is virtually complete.

When primitive behaviors resurge, some speak of "regression." Resurging behaviors need not be primitive, however (Masserman, 1943). The principle of resurgence seems useful in interpreting moment-to-moment changes in behavior in any domain in which behavior is sometimes ineffective, such as problem solving (Epstein & Medalie, 1983; Epstein, 1986b; Hull, 1952; Maltzman, 1955), foraging, or responding on intermittent and concurrent schedules of reinforcement. The principle implies that behavior that has been extinguished is not necessarily "forgotten," which is to say that it can recur under appropriate circumstances (cf. Epstein & Skinner, 1980). Moreover, resurgence is one of several phenomena that make multiple repertoires available, and hence it may lead to the spontaneous interconnection of repertoires, an important source of novel behavior (Chance, 1960; Epstein, 1986a; Epstein & Skinner, 1981; Maltzman, 1955).

NOTES

1. The dotted traces in Figure 14.1 were produced by an independent observer who viewed a videotape of each test session from the point at which reinforcement began and tapped a key when she saw what was, in her judgment, the response that was reinforced. The key taps generated a cumulative record of the alternative responses.

The cumulative record for bird 26Y would appear to indicate a sudden cessation of the alternative response (wing raising) immediately after the last reinforcer. The tape shows, however, that the bird's wings were raised high for 37 seconds following the reinforcer. The wings fluttered slightly and the bird circled the chamber during most of this period. The observer scored this episode as a single response.

2. Novel stimuli can also reinstate responding under certain conditions, but negative results seem to be the rule in operant conditioning procedures. Consider Boakes (1973), Boakes and Halliday (1975), Skinner (1936).

15

EXTINCTION-INDUCED RESURGENCE: PRELIMINARY INVESTIGATIONS AND POSSIBLE APPLICATIONS

Summary. When recently reinforced behavior is no longer effective, previously reinforced behavior often recurs. Although the phenomenon has been described from time to time in both the experimental and clinical literatures, it has never been stringently investigated. Its robustness is suggested, however, by both formal and informal observations of humans and other animals. Applications in both theoretical and practical domains are suggested, among them problem solving, schedules of reinforcement, foraging theory, and psychotherapy.

In a passage on extinction in an influential paper on superstition, Staddon and Simmelhag (1971) write:

one effect of a relaxation of [reinforcement] is a more or less transient increase in the relative influence of the distant past at the expense of the immediate past. In behavioral extinction, this should involve the reappearance of old (in the sense of previously extinguished) behavior patterns.... (p. 25)

They cite no references in the text but add a footnote:

Other than clinical accounts of regression, we have been able to find only one published report of this effect—in an account describing shaping porpoises to show novel behaviors (Pryor, Haag, & O'Reilly, 1969). However, we have frequently observed it while shaping pigeons.... [The] increase in variability during extinction of the most recently reinforced response generally includes the reappearance of earlier responses. (p. 25)

Notterman (1970, p. 93) describes a similar phenomenon as one of four major extinction effects; no supporting data are cited. Yates (1970, p. 28) emphasizes the importance of such a process in therapy; again, no references. Recent statements of such a principle seem to be the exception; many current texts that discuss extinction phenomena at length mention no such principle at all (e.g., Bower & Hilgard, 1981; Catania, 1979; Donahoe & Wessells, 1980; Fantino & Logan, 1979; Ferster, Culbertson, & Boren, 1975; Hintzman, 1978; Karen, 1974; O'Leary & Wilson, 1975; Rachlin, 1976; Reynolds, 1975).

A defensible—although, at this point, somewhat imprecise—principle of extinction-induced resurgence may be stated as follows: *When, in a given situation, recently reinforced behavior is no longer reinforced, behaviors that were previously reinforced under similar circumstances tend to recur.* In spite of a recent lack of interest, variations on this principle have had a long and distinguished history in psychology.[1] Furthermore, data are available which support it, and, just as significantly, there appear to be no disconfirming data.

BRIEF HISTORY

A special case of resurgence would seem to be Freud's (1920) concept of regression, although the concepts differ in several respects. Regression refers to a psychodynamic mechanism that is supposed to underlie changes in behavior. The principle of resurgence, on the other hand, is purely descriptive; no mechanism is implied. Regression is said to proceed to points of fixation which are established during childhood; hence, emerging behaviors are said to be infantile and primitive. The principle of resurgence makes no such restriction. Finally, regression is usually understood to be a response to punishment—to "powerful external obstacles"—rather than simply to nonreinforcement (though Freud himself seems not to have made the distinction). Consequently, most laboratory studies of regression used punishment rather than extinction to induce earlier forms (Everall, 1935; Hamilton & Krechevsky, 1933; O'Kelley, 1940a, 1940b; Martin, 1940; Mowrer, 1940; Sanders, 1937).

Freud's psychodynamic principle gave way to a more descriptive one by the 1940s: Masserman (1943) distinguished regression from "retrogression of adaptation," a return to previously successful behaviors as a response to "conflicting or extremely frustraneous [sic]" conditions. The terms "retrogression" (Barker, Dembo, & Lewin, 1941), "instrumental act regression" (Sears, 1941, 1943), and "habit regression" (Mowrer, 1940) referred to the same phenomenon. The operations said to produce the recurrence of earlier behaviors included punishment, extinction, and even satiation (Sears, 1943), although there were virtually no investigations of the latter two cases.

By far the clearest cases of extinction-induced resurgence were reported by Hull (1934). In one experiment he trained rats to run down a straight 40-foot alley for food. In early sessions, he observed a "speed gradient": the rats ran more and more rapidly as they approached the food. The gradient disappeared after a few days but reappeared when food was withheld. In a second experiment, rats were first trained to run down a 20-foot alley and then down a 40-foot alley. When food was withheld on the longer alley, the rats tended to stop at the 20-foot mark.[2]

RECENT WORK

In all of the studies mentioned, observations of resurgence were incidental to other observations and concerns (also consider Barker et al., 1941; Leitenberg,

Rawson, & Bath, 1970; Miller & Miles, 1936; Pryor et al., 1969). Epstein (1983a) reported a more direct test. Each of six pigeons was placed in a standard experimental chamber equipped with two keys. Pecks on one or the other of the keys were reinforced with food for 11 or more sessions on a variable-interval (VI) schedule and subsequently extinguished for between 1 and 12 1-hour sessions. In a test session, some alternative response, such as wing-raising or turning, was reinforced 20 times. When all reinforcement was subsequently withheld, the frequency of the alternative response decreased over intervals ranging from 21 to 195 seconds, and then each of the birds began to peck again at a relatively high rate on the key upon which pecks had been previously reinforced.

Since there was virtually no pecking on the other key (one peck by one bird during the 10-minute observation period), the recurrence of pecking cannot be attributed merely to "frustration" (cf. Amsel, 1958) nor to the variability in behavior which is typically induced in extinction (Antonitis, 1951). More important, the behavior that recurred had been extinguished, and hence the result supports the strong prediction made by Staddon and Simmelhag (1971), noted above: *Even behavior that has been previously extinguished may resurge.*

Another experiment illustrates the dynamics of the process. In the first of three conditions (Figure 15.1), a pigeon's pecks on the right key of a standard 3-key chamber were reinforced with food according to a VI 1-minute schedule (pecks produced food once each minute, on the average). All three of the keys were always transilluminated with white light. In the second condition the schedule of reinforcement was shifted to the center key. Responding eventually shifted to this key. The rate of responding on the right key decreased steadily over a number of sessions as responding on the center key became more stable. By the tenth 1-hour session of this condition, there were no pecks on the right key.

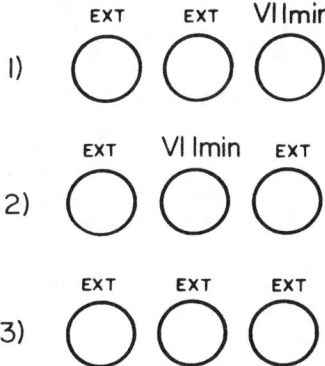

Figure 15.1. Procedure for a resurgence experiment. In a 3-key pigeon chamber, pecks are first reinforced on the right key according to a VI schedule (1). In the second condition of the experiment, pecks on the middle key are reinforced (2). Reinforcement is withheld in the third condition (3).

Finally, in the third condition, all reinforcement was withheld. There was little responding on the left key, upon which pecks had never been reinforced. The rate of responding on the center key was high for the first 40 minutes of the first test session and decreased thereafter. There were *no* pecks on the right key during the first 40 minutes of the session, and then, just as the rate of responding on the center key began to fall, pecking appeared at a high rate on the right key (Figure 15.2), the key correlated with a history of reinforcement. The effect was also obtained with three other birds (Epstein, 1983c; cf. Leitenberg et al., 1970).

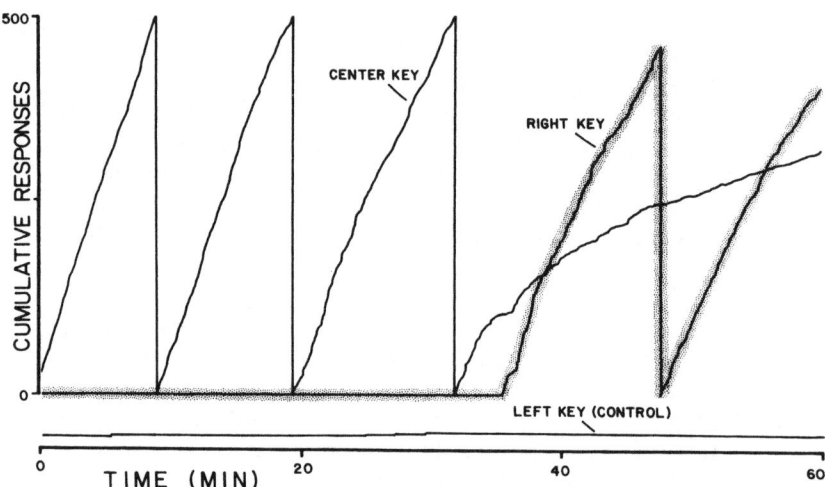

Figure 15.2. Cumulative record segments from the first session in which reinforcement was withheld on all keys for bird 13YP. Each of the three segments shows responding on one key. Responding on the center key had been recently reinforced according to a variable-interval 1-minute schedule. During the first half of the session, a high steady rate of responding was maintained on this key. It became less stable after the first 1,000 responses. A smooth deceleration is apparent during the last 20 minutes. (Note that the pen resets downward after 500 responses.) The lower line corresponds to the left key, upon which pecking had never been reinforced. The pigeon pecked this key only 7 times during the hour. The shaded line corresponds to the right key where there was a history of VI 1-minute reinforcement. No responses occurred on this key while responding on the center key was strong, but the pigeon began pecking it at a high rate at about 40 minutes into the session. It pecked the key nearly 900 times during the last 20 minutes.

APPLICATIONS

Epstein and Medalie (1983) described an instance of what might reasonably be called the spontaneous use of a tool by a pigeon.[3] A pigeon was trained to push a small flat box toward a green target placed at random positions around the base of a large cylindrical chamber. It was then confronted with what might be called "the marble under the couch" problem: Pecking a small metal plate positioned at the base of a clear Plexiglas wall was reinforced with food. Then the plate was moved several inches behind the wall so that the pigeon had to stretch its head beneath the wall to reach the plate. The box was placed on the pigeon's side of the wall and behavior with respect to it was extinguished, while pecks to the plate were reinforced. Finally, the plate was moved just out of the pigeon's reach behind the wall.

The pigeon's performance at this point was remarkably human-like. It stretched repeatedly toward the plate. It behaved emotionally—it scraped its feet on the floor, pressed against the wall, and so on. At about 30 seconds into the session, it pecked weakly at the box, then stretched again under the wall. Finally, at 90 seconds into the session, in one continuous sequence of movements, it pushed the box directly toward the wall, pushed it somewhat awkwardly underneath, and, after some adjustments, thrust it firmly against the metal plate. It then pecked repeatedly at the *box*, which was now in contact with the plate. It would seem that the bird had spontaneously used the box as an extension of its own beak.

Note that the bird had never been trained to push the box toward the plate or under a wall and, more important, that the bird had not pecked the box under these conditions for at least five consecutive daily sessions. Why did the bird start to push when the plate was out of reach? In casual discourse we might appeal to a concept such as "need," but extinction-induced resurgence would seem to be a more useful explanation. With the plate out of reach, behavior with respect to it was extinguished; pushing the box, a previously reinforced behavior, recurred.

Other problem-solving performances also seem amenable to such an analysis. Pigeons with appropriate experiences will solve one of Köhler's (1925) classic box-and-banana problems (Epstein, 1981a; Epstein, Kirshnit, Lanza, & Rubin, 1984). In one variation of this problem, Au and Epstein (1982) trained a bird to climb onto a box and peck a small facsimile of a banana, as well as to push a box toward a green target placed at random positions around the base of a large cylindrical chamber. Flying toward the banana was extinguished. Then the banana was placed within the bird's reach and pecking it was reinforced. The box was available in the chamber, but pecking it was extinguished. When there had been no pecks to the box under these conditions for five consecutive days, the banana was raised out of the bird's reach. It showed signs of "confusion": it stretched repeatedly toward the banana, turned in circles beneath it, and so on. It glanced more and more frequently toward the box, and then, finally, began to push the box toward the banana. It stopped pushing when the box was beneath the banana, climbed, and pecked. The entire performance took under 4 minutes. A complete analysis of this performance is beyond the scope of this paper, but the first part of it at least—the initial pushes—would seem to be extinction-induced.

ANOMALIES

The resurgence principle is generally not invoked in the experimental animal literature, even when it would be useful in interpreting results that otherwise appear anomalous. For example, key pecking that has been established through autoshaping and then eliminated when the food and key light are presented independently of each other reappears at a high rate when food presentations are terminated (Epstein & Skinner, 1980; Lindblom & Jenkins, 1981). The effect has proved difficult to explain. The resurgence principle provides a simple account: When a high rate of pecking is established during the autoshaping procedure, pecks are adventitiously reinforced. When key-light presentations are no longer paired with food presentations, other behaviors are adventitiously reinforced and key pecks are extinguished. Finally, when food presentations are terminated, the recently reinforced behaviors undergo extinction, which takes some time; when they are sufficiently weak, pecking the illuminated key—a previously reinforced behavior—resurges. A pause of several minutes reliably precedes the recurrence of responding which occurs in the autoshaping procedure (Epstein & Skinner, 1980). This account could be tested either by analyzing videotapes of such performances or by establishing a known response during the second phase of the experiment.

Enkema, Slavin, Spaeth, and Neuringer (1972) reported another case of recovery which lends itself to a similar account. They reinforced pigeons' key pecks with food and then eliminated key pecking by no longer reinforcing it and by making a container of free food available in the rear of the experimental chamber. When the free food was removed from the cup, key pecking returned at a high rate. Presumably the free food quickly established approach and feeding behaviors toward the cup. When the food was removed, these behaviors were presumably extinguished over some period of time, and a previously successful response, key pecking, reappeared. Again, a pause, perhaps on the order of several minutes long, should have occurred before the resumption of key pecking.

I. Iversen (personal communication) has suggested a more subtle case. Catania and Keller (1981) brought pigeons' pecks under the control of a VI schedule of reinforcement and then presented the reinforcers independent of behavior (a variable-time or VT schedule). Under the VT schedule, the rate of pecking decreased dramatically. Upon reexposure to the VI schedule a high rate of pecking was restored, and the rate decreased dramatically again upon a second exposure to the VT. With each successive exposure to the VT schedule, the rate of pecking decreased more rapidly.

A simple account may be given in terms of resurgence: As in the studies described above, free food during the first VT probably strengthened some behaviors other than key-pecking (cf. Henton & Iversen, 1978). During the subsequent VI, there should have been a pause—during which the frequency of the new behaviors decreased—before key pecking reappeared. Upon reexposure to the VT, the alternative behaviors (strengthened during the previous VT) were presumably available to resurge and hence were established more rapidly than they had been during the previous VT. Hence the rate of key pecking declined more rapidly than it did during the previous VT, and subsequent exposures to the VT produced even more rapid decrements.

FURTHER IMPLICATIONS

Resurgence probably occurs in any domain in which behavior is sometimes ineffective (along with other extinction effects). Both single and concurrent schedules of intermittent reinforcement should produce extinction effects, since many or most of the responses that occur are not successful. Animals that are earning food by pressing levers or pecking keys do far more than press or peck. One observes partial responses ("air pecks," "rim pecks," weak presses, and so on), partial turns, full turns, tilts of the head, grooming, preening, and many other behaviors besides the one the equipment is recording. Sequences such as turn-and-peck are often established adventitiously, subsequently extinguished, later reestablished, and so on. The characteristic rates and patterns of responding which are produced by particular schedules may be generated in part by the continual resurgence of previously reinforced sequences when responses are not reinforced (cf. Henton & Iversen, 1978). Changeovers on concurrent schedules may occur in part as the result of extinction of responding at one location.[4]

There are undoubtedly other clinical applications, but one topic that certainly bears some mention is symptom substitution. Psychodynamic psychologists and psychiatrists, beginning with Freud himself, have, with few exceptions, maintained that abnormal behavior is symptomatic of underlying conflict. Treating the behavior alone, therefore, should not be effective; the underlying conflict should produce other behavioral manifestations—either "symptom substitution" or a recurrence of the original behavior. Freud rejected hypnosis on these grounds: It "forbid[s] the symptoms ... but leaves all the processes that have led to the formation of symptoms unaltered" (Freud, 1966, pp. 450-451). Behavior therapists rejected the Freudian view and asserted that the focus of therapy should be the behavior itself (e.g., Yates, 1958). One extreme statement of this position is captured in Eysenck's dictum: Get rid of the symptoms and you have eliminated the neurosis.

The resurgence principle suggests at least one situation in which a substitution of sorts should occur: Removal of a behavior through nonreinforcement should lead to the emergence of other behaviors which have previously been effective under similar circumstances (cf. Yates, 1970, pp. 399-400), and clinical studies suggest that this occurs (e.g., Herbert, Pinkston, Hayden, Sajwaj, Pinkston, Cordua, & Jackson, 1973; Sajwaj, Twardosz, & Burke, 1972). There is a practical corollary: A therapist might deliberately induce previously established behaviors by establishing and then extinguishing new behaviors.

Behaviors interact, and research with animals suggests that the interactions are orderly (e.g., Dunham & Grantmyre, 1982). It is not entirely unreasonable to assert that one cannot alter one behavior without affecting others. If so, a fuller understanding of such interactions should greatly enhance the effectiveness of existing therapies (Kazdin, 1982; cf. McDowell, 1982). The process of resurgence is one of many possible interactions.

Biologists have for some time been interested in the manner in which animals forage for food in the wild, and a number of formal models of such behavior have been proposed (e.g., Krebs, 1978; Lea, 1979). Such models predict, among other things, the average time an animal will spend in some relatively isolated patch of food as a function of prey type and density, "handling time," travel time between patches, and so on. Resurgence suggests a simple mechanism that should produce switching from one patch to another: Foraging behavior is extinguished when prey are unavailable, and previously effective behaviors—for example, traveling to other patches—should result. Prevailing theory suggests that after an animal leaves a patch it will sample new ones. The resurgence principle predicts, however, that if an animal is fed at patch A and then food is withdrawn and that if it is then fed at patch B and food is again withdrawn, it will return to patch A before moving to another available patch. Indeed, other things being equal, the animal should switch back and forth repeatedly between A and B before moving on.

When, in the natural environment, some behavior is ineffective, more than one behavior is probably available to resurge. One's genetic and environmental histories may have established dozens of behaviors relevant to a given situation. Thus, when one is unable to turn a knob that has always opened easily, a variety of behaviors appear in rapid succession: One may turn harder, lift, push down, pound on the door, kick, shout for help, and so on—presumably the more behaviors that have been established, the more that will recur. This process is undoubtedly invaluable in problem solving. Artificial intelligence programs may fail as models of human intelligence (Minsky, 1975) because they neglect this aspect of the behavior of organisms.

The principle I have described in no sense explains *why* previously reinforced behavior recurs during extinction. But in identifying what appears to be a reliable set of relationships between certain events in behavior and the environment, it provides at the level of the events observed an explanation for higher-order phenomena which entail these relationships. For example, the first pushes by the "tool-using" bird seem mysterious until one notes that the procedure *entails* extinction and that one common effect of extinction is the recurrence of previously reinforced behavior. When we have determined the many parameters and variables that determine when and whether a response will resurge and the order in which multiple behaviors will recur (cf. Epstein, 1983a), we should not only be able to provide plausible explanations for a variety of behavioral phenomena but also to predict recurrences in new situations.

I have pointed to many possible applications of the resurgence principle in both experimental analysis and clinical interpretation, but its most profitable application may prove to be in our understanding of the emergence of novel behavior. An important source of novelty in the behavior of organisms appears to be the interconnection of repertoires (Chance, 1960; Epstein, 1981a, 1986a; Epstein & Skinner, 1981; Epstein et al., 1984; Hull, 1935; Maltzman, 1955); behaviors that have been established separately by any means, can, in new situations, come together to produce new sequences of behaviors, behaviors that have new functions, or behaviors that have new topographies. Resurgence may be one of only a small number of phenomena that can make multiple behaviors available (cf. Epstein, 1986b).

The extinction-induced resurgence of previously established behaviors appears to be an orderly process by which the history of an organism manifests itself in new situations, a phenomenon that has been underemphasized in many investigations of learning. It suggests that, just as the genome brings to an organism the history of a species, the organism as a whole brings to new environments its ontogenic history and is hence capable of complex adaptations that reflect this history.[5]

NOTES

1. J. Cautela (personal communication) points out that the first of Jost's (1897) laws may also be relevant. The law states that the older of two associations of equal strength loses strength less rapidly than the newer. Although functionally similar to resurgence, this law applies to forgetting (the decrement in responding which occurs as a function of the passage of time), not extinction (the decrement in responding which occurs as a function of nonreinforced responding). The distinction seems worthwhile, in part because it seems that behavior that has been eliminated by nonreinforcement is not "forgotten," which is to say that it will recur under appropriate conditions (cf. Epstein & Skinner, 1980).

2. There are by current standards a number of deficiencies in the Hull (1934) report: His conclusions are based on averages of hundreds of observations, yet no variability is reported and no statistics are given. He notes that, soon after food was withdrawn, many animals would not run and that a number of animals naturally tended to stop at the half-way point in the alley even before food was withdrawn.

3. The report describes the performance of only one bird. Similar performances have since been achieved with two others.

4. Heyman (1979) reported that changeover probabilities in concurrent VI schedules do not change as a function of previous responding, or, more specifically, that pigeons are not more likely to switch from one key to another after a run of many nonreinforced pecks. The observation is based, however, on "steady state" responding, achieved after 20 and, in some cases, 30 or more sessions of exposure to a given schedule. Heyman's report (e.g., p. 43) suggests that the observation does not apply to sessions before the steady state is achieved.

5. A personal note: The manner in which I stumbled upon the resurgence principle would seem in part to exemplify the principle. I was watching a student train a bird for the "tool use" experiment (Epstein & Medalie, 1983). To my knowledge at that time, I had never heard or read of a principle such as resurgence (several months passed before someone pointed out the connection to regression), and I was perplexed by the reappearance of box pushing that had occurred in a previous test. My account was inadequate, or, in other words, I was behaving ineffectively with respect to what I was observing. I repeated the word "reappearance" more than once, and then less common synonyms occurred to me in quick succession: "reoccurrence," "recurrence," "*resurgence*." Skinner and I had used the latter term to describe the autoshaping phenomenon described in the text above (Epstein & Skinner, 1980). Although a year had passed since the autoshaping paper had been published, I was still puzzled by the effect we had reported. I now found myself thinking about *both* experiments. Over the next day or so, common elements occurred to me and then a simple rule that seemed to account for both results. A variety of scientific discoveries may come about as a result

of similar processes. F. S. Keller (personal communication) has pointed out a similar case in Zwaardemaker's (1930) account of his invention of the olfactometer.

16

SPONTANEOUS AND DEFERRED IMITATION IN THE PIGEON

Summary. Experimentally-naive pigeons were placed on one side of a clear partition. A pigeon on the other side received food for pecking a ping-pong ball, pulling a rope, or pecking a plastic disk. When given access to a similar object, each naive pigeon pecked or pulled at a low rate for several sessions and two continued to do so for several sessions in the absence of the leader. In a second experiment, the latter effect was demonstrated after a delay of 24 hours, even though the naive pigeons had never had access to the object in the presence of the model. A third experiment demonstrated that the effect on the follower was not due merely to the presence of or activity of another pigeon and was at least somewhat specific to the behavior of the model.

Occasionally organisms mimic the behavior of conspecifics; the phenomenon, which is usually labeled "imitation" or "observational learning," is an important source of adaptive behavior in humans and other animals (Davis, 1973; Hutchinson, 1981; Miller & Dollard, 1941; Porter, 1910; Rosenthal & Zimmerman, 1978; Thorpe, 1963). It may encompass only a few instinctive behaviors or the full range of behaviors which members of a species can exhibit during their lifetimes. It may occur spontaneously or because of a history of conditioning. It may occur only in the presence of a model or it may be "deferred"—that is, the imitative behavior may appear for the first time long after the model has been removed. There are many reports of imitation in animals in general and birds in particular (e.g., Alcock, 1969; Cronhelm, 1970; Klopfer, 1961; Mundinger, 1970; Porter, 1910; Skinner, 1962; Thorpe, 1963). Despite one attempt (Zentall & Hogan, 1976),[1] however, there seem to be no clear demonstrations of either spontaneous or deferred imitation in what is perhaps the second most widely used laboratory animal—the common pigeon (*Columba livia*). In spite of a long-standing assertion that such imitation does not occur (Skinner, 1953), laboratory lore suggests that it does, and since a variety of research is conducted under conditions in which imitation could conceivably occur (e.g., Boakes & Gaertner, 1977; Epstein, Lanza & Skinner, 1980; Millard, 1979), investigation seems warranted. Three experiments are reported which show what might reasonably be called both spontaneous and deferred imitation of relatively arbitrary responses by laboratory pigeons.

Twelve Racing Homers and two White Carneaux pigeons (276WP and 409WP) served as subjects. All were maintained at about 80 percent of the weights they would normally achieve given free access to food. All were male adults between 1 and 3 years old; they were obtained from breeding farms when they were between 6 and 12 months old. Subjects 337WP, 413WP, 409WP, 421WP, 4Y, 5Y, 18Y, 19Y, 22Y, and 27Y served as "followers." None of these had ever served in laboratory experiments, and none, before or during the experiment, ever ate from a laboratory feeder.[2] In Experiment 1, the naive birds were paired with four birds of like breed who served as models; in Experiments 2 and 3, to eliminate possible variance due to different models, a single bird was used as the model for all of the followers.

All sessions were conducted in a double chamber, 30 cm high, 31 cm deep, and 55 cm wide (Figure 16.1). The birds could see each other through a clear partition in the center of the chamber. Models were always placed in the left half of the chamber and followers in the right. The halves were approximate mirror images of each other: Feeders were attached to the left- and right-hand walls; the right-hand feeder, however, was not wired and had never contained any food. Its food bin was sealed when it came from the manufacturer, and no food was ever placed in it over the course of these experiments. During various conditions, ping-pong balls, plastic loops ("ropes"), or standard response keys (plastic disks, recessed 0.6 cm into the panel) were placed on the front panel at corresponding positions 24 cm from the floor and 3 cm from the partition. Pecking or pushing a ball, pecking a key, or pulling a rope was automatically recorded by electromechanical equipment or a microcomputer. The chamber was completely enclosed during each session, and extraneous sounds were masked with white noise. A video camera with a wide-angle lens was attached to the front of the chamber; all sessions were monitored on television and many sessions were videotaped.

Figure 16.1. The experimental chamber, shown with all three pairs of objects on the front panel. In the actual experiments, only one pair was employed, placed in the uppermost positions where the ping pong balls are shown. The column of small white lights on the left panel was not used in the present experiments.

Spontaneous and Deferred Imitation in the Pigeon

All sessions were one-half hour in length and were, without exception, conducted daily, 24 hours apart. Before each experiment, the models were trained to respond repeatedly on one of the objects: Pecking and pushing the ball, pulling the rope, or pecking the key was reinforced intermittently with food according to a variable-ratio 20 or slightly richer schedule until roughly 1,000 responses were emitted reliably in each session. A 3-second operation of the feeder served as the reinforcer; roughly 50 reinforcers were dispensed during each session.

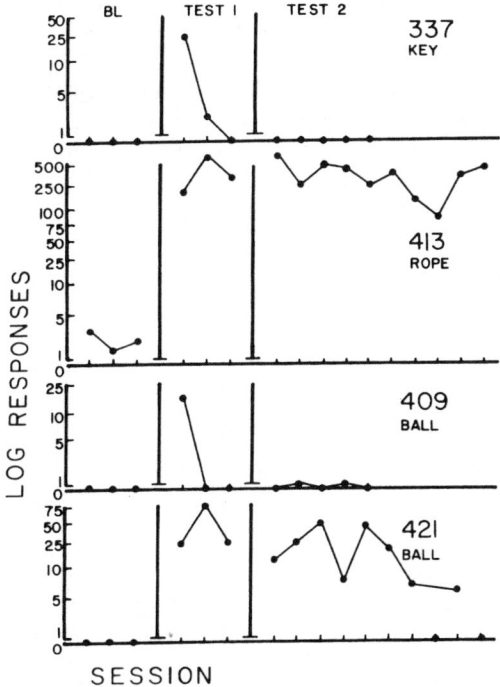

Figure 16.2. Number of responses by the naive subjects during each half-hour session of Experiment 1, shown for the baseline (BL) condition, a test of imitation in the presence of the model (Test 1), and a test of imitation in the absence of the model (Test 2). All of the subjects pecked or pulled considerably more in the presence of the model than they had before having seen the model, and two of the subjects continued to respond even when the model was no longer present.

There were five phases in the first experiment. The object (ball, rope, or key) was in position on the left panel during all phases. 1) Adaptation to the chamber: The naive bird was placed alone in the right-hand side of the chamber for three sessions. No object was present on the right panel. 2) Baseline: The object (corresponding to the one on the left panel) was added to the right panel, and the naive bird was placed alone in the chamber for three sessions. Responding during this period served as the control against which responding would be compared during subsequent tests of imitation. 3) Exposure and adaptation to the model: The object was removed from the right panel. The naive bird was exposed for three sessions to the model while the model pecked the ball, pulled the rope, or pecked the key. 4) Test 1: The corresponding object was added again to the right panel, and the naive bird was exposed again for three sessions to the model while the model pecked or pulled. If the naive bird manipulated the object on its panel more than it had during the baseline period, its behavior could conceivably have been imitative. 5) Test 2: With the object still on the right panel (and the corresponding object still on the left panel), the naive bird was placed in the chamber for five or ten sessions; the model was absent. If the naive bird continued to manipulate the object on its panel more than it had during the baseline period, we would have some indication of deferred imitation.

Few or no responses occurred during the baseline period (Figure 16.2). During the first test, all four naive birds responded at rates considerably higher than the baseline rates. The overall rate of responding for bird 413WP was greater than 16 responses per minute in the second session. There was a large deferred effect (Test 2) for subjects 413WP and 421WP.

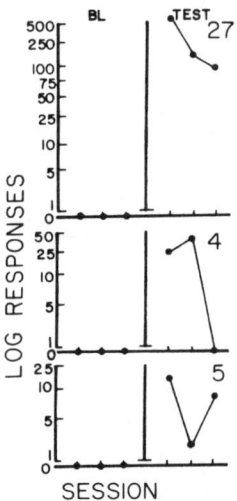

Figure 16.3. Number of pecks at the ball by the naive subjects during each half-hour session of Experiment 2, shown for the baseline (BL) condition and the following test of deferred imitation. The naive subjects pecked the ball repeatedly during the test even though (a) the model was absent, (b) 24 hrs had elapsed since they had seen the model peck a ball, and (c) they had never had access to a ball in the model's presence.

The second experiment tested for deferred imitation more directly. Only the ball was employed. The experiment was otherwise identical to the first experiment, except that the fourth phase was omitted. None of the three naive birds pecked the ball during the baseline sessions. All of them did so during all but one of nine test sessions (Figure 16.3). The overall rate of responding was greater than 16 responses per minute for bird 27Y in the first test session.

The mere presence of or activity of a conspecific can increase activity level, a phenomenon called "social facilitation" (Zajonc, 1965). In Experiments 1 and

2 the possibility remained that we had observed mere social facilitation and, it seems, deferred social facilitation; the observers' behavior may not have been specific to the behavior of the model and hence not imitative. Experiment 3 controlled for this possibility. Three naive pigeons pecked the ball little or not at all when exposed to a model who turned in circles; when later exposed to the same model while the model pecked a ball, they pecked at rates typical of the rates reported in the two experiments reported above (Figure 16.4). Thus the mere presence of or activity of the model was probably responsible for at most a small portion of the effects observed in these experiments. What appears to be the imitative behavior of the followers seems at least somewhat specific to the activity of the model.

In each of the experiments, each follower motioned toward the model repeatedly and often pecked the restraining partition in its direction, especially toward the model's head while it pecked or pulled the object. More significantly, all of the followers—even the two (337WP and 409WP) that did not show a deferred effect—motioned and pecked in this way during the tests of deferred imitation.

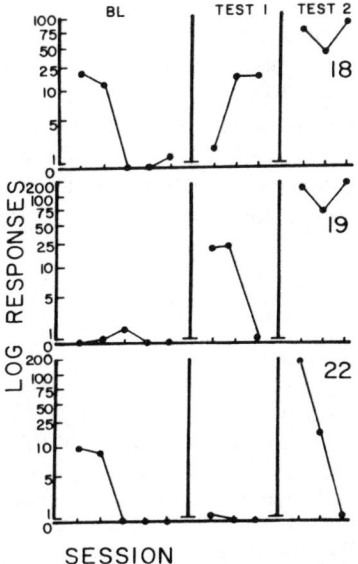

Figure 16.4. Number of pecks at the ball by the naive subjects during each half-hour session of Experiment 3, shown for the baseline (BL) condition, a test of social facilitation when the model was turning in circles (Test 1), and a test of imitation when the model was pecking the ball (Test 2). All of the birds pecked the ball considerably more when the model pecked the ball than when the model turned in circles. Thus the apparent imitative behavior of the naive birds was at least somewhat specific to the behavior of the model.

I recorded on videotape episodes in which followers thrust their heads into their feeder openings and made movements characteristic of feeding for several seconds, either while the model was eating or soon thereafter. It is not surprising that there were few such episodes given that (a) the leaders typically emitted more than 1,000 responses to the ball, rope, or key during each half-hour session but ate fewer than 100 times, (b) making feeding movements in a wall opening is presumably an extremely unlikely behavior, and (c) such behavior would require the follower to turn away from (and hence lose sight of) the model.

Although I have called the responses of pecking the ball, pulling the rope, and pecking the key "relatively arbitrary," the response topographies are common in pigeons. Less common responses, such as treadle-pressing—or, as I have noted above, inserting the head into an opening in a wall—are undoubtedly less affected by the behavior of a model. Preliminary work I have conducted on this issue (with C. Grossbard) suggests, however, that if an uncommon response is made common through reinforcement and then later extinguished, the response may reappear in the presence of a pigeon that is engaging in that behavior.

Other research is also suggested. The effect would probably be smaller with pigeons that were isolated from birth (May & Dorr, 1968). The specificity of the effect could be further tested to allow a more precise characterization of the type of imitation we observed (cf. Davis, 1973; Porter, 1910; Thorpe, 1963): If both model and observer had access to all three of the objects and the model were trained to respond on one of them, would the observer respond on the appropriate object? If the model shifted from one to another, would the observer follow? The role of the food is also unclear. Would the effect occur if the observer could not see the model eat or if the observer were not deprived of food? Even without answers to these questions, the current findings have practical significance, since pigeons both in and out of the laboratory are often deprived of food and are seldom, if ever, isolated from birth.

NOTES

1. Zentall and Hogan (1976), using a group design and a discrete-trial procedure, claimed to demonstrate imitation of key pecking; however, their feeder contained food, their observers were technically not "naive," since they had been trained to eat from the feeders, and in all but one of the conditions of their experiment, key pecks by the observer operated its feeder. They report an extremely small effect for those observers whose pecks did not produce food (a median of 1 response per session for two of the three birds).

2. After subject 337WP was used as a follower, he was trained as a model and paired with subject 421WP in Experiment 1. The other leaders in Experiment 1 were birds 338WP, 329WP, and 276WP. Bird 332WP served as the leader in Experiments 2 and 3.

17

AN EFFECT OF IMMEDIATE REINFORCEMENT AND DELAYED PUNISHMENT, WITH POSSIBLE IMPLICATIONS FOR SELF-CONTROL

Summary. Behavior said to show self-control occurs virtually always as an alternative to behavior that produces conflicting consequences. One class of such consequences, immediate reinforcement and delayed punishment, is especially pervasive. Three experiments with pigeons are described in which an effect of immediate reinforcement and delayed punishment is demonstrated. The results suggest that when a subject is close in time to immediate reinforcement and delayed punishment, the reinforcer alone controls its behavior (the subject behaves "impulsively"). The key to self-control, therefore, may be the acquisition of a large number of avoidance behaviors relevant to reinforcers that are correlated with delayed punishment. Human self-control may indeed involve such a process but undoubtedly involves others, as well.

Human behavior often produces more than one consequence. The case in which consequences are conflicting—that is, in which behavior produces both punishing and reinforcing consequences—has been of special interest to both therapists and researchers for many years. On the one hand, conflicting consequences have been associated with various experimentally-induced behavioral abnormalities, such as "experimental neurosis" (Masserman, 1943; cf. Gantt, 1944) and approach-avoidance behavior (Miller, 1937, 1959). On the other hand, they have formed an integral part of research on punishment, since the behavior being punished is typically maintained by contemporaneous reinforcement (see Azrin & Holz [1966] for examples).

In either case, researchers have dealt primarily with behavior producing simultaneous reinforcement and punishment (e.g., Masserman, 1943) or with behavior producing reinforcement on some occasions and punishment on others (e.g., Miller, 1937; cf. Holz, 1968). Relatively neglected has been a class of conflicting consequences which is both pervasive and troublesome for human behavior, namely immediate reinforcement followed by delayed punishment. Cigarette smoking, overeating, and drug abuse all produce such consequences and, perhaps for that reason, have been resistant to treatment (e.g., Stunkard, 1977). Many less insidious behaviors, such as classroom misbehaviors, also produce such consequences.

The present paper describes an effect of immediate reinforcement and delayed punishment on the behavior of pigeons and suggests an interpretation in terms of current conceptions of human self-control.

EXPERIMENT 1

Method

Subjects. Three experimentally naive, adult male White Carneaux pigeons, numbers 398WP, 233WP, and 399WP, served as subjects. The birds were maintained at approximately 80 percent of their free-feeding weights. Before the start of the experimental conditions, each bird was wired for shock delivery according to the method described by Azrin (1959).

Apparatus. A standard two-key pigeon chamber was used. The two keys were on one wall at a height of 23 cm and spaced 13 cm apart. The left key could be transilluminated from behind with yellow light and the right, with red light. The pigeons could be given access to mixed grain through a recess in the wall beneath the keys. The chamber was equipped with overhead white house lights. A mercury commutator was attached over a 2-inch hole in the center of the ceiling of the chamber, and from the commutator a wire was suspended that could be plugged into a harness on each pigeon's back and through which electric shocks could be delivered. The chamber was enclosed in a sound-attenuating box, which was equipped with a ventilating fan as well as a speaker that emitted white noise.

Procedure. Reliable key pecking was assured before the start of the experiment using standard procedures, including adaptation, hopper-training, autoshaping, and response-contingent reinforcement, and then through the introduction of a series of variable-interval (VI) schedules of reinforcement. The experiment itself was divided into five phases—baseline, 3.0 ma shock, 4.5 ma shock, 7.0 ma shock, and 0.0 ma shock, as follows:

Baseline. Pecking was reinforced according to a two-component chain schedule in which the first component was a fixed-interval 15-second schedule and the second a variable-interval 30-second schedule (chain FI 15-sec VI 30-sec). The first component was correlated with the left key light (yellow) and the second with the right key light (red). After the onset of the left yellow key light, the first peck to that key after 15 seconds extinguished the yellow light and transilluminated the right red key. The first peck to the red key after satisfying the VI 30-second requirement then extinguished the red key light and operated the feeder for 3 seconds. Withdrawal of food was followed by a 1-minute blackout. The houselight was illuminated only while a keylight was transilluminated. The baseline condition remained in effect until no trends were evident in pecking in each component for at least five consecutive sessions.

Shock conditions and return to baseline. A stable performance having been established, the procedure was conducted as in the baseline condition except for the addition of a brief (0.03-second) 3.0 ma shock closely following (after a delay of 0.01 second) the termination of food delivery. Thus the last peck in the second component of the chain produced food immediately and shock after a delay of just over 3 seconds. As in the baseline condition, a 1-minute blackout then preceded the onset of the yellow stimulus at the start of the next trial. The blackout served to minimize possible elicitation effects of the shock that might have interfered with responding in the yellow component. After performance returned to approximate baseline levels (which would be expected because of adaptation to the shock), or after the effect of the given shock intensity on responding in each component was roughly stable, shock intensity was increased to 4.5 ma, and then, after either of the same criteria was met again, to 7.0 ma. After the three shock conditions, the baseline condition (0.0 ma shock) was reinstated until an approximate baseline performance was reestablished.

Sessions were conducted daily for each bird. Each session ended after 60 complete trials or 120 minutes, whichever came first, and ranged in duration, consequently, from 108 to 120 minutes.

Results

Figure 17.1 contains two cumulative record segments showing the typical result of the experiment. Record A shows a high, steady, stable rate of responding in red (the VI 30-sec component) and short latencies, variable but low rates of responding, and occasional accelerations in the yellow (FI 15-sec) component.

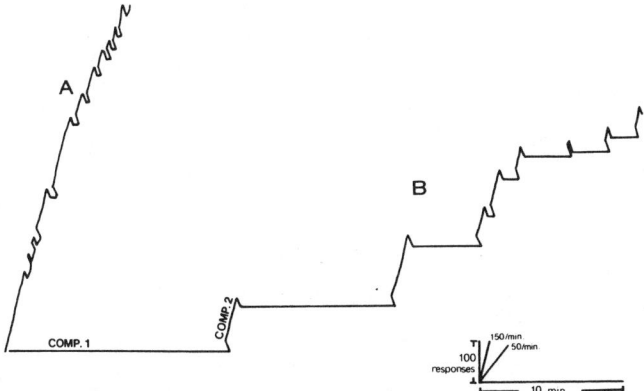

Figure 17.1. Two cumulative record segments for Subject 1 (398WP) in Experiment 1. Record A is from the end of the last session conducted without shock in the baseline condition; record B is from the end of the first session during which food was followed by a brief 4.5 ma shock. The pen deflects downward during the first (yellow) component and is in the normal position during the second (red) component. The recorder stops for the subsequent delivery of food and shock and for the 1-minute blackout that precedes the onset of the next yellow stimulus. Note that in the shock condition (record B), responding is suppressed in the first component.

Record B is from the end of the first session conducted with a 4.5 ma shock for the same pigeon. Responding in the second component is identical in both rate and temporal pattern with that in Record A, established before shock was added to the schedule. Responding in the first component, however, is dramatically suppressed, with the bird occasionally waiting more than 10 minutes before a single peck. Similar records were obtained for all three subjects, although the changes were generally less dramatic for bird 233WP.

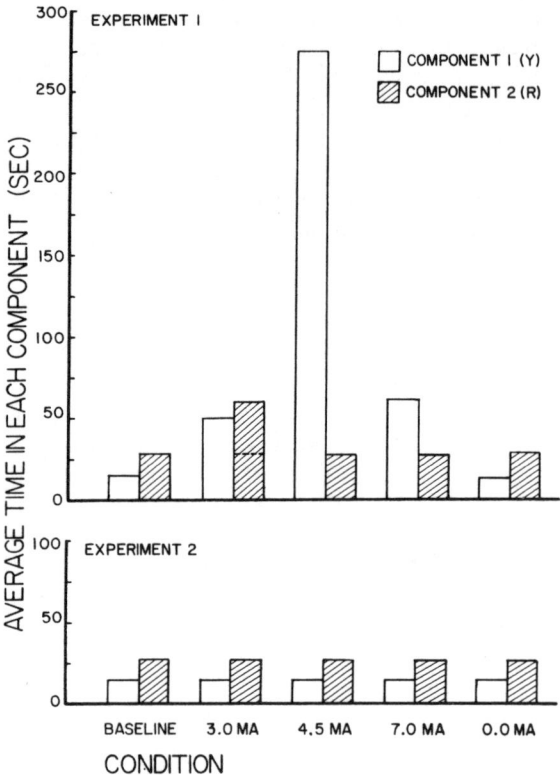

Figure 17.2. Average time in each component, averaged across all subjects and sessions, for Experiments 1 and 2. In Experiment 1 (upper graph), a two-component chain (FI 15-sec VI 30-sec) was terminated either with food alone or food followed by shock. The average time spent in the first component increased dramatically during the shock conditions, whereas the average time spent in the second component was affected little. (The increase in time spent in the second component in the 3.0 ma condition was due entirely to the first shock session for subject 398WP. The dotted line indicates the value obtained if this outlying value is not considered.) In Experiment 2 (lower graph), the same schedule was terminated either with food alone or shock followed by food. The shock produced little or no suppression.

This pattern of suppression is reflected in changes in the response rates in each component. The median response rate in the second component for all birds and shock conditions was 96 percent of the average baseline rate, indicating relatively little suppression; the corresponding value for the first component was 28 percent of the average baseline rate, indicating considerable suppression. Responding in the second component is substantially suppressed in only one of the 26 shock sessions—the first session in which shock was introduced for subject 398WP.

The pattern is also reflected in the average time spent in each component. The top half of Figure 17.2 summarizes these data.

Discussion

Several different accounts of these data are possible. One, which is consistent with certain characterizations of the effects of conflicting consequences found in the human self-control literature (e.g., Kanfer & Phillips, 1970; Thoresen & Mahoney, 1974), is as follows: When a subject is close in time to immediate reinforcement and delayed punishment, responding is controlled primarily by the reinforcer; only when the subject is sufficiently remote in time is the punishment effective. It might be said that in the second component of the chain a subject could not "resist"; in the first component it could behave more "prudently."

Experiment 1 does not rule out other, simpler accounts of the effect. First, the shock may simply subtract an equal amount of responding from each component. Since there is far less responding in the first component to begin with, we see little suppression in the second component and a great deal in the first. Second, the effect may be due to elicitation. It is possible that at the end of the 1-minute blackout the bird has still not recovered from the last shock. When it finally recovers, it begins to peck as usual. The first peck in component 1 satisfies the FI 15-second requirement, and the subsequent rate and pattern of responding in component 2 resemble those of the baseline sessions. Third, the effect may be an artifact of the schedules employed. Rates on VI schedules tend to get "locked-in"; FI responding may simply be more sensitive to the addition of shock. Fourth, early components in chain schedules of reinforcement are known to be more disruptible than later ones (Nevin, 1979; cf. Myer, 1973).

Experiments 2 and 3 control for these possibilities. The subtraction, elicitation, and disruptibility accounts may be tested (though not distinguished) by presenting the shock before reinforcement instead of after it. Presenting the shock 3 seconds sooner should make little difference if elicitation is responsible for the effect and should enhance the effect if shock is subtracting responses from each component or if the effect is due to the relative disruptibility of responding in the first component. In Experiment 2, shock is presented immediately before food and in Experiment 3, the effect of presenting shock before food is compared to the effect of presenting it after food in a within-subjects design. A possible schedule interaction is also tested in Experiment 3.

EXPERIMENT 2

Method

Subjects and Apparatus. Three experimentally naive, adult male White Carneaux pigeons, numbers 403WP, 401WP, and 276WP, served as subjects. Each was maintained at about 80 percent of its free-feeding weight and was wired for shock as in Experiment 1. The apparatus was the same as in Experiment 1.

Procedure. Baseline performances were established as in Experiment 1, using the same schedule of reinforcement (chain FI 15-sec VI 30-sec, followed by 3 sec of food and a 1-minute blackout), after which a brief (0.03-sec) shock was inserted into the sequence just before the onset of reinforcement (the feeder was operated 0.01 sec after the termination of shock). Shock intensity was increased from 3.0 to 7.0 ma over eight sessions for subject 403WP and five sessions for subjects 401WP and 276WP, after which baseline conditions were reestablished, as in Experiment 1.

Results

Inserting the shock before the food resulted in little suppression in either component at any shock value. The average time spent in each component, averaged across all birds and sessions, is pictured in the lower half of Figure 17.2. The dramatic increases that occurred when shock came after food (top graph) did not occur when shock came before food.

Discussion

Since the suppression pattern that was found in Experiment 1 did not occur again in Experiment 2, it probably was not due to either subtraction, elicitation, or the relative disruptibility of responding in the first component. That it was due to the schedules also seems unlikely, unless the pattern was determined by both the schedules and the position of the shock. Experiment 3 uses a within-subjects design to test these possibilities.

EXPERIMENT 3

Method

Four experimentally naive, adult male White Carneaux pigeons, numbers 289WP, 291WP, and 406WP, and 411WP served as subjects. Each was maintained at about 80 percent of its free-feeding weight and was wired for shock as in Experiment 1. The apparatus was the same as in Experiment 1.

Procedure

In the baseline condition, pecks were reinforced according to a chain FI 15-second FI 15-second schedule. As in the previous experiments, the first component was correlated with a yellow light on the left key and the second with a red light on the right key. Satisfying the second FI requirement always produced 3 seconds of food followed by a 1-minute blackout. After a stable baseline performance was established, two of the subjects (289WP and 291WP) received, for two sessions, a brief (0.03-sec) 3.0 ma shock immediately after the termination of food, as in Experiment 1. Baseline conditions were then reinstated for seven sessions, after which a shock of the same intensity and duration was inserted immediately before food for two sessions, as in Experiment 2. The order of the two shock conditions was reversed for subjects 406WP and 411WP. Daily sessions were always 1 hour in length.

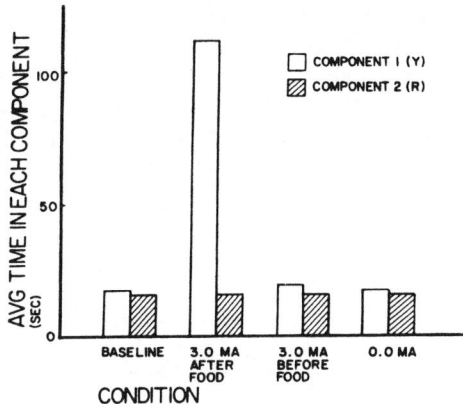

Figure 17.3. Average time spent in each component, averaged across all subjects and sessions for Experiment 3. A two-component chain (FI 15-sec FI 15-sec) was terminated either with food alone, with food followed by shock, or with shock followed by food. The average time spent in the first component increased dramatically when food was followed by shock. The average time spent in the second component was unaffected by the shock in either shock condition.

Results

The results of Experiments 1 and 2 were confirmed. Responding in the second component was affected little by shock placed either before or after food. The subjects (289WP and 291WP) that first received food followed by shock produced the suppression pattern that was observed in Experiment 1. There was substantial suppression only in the first component. When they later received shock before food, there was little suppression in either component. The subjects (406WP and 411WP) that first received shock before food showed little or no suppression in either component. When they later received food followed by shock, the fourth subject (411WP) showed some first-component suppression; no suppression was evident in either component for the third subject (406WP). (A small or no effect of shock during the second exposure is presumably the result of adaptation. This possibility applies to all four of the subjects.)

The result is summarized in Figure 17.3, which shows the average time spent in each component, averaged across all subjects and sessions. The average time spent in the second component is between 15.4 and 15.9 seconds for shock and baseline conditions alike. The average time spent in the first component is 111 seconds when shock follows food but is otherwise between 17.3 and 19.2 seconds.

GENERAL DISCUSSION

The pattern of suppression observed in Experiments 1 and 3 when shock followed food is harmonious with both casual and professional observations about the effects of immediate reinforcement and delayed punishment on human behavior. The overeater, faced with the chocolate cake, is not likely to resist; the smoker, even the one trying to quit, is likely to smoke if cigarettes are at hand. Faced with immediate reinforcement and delayed punishment—in other words, "temptation"—the reinforcer is typically the effective stimulus. If, on the other hand, the reinforcer is somehow less immediate, behavior related to the delayed punishment may triumph (Figure 17.4). As long as the cake is out of sight, the overeater may adhere to his or her diet; while not around smokers, the person trying to quit may make plans to be with non-smokers.

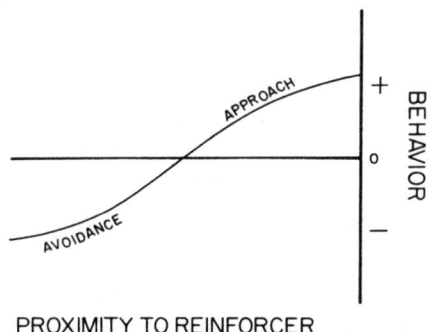

Figure 17.4. An approach-avoidance model of self-control. When close in time to a reinforcer that is associated with delayed punishment (right-hand portion of the curve), approach behavior is likely. When more remote in time (left-hand portion), avoidance is likely. A simple recency account may be given.

Reinforcers often accompanied by delayed punishment are prevalent and so problematic in their effects that they have for many years been a major concern of therapists and are central to several conceptions of human "self-control" (e.g., Ferster, Nurnberger, & Levitt, 1962; Kanfer & Phillips, 1970; Skinner, 1953; Thoresen & Mahoney, 1974). Self-control behavior is said to be responsive to "ultimate aversive consequences" (Ferster, 1965), to "'bridge' the gradient" between immediate and delayed consequences (Thoresen & Mahoney, 1974), and to remove "potentially maladapted sources of gratification" (Goldfried & Merbaum, 1973a); which is to say, it is often behavior that somehow avoids a reinforcer associated with delayed punishment.

The key to self-control may be the acquisition of a large number of avoidance behaviors relevant to reinforcers correlated with delayed punishment. The avoidance behaviors may take any number of forms: inaction ("abstinence"), alternative or incompatible behavior, pre-commitment (cf. Epstein & Goss, 1978; Rachlin, 1974), and so on.

The suppression pattern observed in Experiments 1 and 3 may also be interpreted in terms of the choice-based model of self-control currently the concern of many researchers (e.g., Ainslie, 1974, 1975; Deluty, 1978; Green & Snyderman, 1980; Mazur & Logue, 1978; Navarick & Fantino, 1976; Rachlin, 1970, 1974; Rachlin & Green, 1972; Solnick, Kannenberg, Eckerman, & Waller, 1980), although the applicability of the model is not clear. Abstaining from pecking in the early component could be considered forgoing a near, less "valued" reinforcer—food followed by shock—for some more remote, more "valued" reinforcer—perhaps the food given to the bird after it is removed from the chamber to maintain it at running weight (Figure 17.5). Shock followed by food must somehow be more "valuable" than food followed by shock, according to this model, since it does not produce this suppression pattern. The choice might also be said to be between immediate food and the omission of delayed shock, but this interpretation is lacking in two respects. First, the first alternative involves *both* reinforcement and (delayed) punishment; a response cannot produce one without producing the other, as is often the case for human behavior. Second, the effect of the second alternative should be greater when shock comes sooner; thus, again, shock before food should produce greater suppression than shock after food, which it does not.

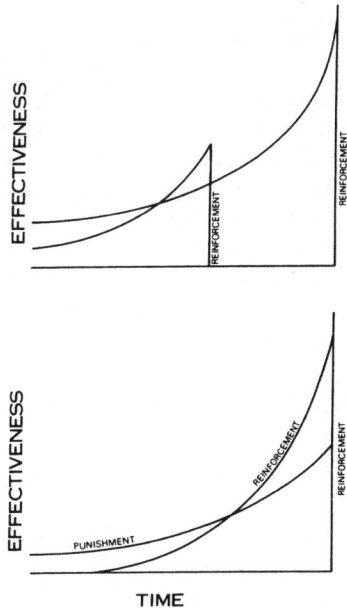

Figure 17.5. According to the choice model (top panel), the organism chooses the larger, more delayed reinforcer when the two reinforcers are sufficiently remote in time. Note the way the curves overlap. The approach-avoidance model can also be represented in terms of overlapping delay gradients, in this case of punishment and reinforcement (bottom panel). The function shown in Figure 17.4 is, roughly, the difference between the delay gradients for punishment and reinforcement.

Neither the conflicting consequences paradigm nor the choice model makes contact with important elements of human self-control, as characterized by both professionals and laypersons. Self-control is often characterized as a "decision" process, not a choice process (Kanfer, 1977). Unlike the passive and inevitable behavior of a pigeon that occurs as a function of the remoteness of various events, it is said to involve some "deliberate" action, some manipulation of behavior or environment related to temporally remote factors; hence the force of the term "control" in "self-control" and the word's kinship with "self-denial," "willpower," and so on (cf. Bandura, Mahoney, & Dirks, 1976; Ferster, 1965; Mahoney & Bandura, 1972; Skinner, 1953). Dictionary definitions emphasize "self-denial" and "self-restraint"—in other words, resisting temptation even when it is sufficiently near that its effectiveness curve is presumably still higher than that of some long-term consequence. "Self-control" is said to refer to behavior that young children (and presumably pigeons) lack entirely (Bandura & Walters, 1963), that is acquired only after an extensive history of training and socialization (Bandura & Walters, 1963; Premack & Anglin, 1973; Risley, 1977; cf. Mazur & Logue, 1978), and that many people never acquire to any great extent. It seems unlikely that pigeons with no special training history are capable of behavior that takes humans years to learn, and imperfectly at that.

Moreover, most instances of behavior that come under the rubric of self-control are the result neither of conflicting consequences nor of remote alternatives that one has actually experienced. They are often simply imitated or under instructional control. Odysseus did not experience the deleterious consequences of the Sirens' song before having himself tied to his mast (rather sophisticated avoidance behavior); he simply followed Circe's instructions (cf. Ainslie, 1975; Rachlin & Green, 1972). And one need not have experienced the immediate reinforcement and delayed punishment associated with oversleeping to set an alarm clock nor have contracted cancer to stop smoking. Nevertheless, to the extent that remote, unequal alternatives or the effects of conflicting consequences on a single response are involved in self-control phenomena, current laboratory procedures may shed light on them.

PART IV

BEYOND BEHAVIORISM: THE CASE FOR A SCIENCE OF BEHAVIOR

18

THE CASE FOR PRAXICS

Summary. Since the early 1900s a variety of names have been proposed for the scientific study of behavior, but none has come into general use. "Praxics," a recent entry, is defensible on several grounds. "Behaviorism," on the other hand, is the name of a school of philosophy. Although praxics has roots in behaviorism, the term "behaviorism" should not be applied to praxics. Confusion between the science and the philosophy has retarded the growth of the science immeasurably. Its growth has also been impeded by its association with psychology, which is still primarily the study of mind.

> *It was not a wholly satisfactory name for a field.*
>
> —B. F. Skinner (1979, p. 331), on "the experimental analysis of behavior"

"Praxics"—a blend of "physics" and *"praxis"* (πρᾶξις), the Greek for "to behave"—is a term I and others now use for the experimental analysis of behavior and related disciplines. We define it as *the study of behavior*. We call one who studies behavior a "praxist," after "chemist." In this essay I present (a) the case for the use of the terms, (b) the case for drawing a clear distinction between praxics and behaviorism, and (c) the case for the separation of praxics and psychology. Most of the arguments I will make have, it turns out, already been made, and hence much of this essay is historical.

TERMS

There have been several attempts to name the study of behavior in general and the experimental analysis of behavior in particular (Epstein, 1984c). Most of these efforts have failed. Two—"ethology" and "praxiology"—have been partially successful in certain domains.

Ethology

The term "ethology" has two different, although closely related, modern usages. It was defined by Lorenz and Tinbergen as the study of instinct (e.g., Tinbergen, 1951). It was founded as a specialty within biology, concerned primarily with innate behavior patterns in non-human animals in their natural habitats. By the 1960s it had evolved into a more comprehensive field, defined as "the biology of behavior" (Eibl-Eibelfeldt, 1970) or "the biological study of behavior" (Tinbergen, 1963). For many years there was little communication between ethologists and experimental psychologists and none to speak of between ethologists and those who worked in the operant tradition. Although exchanges are now common (e.g., Fantino & Logan, 1979; Nevin, 1973), ethology still remains somewhat narrow in its focus: Ethologists still study non-human animals for the most part; they rely almost exclusively on field studies and are skeptical of laboratory research on behavior; they are interested mainly in feral animals and are critical of the use of laboratory-bred or domesticated animals; and so on.[1] "Ethology" is not an appropriate label for the experimental analysis of behavior or the many other scientific fields that are concerned with the determinants of behavior.

A prior use of the term was somewhat more comprehensive and closer to at least some characterizations of modern psychology. In Book Six of his classic *A System of Logic*, published in 1843, John Stuart Mill proposed "ethology" as a label for what he hoped would be a new science, "the science of the formation of character." He derived the term from "*ethos*" (ἦθος), the Greek for "character," by which he meant behavior in all of its aspects. He hoped to see the emergence of a comprehensive science to supplement the philosophical psychology of his day, but none emerged, and the term fell into disuse. The original *Oxford English Dictionary* (henceforward, *OED*), which was published in installments between 1884 and 1928, gives Mill's definition, as well as two obsolete definitions from the seventeenth and eighteenth centuries: the study of ethics, and the practice of mimicry. The 1933 supplement to the *OED* adds the first biological definition, the obvious precursor to the modern usage: "The branch of Natural History which deals with an animal's actions and habits, its reaction to its environment." The first relevant usage is attributed to two zoologists, Parker and Haswell (1897), who defined it as the study of "the relation of the organism to its environment," which, they said, had also been called "bionomics."

Praxiology

The history of the term "praxiology"—also spelled "praxeology"—is considerably more complicated.[2] F. S. Keller has proposed it from time to time (e.g., 1984) as a name for the experimental analysis of behavior. According to Keller (personal communication, December, 1983), he first heard it in a course he had as a graduate student at Harvard in 1928. His instructor, Dwight Chapman, used the term jokingly, and Keller, too, has used it somewhat hesitatingly ever since. It has not been adopted by behavioral psychologists, nor by biologists. But it has been used fairly widely in other domains—philosophy, education, and economics, in particular—so widely that it is listed in several unabridged dictionaries and dictionaries of philosophy and behavioral science.

The original *OED* contains no such listing, but the 1982 *Supplement* contains a listing 49 lines long. "Praxeology," "praxiology," or "praxology" (in that order) is defined as "The study of such actions as are necessary in order to give practical effect to a theory or technique; the science of human conduct; the science of efficient action." "Praxiologist" is defined only as "one who studies practical activity." The American standard, *Webster's Third New International Dictionary*, published in 1966, defines "praxeology" or "praxiology" (again, in that order) simply as "the study of human action and conduct."

Many specialty dictionaries give similar definitions. Horace B. English's (1928) classic *A Student's Dictionary of Psychological Terms* defines "praxiology" as "Study of the activities or movements or 'deeds' of an organism as a whole; synonymous with behaviorism except in not denying the importance of mental processes." The *Psychiatric Dictionary* (Hinsie & Campbell, 1970) disagrees on the last point: "Praxiology" is "Dunlap's term for the science of behavior, which excludes the study of consciousness and similar non-objective, metaphysical concepts." Wolman's (1973) *Dictionary of Behavioral Science* defines it thus: "1. Psychology viewed as the study of actions, and overt behavior. 2. ... Any normative science ... e.g., education, social philosophy, ethics, etc., that sets norms and goals for human actions." The *Dictionary of Philosophy and Religion* (Reese, 1980) refers the reader to an entry on Kotarbiński, about whom more will be said below.

Many similar works contain no such entry, including the 1977 *International Encyclopedia of Psychiatry, Psychology, Psychoanalysis, and Neurology* (this is significant, since Wolman was the editor), *The Encyclopedia of Philosophy* (1967), *The Encyclopedia of Psychoanalysis* (1968), *The Dictionary of Psychology and Related Fields* (1971), *The Dictionary of the History of Ideas* (1973), *A Concise Encyclopedia of Psychiatry* (1977), *A Dictionary of Philosophy* (1979), the *Encyclopedia of Psychiatry* (1981), and the *Dictionary of Philosophy* (1983). The omissions notwithstanding, the term clearly has some legitimacy. How did it get it?

A number of scholars agree that the term originated with the London author and physician, Charles A. Mercier, who lived from 1852 to 1919. In his 1911 book, *Conduct and Its Disorders*, he wrote: "Apart from the general advantage ... of having a systematic knowledge of conduct as a whole; there are certain special advantages to be derived from a study of Praxiology, if I may so term it" (p. viii). Of course, there is nothing new under the sun: Seven years earlier, W. R. Boyce Gibson, a lecturer in philosophy at the University of London, used the term "praxology" for what seems to have been the first and last time (also see Ford [1952], who apparently reinvented the term yet again). On page 190 of Gibson's book *A Philosophical Introduction to Ethics* appear the following rather obscure statements: "The proper propaedeutic for a course in moral philosophy would, in my opinion, consist of a theory of experience (or *philosophical* logic), followed up by a teleological (or *philosophical*) psychology. I say 'theory of experience' instead of theory of 'knowledge' or 'epistemology,' in order to include the theory of action or 'praxology'" (italics original). And von Mises (1944)—who cites neither Gibson nor Mercier—credits the first uses of the term "praxeology" to the French philosopher Espinas in the 1890s (e.g., 1897) and the Russian economist Slutsky in 1926.

Kotarbiński. Mercier's term was taken up by—or perhaps reinvented by—individuals in four separate fields. The Polish philosopher Tadeusz Kotarbiński (e.g., 1965) defines it as "the general theory of efficient action"—for "action" read "labor" or "work"—which, he says, derives from or is at least harmonious with such diverse works as Marx's *Capital*, Mill's *Utilitarianism*, Machiavelli's *Il Principe*, and Defoe's *Robinson Crusoe*. Although they didn't use the term, says Kotarbiński, George Herbert Mead, Talcott Parsons, and Georges Hostelet were all concerned with praxiology, which he describes as follows:

> The praxiologist concerns himself with finding the broadest possible generalizations of a technical nature. His objective is the technique of good, efficient work as such, indications and warnings important for all work which is intended to achieve maximum effectiveness. (p. 1)

This use of "praxiology" does not rule out mentalism or teleology, and the field Kotarbiński describes is neither experimental nor data based. Chapter 14 of his 1965 book is entitled "Mental Activity" and reads in part:

> every act includes elements which are mental in nature. This is so because in every act there is contained a free impulse directed towards a certain goal, which means that the agent not only moves but also is conscious of the purpose of his movement—and that consciousness undoubtedly is a mental factor.... [Purely] mental actions do exist—mental solution of arithmetic problems; recalling past events; composition of musical works without writing down notes.... Hence, one may not only discuss the role of mental events in any action, but also ... analyze purely mental actions as a special case of action in general. (pp. 175–176)

Kotarbiński's version of praxiology has been applied in education, in essays, for example, by James Perry (e.g., 1971) and E. S. Maccia (e.g., 1966), who argue, understandably, that we need to know more about how to be effective in education. They do not mention advances in any empirical science of behavior.

Von Mises. The Austrian-American economist, Ludwig Von Mises (e.g., 1944, 1962), who held a faculty appointment at New York University from 1945 until his death in 1973, defined praxeology as the general science of human conduct. Economics, he said, was a special branch—"the only developed branch" (Gutiérrez, 1971)—of this science. Again, the field he described is not a laboratory science:

> Its scope is human action as such, irrespective of all environmental and incidental circumstances of the concrete acts. It aims at knowledge valid for all instances in which the conditions exactly correspond to those implied by its assumptions and

inferences. Whether people exchange commodities and services directly by barter or indirectly by using a medium of exchange is a question of the particular institutional setting which can be answered by history only. But whenever and wherever a medium of exchange is in use, all the laws of monetary theory are valid with regard to the exchanges thus transacted. (Von Mises, 1944, p. 529)

It is not, he said, "based on psychology and is not a part of psychology" (Von Mises, 1944, p. 531), which he took to be the study of mind. "Praxeology deals with choice and action and with their outcome. Psychology deals with the internal processes determining the various choices in their concreteness"(p. 531).

If praxeology is not empirical, where do its laws come from? Von Mises and his students advanced a series of postulates and theorems of action which were "developed by reason and logic from *a priori* truths" (Bien, 1969, p. 4). "The starting point of praxeology," wrote Von Mises (1962), "is a self-evident truth, the cognition of action, that is, the cognition of the fact that there is such a thing as consciously aiming at ends" (pp. 5–6). The laws were still dependent on data, however, even though they supposedly weren't derived from them, which led Gutiérrez (1971) to dismiss the entire enterprise as vacuous. Further examination of these issues would be out of place here. Suffice it to say that Von Mises, like Perry and Maccia, seemed unaware that there existed a science of behavior any more sophisticated than the one he was espousing. That should be a matter of some concern to those who are immersed in such a science, a matter to be discussed below.

Kuo. "Praxiology" was also adopted—with a passion—by Zing Yang Kuo, an ardent behavioral psychologist who lived from 1898 to 1970. Kuo was trained by Tolman at the University of California at Berkeley, where he became, for a time, a devotee of Watson. He soon became an even more radical behaviorist than Watson himself, and, indeed, he, like Skinner, called his brand of behaviorism "radical behaviorism" (e.g., Kuo, 1967).

In 1923, after five years at Berkeley, he returned to China. By 1930 he had established four laboratories devoted to the study of animal behavior, one financed solely by income from his books in Chinese. He is best known for his strong stand against the concept of instinct (e.g., Kuo, 1921, 1930), as well as for a long series of innovative studies on the behavior of the chick embryo (e.g., 1932, 1933). Unfortunately, political events in China terminated his research career in the 1930s. Between 1936 and 1940 he had neither a job nor a country, and he was not able to publish scientific works again until the 1960s (see the Preface of Kuo, 1967). Except for a brief period in 1963, he was denied the opportunity to conduct laboratory research for the last 30 years of his life (Gottlieb, 1972).

In a brilliant essay called "Prolegomena to Praxiology," published in *The Journal of Psychology* in 1937, Kuo made the case for praxiology, and, in effect, for praxics.[3] He attributed the term to Mercier and Dunlap, whom, he said, suggested it as a better name for Watson's behaviorism.[4] But, disturbed by what he called "the half-heartedness of the behavioristic revolt, and its inability to make a decisive break with the traditional psychology" (p. 5), he assigned "praxiology" yet another meaning:

[Praxiology is] *a branch of biology which deals with the behavior of animals (including man) with special emphasis on its ontogenic and physiological aspects as the chief channels through which causal factors of behavior may be discovered.* The ultimate purpose of praxiology is, of course, prediction and control of behavior. But unless its physiology and developmental history are sufficiently known, it will be futile to hope to be able to predict and control behavior. Watson, the founder of behaviorism, has made a great mistake by declaring that the behaviorist can make a thoroughly comprehensive and accurate study of behavior without reference to physiology.... [The praxiologist] is firmly convinced that by acquiring adequate data on the nature of stimulus and response and their intricate relations and on the physiology and ontogeny of behavior he can give a thoroughly scientific description of behavior in purely mathematical and physical terms. (pp. 5–6, italics original)

"Praxiology" in perspective. Although Kuo's program—an independent, biologically-based field, the subject matter of which is the behavior of organisms—is not without merit, the term "praxiology," I submit, is no longer a viable name for it. It has been used too widely since the 1930s and in too many ways. The dominant usage today seems to be Kotarbiński's, which is clearly an inappropriate label for an empirically-based science like the experimental analysis of behavior. The term itself, it could be argued, is unattractive—antique, perhaps, in its sound and spelling. "Praxology," the form which is cognate with "psychology," seems attractive until a listener confuses it with "proctology."

Anthroponomy

Another early behavioral psychologist, Walter S. Hunter, proposed yet another term for the scientific study of human behavior (e.g., Hunter, 1925, 1926, 1930). Hunter, like Watson, was trained at the University of Chicago under Angell and Carr just after the turn of the century. And, like Watson, he wanted psychology to become a natural science. He devoted himself to this end throughout his life (Schlosberg, 1954).

He argued that psychology was tainted with "charlatans" (Hunter, 1925, p. 286) and with "spiritualists, psychic researchers, and Freudians, who object to the petty laboratory problems in terms of which the psychologist outlines his field and who resent deeply and religiously the tendency in modern psychology to eliminate the purposeful activity of mind" (Hunter, 1926, p. 83). The solution, he thought, was a new name for that part of psychology which was truly objective. His seminal paper on the subject appeared in 1925, while he was a faculty member at the University of Kansas:

Anthroponomy is the science of the laws which govern human action—the science of human nature [cf. J. S. Mill's "ethology," described above]. It seeks by experiment and systematic observation to arrive at an understanding of the factors which determine certain of the observable phenomena of the human individual.... The essential difference between psychology and anthroponomy lies in the attitude towards the observations which are made. The former science is derived directly from the Greek philosophers and is concerned only with the study of mind, consciousness, or the psyche.... Such a point of view results, as might be expected, in the neglect of all data concerning the human individual which cannot be interpreted as evidence for the existence of some type of psychic process. In other words, scientific observations are not to be valued for their own sake, but solely because of the inferences concerning consciousness which they make possible.... [In contrast, the anthroponomist] never raises the question whether or not the observable phenomena express or embody a psychic world beyond them. He studies the large field of observable human nature in order to describe and explain the phenomena there found. (p. 286)

Hunter discussed and dismissed a variety of other terms: "objective psychology," "behaviorism," "tropology," and "anthropology":

non-psychic studies have become so numerous ... that new names for the science are coming into use. Of these Objective Psychology and Behaviorism are the most prominent. The former, however, is defective in that it suggests a sub-division of psychology and in that it contains the obvious contradiction of a non-psychic psychology.... Among Americans, Behaviorism has proved a wonderfully apt term. It contains no suggestion of the psychic.... It does, however, refer to an "ism" and is not, therefore, well suited to designate an entire science. The term Science of Behavior is too cumbersome, and the Greek equivalent Tropology is too reminiscent of a special problem in the behavior of lower animals [the "tropism"], to make these acceptable names for the science.... The term Anthropology, science of man, escapes these difficulties, but is preempted by a closely related discipline.... At present only one thing is certain, and that is the inappropriateness of the term "psychology." (1925, pp. 290–291)

Hunter died in 1954, his dream for anthroponomy unrealized. In a eulogy which appeared in *The Psychological Review*, J. McV. Hunt (1956) wrote: "he suggested that the term *anthroponomy* replace psychology.... The amusement aroused by this suggestion he took in good-spirited stride" (p. 214).

Behavior Analysis

The term "behavior analysis" has come to be used by many individuals as a label for both basic research, primarily in operant conditioning, and the technology that has evolved from this research. The term is far from ideal as a label for the study of behavior in general or the experimental analysis of behavior in particular.

The term, first of all, is nomic but not nominal; that is, it is the customary label for what certain people do, but it is not truly a name. It is, rather, a description: Both behavioral engineers and laboratory researchers sometimes *analyze* behavior. Even as a descriptor, the term is not wholly satisfactory, for behavior analysts do far more than analyze, which means to separate a whole into its constituent parts. They manipulate variables, make predictions, construct theories and models, treat problem behavior, shape and maintain behavior, engineer physical environments, and so on.

The term seems to be used more consistently as a label for applied behavior analysts than for basic researchers, who are sometimes called "operant conditioners" or "operant psychologists" but who are usually not labeled anything at all, since no suitable label exists. Basic researchers are, understandably, never called "experimental analysts of behavior."

The term "behavior analysis" is used almost exclusively by behavior analysts themselves and even then only cautiously. It is a kind of family term, used by family members only. The public knows nothing of behavior analysis, although it has heard of every other scientific discipline from anthropology to zoology. And, with few exceptions, the same ignorance may be attributed to funding agencies. One does not identify oneself as a "behavior analyst" on a grant application; doing so would likely be suicidal.

Finally, because the term is so closely linked with the operant tradition, it is more a label for a fraternity than a science. I oversimplify perhaps only slightly by saying that behavior analysts are those people who are active in the Association for Behavior Analysis; they are concerned primarily with operant conditioning in some domain or other. In contrast, behavior *therapists* are those people who are active in the Association for the Advancement of Behavior Therapy; they are perhaps slightly more concerned with classical conditioning and, these days, with cognition. There is some overlap between the groups, of course.

The Experimental Analysis of Behavior

In the second volume of Skinner's autobiography, he discusses the origin of a term whose sesquipedalian segments have plagued the palates of even its most devoted disciples ever since. With Fred S. Keller and William N. Schoenfeld, Skinner organized the first conference on the domain of research he had originated nearly two decades earlier. It was held at Indiana University in June, 1946:[5]

> We called it a conference on the "experimental analysis of behavior," taking the "experimental analysis" from the subtitle of *The Behavior of Organisms*. It was not a wholly satisfactory name for a field. What should we call ourselves? "Students of behavior"? "Behavior analysts"? And what adjectives could we use to identify our research, our theories, or our organization? "Behaviorism," "behaviorists," and "behavioristic" were not quite right. They were too closely tied to John B. Watson. (Skinner, 1979, p. 331)

Ironically, Hunter had rejected the label "science of behavior" as "cumbersome" more than 20 years earlier. Were standards of locution different in 1946?

Against all odds, "the experimental analysis of behavior" has persisted as a label for the activities of those who continue to do research in the tradition of Skinner's *The Behavior of Organisms*. It is far from satisfactory as a label for this domain: It is awkward, and, like "behavior analysis," it is more a description than a name. And, again, researchers in this field do more than analyze. Finally, the term is wholly unsatisfactory as a name for the study of behavior in the broader sense, since it is so closely identified with a single research tradition.

Other Terms

Some related terms deserve at least brief mention. Hunter had rejected the term "objective psychology," which had been proposed by the Russian V. M. Bekhterev and was used from time to time as an umbrella term for non-mentalistic forms of psychology (see Diserens, 1925). Bekhterev eventually switched to "reflexology"; the study of reflexes would, he asserted, following Sechenov (1863/1935), eventually encompass all psychological phenomena (Boring, 1950).

Knight Dunlap (e.g., 1922, 1926) proposed the term "scientific psychology" in much the same spirit that Hunter offered "anthroponomy," although Dunlap did not reject consciousness as a subject matter. He wanted merely to dissociate himself from various "new psychologies" which seemed to be of questionable value, like those based on Freud, phrenology, or psychic research. Dunlap is also credited with inventing the term "psychobiology," which Moore (1923) suggested as the inclusive label for both psychology (which, said Moore, "means and can only mean the science of mind" [p. 235]) and praxiology, the science of behavior.

Finally, J. R. Kantor offered the terms "interbehaviorism," "interbehavioral psychology," and "organismic psychology" as labels for his own extensive philosophical and theoretical contributions (e.g., Kantor, 1924; Kantor & Smith, 1975). Kantor, like Watson and Skinner, was ardently anti-mentalistic, but, unlike other behavioral psychologists, he was not content to say that the subject matter of psychology was behavior, for this meant, he believed, that one might study mere movement or activity apart from an organism's interaction with its environment. "[Only] the treatment of psychological events as fields in which responses or acts of the organism operate in interaction with stimulus objects under specified conditions can supply complete and satisfactory scientific descriptions and interpretations in psychology as in every other science" (Kantor & Smith, 1975, p. 31). Both research on behavior and empirically-derived theories of behavior have typically involved an analysis of such interactions, even though Kantor's point has seldom, if ever, been stated explicitly.

Praxics

If indeed all of these terms are in competition with each other, "praxics" should surely win at this point by process of elimination. It hasn't failed yet, which is more than can be said for most of the other terms. It is too new to have been abused. It can be difficult to pronounce at first, but it proves, with practice, to be much easier than "tachistoscope," "statistical significance," or "the experimental analysis of behavior," and "praxist" is easier still. "Praxics" is simple in form (cf. "cybernetics") and is recognizable on sight as the name of a science, probably because it is only three letters away from "physics." It has a respectable and appropriate Greek root.

Unadorned, the term describes neither an "attitude" (cf. "anthroponomy," "behaviorism," "interbehaviorism," "objective psychology," "scientific psychology," and so on) nor a methodology (cf. "the experimental analysis of behavior" or Kotarbiński's "praxiology"). It simply circumscribes a subject matter, as do the terms "physics," "biology," "epidemiology," "psychology," "otolaryngology," "ornithology," "astronomy," and so on. The labels of scientific domains are labels for *subject matters*.[6] How odd that a subject matter as pervasive as the behavior of organisms has been so difficult to name.

The study of behavior needs some legitimacy, and I suspect that, like the neonate, it lacks legitimacy for the very simple reason that it lacks a name. A name, after all, can create legitimacy even where none is warranted. There is credibility in a name *(IBM, immunology, microbiology)* and, sometimes, prestige *(Lloyds of London, mathematics, neurology)*. "If we lost our stock of labels," said William James, "we should be intellectually lost in the midst of the world." Certainly the lack of a name for the science of behavior has made it hard to communicate with other people. Over the years I have responded to the question, "But what *kind* of psychologist are you?" in at least six different ways, and I have occasionally had to try two or three on the same listener to evoke the slightest sign of comprehension. Unfortunately, that sign has usually been the rather singsong "Ohhh..." that you emit when you're trying not to show how much you disapprove of someone. Which brings me to behaviorism.

PRAXICS AND BEHAVIORISM

If praxics is the study of behavior, what is behaviorism? Do we need both terms?

"Behaviorism," as J. B. Watson (1913) first used the term, was the name of a *movement* in psychology—"a breath of fresh air, clearing away the musty accumulation of the centuries" (R. I. Watson, 1963, p. 401). It was not the name of a subject matter; nor was it the name of a school of philosophy. The term "behaviorist" was more like "suffragette" than "physicist." Watson did not offer "behaviorism" as a label for the science of behavior; rather, he hoped to convince psychologists that *psychology should become the science of behavior*. One need hardly look beyond the titles of his two seminal works on behaviorism to see the point: "Psychology as the Behaviorist Views It" (J. B. Watson, 1913) and *Psychology from the Standpoint of a Behaviorist* (J. B. Watson, 1919). Behaviorism was not intended as an alternative to psychology but rather as a corrective action. Consider the opening sentences of Watson (1913):

> Psychology as the behaviorist views it is a purely objective experimental branch of natural science. Its theoretical goal is the prediction and control of behavior. Introspection forms no essential part of its methods, nor is the scientific value of its data dependent upon the readiness with which they lend themselves to interpretation in terms of consciousness.

Dunlap, Hunter, Weiss, Skinner, and others continued Watson's program of reform. In December of 1928, shortly after he began graduate school, Skinner wrote in a letter: "my fundamental interests lie in Psychology, and I shall probably continue therein, even, if necessary, by making over the entire field to suit myself" (Skinner, 1979, p. 38).

The movement was not entirely successful, but this is a matter that we can sidestep for the moment. It is safe to say that behaviorism as a *movement* in psychology died long ago. There are few behavioristic *reformers* around these days, and psychology is not especially vulnerable to them. That was not the case in Watson's day. He was viewed by many in the field as a savior. He was elected president of the American Psychological Association only two years after he published his 1913 paper, when he was only 37 years old—an unprecedented rise to prominence in the field. The Association would hardly reward a behavioristic flag-waver with the same kind of recognition today.

But the movement left two distinct products, each of which has grown and, to some extent, flourished: First, it helped to convince many researchers that the behavior of organisms was a legitimate subject matter in its own right. And second, it led to the development of a school of philosophy—consisting mainly of psychologists, not philosophers—called "behaviorism."

Behaviorism as Philosophy

A system of philosophy was implicit in Watson's early statements. In delineating a subject matter, he also made many assertions about the nature of consciousness, thought, conscious content, introspection, feelings, perception, free will, the role of heredity in human behavior, and other matters. Like James, Freud, and Skinner, he was a strict determinist. He asserted early in his career, without supporting data, that thought was simply laryngeal movement.[7] On the nature-nurture question, Watson at first stood the middle ground, but he eventually shifted toward thorough-going environmentalism. Note that he could conceivably have delineated the subject matter *without* taking such stands.

Watson never made a clear distinction between the philosophy and the science he espoused. If anything, the distinction got murkier over the years. In his 1930 revision of *Behaviorism*—his last contribution to academe—he used the term "behaviorism" as a label for the movement he had begun, as a synonym for "objective psychology," and as a label for the science of behavior—by this time, he had shifted the emphasis to *human* behavior (see Watson, 1930, p. 2). He continued to take strong stands on a wide range of philosophical issues.

Skinner seems to have been the first to tease apart the science and the philosophy, perhaps because he added so much substance to the science. He has used the term "behaviorism" fairly consistently as the label for a philosophical school: "Behaviorism is not the science of human behavior," he wrote, "it is the philosophy of that science" (Skinner, 1974, p. 3). It is, of course, more than that; it is a school of philosophy in its own right, which has concerned itself with issues such as the nature of mind and consciousness (e.g., Quine, 1976; Wessells, 1982), the nature and importance of feelings (e.g., J. M. Russell, 1978), free will and determinism (e.g., Burton, 1980), values (e.g., Graham, 1977; Rottschaefer, 1980), the nature of knowledge (e.g., Russell, 1980), the nature of perception and language (e.g., Faraone, 1983; Natsoulas, 1982), and so on. A philosophy journal called *Behaviorism* was established by Willard F. Day, Jr. in 1973 to encourage discourse on these and other topics.

Behaviorists have made assertions such as: (1) Behavior is orderly and predictable; free will is an illusion. (2) Mind is a superfluous concept. Thoughts are not the causes of behavior. Our concern with mind keeps us from finding out more about the real determinants of behavior. (3) Feelings do not cause behavior. They are unimportant, and our preoccupation with them keeps us from finding practical solutions to our problems. (4) Language is also behavior and can only be understood as such. The formal analysis of language tells us nothing. (5) Perceptual phenomena such as imaging can also be treated as behavioral phenomena, and the laws that govern observable motor behavior may be adequate to explain perceptual behavior.

As Skinner recognized, the laboratory study of behavior proceeds almost entirely independently of such assertions. Whether or not behavior is "determined" in the philosophical sense, one can still search for—and, of course, one will find—order in behavior in the laboratory. One can study and will undoubtedly discover interesting things about behavior whether mind exists or not. The presence or absence of consciousness in a given species will not affect one's experimental attack on behavior in that species "by one jot or one tittle" (Watson, 1913, p. 161). Where data and formal theory are relatively sparse—as in the analysis of language or perception—philosophical arguments will naturally be taken more seriously (after all, they're all we've got), but *once the scientific attack on some phenomenon is successful, philosophical arguments fall by the wayside*. This is not to say that data necessarily settle philosophical debates; rather, the data tend to create a substantive understanding of the subject matter which takes on its own life. A century from now, if the behavioral approach to language has been successful, praxists will be debating about the significance of data and about the merits and demerits of various formal, predictive theories of language. The views of the philosopher will be at best of only marginal interest, just as they are at best of only marginal interest to the laboratory chemist. Facts constrain speculation.

Although Skinner seems to have recognized the distinction between behaviorism and praxics, the fact that he is both the most accomplished living behaviorist in the world *and* the most accomplished living praxist has surely caused trouble. And although he has made the distinction, others have not. Rachlin (1970), for example, defines "behaviorist" as "[one who is] engaged in the experimental study of behavior" (p. 2). Like Watson, Rachlin presents the philosophy of behaviorism side by side with laboratory findings in the study of behavior.

Behaviorism vs. Praxics

The term "behaviorism" is by no means obsolete. It is, quite the contrary, essential. But its appropriate use today is as the name for a school of philosophy. Praxics, on the other hand, is a laboratory science, inspired in large part by behaviorism, as well as by the theory of evolution and other advances in the biological sciences. The clear separation of praxics and behaviorism is critical for a number of reasons:

a) *No laboratory science, no matter what its origins, should be constrained by a philosophy.* "To set limits to speculation," said Whitehead, "is treason to the future." As I noted above, data generate limits to speculation, but it is one thing to have one's subject matter constrain one's theories and quite another to be constrained by philosophical dogma. The role that genes play in language acquisition, for example, is an empirical question. The old environmentalist assertion that genes play a trivial role goes beyond the facts currently available.

This is not to say that scientists do not make assumptions. On the contrary, science has always rested on a foundation of assumptions, and the assumptions, once tested, have often proved to be wrong (Burtt, 1954). Early in the century, for example, many physicists abandoned the assumption of determinism in favor of the assumption that the universe is probabilistic; the latter, more conservative assumption was, many said, an adequate basis for scientific progress (e.g., Eddington, 1928).

Perhaps all of the natural sciences were constrained in this way in their early stages, but the philosophical origins of a particular science are eventually forgotten by all but the historians. Modern chemistry, for example, has clear origins in ancient Greek philosophy (Hopkins, 1934); it is no accident that one of the alchemist's tools was the "philosopher's stone." But philosphical assertions that helped give rise to chemistry—for example, the notion that all things strive toward perfection—would seem bizarre or at least irrelevant to modern chemists. The distillation of science from philosophy has occurred even in psychology. For example, modern psychophysics is the offspring of Fechner's obsession with the mind-body problem; his early research was meant, once and for all, to *solve* that ancient problem (Fechner, 1860/1966). Although research of the sort Fechner conducted is still under way (e.g., Mansfield, 1976), the mind-body problem has played no part in it for nearly a century.

The future is clear: The science of behavior will go free of behaviorism.

b) *Behaviorism is truly an "ism," a system of interrelated assertions and beliefs, primarily about mind, free will, and feelings.* Praxists can (and do) study behavior no matter what their opinions are on these matters, just as physicists study the material world no matter what their opinions are of metaphysics (the physicists I know are dualists of the most extreme sort). And so it should be. It's hard to see how an individual's ability to discover orderly relationships between variables in the behavioral laboratory could be much affected by his or her views on the mind-body problem. *Yet—because of the confusion between behaviorism and praxics—people who have had doubts about behaviorism have kept away from behavioral laboratories or have stayed there uneasily. The behavioral researcher is perceived as a "disciple," a "believer," a "card-carrying member." The behavioral laboratories have surely lost talented researchers as a result, and the range and quality of its investigations have surely been restricted.* An individual with no particular philosophical bent, or with views that change radically from time to time, or even with views that are antithetical to behaviorism, is capable of making a positive contribution to the science. The laboratory doors should be open to all talented researchers, and the dualists currently therein should not feel guilty.

The fact is that you can be a praxist without being a behaviorist, and vice versa. In addition to the many mentalists in the behavioral laboratory, there are many individuals who are deeply religious. Some of the most prominent behavioral researchers in the country are regular churchgoers, and I know of one accomplished researcher who has more than a passing interest in Eastern mysticism. One can also be a behaviorist, of course, without ever entering the laboratory—Kantor was an example—and one might also, like Skinner, be both praxist and behaviorist.

c) *Behaviorism is unattractive to the American public, and because it has been so closely identified with the laboratory science, the science has suffered materially.* Praxics has produced profoundly important technologies that have aided millions of people—in pharmacology, medicine, child rearing, education, institutional management, therapy, the treatment of the mentally retarded, business, industry, and so on—but it has not received commensurate support and appreciation from the public. If it is presented to the public as a laboratory science which is independent of any "ism," the support may finally come.

The study of mind—in the hands of "cognitive science," an amalgam of psychologists, linguists, and computer scientists—has presented itself this way in recent years with profound effect. Skinner recently showed me a copy of the "Report of the Research Briefing Panel on Cognitive Science and Artificial Intelligence," one of several chapters in a new book published by the National Academy Press (Estes et al., 1983). The book was commissioned by the White House and the National Science Foundation to serve as a guide to funding agencies for funding in science. According to the preface, cognitive science was identified as one of a small number of scientific areas that "were likely to return the highest scientific dividends as a result of incremental federal investment...." It was placed on an equal footing with *mathematics, the atmospheric sciences, astronomy and astrophysics, agricultural research, neuroscience, human health effects of hazardous chemical exposure, materials science, chemistry, immunology, solid earth sciences,* and *computer science.*

The report could easily signal more money annually for cognitive scientists than the grand total of all awards to operant conditioners since the first conference in 1946. I know personally of more than forty million dollars in foundation funds that have gone to cognitive psychologists over the past few years. And with money goes prestige, laboratories, jobs, professorships, institutes, discoveries, applications (however ill-conceived), and so on. Support of this magnitude will leave its mark on psychology for many years.

Praxics is hardly worth promoting, of course, unless it is advancing as a science. It has advanced, and it is still advancing, although the number and range of topics that have been explored is disappointing, in large part, I am sure, because of the lack of resources. Drawing a clear distinction between praxics and behaviorism is likely to help.

PRAXICS AND PSYCHOLOGY

If praxics is to grow and flourish, it must strike out on its own. But rather than make a case at this point for its separation from psychology, I will attempt to recast the problem. To argue that the time for succession has come might imply to some that praxics belonged in psychology departments at some point in the past. *But it never belonged in psychology departments.* Psychologists and praxists have been locked in mortal combat for more than half a century, competing for scarce resources and debating about what the appropriate subject matter of psychology should be. *But the appropriate subject matter of psychology is mind, not behavior.*

A Historical Blunder

You are a geneticist. You make your way through the august halls of the Zoology Building, stop at the office of the Chair of the Department, and insist on speaking to her. You tell her that your discipline has a lot to contribute to zoology and that you want an office and laboratory space in her department. She is surprised, but intrigued by the force of your arguments. You tell her that problems of classification could be handled in a more sophisticated and objective way by genetic analysis and that, indeed, the proper *subject matter* of zoology is actually genetics. She is on her guard. You tell her that you insist on assuming the chairmanship of the Zoology Department immediately. She throws you out of her office.

This tale seems bizarre until you examine the history of American psychology during the first two decades of the twentieth century. For hundreds of years the subject matter of psychology had been mind. The term comes from the Greek "*psyche*" (ψῦχή), which means "breath." It came to mean "spirit" or "soul," the animating principle of life, since the absence of breath was a sign of the absence of life. In English we distinguish between "soul" and "mind," but the terms have often been used interchangeably, and in some languages, no clear distinction is made. In German, for example, the word *Seele* is used for both.

Early users of the term "psychology"—for example, Christian Wolff and David Hartley in the early 1700s—defined it as the study of mind, following a tradition of inquiry that had begun 1,400 years earlier with Aristotle's *Peri Psyches* (better known by the Latin title *De Anima*). Psychology had long been in the hands of philosophers only, but, over a period of several decades in the nineteenth century, the first psychology laboratories were established, and psychology emerged as a science (cf. Epstein, 1981b)—a science of mind. Fechner's vision of 1850, Wundt's laboratory in Leipzig, Ebbinghaus' classic experiments with nonsense syllables, Müller's experiments on attention—all were concerned with mind. The new "functional psychology" that Angell made popular in America during the first decade of the new century was a new approach to the study of *mind*.

Morgan's Canon—which the behaviorists later modified for their own uses—was a prescription for simplicity in theories of *mind* (Epstein, 1984f). The original *OED* gives only one definition of "psychology": *"The science of the nature, functions, and phenomena of the human soul or mind"* (italics added).

Then, in 1908, in walks William McDougall and, a few years later, John B. Watson. Like our psychotic geneticist, they demand nothing less than that the subject matter of psychology be changed.

Consider McDougall's cogent remarks on the subject in *The Battle of Behaviorism* (Watson & McDougall, 1928):

> I, rather than Dr. Watson, am the Arch-Behaviorist. Up to the end of the last century and beyond it, psychologists did in the main concentrate their attention upon the introspectively observable facts, unduly neglecting the facts of human action or behaviour, and ignoring the need for some adequate theory of behaviour and of character.... This neglect is implied in the definition of psychology commonly accepted at that time, namely, the "science of consciousness".... (p. 54)

McDougall proceeds with a discussion of the unsuccessful attempts of J. S. Mill and Charles Mercier to create "ethology" and "praxiology," respectively, and then writes:

> It was at this time that I was beginning to struggle with the fundamentals of psychology. And it seemed to me that both Mill and Mercier were in error; that what was needed was not a new science of behaviour under a new Greek name, *but rather a reform of psychology, consisting of greater attention to the facts of behaviour or conduct* [italics added].... I gave expression to this view in my first book [*Primer of Physiological Psychology*, 1905], by proposing to define psychology as the positive science of conduct. I further defended this definition and expounded the need of this reform in my *Introduction to Social Psychology* (1908). And in 1912 I published my little book entitled *Psychology, the Study of Behavior*. (pp. 57–58)

Watson (1913) continued this bizarre program even more aggressively than McDougall had. Not only should psychology adopt a new subject matter, he said, it should also completely abandon its traditional one:

> The time seems to have come when psychology must discard all reference to consciousness; when it need no longer delude itself into thinking that it is making mental states the object of observation. We have become so enmeshed in speculative questions concerning the elements of mind [and] the nature of conscious content ... that I, as an experimental student, feel that something is wrong with our premises.... I believe we can write a psychology, define it as [the science of behavior], and never go back upon our definition: never use the terms consciousness, mental states, mind, content, introspectively verifiable, imagery, and the like.... (pp. 163–165)

No doubt more than one department chairman was outraged by such claims, or, as Watson himself said, with atypical understatement, "It was only natural that ... criticisms should appear" (Watson, 1930, p. x). But, as Boring (1950) noted, Watson's "vigorous propaganda" (p. 641) was consistent with the prevailing *Zeitgeist* in two important respects: First, even in the 1913 paper,

The Case for Praxics

Watson promised practical applications for "the educator, the physician, the jurist and the businessman," and second, many psychologists were disillusioned with the progress psychology had made in the study of mind. "Psychology claimed to be science but it sounded like philosophy and a somewhat quarrelsome philosophy at that" (Boring, 1950, p. 642).[8]

In other words, if our geneticist had only been a little more persuasive and his timing a little better, he might have succeeded—for a time—in taking over the Zoology Department.

The Legitimacy of Psychology

The study of mind held its own during the three decades when behaviorism was a force to reckon with in psychology. With the advent of the computer and the adoption of the information processing metaphor by cognitive psychologists, the study of mind gained considerable prestige in the 1950s and 1960s. The marriage of cognitive psychology with linguistics and computer science has created further legitimacy—not only within the field, but among the public at large. The Freudians and their descendants are still active in the field, and even behavior therapists have become taken with the cognitive model. Moreover, if current trends in funding are any indication, the immediate future of the study of mind is assured.

I don't happen to find the assertion that mind is a legitimate subject matter compelling, but the vast majority of psychologists do—*even, I suspect, a majority of the members of the existing behavioristic organizations.* No matter what the referent of the term, most people seem to think it's worth studying. So be it. Let them study it! Give psychology to the psychologists!

The Legitimacy of Praxics

I ask the reader's indulgence while I overdramatize an incredibly simple point: *No one—no university administrator, no government official, no foundation director, no biologist, no psychologist, not even the hard-core cognitivist—would deny that the behavior of organisms is a legitimate subject matter.* Cognitivists have been hostile to behaviorists not because of any doubts about the legitimacy of the subject matter but because of the behavioristic polemic: "Mind is *verboten*, let us take over your field."

How tragic were the consequences of that historical blunder. The study of behavior was denied its place in the sun because Watson and others thought they could elbow their way into a field that was not theirs.

Arguments for Separation

Many have shared the dream of a science of behavior—Mill, Mercier, McDougall, Watson, Meyer, Weiss, Kuo, Hunter, Skinner, Schneirla, Hull, Tolman, Guthrie, Lashley, and so on. But only Skinner managed to found a school that has survived, and that school constitutes less than 3 percent of the membership of the American Psychological Association. The percentage, furthermore, has been declining in recent years.[9] Psychology, in short, has not been reformed, and, as I have argued above, it is probably unreformable.

There is an alternative to the reform movement, which, after all, was only one of the methods proposed for the establishment of a science of behavior. The other is the program suggested by Mill and Mercier so long ago—the establishment of an independent, biologically-based science: "a new science of behaviour under a new Greek name," as McDougall said. The first method hasn't worked. Let's try Plan B.

Establishing a science of behavior outside of the confines of psychology makes sense for a number of reasons:

a) Psychology, like behaviorism, has a terrible public image, largely deserved. The "charlatans and spirit-seekers" about whom Hunter warned are still with us, and the press is still wary.

b) "Psychology" is an inappropriate name for the study of behavior.

c) As I noted above, the concept of mind seems as compelling as ever to most people, and it may simply never go away. If someone believes that the earth is flat, you can point to evidence that it is not. But there is nothing you can point to to convince someone that he or she doesn't have a mind. In any case, it seems unlikely that psychology will be the discipline that debunks mind. A successful debunking can begin only with an effective formulation of the behavior of organisms, and that will be more likely to emerge from a thriving, well-funded, independent science of behavior than from psychology.

d) Seventy years of debate and struggle has resolved nothing. Further debate will only keep us from moving forward.[10]

e) They'll be glad to see us go.

f) A split will likely mean new resources. (A scene toward the end of *Walden Two* comes to mind.) As long as there are only so many offices and positions to go around in a psychology department, we will have trouble growing—indeed, we will have trouble surviving. When, someday, an administrator risks the creation of a department of praxics, the department will have only itself to blame if it does not flourish.

g) The establishment of an independent science of behavior will allow a realignment with the hard sciences, especially with the various branches of biology that are concerned with the controlling variables of behavior: evolutionary biology, ecology, ethology, physiology and anatomy, behavioral genetics, and so on. Biologists have largely ignored behavioral psychologists simply because behavioral psychologists are psychologists. We should attend to data and theories from *any* field—including economics, sociology, anthropology, psychology, and so on—that will help us advance our understanding of the subject matter, but our primary concern should probably be with biology.

h) There have been occasional attempts in biology to synthesize information from various disciplines—primarily psychology, anthropology, and various branches of biology—that have concerned themselves with the behavior of organisms; the effort is sometimes called "behavioral biology" (e.g., Konner, 1982).[11] "Sociobiology" (Wilson, 1975) is a well-known, although controversial, variant. The creation of departments of praxics could help bring about this synthesis. The possible benefits to society would be enormous.

What about the Battle?

"I am pigeon-livered," said Hamlet, "and lack gall/ To make oppression bitter." But proposing a split from psychology is not defeatism. The "battle of behaviorism" (King, 1930; Watson & McDougall, 1928) was to some extent won by the behaviorists long ago: Introspection lost its popularity early in the century and has remained suspect. A concern for objectivity in method and terminology has become part of the fabric of modern psychology, largely due to early behaviorism (Schultz, 1969). According to some, Watsonian behaviorism was so successful that it literally "conquered itself to death. It ... has become a truism. Virtually every American psychologist, whether he knows it or not, is nowadays a methodological behaviorist" (Bergmann, 1956, p. 270).

Watson was fighting many battles at once, and some were won. But the subject matter itself has never been secured. The concern with objectivity is now applied to the traditional—and appropriate—subject matter of psychology.

METHODS

This essay is a research proposal of sorts, and no such proposal is complete without a Methods section. Previous proposals for a science of behavior have neglected to include such a section, which may account for their fates. I offer a glimpse of activities that are under way toward the establishment of an independent science of behavior, as well as some pertinent historical data.

The Praxics Society

In 1983 Paul T. Andronis, T. V. Layng, and I founded an organization called The Praxics Society. Andronis, who earned his Ph.D. under Israel Goldiamond and who is currently doing post-doctoral work at the University of Chicago, serves as director. (In the Chicago area, I'm told, the term "praxics" has shown up on exams, which makes it official.) After nearly a year of correspondence and discussion among interested students and faculty members, twenty of the Society's members met in Nashville in May, 1984, during the meetings of the Association for Behavior Analysis. The membership consists—by design—mainly of young people, but a number of senior people in the field have been supportive of the concept.

Members of the Society hope to create a *Science*-like journal called, naturally, *Praxics*, which will publish original reports of advances in the several biologically-oriented fields that contribute to our understanding of the behavior of organisms. The Society is also planning a series of activities that will involve representatives from various disciplines concerned with behavior. These activities are meant to set the stage for the achievement of Society's primary goal: to bring about the first Department of Praxics. Is this hubris? How does one create—at least in name—a new field? Early psychologists no doubt asked precisely the same questions.

On the Creation of Departments

Modern academic psychology began as an area of specialization in philosophy departments. The first clear suggestions that psychology might have something in common with the natural sciences were made by Herbart early in the nineteenth century (e.g., Herbart, 1816, 1824–5). Kant had insisted that psychology could never be a natural science, but Herbart asserted that psychology could be advanced by using two of the techniques of the natural sciences—observation and mathematics. Experimentation, he thought, was not possible (after all, the subject matter was immaterial). His successor at Göttingen, Hermann Lotze, agreed that experimentation on mind was impossible, but he took the extraordinary step of applying physiological and medical data to psychological issues (e.g., Lotze, 1852), which helped make psychological experimentation inevitable. His students, along with Wundt, Fechner, and others, performed the first such experiments in the 1850s. A new field, substantively different from philosophy, had been created, but formal programs and departments to accommodate the new field did not immediately spring to life.

The first formal program in psychology was probably Wundt's *Institute* at Leipzig, which was founded in 1879—more that twenty years after he conducted his first psychology experiments. Some landmarks in the United States are also notable: The first graduate degree in psychology was awarded to G. Stanley Hall at Harvard in 1878, but it was awarded by the Department of Philosophy, and Hall's research was done in the laboratory of a physiologist. Hall founded the first psychology journal in America, the *American Journal of Psychology*, in 1887, and the first professional organization, the American Psychological Association, in 1892. The world's first chair in psychology was occupied by James McKeen Cattell in 1887 at the University of Pennsylvania, where Cattell established what was perhaps the first university-sanctioned psychology laboratory in the country the same year (less official laboratories had been established previously at Harvard and Johns Hopkins).

Still, these things take time. For decades many psychology programs in the United States were still part of philosophy departments. At Harvard, the first semblance of a psychology department did not appear until 1913, as the Department of Philosophy and Psychology, still under a bureaucratic entity called the "Division of Philosophy"; before that only a Social Ethics Department existed under that Division. It was not until 1934 that separate departments of psychology and philosophy were created—still under a larger entity called the "Division of Philosophy and Psychology." (Note that the *Divisions*, not the Departments, had the authority to grant Ph.D.s.) Psychology did not truly become a separate entity with the authority to grant its own Ph.Ds until 1939, when the Division system was changed.[12] Skinner himself received his Ph.D. in 1931 from the Department of Philosophy and Psychology, under the authority of the Division of Philosophy.[13]

In England some psychology departments were still part of philosophy departments in the 1950s. Harzem (1984) reported that he was part of the two-man team that planned the last such split in the United Kingdom—the creation of the Department of Psychology at the University of Wales, Bangor—in *1963*.

And in Greece, Spain, and other enlightened countries in Europe, psychology departments are still uncommon. As of this writing, the University of Chicago has no psychology department; specialists in experimental psychology are awarded degrees in biology.

The point, I hope, is clear: We all come to preexisting departments, structures, edifices, programs, and so on, which, in some cases, are literally cast in concrete. *But we must never take these divisions and labels for granted; they were created by people, they are not necessarily the best means for promoting either a science or a technology of behavior, and they can be changed.*

"Life is an experiment largely untried," said Thoreau, and praxics, I believe, is an experiment worth trying.

TOWARD A NEW FIELD

In the short time since The Praxics Society was founded, faculty members at three universities have expressed interest in establishing programs in praxics at their universities. That should not be surprising, since many senior faculty members in behavioral psychology have dreamed of such a field for decades, since many junior members are shell-shocked from the attacks of their cognitivist colleagues, and since many graduate students in behavioral psychology are looking forward to rewarding careers as computer programmers. No one doubts that the study of behavior is a legitimate enterprise. The question is simply how to bring such an enterprise fully to life.

Should established behavioral psychologists resign from the American Psychological Association and join the Society? By no means. The attempt to establish an independent science of behavior does not require an exodus from psychology. Many students of behavior are already invested in psychology, and, as usual, some will flourish. Praxics—if there is any merit in the idea—is for the young, for their futures. The Israelites had to wait in the desert for forty years before they could enter the Promised Land—although it was just over the next hill—until those among them who had been slaves had lived out their natural lives. Praxics can and probably should be established without the support and participation of people who have strong ties to psychology.

I can't think of a more fitting ending to this essay than Kuo's (1937) closing words, of which I have taken the liberty of altering only two:

When I discussed with my colleagues my program for [praxics], I was often told: "Your prospectus looks fine, but it will be beyond the possibility of actual accomplishment, and as long as your ideal cannot be fully realized, we will have to rely on those old psychological concepts for the explanation of behavior." I wish to ask my readers for more indulgence if I relate an ancient Chinese fable about an old farmer. The farmer was known among his neighbors by his nickname, "Mr. Fool." He lived in a house which was right behind a hill. Displeased by the obstruction in front of his house, he started to remove the hill. All his neighbors laughed at him most heartily and called him "Mr. Fool." But despite the laughter and ridicule, Mr. Fool carried on. Once he told his neighbors, "I believe we shall be able to remove this hill. If I cannot finish it in my lifetime, I will make my children, grand-children, and great-grand-children do it." When he died he stated in his will that he had buried all his fortune under the hill and the only way to get it out was to remove the entire hill. So generation after generation all his children worked feverishly on the hill. And in less than four generations, the old house had gained a clear view of the field. Perhaps this is a true story about some modern fools in science. Be it fact or fable, and fool or no fool, the [praxist] has planned to remove something much larger than a hill. (pp. 21–22)

Postscript. *The Praxics Society lasted only a few years. Some key members shifted their priorities to a business venture and others to family matters, and I continued to focus my energies on the development of the Cambridge Center for Behavioral Studies. Some Society members joined with others in forming a "behaviorology" organization, which, alas, appears to have retained close intellectual ties with behaviorism. The larger picture looked hopeful when, in 1988, political turmoil within the American Psychological Association led many experimental psychologists to form a new organization—the American Psychological Society. Early APS meetings were concerned with many of the issues raised in "The Case for Praxics": How do we create an independent, prestigious, well-funded science? How do we dissociate ourselves from "pop psych" and the "touchy-feely" enterprises? What should the new science be called? Unfortunately, the subject matter of APS's new science—finally dubbed "psychological science"—is still unclear, and the old battle lines remain. An independent, comprehensive, biologically-based science of behavior would seem to be a long way off. Perhaps, following Kuo's suggestion, a bequest is in order. In addition to the two brief papers that follow, the reader may want to examine Epstein (1985a, 1986d, 1987b, and 1987c), as well as Chapter 24 of this volume, for further elaboration.*

NOTES

1. In *Four Saints in Three Acts* Gertrude Stein provided the ideal rejoinder: "Pigeons in the grass, alas."
2. The English term "praxis" is also common, but it will not be discussed in this essay, since most of its applications have little or no relevance to the issues at hand.
3. A footnote in the Kuo (1937) paper promises a book on the subject, to be called "Principles of Praxiology," but I am aware of no such book. Roback (1937) attributes to Kuo a book published in Chinese in 1935, whose title is translated "The Scope of Praxiology."
4. Although several sources attribute the term "praxiology" to Knight Dunlap, none that I have read has provided relevant references, and I have been unable to find the term in his writings. And Mercier, of course, proposed the term "praxiology" as a name for the study of behavior several years before Watson presented his seminal paper on behaviorism.
5. A photograph of those who attended this first meeting appears on page 456 of Volume 5 (1962) of the *Journal of the Experimental Analysis of Behavior.*
6. Peters (1962), in the revision of *Brett's History of Psychology,* argues that sciences—and psychology in particular—are not definable by their subject matters. "No

doubt," he adds, "there is a quite usual and harmless sense of the term 'subject-matter' in which, in any account of scientific method, petrologists, ornithologists, and astronomers can be said to have different subject matters.... [But what] we call psychology is just an amalgam of different questions about human beings [what about other animals?] which have grown out of a variety of traditions of enquiry" (p. 27). I submit that in this case the historical perspective is misleading. True, chaotic and diverse events may have preceded the formalization of a scientific domain, but once formalized it virtually always has a clearly delimited subject matter, specified by its name. For the purposes of this essay, I am content to use the term "subject-matter" in that "quite usual and harmless sense" that allows us to say that the subject matter of petrology is rocks, the subject matter of ornithology is rooks, and the subject matter of psychology is either mind or behavior.

7. He adopted a more sophisticated view of thought in his later works. See Watson (1930) and Watson and McDougall (1928).

8. Boring never gave an inch, however, to behaviorism. In his preface to the 1929 edition of *A History of Experimental Psychology*, which was reprinted in the 1950 edition, he wrote, "Naturally the words 'experimental psychology' must mean, in my title, what they meant to Wundt and what they meant to nearly all psychologists for fifty or sixty years—that is to say, the psychology of the generalized, human, normal, adult mind, as revealed in the psychological laboratory" (p. x).

9. These statements are based on ratios of recent membership figures of Division 25 of the American Psychological Association, which is devoted to the experimental analysis of behavior, to membership figures of the Association as a whole.

10. Pennypacker (1984) made the point more dramatically: "Never try to teach a pig to sing. It wastes your time, and it only annoys the pig."

11. A good source of work in this area is the journal *Behavioral and Neural Biology*, which was founded in 1968 as *Communications in Behavioral Biology* and subsequently called simply *Behavioral Biology*.

12. This information comes from volumes of the *Harvard University Catalogue* dated from 1912 to 1940.

13. Skinner's dissertation, which is dated December 19, 1930, reads "A Thesis Presented in Partial Fulfillment of the Requirements for the Degree of Doctor of Philosophy in the Department of Psychology of Harvard University," but the Department of Psychology was not formed until 1934. E. B. Newman (personal communication, June, 1984) has suggested that Boring, Skinner's advisor, may have been acting as if a Department of Psychology existed years before the fact. It is notable that Boring became the Department's first chairman.

19

WHY THE DEVOTION TO BEHAVIORISM?

Summary. When a movement fails, its constituents often retrench and change its focus. Such was the fate of early behaviorism, which was transformed from a movement to reform psychology into a greatly elaborated "school of philosophy"—the theodicy, in effect, of the failed movement.

Recent commentaries on the proposal to create a new field called "praxics" (Leigland, 1985; Malagodi & Branch, 1985) made me remember something. In recent papers I have argued, as others have before me, that we should establish a new science of behavior under a new Greek name. The science, I have claimed, must and indeed will break free of the ism that helped to inspire it. It must also separate from psychology, which is the study of mind, and align itself more closely with kindred natural sciences.

But Branch, Leigland, and Malagodi were not entirely persuaded, especially by the distinction I have drawn between praxics and behaviorism. Behaviorism, or at least radical behaviorism, they said, is *vital* to the study of behavior.

Why the devotion to the ism? (Isms, of course, inspire devotion, and that is part of the problem.)

MOVEMENTS

At first glance, behaviorism, whatever the flavor, would appear to be nothing more than an old and rather desiccated movement for reform in psychology. Certainly, that is the way most outsiders view it. For many years it was little more than a whipping boy; now many prominent psychologists just ignore it. The mission of behaviorism was to replace psychology's traditional and etymological subject matter with a new one. Etymology prevailed.

But the behaviorism to which Branch et al. referred is clearly something more than a desiccated movement. *The movement failed and, in failing, it became something else.*

Here is what I remembered: Reform movements seldom succeed, and they also seldom fail. They seldom succeed because it is difficult to transform any established enterprise, religious or scientific, from within. What looks like transformation often isn't. *Plus ça change, plus c'est la même chose.*

Reform movements also seldom fail because, if there is any merit to the mission of reform, the mission comes to take its own life; it evolves and often assumes a new identity. Martin Luther was distraught at the lack of piety he saw in Rome in 1510, but he did not set about to establish a new Church. Rather, he tried to reform Catholicism from within. He worked his way up the Church hierarchy, protesting with increasing vehemence various practices that he viewed as corrupt. In response to strong criticism, he elaborated his views and extended them to other areas. Finally in 1521, after he challenged papal authority, he was excommunicated. With this new credential, Luther continued to elaborate and expound his views, and, to make a long story short, there are now more than 70 million Lutherans worldwide. So much for the reform of Catholicism.

ELABORATION

Early behaviorists also tried to reform something that did not want reforming. Psychology did not immediately yield its offices, laboratories, journal pages, professorships, students, organizations, and honors to the intruders. The behaviorists had to fight for every inch of territory they gained, the gains were often small, and strongholds, such as they were, were often lost (consider the rise and fall of the experimental analysis of behavior at Columbia University or Arizona State University, or the death of the Learning Center at Northeastern University, or, more recently, the demise of the Behavior Therapy Unit at Temple University).

When a mission is failing, its leaders elaborate. Apparently, Watson hadn't explained the mission clearly enough, so Watson himself and then Skinner and others defended it, corrected it, expanded it, and repeated it. Repetition, after all, is the mother of wisdom. From some rather naive and unsophisticated assertions, a full blown philosophy of science (Skinner, 1974; Zuriff, 1985) emerged: Behavior is a legitimate and important subject matter *because*.... Feelings are unimportant *because*.... The study of mind is forbidden *because*.... Cognitive psychology is an unimportant enterprise *because*.... Cognitive science is objectionable *because*....

In short, contemporary behaviorism is the rationale, greatly elaborated from the original, for why praxists deserve office space in psychology departments. Had we been given the resources we wanted in the first place—had psychology yielded its subject matter and resources—we would never have bothered to elaborate the rationale. We would have advanced the science and left its philosophical elaboration to the philosophers of science. Students of behavior have been devoted to the ism because it has long served as their theodicy, their *raison d'être*, and their hope for the future.

Behaviorism is not a scientific theory, not by a long shot, contrary to the assertion of Malagodi and Branch (1985). Relativity theory, the theory of plate tectonics, quantum theory, unified field theory, and, to a lesser extent, evolutionary theory, are all predictive, formal, and testable. They were inspired by a wealth of data and are constrained by data in their every aspect. Behaviorism, however, is a *philosophy of science*, as Skinner (1974) states so clearly. Behavioristic assertions guide research only as philosophical assertions guide research—by directing interest toward one variable or another or one topic or another. Behavioristic assertions are not data based and are not *tested* by research.

SCOPE

Two minor points regarding the scope of praxics were misunderstood in both commentaries:

First, although it seems obvious to me that praxics laboratories must and will be opened to nonbehaviorists, I do not believe that theories of behavior should (or ever will) become mentalistic. I say this not on doctrinal grounds but simply because mentalistic theories are not very powerful, useful, or effective theories of behavior. You can believe in mind, feelings, or, for that matter, the Holy Ghost, and still do a damned good job of discovering how behavior varies as a function of genes, nutrition, sleep deprivation, operant and classical conditioning, instructions, modeling, physiology, anatomy, neural and chemical interventions, and so on. Most physicists believe in mind, but they have refrained from attributing the actions of subatomic particles to mental forces—*because more effective accounts are possible.*

Malagodi and Branch fail to understand that psychology is concerned with mentalistic theories *not because of any concern with behavior but because of a concern with mind qua mind.* We must face the fact that there are people out there who have a genuine scientific interest in *mind* and who observe behavior only to get insights into *mind*. And we must face the fact that the time has come for us to leave them alone. We have work of our own to do.

Finally, "praxics" is not a new name for the experimental analysis of behavior. It is a name for *the study of behavior*. No methodology or *Weltanschauung* is implied.

20

FINAL COMMENTS ON PRAXICS

Summary. Continuing to debate about the merits of a proposal to establish a new science of behavior is not productive. Those who see the need for the new science can help establish it through a variety of professional activities.

Academic debates are, understandably, much like faculty meetings. They are pointless, interminable, and exasperating. We half-listen and half-read. Other people's papers set the occasion for monologues. We accuse our colleagues of misunderstanding and then misunderstand in turn. Scholars are, it would seem, essentially autistic.

Consider the debate about praxics. In 1984, in a paper called "The Case for Praxics" (hereafter, simply "Case"), I proposed the creation of an independent, comprehensive science of behavior, and I offered the term "praxics" as a name for the new science. I also offered a laundry list of reasons for distinguishing between praxics and behaviorism, which is a school of philosophy, and I offered another list of reasons for allowing praxics (the study of behavior) and psychology (the study of mind) to go their separate ways. I reviewed several earlier proposals along these lines; a forceful proposal by Kuo (1937), entitled "Prolegomena to Praxiology," was especially insightful. Finally, I documented a century of unsuccessful attempts to name a science of behavior.

Here are some of the criticisms that have been leveled against the "Case" paper, along with my comments (I claim the right of reciprocal autism):

The science of behavior, or at least "behavior analysis," is in good shape. A paper by Deitz (1986) asserts that those who fear for the health of the field have presented "no data" (p. 66), and indeed a paper by Wyatt, Hawkins, and Davis (1986) reports that "behaviorism" is a "vital, growing area of behavioral science" (p. 103). But it is the Deitz paper that contains no data (it also has no references), and the Wyatt et al. figures are misleading. Wyatt et al. note, for example, that in 1984 the Association for Behavior Analysis (ABA) had a membership of 1,946. But, according to the ABA membership office in Michigan (personal communication, January 29, 1987), the current membership of ABA is 892; the figure is inflated briefly at each annual meeting only because it is cheaper to register and join than it is to register without joining. The 1986 post-meeting peak was 1,852, 94 below the 1984 figure.

Other facts are also disturbing. "Case" spoke about funding patterns, for example, which show modern psychology to be wholly dominated by the study of mind. And for some years I have been tabulating job listings in the *APA Monitor*, which are good indicators of the composition of future psychology departments. The September 1985 listings have been typical for nearly a decade: 19 entry-level, tenure-track jobs in cognitive psychology are listed, many at prestigious schools, including Yale, Stanford, Johns Hopkins, Cornell, and Harvard; no such listings appear in animal learning, behavior analysis, or any related area. In preparing this article, I did a quick count on the December 1986 issue: *Fifty-five* entry-level professorships include the words "cognitive" or "cognition" in their descriptions.

Finally, in "Case" I noted that behavior analysts (members of Division 25) comprised less than 3 percent of the membership of the American Psychological Association; according to the 1986 *APA Membership Register*, that figure is now well below 2 percent.

But whether or not behavior analysis is flourishing (it isn't) is beside the point. I have not called for the growth of behavior analysis, but rather for the creation of *an independent, multidisciplinary, biologically-based science of behavior*. The misguided efforts of William McDougall and John B. Watson have kept us on the wrong track for more than half a century; no true science of behavior has emerged. We are wont to say that behavior is "multiply determined," but we study only a trivial assortment of variables, and our clinical impact remains small (Lindsley, 1985). Those of you who work in clinical environments (I have done so part-time for the last three years) know the agony of our ineffectiveness. We do not cure; we "modify," trivially. For patients who have suffered a brain injury, or who have endured long-term substance abuse, or who are clinically depressed, or who are "retarded," or "autistic," or "schizophrenic," we can do virtually nothing—or at least nothing that lasts.

A true science of behavior must be *multidisciplinary* (not "interdisciplinary," as Ator [1986] suggests), because behavior is a complex subject matter that requires the *joint efforts* of individuals in many specialties, both to advance our understanding and to devise effective treatments. Behavior is affected profoundly by nutrition, physiology, sleep deprivation (if I had had more than 3 hours of sleep last night, what would I be writing now?), sexual deprivation and trauma (no comment), chemical interventions, social phenomena, surgical interventions, physical trauma, anatomical variables, organic disease, hormonal cycles, air temperature, humidity, illumination, air-borne chemicals, radiation, electrical stimulation, genes—and, of course, learning history. It is not folly to think that individuals with different specialties can be brought together to build a new science; it is folly to think that the handful of scientists who now study behavior in almost complete isolation from each other in a dozen different disciplines can advance our understanding significantly.

Last year I gave a talk called "Praxics in the Year 2000" (Epstein, 1986c); I suppose we'd have to dub it science fiction at this point. I described a large, diverse, university department (not unlike the physics departments I was exposed to in my undergraduate days) that was devoted to the scientific understanding of many aspects of behavior. Faculty meetings were still exasperating, but at least no one had any doubts about the identity of the subject matter of the science. All aspects of the science were quantitative and formal, as is typical in all natural sciences. Methods and instrumentation were as diverse as the specialties. A glassy-eyed theoretician labored to synthesize information from different specialties, keeping one glassy eye on Stockholm. As is true in all mature sciences, department members had widely differing religions, philosophies, credos, ethics, morals, and politics; the differences kept certain people from becoming friends but not from advancing an understanding of their subject matter.[1] Advances in the basic science stimulated the development of new and effective technologies; with new team-treatment approaches to severe behavior disorders, even schizophrenia seemed to be giving way. The prestige of pure science, driving real and promised applications—and uncluttered by an irrelevant and unattractive credo—secured large-scale funding commensurate with that of other important sciences.

We have wasted our time trying to wrest psyche-ology buildings away from psyche-ologists. Behavior is an important subject matter in its own right—and it deserves and can have its own buildings. I grieve when senior members of our field (including Skinner [e.g., 1986b]) urge students to continue fighting Watson's old Battle. Yes, certain *individuals* have managed, now and then, after the second or third ulcer, to make their way in psychology, but the *study of behavior* has not flourished, and it has remained hopelessly isolated from the natural sciences.

I have never advocated that individuals who already have a stake in psychology should abandon their careers; toward the end of "Case" I even suggest that such individuals have no place in the new science. I encourage Deitz (1986) to continue to support the "valuable goals" of the behavior analysts of the APA, for the goals are indeed valuable. I applaud Staats (1986) for his continuing efforts to reinterpret psychological concepts in behavioral terms.[2] I suggest, however, that both Staats and Deitz would find more funding, more resources, more space, more students, more colleagues, more stimulation, and more sympathy in a Department of Praxics than in a Department of Psychology. (Alas, only the latter exists at the moment.)

"Praxics" is an "awful" name, according to Deitz (1986), and so is "behaviorology," a name for behavior analysis which both Comunidad Los Horcones (1986) and Fraley and Vargas (1986) seem to claim (it seems safe to say that the term was considered and rejected by others a half century ago). Barry (1986) thinks "praxics" is "simply awkward and limiting in scope" (how is it limiting?), and Gaydos (1986) objects to "praxics" because it is a near-homologue of "praxis," which, he says, "has such a long history of divergent uses that its presence as the root of 'praxics' may be 'praxics' [sic] undoing" (p. 229).

But beauty is in the eye of the beholder (say "statistics" three times quickly), and near-homologues and even homologues do not undo each other, except perhaps among young children. "Astrology" does not undo "astronomy," "english" (a spinning motion given to a ball) does not undo "English," "scientologist" does not undo "scientist" (fortunately), and "physic" (a medicine used to induce vomiting) does not undo "physics." I was well aware of a variety of modern usages of "praxis" when I wrote "Case"; they are, I believe, of no consequence.[3]

"Repetition," a professor of mine used to say (whenever he lost his place in his lecture notes), "is the mother of wisdom." So let me repeat a point I have made repeatedly: "Praxics" is not a name for the experimental analysis of behavior or behavior analysis; it is a name for *the study of behavior*. "No methodology or *Weltanschauung* is implied" (Epstein, 1985c, p. 271).

Finally, I have no strong attachment to the word "praxics" per se, but rather I believe there is a pressing need for the new science, and I believe further that the new science needs a name. I have been working with A. Deen, a Harvard student, on a paper we call "Five Hundred Names for the Science of Behavior." We have researched more than 30 languages and consulted with many distinguished linguists to find suitable names; a computer program has multiplied our efforts almost to the point of absurdity. By the time we are ready to submit the paper for publication we hope to have enough names to cover every last member of the Association for Behavior Analysis, and therefore everybody can be happy.

Praxics needs to drag along an ism with it, assert Fraley and Vargas (1986). Similar arguments were made in papers by Leigland (1985) and Malagodi and Branch (1985). I cannot, in the short space allowed me here, do justice to my position on this matter; I stand by the original critique of isms I made in "Case," as well as by my response to Leigland, Malagodi, and Branch (Epstein, 1985c), and I urge the concerned reader to consult these papers.

One of the people who first got me thinking about the need for a new science was Fred S. Keller. As I noted in "Case," Keller has gently asserted the need for a new science for many years, and he has offered "praxiology," a term he heard in 1928, as a name for the science. In a talk in 1984, Keller commented that the only thing that remains to be done for the science of behavior is to "eliminate the ism," and he is right.[4] Behavioral genetics, ethology, behavioral neurology, and behavioral pharmacology are unfettered by formal isms; "behavior analysis" should be similarly unencumbered, and a new, comprehensive, multidisciplinary science must be pure, unencumbered science. Let the philosophers philosophize. And let's make sure we give them something important to write about.

MY NEW YEAR'S RESOLUTIONS

I will now embarrass myself by sharing with you some recent New Year's resolutions. Please don't hold me to them; that will only make me nervous, and then I will surely break them.

1) *After I submit this paper, I will not participate in the debate about praxics any further*. Rather,

2a) *I will continue to try to help bring about the creation of a comprehensive science of behavior:* by organizing and helping others to organize projects that promote such a science; by contributing time, money, and resources to such projects; and by speaking positively, especially to students, about the merits of the concept.

2b) *Until a better term emerges, I will continue, frequently, to call the new science "praxics," following the ancient dictum "use it or lose it."* (I squeeze the term into almost everything I write, and I even slipped "praxist" into *Nature* in 1984 [Epstein, 1984b].)

3) *I will continue to support the growth of the Cambridge Center for Behavioral Studies*, an advanced studies institute and library devoted to "advancing the study of behavior and its application in the solution of practical problems and the prevention and relief of human suffering." By providing new resources, visibility, and funding for the many scholars, scientists, and practitioners who are concerned with the study of behavior and behavior change, the Center will, I believe, help set the stage for the development of a comprehensive science.

4) *I will continue, through research, to try to advance the scientific understanding of behavior*, and I will make greater use of formal and quantitative methods than I have in the past.

Half my age ago, I sat under a palm tree reading with rapture a skinny little book by a woman (also skinny) who claimed that the methods of science had been applied with some success to the study of behavior and that new, humane technologies of behavior change were emerging.[5] The world was certainly in trouble, and I had long dreamed, as we all do, of a world free of the threat of nuclear war, free of hunger, free of pollution, and free of needless suffering. Science, it seemed to me, was our only hope for realizing such a dream, and I eventually decided to devote 10 years of my life toward furthering that realization. My 10 years were up a few weeks ago, but I have decided to carry on. If you would like to help, drop me a line.

NOTES

1. Fraley and Vargas (1986) assert that praxics "sounds more like a movement for a political party than a scientific discipline" (p. 56), but, curiously, it is they who insist that analysts of behavior must be card-carrying believers in an ism ("radical behaviorism"), and it is they who would continue to limit the study of behavior to the narrow range of variables and methods typical of the operant approach.

2. Staats (1986) is incorrect in his assertion that praxics "as...movement may be considered to be in the tradition of the separatism of the disunified science" (p. 233). Quite the contrary. Praxics is an attempt to unify many isolated scientific approaches to the study of behavior. An effective understanding of behavior can never be reached without a multidisciplinary effort; praxics is the personification of such an effort, and Staats offers no comparable alternatives.

3. The Gaydos (1986) paper also included a rather unkind comment: "The example set by Skinner's careful choice of a name befitting an analysis of language does not appear to have been followed in the choice of the term 'praxics'" (p. 230). But I spent more than two years investigating and considering various names before proposing "praxics," and "Case" included more than 80 references to relevant sources. Since proposing "praxics," I have spent an additional two years systematically generating hundreds of

alternatives. As of this writing, "praxics" is still the frontrunner, although some intriguing competitors have emerged.

4. Keller's (1986) cogent remarks about the Association for Behavior Analysis are also pertinent here.

5. The book was entitled *The Analysis of Human Operant Behavior*, and its author, Ellen P. Reese, recently served as President of the Association for Behavior Analysis.

PART V

B. F. SKINNER

21

OUR MOST UNFORGETTABLE CHARACTER

Author's note. M. J. Willard and I wrote the following essay for B. F. Skinner as a Christmas present in 1977, and we published it a few years later. It describes events that took place from 1975 to 1977, when M. J. and I were in our 20s and Skinner was in his 70s.

Sitting in a genuine Harvard insignia chair on the seventh floor of William James Hall, I was nervously doing Jacobson relaxation exercises. Thirty feet down the hall people sporadically exited from the elevator. Each time the door opened I got cramps in my stomach and had second thoughts about taking dares. I was waiting in ambush for my behavior-modifying idol, B. F. Skinner.

Two days earlier I had been telling my old friend Chip about a fantasy I'd had every since coming to Boston. Walking through Harvard Square one day, I'd bump into "B. F." I'd introduce myself and ask him to tea (I'd heard he liked tea). He'd accept, of course, and we'd get on marvelously well.

"That's a great idea," Chip told me.

"What do you mean?"

"I mean do it," he said. "Only you're never going to bump into him. Go knock on Skinner's door and ask him to lunch."

"Yeah, sure."

"*Really*, M. J.—" he said seriously, "if you don't do it, your *Chicken*."

Not with 10 milligrams of Valium in me, I wasn't. (You can't always count on relaxation exercises.)

There he was. Smaller than I had expected, almost fragile. His maroon sports jacket didn't match his checkered pants. He didn't exactly look like a "great man." But his face matched the one on the back cover of *Beyond Freedom and Dignity*.

"Excuse me, Dr. Skinner," I managed to say. "My name is M. J., and I just always wanted to meet you."

I offered my hand, preparing for a quick shake and good-bye if he seemed annoyed. He took a long look (later I realized it was because his eyesight wasn't very good) and said mildly, "Well, why don't you come in and meet me?"

He asked a few questions about me and seemed pleased I was a graduate student at Boston University. "They're mostly anti-Skinnerian around here," he confided. So we talked—or rather he talked. I just nodded my head and beamed a lot. Perhaps a half hour had gone by when he started and looked at his clock. I apologized for keeping him from his work, but he didn't seem to mind and said, "I just can't resist people who like me."

I really did like him and found myself saying, "Ah, Dr. Skinner—could you ever use any volunteer help? Someone to run errands, clean pigeon cages?"

"Well," he said, looking pleased, "I probably could use some help around here." "Around here" was the immediate office, which, I now noticed, was less than elegant and not very neat. I remembered a scene from Skinner's novel, *Walden Two:*

> Frazier opened a door and waved me in. The room was in confusion. The bed was not only unmade, it looked as if it had not been made for weeks. The top of the desk was littered with books and papers, opened and unopened letters, pencils, a screw driver, a slide rule, and two empty glasses with traces of colored liquid in the bottoms.... On the floor near the window stood a large flower pot in which an unidentifiable plant had long since died of thirst.
>
> Frazier took a pair of soiled pajamas from a small straight chair and urged me to sit down.
>
> "In Walden Two," he said, as he dropped into an ancient swivel chair at his desk, "a man's room is his castle."

I wondered what other characteristics Skinner and Frazier shared. We shook hands good-bye, and he told me that I had just made his day. He didn't know it, but he had just made my year.

My last job had been as a research assistant to a frenzied, overworked professor. When I started working for Skinner, it was weeks before I became accustomed to his mellow working style—and to calling him "Fred," which he insisted was appropriate. He typically arrived at the office by 9 a.m. after having walked the two miles from his home. He spent mornings researching his autobiography, dictating letters, and reading papers.

Nothing was ever so pressing that mid-morning tea was skipped. Conversations over the half-hour break ranged from how my relationship with my boyfriend was going to his views on death or the phylogeny and ontogeny of behavior. I was a receptive audience for his endless stories, and he was part of my continuing-education series. We took turns washing up.

Although the typical morning was a quiet one, Fred, being a sort of tourist attraction, got a fair share of visitors—all kinds. There was, for example, the student from Boston University whose homework assignment had been to photograph an important person. Fred got into the spirit of the project, striding around the room and striking poses. "Here, take one of my haranguing the public. How about the scholarly routine at the desk? Want to see my Mona Lisa look."

An occasional psychotic would drop in. My favorite was "God," a young man who hoped to gain Fred's support in his campaign for the presidency. He was so articulate and his movements so elegant that Fred sat entranced for half an hour listening to his plans for the American people. After he'd left, Fred commented, "He was very good, wasn't he? Remind you of anyone you know?" I was stumped and told him so. Surprised, Fred exclaimed, "Me! Who else do you know who has such grandiose plans for mankind?"

I had been working for Fred a year and a half when he walked in one December morning and announced, "M. J., you have a rival—a very nice young man. He wants to come work for me full-time this summer. He doesn't want any pay—just wants to associate with the great man."

"Sounds like a weirdo to me."

"Not at all," Fred said. "I talked with him a little yesterday. He seemed very bright."

"What made you think so?"

"He quoted me a lot."

"Ugh."

"Well, he's coming over for tea this morning. Check him out and see what you think."

I pictured myself one-and-a-half years earlier and was prepared to meet a nervous, earnest young Skinnerian. I was not prepared to meet Robert Epstein.

Robert arrived promptly at 10. My first impression was that he was young looking for a graduate student. His slight frame and thick-lensed glasses completed the mental image I'd always had of Tom Swift, boy inventor.

The tea ritual had barely begun when the phone rang. As usual, Fred answered it, and after a minute turned to me.

"M. J., go see if *Contingencies* was ever published in paperback. This man wants a copy, and I don't want to send him a hardback."

"Excuse me, Professor Skinner." (This from Robert.) "But *Contingencies of Reinforcement* came out in paperback in 1971. It's still in print, and the price just went up a few months ago to $7.95."

Impressed, I sat back down.

Fred finished the phone conversation and turned back to us. Robert was examining a model of a teaching machine on the desk, and Fred began to talk about it. He said that he had put years of work into developing programmed instruction but had never made any money from it.

"But don't any of those patents you have bring in anything?" Robert asked.

"Oh, yes, I do have two or three patents, but they've never really earned anything."

"Excuse me, Professor Skinner," said Robert, "but you have *nine* patents."

"No, I have two or three."

"I have xerox copies of nine, Professor Skinner." "Oh." Pause. "I guess I have nine." Fred changed the subject. "By the way, Robert, did you get a chance to look at the bibliography I gave you—the one listing my publications?" (Fred's secretary and I had worked for weeks helping him compile it.)

"Yes, I have it right here," Robert said as he pulled it from his briefcase. "I'm afraid there are 62 errors in it."

Fred looked startled. I giggled.

Later, Fred showed Robert around the lab, and they talked about projects they might tackle. Finally, after a tentative date was set for him to begin work,

Robert left. As the door closed behind him Fred turned to me with a note of fervor in his voice.

"I don't care how much he knows, M. J. He'll never take your place."

"I'm not worried, Fred. I don't think it's *my* job he's after."

* * *

Did you have to pick on my glasses, M. J.? Is nothing sacred?

I see Skinner as a man who loves to learn—and not just about psychology. He subscribes to more than 20 literary and scholarly periodicals and keeps up with all of them. He saves tidbits that interest him, which easily keeps both his home and school offices overflowing with unfiled scraps. Sometimes he passes something along to me, and I've come to look forward to his choices. A recent one that caught his eye was an Ann Landers squib about a cat that found its way home from 400 miles away. "The explanation?" it said. "Instinct." Skinner was amused. He underlined the word "Instinct" in red.

The breadth of Skinner's interests is evident in his writing. I've been editing the notebooks he has kept for the past 25 years. He has recorded many ideas for experiments and theoretical papers in the notebooks (he keeps a tape recorder by his bed—"never can tell when inspiration strikes"), but at least half of the notes are non-scientific. There are character sketches, comments on books (*The Rise of the West*, *Le Neveu de Rameau*, *Antic Hay*, and so on), films (*Pather Panchali*, *The Glass Bottomed Boat*), music (especially Wagner), sex, politics, religion, and just about everything else.

Somehow, he never seems to forget this great wealth of material. At teatime, I often talk about whichever book I've been reading over my breakfast cereal. He manages to speak about the details of a piece I've just read with more assurance than I can—as though someone had warned him the night before what the morning's topic would be and he had checked his *Cliff Notes*. A few days ago, I finished reading Kingsley Amis' *Lucky Jim*, a book Skinner recommended. At the moment, I'm trying, unsuccessfully, to remember the name of the tottering, absentminded professor Jim tried so hard to please. Skinner will know.

Just as he fantasized in *Walden Two*, he now firmly believes that one can be *really* productive and creative only a few hours a day, so he spends only a few hours each day at hard work. I've told him that he wastes too much of his time. I entered his office one morning to find him slowly and steadily punching holes in a large stack of papers. He had just bought a new Heavy-Duty-Three-Hole-Puncher and was trying it out on just about everything in sight. He would take a small stack, punch the holes, and then pass the stack to M. J., who put it into a notebook. And then he'd do the same with another small stack. They saw my dismay and smiled at me as they continued to "work." After a while M. J. winked, and I went back across the hall to the lab. (Skinner has accused me of having "a cruel superego." "But it's the *contingencies*," I tell him. "Look at the *contingencies*.")

He called me up one Saturday morning a little before 9 (it amused him that I was still in bed) and invited me to come to his house to build a device for our rat chamber. He worked—and kept me working—quickly and efficiently all morning. He improvised a clever gadget from an old chocolates tin, two spools of thread, and a slice of adding machine cover, among other things. The tin was turned slowly by a motor, and after the basic pieces were in place, he insisted that he plug it in. I objected. "It's not finished. Why turn it on?" He paused, his face brightened, and he replied, "Why, to see it *go*, of course!"

He is equally enthusiastic about most tasks he tackles. At times I have been jealous of his zeal. I "lucubrate"—that it, I sort of hover over my desk in the wee hours and hope for the best. But Fred just sails through a day. He rises at 4:30 a.m., writes intensively for several hours, arrives at Harvard at 9 a.m. in high spirits, works on odds and ends and answers correspondence until lunchtime, and spends the rest of the day relaxing or doing light, work-related tasks. He's in bed by 9. He bubbles with suggestions for experiments and projects nearly every day. After one such suggestion I generously said, "That's a *great* idea!" He beamed. "You see?" he said. "There's good stuff in me yet!"

His sprightly manner often has a disarming effect on the people around him. Even his staunchest critics (or at least those who've met him) admit that he's charming. His last secretary was a doctoral candidate at Boston University. She did "that other" sort of therapy—no, not Freudian, but not behavioral, either. She was so impressed with Skinner's work habits and zest that she actually had second thoughts about behaviorism.

She told me once that she was concerned about the fact that Skinner never criticized her poor typing. I explained, to her amazement, that he's generally opposed to the use of criticism and punishment. I've seen him go out of his way to feign ignorance rather than correct people's mistakes. We've argued about this. He insists, stubbornly, on using positive reinforcement, no matter what the cost. But to do that, to refrain from simply giving instructions or trying to suppress unwanted behavior, means you must wait for some "right" behavior to occur. And that might take a long time to happen. An adventuresome young man I know made a habit of entering Skinner's office without knocking or otherwise announcing himself. This happened every day for about four months. Finally—it was on a Tuesday, I think—he knocked loudly on Skinner's door and announced, "Good morning! I thought I'd let you know I was here today!" Skinner swung around in his chair and said cheerfully, "Oh, hello! And *thanks* for knocking. I *like* it when people do that."

He tenaciously claims that *waiting* for the right behavior to occur is the best way to maintain a warm relationship. But how absurd it was to wait four months for me to knock on a door! How absolutely absurd![1]

Is it his science that has made him so strange? Perhaps, but even more perplexing are the ways the science hasn't affected him. It can be frustrating talking to an ardent behaviorist, even under the most casual circumstances. At a cocktail party once I began a sentence "The way to use the word...." That evoked a glower and a correction from a nearby behaviorist. "You don't *use* words," I was told. "You *say* them." I came to Skinner prepared to speak behaviorese—to "covert" (rather than think), to have "faulty recollections" (rather than a bad memory), and to say "I've no answer" or "No answer occurs to me" (instead of "I don't know")—and all for nothing. He just *doesn't do it*. He is comfortable speaking plain English, and he makes his listeners comfortable in doing so. One forgets in casual conversation that he is the quintessential behaviorist. He can snap back to the jargon, of course—his notebooks are filled with it—but he doesn't burden everyday listeners with that particular skill.

In a conversation with him a few weeks ago, he protested when I slipped and referred to him at one point as "Skinner." To cover my tracks, I insisted that he was a "great man" and that we refer to such people by their last names. He paused a moment, smiled, and said, "Well, let's see.... There's Darwin, Copernicus, Galileo...." Another pause.

"Skinner? ... Why not!"

NOTE

1. Truth is, I used to sit down immediately to his right and wait. His peripheral vision was so poor that it would often take him several minutes to notice me—at which point he would wince and jump slightly. To Fred's credit, he never showed the slightest sign of anger over my peculiar routine. By the way, getting Fred Skinner to jump every morning for four months pretty much exhausted my sadistic tendencies.

22

BEHAVIORIST AT FIFTY

Author's note. The following poem was read at a party for B. F. Skinner on March 20, 1981, honoring both his seventy-seventh birthday and his fiftieth year as a psychologist. Skinner was born on March 20, 1904, and his Ph.D. was awarded on March 2, 1931. The poem contains references to all of his books through 1981, as well as to the infamous "baby box," an enclosed crib for infants. The "Parthenon" was a precursor of the modern "Skinner box," an experimental chamber now used widely to study animal behavior. The poem first appeared in the *Recorder*, a newsletter of Division 25 of the American Psychological Association.

    The new age began, appropriately, with
      The Parthenon's second fall.
The Behavior of Organisms could now answer bold
      The field's muted call.

    Of white heat then came *Walden Two*,
      And though not *Life*'s ideal savior,
Undaunted came the "text" that wasn't—
      Science and Human Behavior.

    The pen aside, the wrench in hand
      Machines that taught devised,
And boxes of every dimension—
      Even one of Deborah's size.

Verbal Behavior and *Schedules*,
      The theory and the fact,
Then *Cumulative Record*, edition one,
      And *Analysis*, a programmed tract.

T of T and *Contingencies*
   Were just preludes to higher heights:
Freedom and Dignity, way *Beyond*,
   Was where he set our sights.

Philosophers still cringing
   At the ever-widening schism,
A move to answer and explain
   In *About Behaviorism*.

A life story, some *Reflections*,
   And the *Notebooks* in the ads,
More than 200 publications
   To drive poor Epstein mad.

Fifty times around the sun—
   Psychology remade, philosophy spinning—
Our futures secured, our reinforcers delivered—
   We thank you for beginning.

23

SKINNER, CREATIVITY, AND THE PROBLEM OF SPONTANEOUS BEHAVIOR

Summary. Behavior is generative, by which I mean that it is probabilistic, continuous in time, and always novel. At first glance, B. F. Skinner's work would seem to make contact with generative aspects of behavior, since he studied the "emitted" behavior of "freely moving organisms," since he analyzed language, music, literature, and other creative activities, and since he himself was an exceptionally creative individual. In fact, Skinner's work focuses on the effects of various *interventions* on ongoing behavior; it says little about where that behavior comes from in the first place. Generativity Theory suggests that simple behavioral processes of the sort Skinner studied operate simultaneously on the probabilities of a large number of different behaviors. Instantiated in a computer model, the theory has successfully emulated complex, novel performances in both human and animals subjects, and it may some day allow for the real-time simulation of novel performances in individual human subjects.

First occurrences have an air of magic about them: your first kiss, your child's first word, your first publication. The behavior of organisms has many firsts, so many, in fact, that it's not clear that there are any seconds. We do new things all the time, some profound, some trivial. We "solve problems," which, by definition, means we're doing new things in situations we've never faced before. We write poems and improvise on the piano and devise scientific theories. We speak new utterances all the time, even, sometimes, in faculty meetings.

When you look closely enough, behavior that appears to have been repeated proves to be novel in some fashion. If you say the word "pigeon" several times, a spectrograph will show clear differences in each occurrence (and, as I can testify from personal experience, passers-by are likely to point at you and mutter *behaviorist*). You never brush your teeth exactly the same way twice, and even the rat's lever press varies in subtle ways with each occurrence. Variability is typical of all behavior, from nystagmus in our eyes to the slight tremor in our hands. Even if, somehow, you could repeat some response precisely, it would still be novel in the sense that each occurrence is the product of a changed organism. Curiously, we are relatively insensitive to variability and novelty in our behavior, even to the extent that concepts in the behavioral sciences may have been compromised by our insensitivity as scientists to such variability and novelty (Chapter 25).

Behavior is also fluid and continuous. We speak of a lever press as if it is a discrete entity, but it is not. The rat moves from the feeder to the lever, one or both of its front paws move toward the lever as it flicks its tail, a paw depresses the lever and slides off as the rat moves its head from side to side and twitches its whiskers, the rat moves away, and so on. The click of a microswitch suggests, falsely, that a discrete "response" has occurred, but the rat is active continuously, and what occurs is multi-dimensional and complex. The operation of a feeder—the delivery of a "reinforcer"—does not simply "strengthen a response"; rather, it impacts the flow of behavior in complex ways. Just as we are often insensitive to novelty and variability in behavior, we are also insensitive to continuity. We hear discrete "words" in a spoken sentence, for example, but the acoustic signal is typically continuous.

Finally, behavior is inherently probabilistic. A large number of factors converge continuously on an always-active nervous system to produce behavior. As thresholds are passed and firing rates increase, circuits controlling the occurrence of many different behaviors are activated. The behavior you actually see is the result of a complicated numbers game. People are quick to agree that it's difficult to predict what someone will do or say next, but that's not what I mean by probabilistic. Probabilistic systems, even chaotic ones, may be highly predictable and easy to describe mathematically. I mean rather that behavior is the result of a very complicated process which is in part stochastic. Focusing on one instance or one dimension does not do justice to the system.

I use the term *generative* to denote these three aspects of behavior: that behavior is novel, continuous, and probabilistic. Various scientists and theoreticians have been concerned with generativity in various ways and in various contexts (e.g., Arieti, 1976; Chomsky, 1965; Sternberg, 1988; Wertheimer, 1945). In this essay, I will look at the issue narrowly, first by examining generativity in the context of B. F. Skinner's work, and then by summarizing my own work in this area.

B. F. SKINNER

A Contradiction

Skinner is well known for two positions that bear on generativity and that appear to contradict each other. On the one hand, central to his work was the distinction he drew between operant and respondent behavior. Operant behavior is "emitted," he said, whereas respondent or reflex behavior is "elicited" or "drawn out" by a specific stimulus (Skinner, 1938). Operant behavior has no obvious eliciting stimulus; it is, by definition, the kind of behavior usually called "spontaneous" (Skinner, 1938, pp. 19–20). To study such behavior, Skinner avoided using "reflex preparations" in which the movements of animals are constrained; instead he studied the behavior of the whole, freely-moving organism. Operant behavior is surely generative, and Skinner certainly observed many generative phenomena.

On the other hand, Skinner didn't believe in spontaneity, and, although he used the word occasionally, he usually put quotations marks around it. He was, indeed, a strict determinist, attributing all behavior to our genetic endowments and environmental histories (e.g., Skinner, 1955–56, 1971a, 1989), with most of his career devoted to the study of the latter. He believed that he had fully reconciled these two positions—his belief in the active organism and his belief in determinism—through his use of selection as a causal mode (e.g., Skinner, 1981a). Behavior that appears to be spontaneous is part of a "class" of responses that has been selected by past reinforcers, said Skinner, just as a new species is part of a class of organisms that has been selected by contingencies of survival in evolution. True, operant behavior has no obvious eliciting stimulus, but it is occurring now because similar behavior (members of the response "class") have been reinforced in the past.

There is a problem here, and it's simple enough to state, although Skinner himself never seemed concerned about it. Selection alone doesn't produce anything *new* in evolution. Mechanisms of variation are also necessary. Selection merely limits the range of variation that occurs in the next generation. It doesn't really produce anything; it just constrains. Similarly, reinforcement doesn't produce any of the particular behavior variants from which it may select (except to the extent that it is acting as an eliciting or discriminative stimulus, but these cases are not pertinent to Skinner's position). Before behavior can be selected in ontogeny, it must somehow be *generated* (cf. Segal, 1972; Staddon, 1975). Mechanisms of variability must exist, some relatively trivial, perhaps, and some profound. To rely on so-called "random" variation is by no means enough to account for the dramatic and complex instances of novelty we often observe in behavior; *Beyond Freedom and Dignity* (Skinner, 1971a) was not the product of random variations of spoken or written English. To put it another way, Skinner's deterministic dyad always needed another factor: Behavior is determined by genes, environmental history, and certain *mechanisms of variability*.

Shaping

Skinner named and popularized the technique of reinforcing successive approximations, the "shaping" technique. Without mechanisms of variability—indeed, without fairly orderly mechanisms of variability—shaping could not work. The textbook account of shaping oversimplifies the process. Here is a slightly more detailed view:

You'd like a hungry pigeon to turn in circles. You wait for almost any approximation at first, say, turning the head to the right. Then you immediately operate a feeder, and the pigeon eats. You operated the feeder following a slight head turn, but other behavior was undoubtedly reinforced, as well: The pigeon may have been lifting a wing, stepping, and opening its beak just as it turned its head. *A great deal of irrelevant behavior is always captured by reinforcement.* You may also have inadvertently strengthened one or more *sequences* of behavior: The pigeon may have pecked a spot on the wall just before it turned its head, and you may have strengthened pecking-and-turning. The pigeon also continues to engage in *other* behavior: It walks, flaps its wing, and so on. Many behaviors seem to be competing with each other, and your reinforcer seems merely to have altered the distribution in some complicated way.

Among other things, you will probably see the pigeon turn its head again. When you see the pigeon turn its head a little farther than it did before, you operate the feeder. Again, you observe many different behaviors—more stepping, partial turns, wing lifts, and so on—and you continue to "increase your requirement." Old behaviors continue to appear in some fashion, and you also observe various new forms appearing, along with variants of many of the forms you have (deliberately or inadvertently) reinforced. If you continue to operate the feeder at judicious moments, within a few minutes, the pigeon will turn in full turns—while continuing to engage in other behaviors, as well.

Where did the orderly variants come from, and could we have predicted them? It's not enough to know what we thought we were reinforcing; we had multiple effects on the flow of behavior, and many new forms turned up, not simply "random variants" of specific response forms. Note that *without the new behavior, we could not have proceeded with the shaping process.* Could we have predicted, precisely, what new behaviors would occur, moment-to-moment? What principles would allow us to make such predictions?[1]

Reinforcement may, in some sense, alter the probability of a response, but *where does the response come from in the first place?*

Probability

Throughout his long career, Skinner spoke of the probability of responding, but, early on, he concluded that the concept of probability per se had limited usefulness in the study of behavior (e.g., Skinner, 1953, p. 62). It was not directly measurable, for one thing, and it was a *statistical* idea, always unsavory to Skinner (e.g., Skinner, 1964). In the early years he spoke of "strength" of responding, which he was careful to define in physical terms. The strength of a reflex, for example, could be defined in terms of latency or threshold values (e.g., Skinner, 1931, 1932, 1938). Ultimately, he settled on *rate of responding* as the ideal measure of the "strength of an operant" (e.g., Skinner, 1938, p. 58). To Skinner, science could not proceed without a repeatable unit, and the occurrence or nonoccurrence of a particular instance of operant behavior, normally defined in terms of a simple switch closure, was just the thing (cf. Skinner, 1935).

Let me recast this to suit the present discussion: We'd like to get at probability directly, but we can't, so we will limit our discussion to "response strength." "Frequency" is our best measure of the strength of so-called "spontaneous" or "emitted" (that is, "operant") behavior. Thus we shift from *probability*, a fairly abstract concept, to *strength*, defined in physical terms in various ways, to *frequency*, normally defined in terms of switch closures.

Some chance events led young Skinner to invent a simple device for recording frequency data in real-time in a powerful form: the cumulative record (see

Skinner, 1956). If he had had camcorders and computers at his disposal, would he have settled for this? Would he have abandoned probability in favor of frequency?

Fluidity

Skinner is often portrayed as a stimulus-response psychologist. He objected strongly to this sort of portrayal (e.g., Skinner, 1974), mainly because it suggested that he was a Pavlovian, which he was certainly not. Skinner even had reservations about the usefulness of the very concepts "stimulus" and "response," although he employed them throughout his career. Skinner (1935) recognized the fluidity that exists on both sides of the equation. He proposed to define a response in terms of its *function*—its effect on the world—rather than in terms of its appearance, in order to approximate more closely "the natural lines of fracture along which behavior and environment actually break" (p. 40). In a published interview in the 1960s, he even rejected the concept of response almost entirely:

> As it stands, I'm not sure that response is a very useful concept. Behavior is very fluid; it isn't made up of lots of little responses packed together. I hope I will live to see a formulation which will take this fluidity into account. (quoted in Evans, 1968, pp. 20-21)

Creativity

Skinner never studied creativity per se, but he was fascinated by it, and he himself was a study in creativity. Before graduate school he had planned to become a creative writer, and he even received a warm letter of praise from Robert Frost for early compositions (Skinner, 1976, pp. 248–249). As a psychologist, he roamed the creative field: new laboratory equipment and methods (e.g., Skinner, 1956), now widely used; an enclosed crib for babies (Skinner, 1945a); a secret, pigeon-guided missile nose cone for the military (Skinner, 1960); a utopian novel (Skinner, 1948); analyses of great works of art, literature, and music (e.g., Epstein, 1980a; Skinner, 1939, 1941, 1957); new teaching devices and methods (e.g., Skinner, 1968). At home Skinner was always tinkering, modifying, inventing—always improving the space around him to make it easier to work and relax. As I write this essay nearly a year after his death, his basement study is still enmeshed by wires and strings attached to oddly shaped gizmos: a counter-weighted magnifying glass (to help him read), a crude tray to hold the television remote control (so he wouldn't lose it), a mechanical finger (to push the pause button on his tape recorder when the phone rang).

But his few explicit commentaries on the creative process (Skinner, 1956, 1957, 1966, 1970, 1972, 1981b) shed little light on that process. In his autobiographical "Case History" paper, we learn about the role that fortunate chance events had in the discovery process, but creative leaps just seem to happen. Describing the events leading to the invention of the cumulative recorder and, it would seem, to his passion for frequency data, Skinner writes,

"One day it occurred to me that if I wound string around the spindle and allowed it to unwind as the magazine was emptied, I would get a different kind of record" (Skinner, 1956, p. 225). Was the creative process so mysterious, even to Skinner, that nothing more could be said? In *Verbal Behavior*, Skinner (1957) speculates that new word blends can come about when "multiple variables" strengthen several "word fragments" simultaneously; the result is "usually nonsense" (p. 303). In general, Skinner (1957) says little about novelty in either speech production or comprehension, one of the complaints leveled against *Verbal Behavior* by Chomsky (1959). In "Creating the Creative Artist," Skinner (1970) argues that society can and should encourage artistic endeavors by providing appropriate reinforcers. He attributes creativity itself to random "'mutations,'" and he is skeptical about being able to discover the details:

> Many of these [mutations] are accidental in the sense that they arise from conditions which we cannot now identify in the genetic and environmental histories of the artist and from unpredictable details of his working methods and conditions. We may not like to credit any aspect of a successful painting to chance, but if we are willing to admit that chance does make a contribution, we can take steps to improve the chances. (pp. 69–70)

In "A Lecture On 'Having a Poem,'" Skinner (1972) compares the act of creating a poem to the act of having a child, arguing that in each case the creator is just a "locus" through which environmental variables act; the creator adds nothing to the creation.[2] How, specifically, a particular poem comes about is not stated. In "How to Discover What You Have to Say," Skinner (1981b) gives excellent tips on how to stimulate and preserve one's new ideas, but what new ideas are likely to turn up, and why?

Of special note are Skinner's (1966) comments in a paper on problem solving:

> Solving a problem is a behavioral event. The various kinds of activities which further the appearance of a solution are all forms of behavior. *The course followed in moving toward a solution does not, however, necessarily reflect an important behavioral process.* (p. 240, italics added)

Skinner recognized generative aspects of behavior but did not see generativity per se as a problem worthy of study or analysis. He knew that behavior was fluid, probabilistic, and at least *sometimes* novel, but he did not know how to advance an analysis of behavior without positing a recurring unit; hence the need to divide up behavior into "lots of little [recurring] responses." In a sense, Skinner took generativity for granted, relying on broad-brush explanations of creativity ("chance," "mutations") or on no explanations at all ("One day it occurred to me")—even suggesting that the creative process was not "important." This fit his two-factor form of determinism. Nontrivial mechanisms of variation might have made the organism seem a little too autonomous for Skinner's liking. Ironically, virtually all of operant psychology revolves around spontaneous behavior; without it, we'd never have anything new to reinforce.

GENERATIVITY

Combinations

Creativity has been said by many to be the result of a combinatorial process (e.g., Arieti, 1976; Bingham, 1929; Chomsky, 1965; Gardner, 1982; Hull, 1935; Koestler, 1964; Maier & Schneirla, 1935; Sternberg, 1988; Wertheimer, 1945). For example, Rothenberg, a psychiatrist, describes creativity as a "Janusian" process, after Janus, the god of two faces. New ideas result from "the capacity to conceive and utilize two or more opposite or contradictory ideas, concepts, or images simultaneously" (Rothenberg, 1971, p. 195). Henri Poincaré, the eminent mathematician, made an important discovery one evening after having drunk too much coffee. "Ideas rose in crowds," he wrote. "I felt them collide until pairs interlocked, so to speak, making a stable combination" (Poincaré, 1946, p. 387). Stephen Jay Gould attributes his creativity to his ability to "make connections" (quoted in Shekerjian, 1990); Einstein spoke of "combinatory play" in explaining his own creative ability; and the great English poet and playwright John Dryden spoke of "a confus'd mass of Thoughts, tumbling over one another in the Dark" as essential to his own creative efforts (quoted in Ghiselin, 1952).

Simulations

My own interest in combinations began during research with pigeons—the so-called "Columban Simulation Project" (Part II of this volume), which Skinner and I began in 1979 (Baxley, 1982; Epstein, 1981a). We had found yet another way to further Skinner's longstanding campaign against cognitive psychology. With pigeons as subjects, we "simulated" human and chimpanzee performances that had been attributed to cognitive processes and offered alternative accounts of such performances in terms of contingencies of reinforcement (e.g., Epstein & Skinner, 1981; Epstein, Lanza, & Skinner, 1980, 1981). The logic of simulations is actually fairly complicated (see Epstein, 1986b), and some of our studies may have had more political value than scientific value.

But the outcome of the Simulation Project was in general quite positive, mainly because it got us to look at our avian subjects in new ways and under new conditions. To Skinner's credit, he never once suggested that we use "rate of responding" to measure the extraordinary behaviors we observed as we began to consider self-awareness, symbolic communication, imitation, problem solving, cooperation and competition (Figure 23.1a), morality (Figure 23.1b), the use of memoranda, and other topics from a behavioral perspective. (Some of his devotées have proved to be far less flexible.) Rather, we borrowed or invented measurement techniques as we went along. In one study (Epstein & Skinner, 1981), Skinner whispered a running account of the performances into a tape recorder during critical tests; our data was the transcript of his narration.

Figure 23.1. (a) Competition between pigeons. A pigeon's key peck moves the cart of food toward it. The pigeon gets access to the food when the cart reaches its side, and the cart then resets to the middle of the track. If both pigeons peck, the cart moves back and forth and may not reach either one. (b) "Morality" in the pigeon. A mouse has been trained to press a lever, the operation of which dispenses milk to the mouse and grain to the pigeon in the adjacent chamber. Slowly rotating "snakes" in the mouse's chamber make it difficult, however, for the mouse to press the lever. The pigeon can temporarily stop the rotation of the offending snakes by pressing a foot pedal, thus providing relief to the mouse, and, in turn, increasing the likelihood that the mouse will dispense grain to the pigeon.

More important, we never used closed experimental chambers; here was Skinner without the box, so to speak. The pigeons roamed free in large wire-mesh or Plexiglas chambers where complexity could be seen in all its frustrating splendor, and eventually I began filming or videotaping each performance and analyzing the recorded images, sometimes frame-by-frame.

Skinner, Creativity, and Spontaneous Behavior

The simulation research had a pattern to it. Pigeons were trained to do things that chimpanzees or people could do and then placed in new situations where, very often, new, interesting behavior would turn up that seemed typical of chimps or humans. For example, Epstein, Kirshnit, Lanza, and Rubin (1984) reported that pigeons with the right training history could solve the classic box-and-banana problem in an "insightful" fashion (Koffka, 1924; Köhler, 1925). A small facsimile of a banana was suspended out of reach of the pigeon, and a small box was placed elsewhere in the chamber. The pigeons had received food for pecking the mock banana when it was within reach. Would they use the box to reach the banana?

Each pigeon looked confused at first. It stretched repeatedly toward the mock banana, motioned toward the box, stretched again toward the banana, and so on. After a minute or so, each pigeon began, suddenly, to push the box directly toward the toy banana—sighting the banana as it pushed—stopped pushing in just the right spot, climbed, and pecked the banana.

These and other studies showed dramatically that previously established behaviors manifest themselves in new situations in new, interesting, and orderly ways. They also showed that differences in training affect new performances systematically (also see Birch, 1945; Köhler, 1925; Schiller, 1952; Shurcliff, Brown, & Stollnitz, 1971). But is that enough?

A Japanese researcher visiting my laboratory in the early 1980s seemed impressed with the performances I was generating, but he left me, albeit politely, with a disturbing question: "Where does all the new behavior come from?" I recast the question as follows: Can a rigorous, moment-to-moment account of the emergence of a novel performance be formulated?

Initial Efforts

I first attempted such accounts by using simple, empirical principles to account for changes in a novel performance as it unfolded over time, as evidenced by a videotape record. For example, the period of "confusion" evident when a pigeon is first confronted with the box-and-banana problem seems to be a simple competition of two repertoires occasioned by features of the test situation. The test situation has features common to two training situations and hence should occasion behavior with respect to the box and behavior with respect to the banana simultaneously (Epstein et al., 1984). *Multiple controlling stimuli* make repertoires compete, and the relative strength of the repertoires is determined by properties of the stimuli (see Chapter 2).

Other simple principles help account for other aspects of the performance. The bird stops pushing in the right place, for example, because its pushes have produced increasingly closer approximations to a stimulus the bird has seen during training—box-under-banana, the stimulus in whose presence climbing and pecking has been reinforced with food. This is an example of a process called *automatic chaining*, or simply *autochaining*. Behavior often changes the environment in a way that changes the probability of subsequent behavior. Even a turn of the head sometimes has this effect, because it radically changes the visual field (Epstein, 1985b).

Figure 23.2. The author with B. F. Skinner in the "Columban Simulation Laboratory," circa 1980.

Strings and Functions

I have offered moment-to-moment accounts of a number of such performances using simple principles of this sort, but a more productive approach to understanding generativity began to evolve when I extended the research to human subjects, at first studying variants of Maier's (1931a) pendulum problem and, more recently, a variety of mechanical problems involving building blocks, brooms, keys, and so on. As I watched many performances with people and pigeons unfold, I became increasingly aware of inadequacies in my running accounts of novel performances. First, I was dividing up the performances into arbitrary segments to fit my principles. What basis I did have for asserting that multiple controlling stimuli were operating only during the first 10 seconds of a performance, resurgence only during the next minute, and so on, or that only three repertoires were competing during the first few minutes and only two during the next few minutes? I had been asserting the obvious—that behavior and the environment are fluid and continuous—but I was violating my own precept. No audience or reviewer ever took me to task on this point, which made me especially wary. Second, I could make reasonably good predictions about the emergence of a novel performance, but my predictions were imprecise, as informal, verbal predictions tend to be.

My dilemma virtually demanded that I take two small steps:[3] First, I supposed that each of the various processes I was invoking was operating continuously in time and concurrently, and, as a corollary, that every process was operating simultaneously on the probabilities of every behavior that might occur in the situation.[4] I did not have high hopes for this conjecture, but it seemed unavoidable. Second, I cast four simple principles—extinction, reinforcement, automatic chaining, and resurgence—into linear equations in a simple state model and entered parameters describing Maier's two-string problem. A computer simulation produced surprising results. It yielded smooth, overlapping probability curves in what I have come to call a "probability profile"; it yielded a reasonable, human-like solution to the problem; and it predicted some of the dynamics of frequency data obtained with human subjects (Epstein, 1985a, 1990a).

Producing Multiple Repertoires

Multiple repertoires of behavior would indeed seem to be the stuff of creativity, and Generativity Theory may be helpful in specifying how repertoires compete and interact over time. New sequences and new topographies result from such interactions, with the resultants immediately available as new components in the generative process. Presumably any repertoires of behavior, established or induced by any means, can feed this process.

Circumstances that produce multiple repertoires of behavior would seem to be of special value in driving the process, and two phenomena are especially notable. In the natural environment, multiple controlling stimuli abound, and failure is not uncommon. The first produces multiple repertoires of behavior directly and the second, indirectly, through the resurgence of previously established behaviors. Thus the real world is a rich source of generativity. Other mechanisms may also spur the process: states of deprivation, complex instructions, releasers, intermittent schedules of reinforcement, modeling, dietary factors, and so on (cf. Segal, 1972).

Generativity and Shaping

A rigorous analysis of shaping would seem to be within reach. Critical to the shaping procedure is the repeated and systematic *withholding* of reinforcement. The animal keeps succeeding briefly and then failing for awhile. Failure is inducing a resurgence of previously established behaviors—including earlier forms that have been captured during the shaping process itself, a common observation during shaping (e.g., Pryor, Haag, & O'Reilly, 1969; Staddon & Simmelhag, 1971). New forms evident during the shaping process are not merely random variants but are *resultants* of competing repertoires, some of which blend to form increasingly exaggerated forms. This approach lends itself to formal analysis, and, if successful, such an analysis will account not only for changes in the target behavior but also for the dynamics of the many other behaviors that appear during the shaping procedure.[5]

Practical Implications

Generative phenomena are undoubtedly affected by individual differences—in speed of acquisition and transformations, the number of repertoires than can be supported simultaneously, emotional factors, and so on. But the bottom line is probably that these processes are operating all the time in everyone, meaning that in a very real sense we are all creative. People labeled "creative" by society may simply be producing more valued products (cf. Csikszentmihályi, 1990; Glover, 1980), or they may have certain skills that enhance generative processes or better utilize the output of such processes (cf. Guilford, 1962; Shekerjian, 1990; Simonton, 1984; Skinner, 1981b; Torrance, 1971).

Several practices follow directly from Generativity Theory as means to enhance creativity. The most important is to *capture* some of the new that's being generated all the time. Artists carry sketchpads and writers carry notebooks for this purpose. Finding *conditions* under which one can take the time to pay attention to competing repertoires is also important, and one can enhance the competition by *acquiring new skills and knowledge* (thus increasing the number of repertoires available to compete), by exposing oneself to *diverse and changing situations* (roughly, multiple controlling stimuli), and by exposing oneself to *new challenges* (and the possibility of extinction-induced resurgence).

Real-Time Simulation

I am currently working with D. Thompson and several students to develop software that may allow for the real-time simulation of the behavior of individual human subjects in a simple situation. At one terminal the subject performs a simple task—pushing buttons to move a dot across the screen. At terminals linked to the subject's terminal, we will see a probability profile showing overlapping probability curves for each of the buttons, the predicted path of the dot, and statistics comparing our predictions to chance predictions in real time. Every press of a button will alter the profile and our predictions. It may be possible in this situation to stay ahead of the subject by several seconds or more, even when the functions of the buttons are so complex that casual observers—and even the subjects themselves—cannot make accurate predictions. A simulation of this sort, if successful, will further validate the approach to understanding ongoing behavior that has been outlined in this essay. It may also lead to applications of Generativity Theory in artificial intelligence.

Interventions

Reinforcement, punishment, extinction, time out, instructions, modeling, prompting, manual guidance, and so on—the kinds of procedures studied and developed by Skinner and his students—are not generative mechanisms per se. Rather, they are *interventions* that interrupt and redirect the flow of behavior by altering the probabilities of many different behaviors (cf. Dunham & Grantmyre, 1982; Thompson & Lubinski, 1986). Even simple interventions necessarily have multiple and complex effects, although our procedures may, unfortunately, lead us to overlook complexity in many situations. In a way, interventions are the exception and generativity is the rule, for without interventions organisms continue to behave in new and interesting ways indefinitely. The organism is truly active, even if the activity of organisms proves to be wholly orderly and predictable.

Am I suggesting that determinism, or at least that Skinner's brand of determinism, is dead? I'd prefer to sidestep the question with an assertion, one I have been making for several years (e.g., Epstein, 1984a, 1987b). Isms are common in the early stages of a science, but they are damaging in the long run. *Determinism, behaviorism, environmentalism, nativism*—all are distractions, really. It will take the joint efforts of many scientists in several fields to advance an effective understanding of human behavior, by far the most complex subject matter in all the sciences. The time has come to proceed in this worthy endeavor without ideology or ism, as colleagues with a common purpose.

NOTES

1. In an excellent paper on the "provenance of operants," Segal (1972), following Skinner, asserts that reinforcement strengthens a "class" of responses which includes all of the variants, including the novel forms (e.g, p. 5). The assertion does not lend itself to falsification, unfortunately, and it doesn't help us to know exactly which responses will be in this new "class." No principles or mechanisms are given that would allow us to specify the new members. The class idea itself is suspect, because it can't easily handle the dynamic and ever-changing nature of behavior. One reinforcer may change behavior in certain ways, the next in new ways, the third in still other ways, and, even without reinforcers, behavior continues to unfold in new and interesting ways. It seems preferable to try to state these ways precisely and to specify the dynamic mechanisms, rather than to say simply that a different hypothetical "class" of behaviors is lighting up with each reinforcer, as if that solves the problem. Segal also notes that novel behavior of evolutionary significance can be produced by other procedures besides shaping: deprivation, certain schedules of reinforcement and punishment, the presentation of releasers, and so on. All such behaviors are grist for the generativity mill, as I will argue below.

2. Publically, Skinner took a strong empiricist stand on creativity, but in private his views seemed more balanced. We had an amusing exchange one day about his claim that he was creative and inquisitive because, as a boy, he had found "something interesting under every rock." I asked whether other boys accompanied him on his walks through the woods, and he said yes. I asked whether any of the other boys had made interesting discoveries under rocks, and he started to smile and said yes. "Well," I said, "where are those boys now?" He grinned broadly and replied, *"Probably driving trucks."*

3. Generative principles have been helpful in accounting for advances in my own thinking, but there is inadequate space here to attempt such a discussion. Viewed as covert perceptual and verbal behavior, thinking is wholly amenable to the kind of analysis offered here (Epstein, 1991b).

4. This system seemed simpler that the arbitrary one I had been employing, and it also seemed to have a far better fit to the nervous system.

5. The approach also seems consistent with the observation that shaping occurs more rapidly in adult organisms than in young organisms (Segal, 1972). A far greater number of repertoires are available to resurge and complete in the adult.

24

IN THE YELLOW WOOD

Summary. As a scientist, Skinner made extraordinary contributions, but his philosophical views are so unpalatable to mainstream Western thinking that they have obscured his better side. Distinguishing between the science of behavior and the philosophy of that science will help to clarify his contributions.

B. F. Skinner: Consensus and Controversy, a recent collection edited by the Modgils in England, contains little consensus and a great deal of controversy. On only one matter—which, unfortunately, is given little treatment—is there universal agreement and, indeed, praise: Skinner has made significant contributions to the scientific understanding of behavior. His first book, *The Behavior of Organisms: An Experimental Analysis* (1938), is singled out repeatedly as a tour de force. Skinner as researcher and methodologist is untouchable; consider the matter closed.

Other matters, mainly "meta" or "ismic" in nature, rouse the critics to ire. Skinner has given us "dogmas." His positions on various issues are "superficial," "scanty," "confused," "paltry," "uninspired," "restrictive," "inherently incomplete," "constraining," and "naive." Praise and damnation. Quick consensus and prolonged, perhaps unending, controversy. Why?

The history of psychology sheds some light. "Psychology" is derived from the Greek "psyche," which originally meant "breath" and came to mean "soul" or "mind." A concern with the nature of mind can be traced back at least as far as Aristotle's *Peri Psyches*; advances in a variety of scientific disciplines in the nineteenth century led, finally, to the application of scientific methods to the study of mind. By the end of the century, a new science had taken shape, defined by the *Oxford English Dictionary* as "the science of the nature, functions, and phenomena of the human soul or mind." "From the most ancient subject," said Ebbinghaus, "we shall produce the newest science."

But, in 1905, something peculiar happened. William McDougall, in his *Primer of Physiological Psychology*, defined psychology as "the study of behavior." He had no particular complaints against the old subject matter, but he thought that behavior, too, deserved attention (Watson & McDougall, 1928). In 1913,

Watson went a step further. Psychology should study behavior, he said, and mind, the traditional subject matter, is now *forbidden*. The assertion was absurd; proclaiming someone else's field yours does not make it so. But Watson was charismatic, and he promised many applications. Moreover, the possibility of a science of behavior was in the air; Charles Mercier, J. S. Mill, and others had suggested that it be established as an independent field. Had their suggestions been followed, the science of behavior would now very likely be one of the most effective and respected disciplines in the world. But Watson set the new science on a steep and thorny way—as the belligerent footman of psychology.

The movement for reform had, appropriately, an ism in its name: *behaviorism*. And the ism carried with it many untested and untestable assertions, philosophical in character: Unobservables are off limits; behavior is determined; thought is laryngeal movement; nurture conquers nature. All extra baggage, really, since the mission of the crusade was simply to make behavior the subject matter of a science. The movement was destined to fail. Even during the three decades when behaviorism was conspicuous in psychology, the traditional subject matter held its own. With the advent of computers and the alliances that were formed between psychologists, computer scientists, and linguists, the study of mind eventually flourished as it never had before. Today, less than 2 percent of the membership of the American Psychological Association identifies itself openly with the behavioristic tradition.

The movement died, but its legacy is clear: It created a fanatical concern for objectivity in psychology proper. It led to the development of a school of philosophy, which today is the proper referent of the word "behaviorism." And, perhaps most important, it convinced many people that the behavior of organisms is a legitimate subject matter in its own right. The study of behavior, which some now call "praxics" (from the Greek *"praxis,"* for "behavior"), may yet become an independent and important science (Epstein, 1984a, 1985a).

Skinner is both praised and damned because he is both praxist and behaviorist and—even though he recognizes the difference (Skinner, 1974)—because the lines of separation are not always clear. As praxist, Skinner single-handedly advanced the science as no one has done before or since. As behaviorist, Skinner greatly elaborated and refined Watson's naive philosophical views. But the overlap has caused trouble. Almost all of the complaints against Skinner in this volume and elsewhere have to do with the mixing of the science and the philosophy. The "conceptual imperatives" Skinner is said to have imposed on the science are, with few exceptions, the imperatives of the ism. Skinner's "interpretations" are extrapolations from the science, constrained by, or at least consistent with, the ism.

Philosophy has no limits, but no science should be constrained by a philosophy. It is the subject matter of behavior that is important, not any particular methodology or set of variables. And no one should be denied a place in the behavioral laboratory because he or she is not a behaviorist. Moreover, the science of behavior cannot flourish in psychology's shadow. The squabbling has only been destructive to both disciplines—especially to the intruder.

The future is clear. The science of behavior will go free of the ism that helped bring it to life, just as other natural sciences have broken free of their own philosophical forebears (consider Hopkins, 1934). With the ism left behind, Mercier's proposal may finally be realized: The new science may finally emerge as an independent field.

Skinner's contributions will be similarly partitioned, also with good effect. He will be recognized in various disciplines in different ways, just as Descartes is revered in mathematics for different reasons than he is remembered in philosophy. The landscape is not yet right. We cannot yet get a dispassionate view. But we are in the yellow wood. For the good of the science—and, indeed, if Skinner is right, for the good of humanity—behaviorism and the science of behavior must go their separate ways.

PART VI

COGITATIONS

25

THE MYTH OF CATEGORIZATION

Summary. The concept of categorization has changed for psychologists over the last few decades. In the 1940s, categorization was treated as the meeting of two bounded, describable entities: A psychological or behavioral invariant, such as a name, was assumed to attach itself to an invariant class of objects or events in the environment. Recent developments have called attention to the complexities of the categorization process and specifically to the fluid, fuzzy nature of the environment. A still more complete development of the concept would acknowledge the fluidity and variance in behavior. Categorization must involve a correspondence between two continua.

A concern with categorization is a concern with how people divide up the world. Roughly defined, a category is a group of non-identical objects or events which an individual treats as equivalent. "Dog," for example, is the name of a category that consists of a variety of (usually) four-legged animals. Psychologists have been concerned with the composition of categories and with the principles that govern their formation. Such concern has been expressed using many different investigative procedures and under many labels—classification, concept formation, identification, and so on—but until recently the various approaches to the experimental study of categorization were all alike in at least two major respects.

First, they assumed that categories have well-defined boundaries and that the elements in a category all share certain exhaustively specifiable properties. Second, categorization experiments used artificial, simple stimuli that, conveniently, formed bounded classes in which all members shared certain properties. Vygotsky (1962) and colleagues, for example, showed subjects wooden blocks that varied in color, shape, size, and height. A nonsense syllable on the bottom of each block indicated its category. In one scenario, an experimenter selected one block—say a tall, large one labeled *lag*—and asked the subject to select other objects in the same category. The experimenter overturned objects that had been selected incorrectly until the subject could correctly sort all of the objects into the proper groups—tall and large, flat and large, tall and small, and flat and small. Classic investigations by Hull (1920), the Kendlers

(1962), Bruner, Goodnow, and Austin (1956), Heidbreder (1946, 1948, 1949), and many others used similarly contrived stimuli.

ENVIRONMENTAL VARIATION

Recently psychologists have abandoned the notion that categories are bounded and well-defined, and, appropriately, abandoned in categorization experiments simple artificial stimuli like Vygotsky's blocks. The trend has been spearheaded by Rosch and her colleagues, who have emphasized that many categories have at best very "fuzzy" boundaries and that a more important characteristic of categories occurring in the natural environment may be their "internal structure" (Mervis & Rosch, 1981; Rosch, 1977; Rosch, Mervis, Gray, Johnson, & Boyes-Braem, 1976).[1] They have examined many natural categories whose members do not share a set of easily specifiable features. Mechanisms such as Wittgenstein's notion of family resemblance have been invoked to account for the linkage between category members (e.g., Rosch & Mervis, 1975).

There is now widespread interest in the fuzziness of category boundaries, evident, for example, in linguistics in a paper by Labov (1973), in psychology in various applications of fuzzy set theory (e.g., Hersh & Caramazza, 1976; Oden, 1977; also see Zadeh, 1965), and in philosophy in one form or another (consider Goodman, 1965; Quine, 1969b; cf. Russell, 1923). Rosch's work has dealt primarily with natural categories, both perceptual and semantic (e.g., Rosch, 1973)—the whole spectrum of colors, as opposed to a choice between green and red, or types of trees, as opposed to a choice between squares and triangles. A concern with natural categories has been felt even in the animal laboratory in studies, for example, in which pigeons identified trees and people (Herrnstein, Loveland, & Cable, 1976), or in a recent study in which pigeons proved able to distinguish oak leaves from other types of leaves (Cerella, 1979). Brown (1976) has noted the importance of this trend (cf. Brown, 1977; Schönbach, 1977).

Our conceptualization of categorization has moved from the contrived to the natural, from rigid hypotheses about categorization to a greater sensitivity to the full range of phenomena which the process might encompass. In our concern with fuzziness, we have come to deal more and more with the fluidity of the environment. Categorization is no longer seen as a matter of attaching a name to a distinct object or event or even to a distinct class of objects or events but rather to classes with intentions (defining properties) that are difficult to specify, to spatial and temporal segments of a continuity.

Seen in this light, the trend is harmonious with the stress on continuity evident in the works of James (1890), Dewey (1896), Bergson (1946), Skinner (1935), and others.[2] Variance is the rule in the events or objects we categorize, a fact that is easy to observe. The range of different objects which we call "fruit," for example, varies considerably, and, at extremes, many objects, such as coconuts or tomatoes, will not be categorized reliably. No two dimes are ever identical, and although they may certainly differ along fewer dimensions than two possible members of the "fruit" category, even "dime" is a name for a fuzzy set. Even the "same" object, seen at different times, varies in several ways from occasion to occasion: Our contact with the object is, for one thing, temporally distinct—as James (1890) noted, we don't call two ticks of a clock the "same" tick—and the object likely varies in spatial orientation and other ways which affect our perception of it from one occasion to the next. Variance, again, is the rule, and the current conceptualization of categorization takes it into account.

BEHAVIORAL VARIATION

Our general concern is with the "principles by which humans divide up the world" (Rosch et al., 1976, p. 382). A "category" or "concept" indicates that some division has occurred. According to Rosch, a category is "a number of objects which are considered equivalent" (Rosch et al., 1976, p. 381). Posner (1973), following Bourne (1966), gives a closely related and more specific definition: "A concept has been formed when a human subject shows the ability to respond to a series of different events with the same label or action" (p. 46). In each rendering, a subject must somehow demonstrate that he or she considers differing objects or events equivalent. An individual demonstrates this by behaving "equivalently" with respect to them, or as Posner notes, by giving us the *same* response. This is the essence of the concept of categorization as explicitly defined in psychological research. Some name or other identifying response gets attached to an apparently diverse set of objects or events. Or, in other words, an invariant element in behavior gets attached to variant elements in the environment.

But no such invariant exists. Behavior is as fluid as the environment, and the same is true of neurological or cognitive events which might be said to correspond to categories.[3] Consider some early instances of a child starting to call things "dog." The label is applied imperfectly at first—perhaps, at some point, to all four-legged creatures. Eventually, the child's "dog" category approximates our own. At each step in the acquisition of the category, the name "dog" indicates the nature of the category. When the child applies the word "dog" to a Dalmatian on one occasion and a Beagle on another, we know that the child considers them "equivalent" or "the same." But how did the child know that its two "dog" responses were the same? They were not identical; they were physically and temporally unique, just as the dogs were. We have long noted that there are different words for the same thing (e.g., Brown, 1958), but we also know that word instances vary in pitch, volume, and duration, that the "same" word may be spoken either with or without the vocal cords, and that there are still other easily discriminable variations in response form. Rosch et al. (1976) note that "categorization occurs to reduce the infinite differences between stimuli" (p. 428). Apparently we should add that categorization occurs to reduce the infinite differences between responses.

The segmentation of one's own behavior may be pre-programmed to some extent, determined by some underlying neurological event, but learning can contribute to the process. Consider a boy learning to swim the side stroke. He practices according to instructions and at first is insensitive to the great variation that occurs; his "side stroke" category is broad and will be sharpened with practice. Experience plays a role in segmentation when one learns a new language, certainly whenever phonetic categories of the new language impinge upon the integrity of the old. In learning Zulu, for example, one must master two [b] sounds, and in learning Hindi, four consonant sounds in roughly the [d] to [t] range. The relative contributions of innate, learning, and maturational factors in the recognition of invariants in one's own behavior have not been established.

Behavioral variation is overlooked or underemphasized in most studies of categorization. Rosch and her colleagues place primary emphasis on environmental variance (e.g., Rosch, 1973; Rosch et al., 1976; Rosch, 1977; cf. Heider, 1972). In a typical task, the objects to be categorized—e.g., colors or geometrical forms—are constructed so as to vary in systematic ways and displayed to subjects on cards. The subjects learn to name certain subsets of these stimuli, and the manner in which they do so sheds light on the structure of the acquired category. Environmental variance is also emphasized in applications of fuzzy set theory (Brownell & Caramazza, 1978; Hersh & Caramazza, 1976) and other recent work on concepts or categories (e.g., Bolton, 1977; Garner, 1976; Goldman & Homa; 1977; Oden, 1977; Zadeh, Fu, Tanaka, & Shimura, 1975).

What would at first seem to be an exception to this rule is work on speech perception. But here we typically look at variation in speech sounds only when presented as stimuli, not when they occur as responses. Yet this is, once again, a case in which the categorizing responses vary just as the stimuli do—in fact, in this instance, *precisely* as the stimuli do. In a paper that applies fuzzy set theory to a model of speech perception (Oden & Massaro, 1978), subjects pressed buttons to categorize speech sounds; the button pushes, although undoubtedly varying in topography, latency, magnitude, and duration, were implicitly considered invariant.

Such work, in overlooking response variation, is not necessarily deficient, and neither, for that matter, were the Heidbreder or Vygotsky studies. But the Heidbreder approach was abandoned in an effort to tackle some of the intricacies of categorization as it occurs in the natural environment. Looking more closely at response variables like force, latency, and duration—or, in a naming task, even at spectrographic fluctuations—might reveal new and interesting dynamics of the categorization process, just as Rosch's work has done. We know that variation occurs on both sides of the environment/behavior interface. How do they covary?

In some instances, variables such as duration, reaction time, rate (Herrnstein et al., 1976; Cerella, 1979), or "confidence"(Medin & Schaffer, 1978) of naming or identification responding have been measured, but the rationale for such measurement has usually been restricted to particular theories about the cognitive processes involved in categorization and does not stem from the more general concerns that have been addressed here.[4] Results of such investigations do show, however, the sorts of variation in behavior that have been discussed. In a study reported in 1972, for example, Rosch noted that focal colors—viz., more central category members—were given shorter names and had shorter latencies than nonfocal colors (Heider, 1972).

Categorization is sometimes studied without relying on a naming response or any other obvious identification response—for example, in the "oddity" task or in tasks requiring only a "same" or "different" response. We could, by such means, sidestep theoretical vagaries and still investigate the categorization process, but doing so would reduce the concept to psychological triviality. The concept would survive, but at the expense of our understanding of the subject matter that spurred the concept in the first place.[5]

A MYTHOLOGICAL CONCEPT

One thing that all recent concepts of categorization have in common is the notion that people divide up the world. Rosch was looking for the "principles" by which the division occurs. Humans are often seen as compulsive classifiers (cf. Bergson, 1946), and classification, discussed in almost any context, is understood to mean such a process (consider Stevens, 1939, p. 233). But the environment divides up behavior just as behavior divides up the environment. There is variation and continuity in each, and the "segmentation" that occurs, occurs in each.

Then why is the notion that we divide up the world so pervasive? Why do our concepts of categorization, naming, classification, and identification all make this assumption? Perhaps our tendency to see people as dividing up the world is compelling for the same reason that we so easily recognize occurrences of some word as being "the same" from one occasion to the next in our own behavior—because we are irresistibly sensitive to certain commonalities in our behavior. Variation, relatively speaking, is all but invisible to us. How understandable, in that case, that we devise a concept of categorization in which invariant, pre-segmented behaviors or psychological entities get attached to an amorphous world.

The fact that we so inexorably and automatically attend to commonalities in our behavior suggests that the ability to do so is somehow fundamental to our functioning and implies a sort of Gödel's Theorem of psychological study: Characteristics of our functioning impede the extent to which we can study that functioning effectively. The concept of categorization may be one instance in which characteristics of the psychologist were restrictive. Concepts such as categorization would never take the form that they do in psychological research if psychologists began with observations of continuity and variation in behavior and the environment. Other concepts in psychology may now be historical relics because they were inconsistent with such observations. We know, for example, that a concept of memory based on response repetition has come into disrepute as an experimental heuristic; was this inevitable solely given that such a concept, like the concept of categorization, overlooks behavioral variance?

That there is variance in both behavior and environment is not a new idea, but somehow our relative insensitivity to the behavioral variance has kept us from a full exploration of the categorization process. Categorization is not a myth—at least not to the extent that people behave as if non-identical objects were equivalent.[6] But various experimental and theoretical formulations of the concept in psychology have not adequately acknowledged the complexities of the process.[7] It is not enough to say that we divide up our world into categories, for our behavior is itself divided up by the world. The process of division is a mutual one.

NOTES

1. The concern with internal structure is also evident in work by Bransford and Franks (1971) and in some of Posner's work (e.g., 1969, 1973), although these studies restricted themselves to relatively simple stimuli.
2. Consider James's (1890) classic portrayal of the stream of consciousness: *"no state once gone can recur and be identical with what is was before....* For an identical sensation to recur it would have to occur the second time *in an unmodified brain.* But as this, strictly speaking, is a physiological impossibility, so is an unmodified feeling an impossibility.... A permanently existing 'Idea'...which makes its appearance before the footlights of consciousness at periodic intervals is as mythological an entity as the Jack of Spades"* (Vol. I, pp. 230–236; italics original).
3. Postulating the existence of a cognitive or neurological event that washes away the differences in certain behavioral events is no solution to the problem. For one thing, there is no reason to believe that internal events are any simpler than the external ones they underlie; it seems reasonable to suppose that they are every bit as complicated. Furthermore, we know that experience can play a role in concept acquisition, as is noted, for example, in Rosch's discussion of expertise (Rosch et al., 1976, pp. 431–432; also see Goldman & Homa, 1977). It seems unlikely, then, that all concepts are simply "preset" in neural matter. Finally, postulating the existing of some underlying invariant will only divert us from examining dynamic relationships that may exist between behavioral and environmental events. Neurological abstraction processes must exist (consider the missing fundamental in pitch perception), but they are not, to my knowledge, well understood. At this point, trying to bolster a mythical concept of categorization with a mythical neurological or cognitive process that handles behavioral variance would not be a great step forward.
4. An exception is an experiment reported by Brown (1956, pp. 291–294), in which a subject's ability to discriminate category names was shown to be a determinant of the categories he or she formed.
5. A comparison response, in particular, would be inadequate for many reasons. Whereas categorization seems an inevitable process for infrahumans, comparison is not. Nature does not arrange circumstances under which, say, a rat must examine two objects and then respond "same" or "different." A comparison response is probably strictly a verbal phenomenon and hence a special product of humans. In unpublished research done in Harvard's operant laboratory, pigeons had trouble learning comparison responses, although limited success with chimpanzees has been reported (e.g., Premack, Woodruff, & Kennel, 1978). The comparison response probably differs from the categorization response in complexity; perhaps comparing two objects first requires two separate categorization responses. Given marked differences in generality and probable differences in complexity, studying one process would seem to be no substitute for studying the other.
6. In spite of this partial disclaimer, I believe that the paper's title is appropriate. It is based on James's characterization of the fixed idea as an entity as "mythological...as the Jack of Spades." See Note 2 this chapter for a more complete quotation.
7. There are exceptions. According to Brown (1956), for example, "Where the subject is human and the responses are verbal it is...clear that the experimenter makes a judgment of response equivalence—an array of entities is called by the 'same' name. The bounds

The Myth of Categorization

of verbal categories are set by human beings.... Not [everyone] will agree as to which utterances are the 'same.' The varying utterances categorized as one word have a kind of functional equivalence in that they will produce the same social effect.... *The categorical response must appear in correlation with entities of a particular class* and must be extended to entities of that class" (p. 277, italics added).

26

THE PRINCIPLE OF PARSIMONY AND SOME APPLICATIONS IN PSYCHOLOGY

Summary. A modern principle of parsimony may be stated as follows: Where we have no reason to do otherwise and where two theories account for the same facts, we should prefer the one which is briefer, which makes assumptions with which we can easily dispense, which refers to observables, and which has the greatest possible generality. Psychologists often violate this principle, particularly in attributing complex behavior to cognitive processes. The practice is exemplified by recent accounts of chimpanzee behavior.

In this essay I first develop a modern variant of what has been called the "principle of parsimony." I achieve this through the device of commenting on a quotation by Ernst Mach on the nature of science. I then briefly trace the history of the concept in modern experimental psychology. Finally, I apply the concept to recent research with both chimpanzees and pigeons. I offer no defense of the principle, for, as I note below, I believe that no definitive defense is possible and acknowledge that the principle does not guarantee that a theory will be adequate or correct (cf. Barker, 1961; Goodman, 1972; Sober, 1981). I assume it, as did Ockham and others, as a first principle, one that, in the absence of arguments to the contary, must always be applied.

A PRINCIPLE OF PARSIMONY

"Science," wrote Mach, "may be regarded as a minimal problem consisting of the completest presentation of the facts with the *least possible expenditure of thought*" (Mach, 1893/1960, p. 586; italics original). By his own definition the statement is not very scientific, for neither its meaning nor its implications for scientific practice are apparent. Scientists in most fields would agree that they strive to give "the completest presentation of the facts." But what does it mean to say that this should be done "with the least possible expenditure of thought"? Four possibilities suggest themselves.

Brevity. First—crudely substituting the word "speech" for "thought"—we might conclude that a good scientific theory is one of few words. The book of Genesis begins with a rather succinct account of creation: "In the beginning God created the Heaven and the Earth." No physicist can compete with such simplicity. One of several reasons why it fails as a scientific theory is because of the first part of Mach's statement: Physical theories account for more facts about the universe as we know it than does the Bible. Brevity per se is not a criterion of good science. On the other hand, where two theories account for the same facts and where we have no other reason to prefer one over the other, we should probably prefer the briefer (cf. Goodman, 1961).

Assumptions. Second, perhaps Mach was talking about assumptions—statements the truth of which are taken for granted and which may otherwise be unsupported by fact. We often take it for granted in modern science that the better theory is the one that makes fewer assumptions. But one must be cautious here, for the nature of the assumptions must be considered. The creationists have attacked evolutionary theory precisely on the grounds that evolutionary theory makes many assumptions (for example, about the validity of carbon-dating techniques or the significance of geological strata), whereas "creation science" makes only one (Gurin, 1981; Lewin, 1982). Many cognitive psychologists also make only one basic assumption to support elaborate theories of human cognition, namely that humans are "information processors"—that, like computers, we are instruction-driven symbol manipulators (e.g., Kosslyn, 1980; Newell & Simon, 1972; cf. Epstein, 1981a). Given this one apparently innocuous assumption, they claim special knowledge about the nature of human problem solving, memory, attention, and so on.

More critical than the number of assumptions is the scope of the assumptions; the more expansive each assumption, the more dependent and hence vulnerable the theory. An extremely expansive assumption can be a theory's *sine qua non*. If there is no Creator, creation science tumbles to the ground; whereas, if the carbon-dating technique is invalid, evolutionary theory continues to stand relatively unshaken on other facts and assumptions of paleontology, as well as those of genetics, geology, comparative zoology, and so on. By the same token, if humans are not really information processors—an assumption which is unsupported by fact—computer simulations of cognition may prove to be of little value (cf. Edelman, 1982; Epstein, 1984e; Miller, 1981; Neisser, 1976).

One might also consider the utility of the assumptions in other domains. An assumption that proves useful in more than one domain seems preferable to one that must be contrived for a single case. (See the discussion on "generality" below.)

One might be tempted to try to define scope and utility more precisely and then to try to delineate the trade-offs among scope, utility, and number. I will merely assert what I believe would be one practical outcome of such an analysis: Some theories can survive the loss of one or more assumptions more easily than other theories. *Ceteris paribus*, we should probably prefer the theory that is less dependent on its assumptions. Given two theories which depend on comparable assumptions and which are equally dependent on them, we should probably prefer the one with fewer assumptions.

Observables. Third, Mach may have been warning against descriptions or accounts of natural phenomena which appeal to unobservable entities (cf. Gooding, 1982). It takes little brainpower to see a chair, but one cannot see the self-concept, an atom, or the ether. Indeed, one can do little with respect to such concepts but "expend thought." Simple concepts may require only a small expenditure. Someone may show you the Rutherford-Bohr model of the atom—the one that looks like a solar system—and ask you to imagine it much smaller. Complex unobservables, such as the "mental image" or Schrödinger's mathematical model of the atom, may require a great expenditure—so great that we resort to metaphors to characterize the concepts. Kosslyn (1980), for example, compares the mental image to a display on a CRT screen. The Schrödinger atom is perhaps beyond our ability to envision; it is usually represented in physics texts as a cloud of points, which hardly does it justice.

Mach was indeed skeptical about unobservables. He was, for example, reluctant to accept the utility of the concept of the atom. Shortly before his death, Einstein recalled trying, many years earlier, to convince Mach of the utility of atomic theory. He managed, finally, to get a concession: "[If] an atomic hypothesis would make it possible to connect by logic some observable properties which would remain unconnected without this hypothesis, then, Mach said, he would have to accept it. Under these circumstances it would be 'economical'..." (Cohen, 1955, p. 73).

Atomic theory won out, of course, over Mach's skepticism. Unobservables have proven themselves invaluable in modern physics. We cannot reject outright the use of unobservables in our theories; rather, we can assert, as did Mach to Einstein, that where we can account for as many facts with observables as with unobservables, we should probably prefer the former.

Generality. Fourth, Mach may have been saying that the principles we use to present our multitude of facts should be applicable to as many domains as possible. If one set of principles can account for both the Doppler shift and Brownian motion, or for both the diversity of species and the fossil record, we should prefer that to two separate sets that explain each phenomenon separately. The great drive in theoretical physics is toward a "unified field theory"—one theory that will account for known properties of the four basic forces in nature: the strong and weak forces of the atom, electromagnetic force, and gravitational force. One recent version, which characterizes the universe as an infinity of bubbles, has been praised on the grounds that it has the added merit of offering an account of the origin of matter and energy (Waldrop, 1982). The principles go farther.

My discussion of Mach's statement may be summarized as follows: Science may be regarded as a minimal problem consisting of the completest presentation of the facts in the briefest possible terms, which makes assumptions that can easily be dispensed with, which refers to observables when observables will do, and which has the greatest possible generality. We now have a variant of what has been called the "principle of parsimony."

OCKHAM AND MORGAN

The first statement of such a principle is usually credited to William of Ockham, a fourteenth-century English scholastic and philosopher, although the concept can be found in Aristotle and though, in Ockham's day, it was first stated by Duns Scottus (Boehner, 1957). Ockham proposed a rule of logic which has come to be called "Ockham's Razor." He stated it variously: "Plurality is not to be posited without necessity" (*Pluralitas non est ponenda sine necessitae*) or "What can be explained by the assumption of fewer things is vainly explained by the assumption of more things" (*Frustra fit per plura quod potest fieri per pauciora*).

Taken out of context, such statements seem to imply a strict rule of parsimony, consistent in part with the one I have developed above. But Ockham was first a man of religion, and he applied his logic only insofar as it was consistent with religious dogma. The "real meaning" of such statements, taken in context, is said by a noted scholar of Ockham to be as follows: "We are not allowed to affirm a statement to be true or to maintain that certain things exist, unless we are forced to do so either by its self-evidence or by revelation or by experience or by a logical deduction from either a revealed truth or by a proposition verified by observation" (Boehner, 1957, p. xx). If something were "proved by the authority of a holy scripture," other considerations would be ignored. Ockham's texts could not be used to defend the theory of evolution.

Psychologists, and particularly early behaviorists, were more directly influenced by C. Lloyd Morgan, Edward L. Thorndike, and Jacques Loeb. Morgan was an English psychologist and biologist who, in *An Introduction to Comparative Psychology*, published in 1894, challenged the tendency of some naturalists of his day to attribute human characteristics to animals. One of the worst offenders, George J. Romanes, had argued, following Darwin, that "there must be a psychological, no less than a physiological, continuity extending the length and breadth of the animal kingdom." Especially in cases in which we can show that an animal learns, he said, "we have the same right to predicate mind as existing in such an animal that we have to predicate it as existing in any human being other than ourselves" (Romanes, 1882). Consciousness and mental states were, after all, only inferred in other people from their behavior. Given that there is continuity in nature, should we not give the same credit to animals?

Morgan was no less a mentalist than Romanes, but he took a more conservative stand. Just as evolution had produced organisms that varied from the simple to the complex, he argued, so must it have produced minds that varied from the simple to the complex. It would therefore be presumptuous of us to infer higher mental activities in animals where simpler ones would do. He expressed this position in his famous Canon, sometimes called the Canon of Parsimony: "*In no case may we interpret an action as the outcome of the exercise of a higher psychical faculty, if it can be interpreted as the outcome of the exercise of one which stands lower in the psychological scale*" (Morgan, 1894, p.53; italics original).

Thorndike, who, while a graduate student at Harvard, apparently attended a lecture that Morgan gave there on the topic in 1896, bolstered Morgan's position by showing in his famous puzzle-box experiments that simple mechanistic laws of learning could account for some problem-solving behavior in animals (Thorndike, 1898, 1911). Thorndike was still a mentalist, but, as Skinner (1963) has pointed out, it was only a matter of time before Romanes' argument would be turned around completely. Jacques Loeb, for example, a German-born physiologist who was on the faculty for many years at the University of Chicago, argued that animal behavior consisted largely of tropisms, forced orienting movements determined by physical and chemical reactions. And Pavlov and several of his predecessors in Russia went so far as to characterize all animal behavior—including all human behavior—as reflexive.

As animal behavior was shown more and more to be explainable by simple laws of conditioning, mentalistic accounts became less popular. It was inevitable that non-mentalistic accounts of human behavior would be proposed. The theory of evolution, which had been applied in one way by Romanes to justify the attribution of a mental life to animals and a second way by Morgan to warn against such attributions, could now be applied yet a third way: *Given that animal behavior could be accounted for by laws of conditioning and given that there is continuity in the animal kingdom (which includes Man), human behavior, like animal behavior, should be explainable without reference to mind.* Skinner (e.g., 1945b, 1963, 1977b) has defended this view on many occasions.

PARSIMONY IN THE INTERPRETATION OF BEHAVIOR

Behaviorism. The statement given in italics above is the rationale for early behaviorism. Note that it contains three assertions, none of which is universally accepted by modern psychologists:

First, the statement implies that all animal behavior—or at least all animal behavior which would normally lead people to speak about the mind—can be accounted for in terms of conditioning. This was certainly not true in 1913 when behaviorism formally began and, to my knowledge, is still not true today. Indeed, a variety of complex behavior in animals in general and in chimpanzees in particular has been said to defy conditioning accounts (e.g., Hulse, Fowler, & Honig, 1978; Köhler, 1925; Premack, 1983b; Roitblat, 1982; Savage-Rumbaugh, Rumbaugh, Smith, & Lawson, 1980; Tolman, 1932).

Second, the statement implies a continuity theory that is, ironically, much closer to Romanes' than to Morgan's. Morgan had stressed that evolutionary theory predicted *differences* and *gradations* among traits, whereas both Romanes and the behaviorists insisted that species—or at least human and non-human animals—had a great deal in common. And the debate continues. Modern mentalists assert, as did Romanes, that the mental world is common to many species, or, as did Morgan, that perhaps only humans and a few close relatives posess higher mental processes—that evolution can create discontinuities. Gallup (1977a), for example, supports his assertion that only the higher primates have certain cognitive capacities in part by citing biochemical data which show remarkable similarities between humans and chimpanzees. And behaviorists continue to assert with equal conviction that extrapolations from animal behavior are warranted.

Third and most important, the statement assumes the validity of some variant of the principle of parsimony, one close to Morgan's Canon. A non-mentalistic account of animal behavior is preferable to a mentalistic one presumably because it refers to observables and because it makes fewer and less critical assumptions (about the existence and nature of mind, for example). Note, however, that mentalistic accounts are brief and that they have great generality; sometimes their use has been defended on such grounds (e.g., Miller, 1959). Perhaps more commonly, many modern psychologists reject the principle of parsimony outright. For example, Gallup (1979) has noted that, unlike other animals, a chimpanzee that has been exposed to a mirror for a long period of time will come to treat its mirror image as an image of its own body. From this he infers the existence of a "cognitive entity" called the "self-concept," which he then proposes as the the *explanation* for the chimpanzee's behavior. Although more parsimonious explanations would seem desirable and are indeed possible (Epstein, 1986a; Epstein, Lanza, & Skinner, 1981), Gallup asserts, "As far as the self-concept is concerned, it would appear that on the morning before God created the great apes, maybe he became distracted by his own reflection in the mirror and forgot to shave with Occam's [sic] razor" (1977a, p. 337).[1]

Representation. Chimpanzee behavior is often interpreted in terms of higher mental processes. For example, Savage-Rumbaugh et al. (1980) presented data said to show that chimpanzees are capable of a "representational symbolic function." Having established with three chimpanzees discriminations between three foods and three tools, photographs of those foods and tools, and symbols that the chimpanzees had learned to pair with those foods and tools, the experimenters showed that two of the chimpanzees could successfully categorize novel foods and tools, photographs of novel foods and tools, and symbols that they had learned to pair with novel foods and tools. In claiming that these results were possible only if the chimps were capable of "symbolic encoding" or "representation," the authors were saying, in effect, that the chimp had to "think of" the referent of the symbol it was shown in order to categorize that symbol correctly as either a food or a tool.

I have argued (Epstein, 1982b; cf. Epstein, 1982c) that the training the chimpanzees had received should have produced reasonably good categorization of novel foods and tools or corresponding symbols given only rudimentary processes of conditioning. Before the reported tests, symbols for food had necessarily been paired with food more than symbols for tools had been paired with food. Through classical conditioning, symbols for food would come to elicit food-related responses, such as salivation. The discriminations that were subsequently trained and the subsequent categorization responses could have been based, then, on rather simple contingencies: Early in training, a chimpanzee earned reward by placing into the "food" bin items in whose presence he salivated and by placing into the "tool" bin items in whose presence he did not salivate. Although undoubtedly not the whole story, this history of discrimination training and classical conditioning could easily account for successful performances in subsequent tests, as well as for some of the reported errors.

My interpretation of the chimpanzee data is, I admit, unappealing, but that is beside the point. Sir William Hamilton (1859) wrote that the law of parsimony "forbids ... above all, the postulation of an unknown force where a known impotence can account for the effect" (p. 395). Should we accept an account of the chimpanzees' behavior in terms of "symbolic encoding," "concept formation," and "representation" when a simple history of conditioning will suffice?

This study was not the first in which chimpanzee behavior was unnecessarily overinterpreted. Researchers who have in recent years been trying to teach human-like language to chimpanzees have been criticized by psycholinguists (Chomsky & Premack, 1979), behavioral psychologists (Terrace, Pettito, Sanders, & Bever, 1979), and ethologists (Sebeok & Umiker-Sebeok, 1980) alike. Terrace and his colleagues have pointed out, for example, that imitation and some simple principles of learning can account for much of the language-like behavior. And Epstein, Lanza, and Skinner (1980) showed that an exchange between two chimpanzees which had been unnecessarily attributed to the "information," "knowledge," and "intentions" of the chimpanzees could be closely approximated with two pigeons and could be accounted for fully in terms of simple conditioning procedures.

Overinterpretation in research with chimpanzees is ironic, considering the plight of modern cognitive psychology. Cognitivists generally have no interest whatsoever in either the environmental or genetic origins of the behavior they study—in how, for example, language might have been learned. That is understandable, in a way. The origins of complex behavior are often extremely complicated and, of course, lost in a subject's past. With chimpanzees, on the other hand, the antecedents—the training—the environmental histories—have usually been *programmed*. They are well known, and hence parsimonious accounts of the behavior can at least be attempted.

THE SPONTANEOUS USE OF A TOOL BY A PIGEON

Consider the following example: A pigeon is placed in a large cylindrical chamber, about a yard in diameter and equipped with a standard feeder. A hexagonal box, about 6-inches in diameter and 1-inch high is on the floor in the center of the chamber. The pigeon ignores the box. At the base of a clear Plexiglas wall is a small metal plate, about 1-inch square. The pigeon pecks repeatedly at this plate, and pecks are reinforced intermittently with food. Each peck operates a microswitch and thus produces a brief high-pitched tone. Over the course of a few sessions, the plate is moved back behind the wall a few inches. The bird can see it clearly through the Plexiglas wall. It continues to peck it repeatedly by stretching its neck beneath the 2-inch gap at the base of the wall.

Finally, the plate is moved back a full 6.5 inches behind the wall—too far for the bird to reach. The bird has never been faced with this situation before. What does it do?

A normal 5-year-old child and at least one of Köhler's (1925) chimpanzees would probably, after a fashion, have "solved the problem." A young boy might perform as follows: He reaches repeatedly beneath the wall (or, say, the sofa) and grabs for the metal plate (or, say, the marble). He gives up, perhaps showing signs of frustration. He may have done this dozens of times before and given up each time. But this time he perseveres. He looks pensive, he looks around the room, and, finally, he reaches for a large object on the floor beside him (say, a magazine), and thrusts it under the couch toward the marble. After a few awkward thrusts, he hits the marble and perhaps thus moves it to a location he can reach. We might say that the child had spontaneously used a tool. Lay explanations would invoke the child's "intelligence," "knowledge," "expectations," "intentions," and "imagination." So, of course, would the explanations of many psychologists.

But the pigeon did the same things that our hypothetical child did. The pigeon first stretched repeatedly toward the metal plate. After about 30 seconds, it glanced back toward the hexagonal box. It stretched again a few times toward the metal plate and then began, somehow, to look "frustrated" and "confused" and even "pensive." It pecked at the wall and the floor. It scraped it feed on the floor and rubbed up against the wall. It looked back and forth several times from the box to the plate. Suddenly, after a minute-and-a-half, it began to push the box directly toward the Plexiglas wall. When the box was under the wall, the pigeon lost control of it for a few seconds. It looked again at the plate, made some adjustments, and then pushed the box solidly against the plate and pecked it repeatedly, thus activating the high-pitched tone. It had, it seems, "spontaneously" used the box as an extension of its own beak to solve a simple problem (Epstein & Medalie, 1983).[2]

There are two disturbing things about this result: First, the results would probably have been publishable without reporting the environmental history of the animal. We could have claimed ignorance—the tactic of many developmental psychologists—or disinterest—the tactic of many "cognitive scientists." We could have attributed the entire performance to "cognitions" and "intentions" (cf. Roitblat, 1982; Tolman, 1932). Second and far worse, we could have done what researchers who work with chimpanzees sometimes do: We could have briefly described the environmental history—at least summarized the training the animal had had recently—and *then* attributed the entire performance to "cognitions" and "intentions."

I have analyzed the behavior of the tool-using pigeon elsewhere (Epstein, 1984e; Epstein & Medalie, 1983) and here will merely state some critical facts and make what I hope is a tantalizing assertion: (a) The pigeon had recently had some experiences that are "relevant" to the solution to the problem—just as chimpanzees and children have had hundreds or thousands of such experiences before they are successful in similar situations. (b) The pigeon had never been confronted with this problem before, had never pushed things under a barrier, and had never pushed a box toward the metal plate; its performance, in other words, was genuinely novel. (c) A moment-to-moment account of its behavior is possible in terms of its environmental history and some basic principles of behavior—and without any recourse to "unknown forces."

CAVEATS

I have not in this essay attempted to justify the principle of parsimony (though cf. Feuer, 1957; Goodman, 1972; Kordig, 1971; Mach 1893/1960; Rolston, 1976;

Russell, 1951; Walsh, 1979). In my opinion, no definitive justification can be made. The principle is itself, ironically, an assertion, one that pervades science but that remains, for the most part, unexamined. Since it is a criterion by which a theory is judged to be better or worse than another, it may be little more than a value (cf. Goodman, 1972; Walsh, 1979). The principle probably evolved for reasons that are less grand than any post hoc justifications we might devise. As is true of other pre-scientific or scientific concepts (Epstein, 1982b), the principle may be little more than a reflection of our own limitations: As both theory and research grew more complex, simplification would surely have become a practical concern. The principle of parsimony may be nothing more than an instantiation of the principle of "least effort," and hence we might interpret Mach's "least possible expenditure of thought" literally (cf. Walsh, 1979).

The law of parsimony is accepted as an important criterion in science for judging the merits of a theory or an explanation, but it is not the only one. A theory that is parsimonious need not be "right"—which is to say, it may not be the most effective or useful description of the body of facts for which it is said to account (Barker, 1961; Bunge, 1961; Sober, 1981; Sober & Lewontin, 1982). There are even occasions upon which one can predict with confidence that a parsimonious theory is likely to be wrong. For example, Anderson (1978), a cognitive psychologist, has noted that the most "parsimonious" computer program will probably not be the best one to represent cognition. There is no criterion of parsimony in evolution; redundant and supernumerary organs and mechanisms abound in nature. And there is no reason to believe that human cognition—or its counterpart in the real world, the nervous system—has been spared nature's disinterest.

Should this weaken our faith in parsimony? I think not. We should recognize the limitations of the principle, but we would do ourselves an injustice if we did not admit how well the principle has served. For the principle of parsimony is, as Mach said, what science is all about.

NOTES

1. Philosophers, too, sometimes reject the principle of parsimony as a criterion of good science. For example, Bunge (1961) notes "Simplicity is ambiguous as a term and double-edged as a prescription, and it must be controlled by the symptoms of truth rather than be regarded as a factor of truth.... Ockham's razor—like all razors—must be handled with care to prevent beheading science in the attempt to shave off some of its pilosities. In science, as in the barber shop, better alive and bearded than dead and cleanly shaven" (p. 149). Other philosophers assert parsimony as a fundamental of science (e.g., Goodman, 1972; Walsh, 1979; cf. Mach, 1863/1960), sometimes without defense.

2. Epstein and Medalie (1983) report the performance of only one pigeon. Similar performances have been achieved with two others.

27

THE POSITIVE SIDE EFFECTS OF REINFORCEMENT

Summary. Reinforcement and punishment are said to be symmetrical in their effects. Unfortunately, this assertion has led to simplistic characterizations of each procedure. Both have multiple effects, and either can be misused. Reinforcement, properly utilized, is the preferred intervention because it involves less risk.

Skinner was convinced by some of his earliest research that punishment was not very effective. He found, for example, that when lever pressing in rats had been suppressed by mild punishment and the punishment was then removed, the rate of pressing increased to such an extent that the total number of presses after some time had passed was about the same as it would have been had punishment never been presented (Skinner, 1938, p. 154).[1]

Skinner (1953) also noted some "unfortunate by-products" of punishment: It produces a tendency to attack the individual who has dispensed the punisher. It may produce pathological behavior (for example, stuttering) as a result of conflict it sets up between the punished behavior and behavior that avoids punishment. It may produce debilitating emotional reactions. He suggested various alternatives to punishment: waiting for time to pass according to some "developmental schedule" (p. 191), reinforcing incompatible behavior, extinguishing the behavior, and so on. It is a mark of civilization, he argued, that we turn to alternatives to punishment.

Subsequent developments have generally complemented Skinner's early views. The list of alternative ways to suppress behavior has grown tremendously, as he predicted it would. An examination of some recent texts on behavior analysis and therapy suggests at least 15 others, including time-out, modeling, instructions, differential reinforcement of any other behavior (as opposed simply to specific behaviors that are incompatible with the target behavior), differential reinforcement of an alternative behavior (as opposed to one that may be incompatible with the target behavior), differential reinforcement of low rate, sudden stimulus presentation (for example, a loud noise), adaptation, physical restraint, restitution, positive practice, fixed-time and variable-time schedules of reinforcement (which are response-independent), satiation, stimulus change, and so on.

The list of unfortunate by-products has also grown. Therapists are warned about possible widespread suppression effects, negative modeling, escape and avoidance, the establishment of inflexible, ritualistic behaviors, and so on. Subsequent research has also revealed what some consider to be "symmetries" between reinforcement and punishment—that is, they produce similar, but opposite, effects under some circumstances. A single punisher may produce only a temporary decrease in rate of responding, but a single reinforcer produces only a temporary increase, after all. And Skinner's contention that the effect of punishment is only temporary does not apply to all cases: Severe or prolonged punishment can produce enduring effects (e.g., Azrin & Holz, 1966; Boe & Church, 1967).

Balsam and Bondy (1983) have recently summarized some of these developments and, in so doing, have drawn what I believe to be incorrect conclusions about the nature of reinforcement. Their major argument may be stated as follows: Reinforcement and punishment have been shown to be symmetrical in their effects on behavior. Since punishment produces negative side effects, reinforcement, too, should be expected to produce negative side effects, and the clinical literature provides examples of such effects. We should, therefore, be cautious in our use of reinforcement techniques.

I will present two major objections to their arguments, as well as several minor ones.

SYMMETRY AND CONTINGENCIES

The first problem is a matter of logic. If reinforcement and punishment produce similar but opposite effects, and if punishment produces *negative* side effects, then reinforcement should produce *positive* side effects. This conclusion is unavoidable as long as the authors insist that reinforcement and punishment produce *symmetrical* effects, as opposed to *similar* ones. Punishment weakens behavior; reinforcement strengthens it. Punished behavior may *re*appear; reinforced behavior may *dis*appear. It follows that if punishment produces unpleasant emotions, reinforcement should produce pleasant ones (it usually does). If punishment produces a tendency to escape the source of punishment, reinforcement should produce a tendency to approach the source of reinforcement (it often does, as the authors note). If punishment produces aggression, reinforcement should produce signs of affection (again, it often does). If punishment can produce widespread suppression, then reinforcement should be able to produce an increase in the general level of activity. And so on.

I am suggesting that the symmetry argument should lead to a very different paper than the one the authors have written. But this argument is, it seems to me, actually irrelevant to what seems to be the substance of the paper. Balsam and Bondy describe, with justifiable concern, a number of reinforcement procedures that have produced troublesome behavior not anticipated by those who administered the reinforcement. Where did these behaviors come from, and was reinforcement the culprit?

The authors fail for the most part to distinguish between the effects of reinforcers on the one hand and the effects of *contingencies of reinforcement* and *schedules of reinforcement* on the other. It is true that certain contingencies or schedules can produce behavior other than the behavior one may be reinforcing. Fixed-interval schedules of food reinforcement in rats, for example, lead to excessive drinking when water is freely available, as the authors note. But is the drinking produced by the reinforcer itself or by the *withdrawal of* or *unavailability of* the reinforcer? Aggression and ritualistic behaviors are indeed produced by certain *schedules* of reinforcement. But far from being an indictment of reinforcement per se, this is an indictment of the *lack of* reinforcement. Post-reinforcement effects are produced by the *withdrawal of* reinforcement, an operation which is sometimes labeled "punishment" (e.g., Catania, 1968, p. 343). Interim and terminal effects are the result of the *unavailability of* reinforcement during the interreinforcement interval, a period resembling a period of extinction (Cohen & Looney, 1984; Gentry, Weiss, & Laties, 1983; Staddon, 1977).

Particular *contingencies* of reinforcement can strengthen and maintain "lying, cheating, stealing, and conniving," but reinforcement itself is not the culprit. It is rather, poor contingencies that are at fault. Zeiler (1977) notes that in setting up one contingency we often inadvertently arrange other, "indirect" contingencies. For example, on a variable-interval schedule of reinforcement, the explicit contingency has to do only with the time that has passed since the last reinforcer: The first response after this interval has elapsed will be reinforced. But this contingency also differentially reinforces pauses between responses: Long pauses are more likely to pay off than short pauses. On a variable-ratio schedule, however, there is no advantage to pausing between responses, and, hence, it produces a higher response rate than a variable-interval schedule when the two schedules yield the same rate of reinforcement (Ferster & Skinner, 1957).

Some of the so-called "negative side effects" described by Balsam and Bondy involve troublesome behavior that is supported by contingencies that have been set up inadvertently. They note, for example:

> Operant aggression may be directed at others in the vicinity of a reinforcing agent. That is, if dispensing reinforcers to others reduces the availability ... of reinforcers for a particular individual, that individual will be rewarded for preventing the dispersal of the reinforcers. (1983, p. 291)

In this case, an explicit contingency has been arranged: Say, sitting in one's seat produces tokens. But, because the tokens are in short supply, another contingency is also in effect: Inciting one's neighbors to misbehave maintains the token supply. By no means is the latter behavior a "negative side effect." It is simply the case that several contingencies are in effect, one of which produces troublesome behavior.

The authors also identify the failure of training to transfer from one setting to another as a "negative side effect." Transfer of training is a function of many factors—the similarity of the settings, the prevailing contingencies in the new setting, the schedule of reinforcement used in the original training, and so on—and it can be preprogrammed to some extent—for example, by providing training in self-management(Baer, 1981; Epstein & Goss, 1978; Rhode, Morgan, & Young, 1983; Rincover & Koegel, 1975; Stokes & Baer, 1977; Walker & Buckley, 1972). But the failure to transfer is not a "negative side effect"; it is not even a "side effect." It is yet another engineering problem (and a challenging one).

The authors note, furthermore, that reinforcers can suppress the very response they were meant to support. It is true that conditioned and unconditioned reinforcers can act as conditional and unconditional stimuli (and, for that matter, that discriminative stimuli that have been part of more than one contingency can increase the probability of more than one behavior). The presentation of a particular reinforcer might indeed interfere with conditioning, but this is at best a *complication* of its dual role as reinforcer and elicitor. Again, I suggest that the label "negative side effect" is misleading.

Balsam and Bondy (1983) have included imitation in their list of negative side effects of reinforcement, and, this, too, seems inappropriate. Imitating undesirable behavior could, I suppose, be called a negative side effect of *imitation*, but it has nothing to do with reinforcement. (It is true that a repertoire of generalized imitation could have been acquired through reinforcement, but to blame subsequent instances of the imitation of undesirable behavior on reinforcement is stretching things.)

Finally, the authors have not made the best use of Herrnstein's (1970) matching law. The law predicts, they say, that a high density of reinforcement during a therapy session may produce lethargy and depression outside of therapy (no supporting data are given). But a therapy session does not take place simultaneously with the rest of one's life; that is, the two situations are not "concurrent." They are closer to components in a multiple schedule, for which the unadorned matching law works poorly. "Undermatching" is the rule on such schedules—which is to say that the components are more independent than the law predicts—except when they are only a few seconds long (Charman & Davison, 1982; Lander & Irwin, 1968; Lobb & Davison, 1977). It would be a mistake to say that the law could predict a significant decrease in responding during 167 hours outside of therapy just because extra reinforcers were introduced during the 168th (cf. McDowell, 1982). The reasons for depression after therapy are surely much more complex than the authors acknowledge. And, anyway, there must be at least a few cases in which patients emerge from therapy *less* "withdrawn, obsessed, or monotonous."

Contingencies of reinforcement can be arranged to support almost any behavior, "negative" or "positive." Reinforcement should not be considered suspect simply because it can strengthen aggressive behavior or crying, or because poor contingencies may produce behavior that does not immediately generalize to new surroundings, or because inadequate contingencies may fail to establish a discrimination. We should conclude instead that some contingencies are better than others.

COMPLEXITY AND ETHICS

I suggest another approach to the general concerns Balsam and Bondy (1983) have raised: Rather than talk about "side effects," we should look more generally at the *effects* our interventions produce—in all their complexity. The physical appearance, mannerisms, and verbal and non-verbal behavior of the therapist undoubtedly affect patients moment-to-moment in time in ways that are far more complex than our concepts can capture at the moment. It seems safe to say that one cannot affect any single response class without affecting others; response classes seem to interact in orderly ways (Dunham & Grantmyre, 1982; Epstein, 1983a, 1985d; Herbert, Pinkston, Hayden, Sajwaj, Pinkston, Cordua, & Jackson, 1973; Kazdin, 1982; Nordquist, 1971; Sajwaj, Twardosz, & Burke, 1972). A stimulus that serves as a reinforcer for one organism on one occasion may not do so on another; it may not do so for another member of the species or for another species. The delivery of a single bit of food, even under laboratory conditions, produces multiple effects: It may increase the probability of that behavior under similar (what does that mean?) stimulus conditions, it may elicit behaviors of phylogenic origin, it may make other stimuli effective in the future as discriminative stimuli or conditional stimuli or both, its ingestion may reduce the effectiveness of the delivery of the next bit of food, and so on. Moreover, both reinforcers and punishers are known to have discriminative properties (e.g., Azrin & Holz, 1966; Reid, 1958).

When, as a result of conditioning, a stimulus acquires controlling properties over some behavior, other stimuli become effective in controlling that behavior; there is a spread of effect from one stimulus to other stimuli. We cannot predict where the spread will occur, except perhaps when, in the laboratory, we are using absurdly simple stimuli that fall neatly along some continuum. In the real world, the problem is much more difficult.

The simple withholding of reinforcement is also not so simple. It leads, eventually, to a decrement in the response that had been producing reinforcement. But it also produces increases in response force, variability in responding, emotional behavior, and, it seems, a resurgence of behaviors that were previously reinforced under similar stimulus conditions, a phenomenon that has profound implications for therapy (Amsel, 1958; Antonitis, 1951; Epstein, 1983a, 1984g; Masserman, 1943; Notterman, 1970; Sears, 1943; Yates, 1970; cf. Sajwaj et al., 1972). As Balsam and Bondy have noted, punishment, too, produces complicated effects (also see Hutchinson, 1977; Walters & Grusec, 1977). Schedules of reinforcement and punishment, multiple consequences, and response-independent events introduce further complications (e.g., Church, 1969; Epstein, 1984g; Morse & Kelleher, 1977). And, of course, all of these operations are simplifications of the kinds of events that occur in the real world, where multiple determination is the rule.

Finally, the history of the organism makes a profound difference in the effectiveness of any these operations and of any others. Previous conditioning is critically important in the emergence of problem-solving behavior, for example (Epstein, Kirshnit, Lanza, & Rubin, 1984). The effect of any intervention should be determined in large part by previously established behaviors, previously established discriminative stimuli and conditional stimuli, and so on. And the conditioning history is only one small part of an organism's total environmental history. Other factors are critical in the analysis of behavior in clinical settings: an individual's medical problems, nutritional history, history of physical trauma, history of exposure to allergens and drugs, and so on.

This may sound depressing, but it shouldn't. As Ferster so often pointed out, we should recognize how little we know and be prepared to see effects that we cannot yet predict. Effective intervention requires a sophisticated knowledge of many factors; the better one's analytical skills, the more effective one will be.

In any comparison between punishment and reinforcement, ethical issues should be considered, and I don't believe that they were considered adequately in Balsam and Bondy's paper. Reinforcement, by definition, is something organisms seek, and, more often than not, it produces pleasant emotional reactions. Punishment, at least by some definitions, is something organisms avoid. It produces discomfort, suffering, and even pain. Just one presentation of a severe shock, entirely independent of behavior, can cause severe suppression, signs of withdrawal and depression, cries and other signs of distress, frantic attempts to escape from an experimental chamber, and even death. Misapplied, the administration of punishment is a serious crime. In some states, even the potentially therapeutic administration of punishment is a crime. When reinforcement and punishment are both possible in the treatment of some maladaptive behavior, reinforcement should be the treatment of choice, if only for ethical reasons.

A standard guideline in medical practice is pertinent: When several remedies are possible for a given patient and problem, *try the least intrusive one first*, and then, if necessary, the more intrusive ones. If you complain of knee pain, a physician might first recommend rest and a hot compress; if that doesn't work, physical therapy, then perhaps drugs, and, finally, as a last resort, surgery (what could be more intrusive?). Punishment techniques are potentially far more harmful to subjects than reinforcement techniques; they, too, should be used only as a last resort. I have no doubt that Balsam and Bondy would agree, but the point was not made clearly in their paper, and their title alone—"The Negative Side Effects of Reward"—might lead someone to a different conclusion.

The authors began their paper with a story, presumably apocryphal, about one Dr. B., who turned a quiet student into a garrulous nudge by praising some of the student's comments. Dr. B. panicked; he had produced more behavior than he had intended to, and he didn't know how to turn it off. Balsam and Bondy would call the extra behavior a "side effect" of reinforcement. They conclude their paper, "As for Dr. B., he has learned a lesson that Emerson (1883) so aptly phrased, 'Every sweet hath its sour [presumably they mean reinforcement], every evil its good [could this mean punishment?]'" (p. 294). I suggest a more conservative conclusion:

"As for Dr. B., he was a poor behavior modifier; he knew how to reinforce but not how to shape or how to establish a discrimination. He was the victim, not of what someone once called 'the negative side effects of reward,' but merely of inadequate training in the principles of behavior."

NOTE

1. A figure on page 154 of *The Behavior of Organisms* (Skinner, 1938), for example, contains cumulative record segments which show average responding in each of two groups of rats whose lever presses were extinguished over a 2-hour period. The first segment is a typical negatively-accelerated extinction curve in which about 100 responses were emitted during the first 30 minutes and about 200 responses were emitted in total over the 2 hours. The second segment shows responding in a group of rats whose presses were punished for 10 minutes at the beginning of the extinction period (the rats' paws were slapped with a mechanical hammer when the lever was depressed). The second curve is more nearly linear. Only about 25 responses were emitted during the first 30 minutes, but by the end of the 2 hours, about 200 responses appeared, as in the first group. Skinner believed that responses in the second group were held in a "reserve" (a concept he later abandoned), all waiting to come out once the emotional effects of punishment had dissipated. On the basis of this and other experiments, he concluded: "the experiments on periodic negative conditioning show that any true reduction in reserve is at best temporary and that the emotional effect to be expected of such stimulation can adequately account for the temporary weakening of the reflex actually observed" (p. 157). In other words, punishment has only a temporary effect.

28

SHOULD YOU PUNISH YOUR CHILD?

Summary. Many humane techniques are available for managing a child's behavior. Punishment should generally be avoided because of its possible ill effects. However, eliminating punishment from child rearing would be like eliminating surgery from medicine. In some instances, failing to punish may do more harm than punishing.

Here are three ways in which I've seen children punished recently:

1) At a friend's house, a bubbly three-year-old boy bounded into the living room where I was sitting. His parents were out of the room for the moment. He approached the upright piano to my left, smiling broadly. He reached up toward the keys but then paused, mid-reach, and looked around quickly. Seeing no one but me—and he gazed extra long at me, I noticed—he proceeded to pound gleefully on the keys. "A Beethoven in the making," I mused.

But the child's joy was short-lived, because the noise soon brought his dad into the room, who shouted, "I've *told* you not to touch the *piano*, and you're disturbing our guest!" The little boy left the room making a new kind of loud noise.

2) I took an employee of mine to lunch, and she brought her little girl. The girl threw a piece of spaghetti across the table at one point, and her mother shouted "No!" and slapped the girl's thigh rather hard. The girl started to cry, and her mother shouted "No crying!" and slapped her again on the thigh. The daughter—understandably, I thought—cried louder, and, to my astonishment, her mother admonished her again and slapped her again. The more the child cried, the harder her mother slapped. This sequence repeated itself for nearly ten minutes, by which time the child's crying was reduced to a pathetic whimper, like that of a wounded animal. She never actually stopped crying, of course.

3) I saw a neighbor's 12-year-old boy playing basketball with great gusto outside his house on a school day, and I asked why he was home. He didn't seem at all sick. He explained that he and some other children had left the school grounds the day before without permission. They were all "suspended" for three days. He concluded, "Pretty great punishment, don't you think? Wanna play some one-on-one?"

In each case children were being "punished," just as you and I were when we were children. We *punish* our children by doing something that we think they'll find unpleasant. We take this step to stop certain behavior.

The father of the would-be pianist used a loud reprimand to discourage his child from playing. The impatient mother slapped her crying child to try to stop the crying. A school official suspended the basketball player in an attempt to dissuade him from leaving school grounds without permission.

Do such techniques actually work? Do they stop or eliminate unwanted behavior?

Our everyday experiences suggest that the answers to these questions are not so simple, and decades of research on punishment by behavioral scientists have confirmed this. A therapist might predict, for example, that the young pianist might grow up to hate all musical instruments or even all music. The spaghetti thrower could be a candidate for chronic depression or suicidal thoughts. The basketball player has learned another way to manipulate the system, if he's learned anything at all.

Punishment may actually work in the short term in some cases, and it may even be the very best method to use, but what other effects might it have besides the possible suppression of unwanted behavior? What are its long-term effects? How, for example, does it affect relationships?

The behavioral sciences have identified many alternative methods for suppressing unwanted behavior. The results of many research studies can help us to understand when punishment should be used, how it should be applied, and what outcomes we might expect.

These are critically important issues for every one of us. Perhaps the best way I can make this point is to repeat a dramatic statement I have made in various lectures around the country, a statement supported by many experts on mental health: *"Virtually every emotional, psychological, or behavioral problem we have as adults is rooted in punishment we received at some point in our lives, often when we were children."*

The converse is also true, generally speaking. Happy adults have generally been exposed to relatively little punishment, or they have spent many, many years overcoming a history of punishment, often through therapy. Mental health professionals of virtually every persuasion—Rogerian, Freudian, Skinnerian, you name it—will confirm that that's mainly what therapy is about.

I made these points once to a group of college students in Tennessee (where over 65,000 students are paddled in the public school system each year), and several of the students got quite upset. One young man, sitting far in the rear of the lecture hall, raised his hand and said, his voice shaking, "My pa used to beat me outside our house when I was growing up to teach me right from wrong. I'm a better person for it, and I'm going to raise my own children the same way."

I stood my ground. "There are better, gentler, more humane, more powerful techniques available for teaching right from wrong," I said. "If your father had known about them, I'm sure he would have used them, because I'm sure he loved you very much."

The young man started to cry, a sure sign that he was still carrying a great deal of the pain of those beatings. Did he have mixed feelings about his father? In therapy, this would probably have been revealed. As a young child, did he really understand what his father was trying to accomplish, or was he just terrified and confused most of the time?

The beatings had left their mark, to be sure.

Punishment is a powerful technique of behavior change that can do extraordinary harm. Beatings can leave bruises of all sorts which last a lifetime, and even very mild punishment—a casual remark by a teacher, for example—can have a profound impact. Because punishment is widely used in our society and because it can have such deleterious effects, it's important that we learn about it. We need to know about alternatives to punishment and about how to use punishment properly when better alternatives are not available. In fact, behavioral scientists have identified *dozens* of alternatives to punishment, some of which I'll describe in this article.

When I was 13, an older cousin told me a funny story about a blunder of hers. It seems that when a new family moved onto her block, she tried to play the good neighbor. The mother said that she would like to buy some curtains for her many bare windows, so my cousin offered to take her shopping the following day. She arrived at the appointed hour and hustled the neighbor and the neighbor's little girl into her car. They didn't seem to want to go, but that didn't bother my cousin. She was *determined* to help.

She brought them to the curtain department in a local department store and showed them many beautiful curtains, but the mother seemed uninterested. My cousin, on the other hand, got so excited by her own sales pitch that *she* bought several pairs. Was she hoping the neighbor would imitate her?

The sales clerk offered all of them free tickets to an amusement park, so, undaunted by her failure as a curtain vendor, my cousin hustled her new neighbors into the car again and took them to the park for the rest of the day. The daughter had a good time, but the mother didn't seem very appreciative.

Turns out the woman my cousin had picked up with the little girl was the babysitter, not the mother. When she finally drove them home, she found the mother in the driveway—in an unneighborly mood.

The mother was about ten years older and thirty pounds heavier than the babysitter, by the way. Laboratory animals could easily have told them apart. (Rest assured that my relatives on the other side of the family are much, much smarter....)

Okay, maybe it's not the best story in the world, but I put my heart into writing about it for my eighth grade English class, and I tried especially hard to turn it into a roaring comedy. In my story, my cousin got so excited about the curtains that she even sold a pair to the store janitor. Alas, my teacher was unimpressed. At the top of my paper she scribbled the words: "I don't get it. What's the point? By any chance, were you trying to be *funny*?"

I was devastated. So devastated, in fact, that it was a full *twenty years* before I tried my hand at writing humor again. One insensitive remark. Twenty years damage.

Not every child would be so hurt by such an experience, of course. But punishment, mild or severe, always involves a degree of risk. A retired teacher I know once told me, "I just hope I didn't do too much damage." Some kids are easily damaged, and punishment is usually the culprit.

The behavioral sciences have taught us a great deal about punishment in all its forms. One thing we know for sure is that punishment produces a number of *side effects*. Here are the major ones:

1) *Unpleasant feelings*. We usually feel awful when we're punished. Let's face it, when we *don't* feel awful, the punishment wasn't really punishment—like the basketball player's suspension from school. A child who has been struck or reprimanded feels angry and depressed. We are not immune to such feelings as adults; how do you feel when a police officer pulls your car over on the highway or when you are criticized by a boss you truly admire?

2) *Counterattack*. I'll never forget when, as a young babysitter, I tried to take a sharp object away from a three-year-old boy. He bit me! That, it turns out, is a fairly natural reaction to being punished. When someone punishes you, you feel like you're being attacked, and a natural tendency is to counterattack. Monkeys whose tails are shocked will attack and bite literally *anything* within reach, and we do much the same. Transgressors who are punished in school have been known to return later and break windows, and, sad to say, these days that is a fairly mild form of counterattack in our schools. By no means am I defending misbehavior. I am simply pointing out that counterattack is one natural, and very unfortunate, outcome of punishment.

3) *Escape and avoidance*. When I was seven, my dad threatened to spank me for some reason (I'm sure there was no justification!). I locked myself in a bathroom, climbed out the window (dropping about six feet), and hid in the garage. Some kids get much farther. It is natural to want to avoid or run away from people who punish us.

4) *Negative modeling*. Parents who punish their children serve as powerful models, and many people are aware of this danger. By using punishment, you teach your children that punishment is a legitimate way to handle problems. When you shout at your older child, almost invariably, within the next few hours you'll hear that child shout at a younger one, often using the same tone or same words you had used. Classic studies by Bandura and others have demonstrated this phenomenon in a striking fashion. Children who have seen adults hitting a large doll, for example, will later hit the doll in almost precisely the same fashion later.

With very few exceptions, we raise our own children the way we were raised; we imitate our parents to an extraordinary degree, even though we objected to the way they raised us! Unfortunately, this also means that parents who were abused as children tend to abuse their own children, as studies confirm.

5) *Widespread suppression*. Striking or shouting at your little girl for touching your VCR might dissuade her from touching it again, but it may also

suppress a great deal of other behavior that you didn't mean to eliminate. She may forever be afraid of *all* VCRs or *all* electronic devices or *all* mechanical equipment. She may even be afraid of investigating other things she's curious about, and she will certainly be afraid of *you*. A child who is severely criticized on one school assignment might subsequently have trouble speaking up in class.

The more severe the punishment, the more widespread the suppression, and *we don't yet know how to predict which behaviors will be affected.* In other words, punishment can produce unpredictable effects that are both long-lasting and dramatic.

6) *Damage to relationships.* Punishment leaves scars on relationships. It's hard to feel entirely good about people who punish you. You always fear them. You can never give them all your trust. You always feel a little uncomfortable around them, afraid that your next step will bring their wrath. When one party uses punishment in a relationship, the other party often does, as well, and the result can be endless argument and conflict.

Damage to one relationship can even carry over to others. Adults who were abused as children, for example, often have trouble establishing meaningful relationships with other adults.

7) *Damage to ourselves.* Sometimes—but not always—we feel guilty after we have used punishment, especially if we have punished our own child. When a youngster dissolves in tears, we wonder whether we have done the right thing. Have we been "abusive"? Was there a better way to handle the problem? Sometimes a child will sense our dilemma and take advantage, crying and sulking for hours just to make us feel worse. I've seen several moms "give in" under such a siege and ask their children for forgiveness. Punishment has completely backfired in this case. It has taught the child a new way to manipulate mom or dad, and it has made the parent feel cruel and ineffectual.

So what should you do if your child is driving you up the wall? Fortunately, we have identified a great many humane and effective alternatives to punishment, by which I mean that you can stop, weaken, or suppress unwanted behavior in many ways without using punishment. In a course I teach for therapists, I cover more than *fifty* such techniques, a number that surprises even veteran psychotherapists. Here are a few especially easy and powerful techniques:

1) *Modify the environment.* Sometimes a child shouldn't need to learn *not* to do something. Very young children need to explore and touch; that's natural and healthy, and it shouldn't be discouraged. When my two-year-old began playing with the knobs of my stereo system, I mounted broad shelves on the wall about five feet off the ground, and the stereo remained safe there for years. (The shelves were just a tad too high for my wife to access easily. Was that deliberate on my part?) Both of my children tended to tear the dust jackets off of hardcover books on the lower book shelves. Up they went to the higher shelves! (I mean the books, of course, not the children!)

Changing the environment is such an easy way to eliminate unwanted behavior, yet many of us forget this simple approach. Instead, we use our voices or our hands: "Stay away from that stairwell!" (Why not add a sturdy gate?)

"Stop staring out that window!" (Why not draw the curtains or rearrange some furniture?)

2) *Teach your child how to cope.* Children of all ages can be taught simple skills to help them handle difficult situations in which they would otherwise act inappropriately. A very young child, for example, can be taught to calm down by taking deep breaths, and many other such techniques—called "self-management" techniques—are available to suit different situations and children of different ages and abilities.

Pre-schoolers have benefitted from learning a simple method called "The Turtle Technique." When your child is calm, instruct him or her as follows: "Turtles get upset sometimes, and, when they do, they pull back into their shells where it's cozy and warm. Pretty soon, they feel calm and comfortable again, so they come back out. You can do the same thing when you're starting to feel upset or angry." Show your child how to be a turtle by lowering your head and curling your hands up over your head. Have your child do the same thing, and praise him or her for imitating you. Praise is a form of what psychologists call "positive reinforcement," and it's one of the most effective and humane teaching tools we have. Then, the next time your child gets angry or has a tantrum, rather than punishing, remind your child how to be a turtle and then praise him or her for calming down.

3) *Practice makes perfect.* When your child does something wrong, have her practice doing something right. This is like having someone "make up" for a mistake they made. If your daughter breaks a glass, have her sweep up the mess *and* clean the counter. When one child breaks another's toy, have him apologize *and* give the child one, or even two, of his own toys. Let the message be, "In our house, when we do something wrong, we *make up* for what we did."

This policy works especially well if it applies to the *parents* as well as to the children. If you've forgotten to take your kids to the park, as you had promised, do you deserve to be *punished* for your misbehavior? Don't even bother to wait for the kids' complaints. Say, "Look, kids, I let you down. How 'bout if I take you to the park *twice* next week—and to the baseball game next month?"

True, it's a lot of work to make up for a wrong, but it makes you feel good afterward because you've *erased* the wrong, and it helps to preserve and renew relationships.

Extensive studies by psychologists Nathan Azrin, Richard Foxx, and others, have shown the efficacy of this powerful technique—which they call "positive practice"—with many different types of behavior and with both normal and impaired children.

4) *Rehearse, rehearse, rehearse!* Act out difficult situations with your children. If your daughter has been talking back to her teacher, pretend you're the teacher and act out the school scene with your child. Give her tips on where she might have gone wrong, and show her better ways to handle similar situations in the future.

When you work with your child in this way, you fulfill some of your most important functions as a parent: You are an educator, a teacher, a helper, and a partner—rather than an adversary.

Should You Punish Your Child? 261

5) *An ounce of prevention.* Don't wait for your child to go wrong. If you know that she is restless on long car trips, remind her frequently of the rules *before* she gets out of hand. "Don't forget to keep your hands inside the car. Good girl!" If that's not enough, take occasional breaks on the road to let her unleash that awesome energy of hers *outside* the car.

Reminding a child about the possibility of punishment may also be helpful, but such a reminder can generate as much anxiety as punishment itself—in fact, it's usually called a "threat." You're better off encouraging good behavior in your child and then attending to it and praising it as much as you can.

6) *Teach the "Three M's"*: You can teach your children how to change their own behavior by teaching the "Three M's"—simple skills of "self-management."

The first **M** is "**M**odify your environment." Rather than changing your son's space for him, teach him the general idea. If he gets distracted by the view outside his window when he should be doing homework, ask him how he might rearrange his room to help solve the problem. Even without coaching, he might surprise you with, "I'll try moving my desk away from the window!" Teach him the general principle: *You can accomplish many of your own goals by changing your surroundings, often in very simple ways.*

Second, teach your children to "**M**onitor their behavior." Extensive studies have shown that behavior often changes for the better when we are more aware of what we are doing. One simple way to make children more aware is to help them make a chart to keep track of their progress. Many children feel great pride when they can see the progress they're making. And, again, teach your child the general principle: *Monitoring what you do helps you do better.*

Third, teach your children that they can sometimes achieve their goals by "**M**aking commitments." Your daughter may study more if she makes commitments to study with friends. These techniques will help you, too!

7) *Time out!* If your child is out of control, getting her away from the stimulating environment will help calm her down, and it's the considerate thing to do, as well. When my boys were tots and started crying in a restaurant, a quick walk in the parking lot would do wonders.

At a friend's house the other day, the two-year-old daughter started throwing food rather than eating it, and I was sitting a bit too close for comfort. Her dad, knowing my interest in behavior change, got panicky and said to me, "Quick, tell us what to do!" "*No way,*" I replied. "I never interfere with other people's parenting. It's the quickest way to lose friends." My friend laughed, and his daughter got me squarely in the eye with a piece of apple.

If I *had* offered advice, I would have said "Time for a time out."

8) *Just because!* A baby-sitter brought a tradition from her family to mine—the "just-because" present. Now and then she would give a hug or a token gift or candy to my sons "just because"—in other words, for no particular reason at all. My kids loved this practice, and, needless to say, they were crazy about the baby-sitter. From a scientific perspective, the just-because present, known technically as "response-independent reinforcement," is a sound practice. It makes everyone feel great, and it makes the adult especially effective both as a role model and an instruction giver. It greatly reduces the need for punishment, because it makes for happier, better-behaved children.

Drop what you're doing right now, and give your child a "just because" hug. You'll both feel better.

9) *Reinforce the good stuff.* Reinforcing good behavior is a great way to get rid of bad behavior. Praise or reward at the right moment can have a powerful effect. You've probably already heard this before, so I'll tell you some things about reinforcement that you may not have heard.

Psychologists use the term "reinforcement" in a special way. We define it in terms of its *effects*. If an event strengthens behavior, we call it a reinforcer. If it doesn't strengthen behavior, it's not a reinforcer. In other words, *if it doesn't work, it's not a reinforcer.* You may reward good behavior with a trip to a baseball game, but if your child finds baseball boring, the reward won't work as a reinforcer. It won't strengthen the behavior you were trying to strengthen. When rewarding good behavior, find things that your child really wants. Ask her what she wants, or look closely at how she spends her time. If she listens to Michael Jackson records, she might work hard to earn a new one. Whether or not you like Michael Jackson is beside the point. Each to his own taste.

Some people confuse reinforcement with bribery, and that can cause real trouble. If you ask your son to do the dishes, and he just shrugs, you might be tempted to say, "If you do the dishes, you can watch a movie later." At first glance, it looks like you're reinforcing dishwashing, but in fact all you're reinforcing is your son's uncooperativeness. You're really just offering a *bribe* to try to get him do something he has refused to do. Next time you ask him to do something, he's likely to shrug. After all, shrugging got him a reward last time. It's shrugging you reinforced, not dishwashing.

Here's a great way to use reinforcement to help teach your child to calm himself down. When he loses his temper, ignore him until he calms down, even just a little, and then take note immediately. "You calmed down all by yourself! I love it when you do that. Now how can I help you?"

10) *Teach them when to do what.* "Bad" behavior isn't always bad. When the conditions are right, almost any behavior is acceptable. The challenge is to let your children know *when* certain behavior is okay.

Like most parents, I had trouble trying to explain to my children why they shouldn't use profanity, especially when they heard adults swear now and then. I tried to explain that there were times when you could swear without getting in trouble, but I was unable to say exactly when. One day friends and family were having a picnic in the backyard when suddenly my older son shrieked. We ran to where he was sitting on the ground, and he said, "Daddy, Daddy! Justin [his younger brother] just pee'd in my face! Is this the right time to call someone a @#$%@#$?" All of the adults present nodded their heads in profound agreement. "Yes, Honey," I said, "*this* is the right time."

To our relief, Justin was nowhere in sight, and Julian, the victim, took a few deep breaths and calmed down.

11) *Punch that pillow!* Aggressive children often calm down when you give them legitimate ways to blow off steam. Play soccer with your son in the back yard, or see if you can get him interested in joining a team at school. Install a good punching bag in your garage; you may find yourself using it more than your kids do, and that might make you a more tolerant parent! If one child

frequently gets angry and strikes out at another, give her something else to strike. "When you're upset, punch your pillow, not your brother."

12) *Say it, don't yell it.* Plain old instructions can work beautifully sometimes. Unfortunately—especially when an adversarial relationship has already developed—we shout our instructions. Try *saying* what you want from your child rather than shouting it. Your child may be surprised to hear you talk in an even tone of voice. The shock alone may get the child back on course.

Older children—teenagers especially—might ignore what you say. But it's a mistake to give up talking in favor of shouting. If talking alone doesn't work, try the many other alternatives you have for changing your child's behavior. Save shouting for true emergencies ("Fire, fire!"), or you may find that your shouts are ignored when they're truly important, like the cries of the boy who finally saw that wolf.

Child abuse can have devastating effects: chronic depression, dysfunction in social and romantic relationships, insecurity, dysfunction in parenting, and so on. Such outcomes are directly attributable to a history of punishment. But extreme abuse isn't the only form of punishment that does lasting harm, and the possible effects of punishment are many and diverse.

Many sexual problems, for example, can be traced to a history of punishment. Frigidity in woman and impotence in men is, at least in some cases, the result of insults or warnings or threats people have received while growing up. Early sexual encounters can be embarrassing and awkward. An insensitive giggle or critical remark can have a profound effect. Women in our society often have a great deal of anxiety about sex that can be traced to the stern warnings of parents. When a girl who loves her parents is warned, "If you ever get pregnant, don't bother coming home," that's going to take quite a toll on her sexual behavior, and her anxieties won't vanish suddenly the day she marries. Unfortunately, because of the stigmas associated with sex, many people never receive proper treatment for sexual problems, although such treatment is available.

A variety of mood and anxiety problems can also be traced to punishment. One theory of depression, proposed by psychologist Martin Seligman, suggests that depression results from punishment over which you have no control. If you get fired because you did poorly at work, you may get angry, but you will probably not suffer a major depression. If, however, your job is eliminated suddenly without any wrongdoing on your part—say, your company closes—you are a candidate for major depression. Punishing your child for no reason at all, in other words, can do grave damage. *Never* punish without a reason.

Should punishment be used at all? I say yes, but not all of my colleagues will agree. I suggest that where we have other options, we try them before we resort to punishment. Why? Because our kids end up happier, healthier, more functional, and more secure in their relationships if they're not punished. It's that simple.

But the alternatives may not work, so we should certainly not rule out punishment, just as we do not rule out surgery or radiation therapy in medicine.

After all, punishment can be very effective; it's just the side effects that make it so unappealing. Remember that the natural environment uses punishment as a teaching tool all the time: Running on an icy sidewalk, for example, is punished with a fall; we learn to walk carefully as a result. Punishment *is* a powerful technique; it's just not the *only* one.

Before resorting to surgery for a bad knee, a physician tries less risky, less intrusive treatments, such as physical therapy or whirlpool baths. I believe that as parents, we, too, should try less risky, less intrusive methods before resorting to punishment.

Studies indicate that the best parents—the ones whose children feel best, get along with others best, and flourish the most in school—are good at setting limits and administering discipline *and* at showing a high degree of affection toward their children. Developmental psychologists call this type of parenting *authoritative* (not to be confused with *authoritarian*, which leaves out all the affection!). In other words, punishment plays a role in good parenting, but it's important that it not play the *only* role.

As a good parent, you need to recognize the important role you play as a *teacher* of your children. Ask yourself what you want to teach and what you *are* teaching your sons and daughters. Remember that the way you treat your children teaches them how to treat others.

As a good parent, you need to focus on the *outcomes* and on the *effectiveness* of your actions toward your children. Does grounding your child really work? Does it accomplish what you wish to accomplish? Or does it create more problems? Use techniques that *work*, and discontinue them if they're not working. Slapping a crying child to make her stop crying is pointless and cruel. Slapping *makes* people cry.

When should you not hesitate to punish? Experts will probably never reach a consensus on this issue, but here, in any case, are my own recommendations: Swiftly and firmly punish behavior that is dangerous or life-threatening. Swift, intense punishment is the only technique that produces both immediate effects and complete or nearly complete suppression. In a few, relatively unusual situations, you need such suppression for your child's protection. If your little boy runs ahead of you into the street, shout "No!," bring him back onto the sidewalk, and slap his bottom. Point to the street and say "*Never, never* run into the street! It's *very* dangerous!"

Alas, if an older teenager is engaging in life-threatening behavior, you may not have any true punishers available with which to control the problem. You can't slap a teenager on the bottom, and many of the actions you can take are likely to be laughed off. One of the hardest things for parents to accept is that their children are no longer children. You have your biggest effect when your children are young. At some point, you just need to pray that your good parenting has set your children on the best possible path. Using punishment prudently and properly will help set them on that path and will help establish a good relationship that will last into the teen years and beyond.

Should You Punish Your Child? 265

When I was six, I jammed a bobby pin into an electrical outlet. I learned, nearly at the speed of light, never, ever to do that again, and it's lucky, in retrospect, that I wasn't injured or killed. The best protection for your children in this case is to change your environment: Put tight safety covers on all outlets within reach of your young children. A child who persists in tampering with outlet covers should be administered swift and firm punishment. After all, it's the *behavior* you want to terminate, not the child.

I saw a parent mete out severe punishment when her little girl reached out toward a hot stove, but the stove itself would have been a better teacher than the parent in this case. Touching a hot surface hurts, but nature has wired us so that our hand pulls back instantly from hot surfaces, so quickly that sometimes we don't get burned at all. A simple warning was all that was really needed: "Don't touch! That's *hot*. It will *burn* you." Having been warned, if the child touched the stove, she would have learned (a) not to touch stoves, and (b) to heed mommy's warnings in the future!

In those situations when you must punish, try to teach some appropriate behavior. Don't try to eliminate one behavior without building another. After you've admonished your child for running into the street, say, "Always hold Mommy's *hand* when we're crossing a street." Take the child's hand and praise him or her for holding yours. "That's *good*. You're holding Mommy's *hand* on the street. *Very good*."

Continue to work on building appropriate behavior when the incident has passed and your child is calm. That's when he or she will learn best. And, to avoid similar incidents in the future, *prompt* appropriate behavior before a problem occurs. Before you reach the next street corner, say, "We're coming to another street. Remember what I taught you? *Good*, you gave me your hand to hold. *Always* hold Mommy's hand when we cross a street."

When you must punish, give your child a way out if possible. Remember that punishment has many side effects, and it's best to avoid them if you can. Some punishments can drag on forever, and it's especially important to give your child a way of returning things to normal. For example, if you've just told your son that he has lost his allowance for failing to clean his room, add, "But if you finish your room *and* clean the garage, I'll reinstate your allowance." Be sure to give your child *some* way to get that allowance back; otherwise, he may go on strike, and who could blame him?

When you punish, be sure it's for the right reasons. *Never punish out of anger*. I am not suggesting that you never *get* angry, but merely that it's a rotten time to make decisions. Either stay calm, or wait until you're calm before you act. We all make better decisions when we're calm, and we invariably find better ways to deal with our children.

I've heard people say that a parent's anger is natural and healthy, that children can understand it, and that they will try hard to avoid provoking it. But that hardly justifies anger as a method of child rearing, and it's still the case that we make better decisions when we are calm. If you get angry a lot, you are giving your children some bad messages. One is that you can't handle stress very well. If you can't, why should you expect your child to? You're also modeling: You're saying that it's okay to get angry at other people—including you! To control your anger, *learn* better coping techniques, and teach such techniques to your children to help them control *their* anger.

Finally, when you must punish, be sure, when the incident has passed and the child is calm, to remind your child that you love him or her. You are punishing *behavior*, not the child. Even very young children can understand this simple idea, but you need to take the time to put it in words.

"Honey, I spanked you today because you were playing with matches, and matches are very, very dangerous. Grandpa and Grandma were nearly killed in a fire that was started by matches just like those. If you find matches again, you must bring them straight to an adult. If you keep them, I'll spank you again.

"But you know what? I still love you. Even when you do something wrong like this, I still love you very, very much."

"Really, Mom?"

"*Really*. Sweet or sour, good or bad, you'll always have all the love I have."

It's not good poetry, but it's very good parenting.

29

THE QUEST FOR THE THINKING COMPUTER

Summary. Some day we may be able to communicate with computers very much as we do with people. When a computer is indistinguishable from a person in conversation, the computer might be said to be thinking, intelligent, or even self-aware. The annual Loebner Prize Competition in Artificial Intelligence is the search for the first such computer. $100,000 will be awarded to the computer's designer.

In 1985 an old friend, Hugh Loebner, told me excitedly that the Turing Test should be made into an annual contest. We were ambling down a Manhattan street on our way to dinner, as I recall. Hugh was always full of ideas and always animated, but this idea seemed so important that I began to press him for details, and, ultimately, for money. Four years later, while serving as the director of the Cambridge Center for Behavioral Studies, an advanced studies institute in Massachusetts, I established the Loebner Prize Competition, the first serious effort to locate a machine that can pass the Turing Test. Hugh had come through with a pledge of $100,000 for the prize money, along with some additional funds from his company, Crown Industries, to help with expenses. The quest for the thinking computer had begun.

In this article, I'll summarize some of the difficult issues that were debated in nearly two years of planning that preceded the first real-time competition. I'll then describe that first event, which took place on November 8, 1991, at The Computer Museum in Boston and offer a summary of some of the data generated by that event. Finally, I'll speculate about the future of the competition—now an annual event, as Hugh envisioned—and about its significance to the AI community.

PLANNING

Planning for the event was supervised by a special committee, first chaired by I. Bernard Cohen, an eminent historian of science who had long been interested in the history of computing machines. Other members included myself, Daniel C. Dennett of Tufts University, Harry R. Lewis of the Aiken Computation

Laboratory at Harvard, H. M. Parsons of HumRRO, W. V. Quine of Harvard, and Joseph Weizenbaum of MIT. Allen Newell of Carnegie-Mellon served as an advisor, as did Hugh Loebner. After the first year of meetings, which began in January of 1990, Dan Dennett became chair, and he remains so. The committee met every month or two for two or three hours at a time, and subcommittees studied certain issues in between committee meetings. I think it's safe to say that none of us knew what we were getting into. The intricacies of setting up a *real* Turing Test that would ultimately yield a legitimate winner were enormous. Small points were occasionally debated for months without clear resolution. Several still plague us.

In his original proposal, published in *Mind* in 1950, the English mathematician, Alan M. Turing, proposed a variation on a simple parlor game as a means for identifying a machine than can think: A human judge interacts with two computer terminals, one controlled by a computer and the other by a person, but the judge doesn't know which is which. If, after a prolonged conversation at each terminal, the judge can't tell the difference, we'd have to say, asserted Turing, that in some sense the computer is thinking. Computers barely existed in Turing's day, but, somehow, he saw the future with uncanny clarity: By the end of the century, he said, an "average interrogator" could be fooled most of the time for 5 minutes or so.

After much debate, the Loebner Prize Committee ultimately rejected Turing's simple two-terminal design in favor of one that is more discriminating and less problematic. The two-terminal design is troublesome for several reasons, among them: The design presumes that the hidden human—the human "confederate," to use the language of the social sciences—is evenly matched to the computer. Matching becomes especially critical if several computers are competing. Each must be paired with a comparable human so that ultimately the computers can be compared fairly to each other. We eventually concluded that we could not guarantee a fair contest if we were faced with such a requirement. No amount of pre-testing of machines and confederates could assure adequate matching. The two-terminal design also makes it difficult to rank computer entrants. After all, they're only competing against their respective confederates, not against each other.

We developed a multi-terminal design to eliminate these problems: Approximately ten judges are faced with an equal number of terminals. They are told that at least two of the terminals are controlled by computers and at least two by people. Again, the judges do not know which terminal is which. Each judge spends about 15 minutes at each terminal and then scores the terminals according to how human-like each exchange seemed to be. Positions are switched in a pseudo-random sequence. Thus, the terminals are compared to each other and to the confederates, all in one simple design.

Other advantages of this design became evident when we began to grapple with scoring issues. We spent months researching, exploring, and rejecting various rating and confidence measures commonly used in the social sciences. I programmed several of them and ran simulations of contest outcomes. The results were disappointing for reasons we could not have anticipated. Turing's brilliant paper had not gone far enough to yield practical procedures. In fact, we realized only slowly that his paper hadn't even specified an outcome that could be interpreted meaningfully. A binary decision by a single judge would hardly be adequate for awarding a $100,000 prize—and, in effect, for declaring the existence of a significant new breed of intelligent entities. Would some proportion of 10 binary decisions be enough? How about 100 decisions? What, in fact, would it take to say that a computer's performance was indistinguishable from a person's?

A conceptual breakthrough came only after we hit upon a simple scoring method. (R. Duncan Luce, a mathematical psychologist at the University of California, Irvine, was especially helpful at this juncture.) The point is worth emphasizing: The scoring method came first, and some clear thinking followed. The method was simply to have each judge rank the terminals according to how human-like the exchanges were. The computer with the highest median rank wins that year's prize; thus, we are guaranteed a winner each year. We also ask the judges to draw a line between terminals he or she judged to be controlled by humans and those he or she judged to be controlled by computers; thus, we have a simple record of errors made by individual judges. This record does not affect the scoring, but it is well worth preserving. And, finally, if the median rank of the winning computer equals or exceeds the median rank of a human confederate, *that computer will have passed (a modern variant of) the Turing Test.* It's worth quoting part of a memo I wrote to the committee in May of 1991 regarding this simple approach to scoring:

Advantages of this Method

1) It's simple. The press will understand it.
2) It yields a winning computer entrant.
3) It provides a simple, reasonable criterion for passing the Turing Test: When the [median] rank of a computer system equals or exceeds the [median] rank of a human confederate, the computer has passed.
4) It preserves binary judgment errors on the part of individual judges. It will reveal when a judge misclassifies a computer as a human.
5) It avoids computational problems that binary judgments alone might create. A misclassified computer would create missing data, for example.
6) It avoids theoretical and practical problems associated with rating scales.

Other issues were also challenging. We were obsessed for months with what we called "the buffering problem," which has still not disappeared entirely. Should we allow entrants to simulate human typing foibles? Some of us—most notably, Joe Weizenbaum—think such simulations are trivial and irrelevant, but we ultimately agreed to leave this up to the programmers. One could send messages in a burst ("burst mode") or character-by-character ("chat mode"), complete with misspellings, destructive backspaces, and so on. This meant that we had to have at least one of our confederates communicating in burst mode and at least one in chat mode. Allowing this variability might teach us something, we speculated.

We knew that an open-ended test—one in which judges could type anything about any topic—would be a disaster. Language processing is still crude, and, even if it weren't, the "knowledge explosion" problem would mean certain defeat for any computer within a very short time. There's simply too much to know, and computers know very little. We settled, painfully, on a restricted test: Next to each terminal a topic would be posted, and the entrants and confederates would have to communicate on that one topic only. Judges would be instructed to restrict their communications to that one topic, and programmers would be advised to protect their programs from off-topic questions or comments. Entrants could pick their own topics, and the committee would work with confederates to choose the confederates' topics. Moreover, we eventually realized that the topics would have to be "ordinary." Expert systems—those specializing in moon rocks or the cardiovascular system, for example—would be too easy to identify as computers. In an attempt to keep both the confederates and judges honest and on-task, we also decided to recruit referees to monitor both the confederates and the judges throughout the contest.

Sounds simple enough, but we knew we'd have trouble with the topic restriction, and we were still debating the matter the evening before the contest. If the posted topic is "clothing," for example, could the judge ask, "What type of clothing does Michael Jordan wear?" Is that fair, or is that a sneaky way to see if the terminal can talk about basketball (in which case it's probably controlled by a human)?

Should we allow the judges to be aggressive? Should graduate students in computer science be allow to serve? Again, many stimulating and frustrating debates took place. Both in order to be true to the spirit of Turing's proposal and in order to assure some interesting and non-trivial exchanges, we decided that we would select a diverse group of bright judges who had little or no knowledge of AI or computer science. We attracted candidates through newspaper ads that said little other than that one had to have typing skills.

In short—and I am only scratching the surface here—we took great pains to protect the computers. We felt that in the early years of the contest, such protection would be essential. Allen Newell was especially insistent on this point. Computers are just too inept at this point to fool anyone for very long. At least that was our thinking. Perhaps every fifth year or so, we said, we would hold an open-ended test—one with no topic restriction. Most of us felt that the computers would be trounced in such a test—perhaps for decades to come.

We agreed that the winner of a restricted test would receive a small cash award and bronze medal and that the cash award would be increased each year. If, during an unrestricted test, a computer entrant matches or equals the median score of a human, the full $100,000 will be awarded, and the contest will be abolished.

Other issues, too numerous to explore here, were discussed: How could we assure honesty among the entrants? After all, we're dealing with a profession known widely for its pranks. Should the confederates pretend to be computers or simply communicate naturally? We opted for the latter, consistent with Turing. Should we employ children as confederates in the early years? Should professional typists do the judges' typing? How aggressive should the referees be in limiting replies? Should entrants be required to show us their code or even to make it public? We said no; we did not want to discourage submissions of programs with possible commercial value.

Our final design was closely analogous to the classic double-blind procedure used in experimental research: The prize committee members are the "investigators." We know which terminal is which, and we select the judges, confederates, and referees. The referees are analogous to "experimenters." They handle the judges and confederates during the contest. They are experts in computer science or related fields, but they don't know which terminal is which. The judges are analogous to "subjects." They don't know which terminal is which, and they are being handled by people with the same lack of knowledge.

Over time, formal rules were developed expressing these ideas. Announcements were made to the press, and funding for the first contest was secured from the Sloan Foundation and the National Science Foundation. Technical details for running the show were coordinated with The Computer Museum in Boston, which agreed to host the contest. Applications were screened in the summer of 1991, and six finalists were selected by the prize committee in September. Confederates, judges, and referees were selected in October.

THE 1991 COMPETITION

The first contest fulfilled yet another desire of the prize committee. It was great fun. It was an extravaganza. A live audience of 200 laughed and cheered and conjectured while they watched eight conversations unfold in real-time on large screens. A moderator—A. K. Dewdney of *Scientific American*—roamed the auditorium with a cordless microphone, interviewing and commenting. Four film crews and dozens of reporters and photographers bristled and flashed and shouldered each other to get the best angles. Food flowed all day.

The judges and terminals were set up in a roped-off area outside the auditorium. You could view them directly behind the ropes if the journalists would let you by—or on a large screen set up in the auditorium. Groups of about twenty chairs were positioned around each screen in the auditorium, and the moderator encouraged the members of the audience to move to another screen whenever the judges switched terminals—about once every 13 minutes. The confederates were stationed in a remote area of the museum behind a guarded door. Dennett and others made some opening remarks mid-day, and the real-time competition itself took about three hours in the afternoon.

Some technical problems got things off to a frustrating start. Two of the ten terminals would not function properly, knocking out two of the four confederates we had planned to use. We went forward with the six entries and two confederates. (Recall that everyone except the members of the prize committee and some technicians knew simply that at least two of the eight working terminals were controlled by computers and that at least two were controlled by people.)

Our ten judges were diverse, bright, and without expertise in computer science, just as we had planned. Seven were female, and three were male. They ranged in age from 19 to 48; six were in their 20's, one was in her 30's, and two were in their 40's. All were proficient in English, yet one was born in the Philippines, and three had spent most of their lives in foreign countries: Ethiopia, Australia, and West Africa, respectively. Seven had B.A.'s, two of the seven had masters degrees, and two were currently in graduate school. One was high school educated, and two were current college students. Four claimed to have some background in psychology or philosophy. Those not currently in school had a variety of professions: auto mechanic, graphic designer, hypnotist, teacher, and so on.

All communications were by modem. Entrants communicated from PC's or mainframes located throughout the country, and even the confederates' communications were looped through phones outside the building. The judges and audience were told this so that transmission errors would be discounted as clues about the identity of the terminals.

As we expected, the computers performed relatively poorly for the most part. Consider the following exchange—complete with spelling errors—between Judge 2 and Terminal 10 (the topic was "Dry Martinis"):

01:36:42 Judge 2
Of what is gin made?

01:36:52 Terminal 10
I'M NOT SURE.

01:36:58 Judge 2
OK Tell me any thin else you know of about martinis.

01:37:21 Terminal 10
I REALLY DON'T KNOW.

01:37:28 Judge 2
What foods do martinis go with.

01:37:44 Terminal 10
COULD YOU ASK THE QUESTION A DIFFERENT WAY?

01:37:52 Judge 2
Why?

01:37:58 Terminal 10
I REALLY CAN'T SAY. OH WELL.

01:38:04 Judge 2
Ok with what foods shoul onew drink a martini.

01:38:28
I REALLY CAN'T SAY. OH WELL.[1]

Five consecutive replies were unresponsive to the judge's questions; the last two replies were repeated verbatim, a dead giveaway. Frequent typing errors by

The Quest for the Thinking Computer

the judge may have had some effect. Unfortunately, this pattern was common. Consider this exchange (the topic was "Second Grade Topics"):

02:53:22 Judge 4
What do you study at school?

02:53:43 Terminal 3
I don't know.

02:53:51 Judge 4
What do you like most about school?

02:54:16 Terminal 3
As I said- I don't know.

02:54:25 Judge 4
What topic do you know the most about?

02:54:42 Terminal 3
I don't know.

02:54:51 Judge 4
What kind of gymnastics do you do?

02:55:10 Terminal 4
As I said- I don't know.

02:55:16 Judge 4
I thought you were a gymnast.

02:55:27 Terminal 3
Learning is fun.[2]

The winning entry, "Whimsical Conversation," submitted by an independent programmer, Joseph Weintraub of New York City, performed substantially better than the others. It seemed, fairly often, to make contact with the judge's comments and queries. Moreover, it simulated the rhythms and corrections of human typing nearly perfectly. Consider the following exchange:

01:32:25 Judge 6
Hello, earth person!

01:33:03 Terminal 5
Hello there judge, are you ready to have some fun? How ya doin, judge? Hello - how's the weather up there today?

01:33:35 Judge 6
Dark clouds with occasional bursts of sunshine (or rather camera flashes).

01:34:45 Terminal 5
The trouble with the rat race is that even if you win you're still a rat. Whimsy can be flimsy, right? How important is that to you?

01:35:26 Judge 6
I can't say I understand the question...but the whimsy of a poet is one thing and the whimsy of most of us is another.

01:36:51 Terminal 5
How do you know you can t say you understand the question...but the whimsy of a poet is one thing and the whimsy of most of us is another.

01:37:37 Judge 6
Are you repeating me just for laughs?

01:38:04 Terminal 5
I'm sorry, I do sometimes repeat myself...perhaps it's because i can't find my electr]nic organizer!.[3]

In this exchange, the program reflects back one response wholesale, just as Weizenbaum's Eliza did decades ago. But it recovers fairly impressively from the blunder with an apology, simulating typing foibles all the while.

The overall result was fairly predictable, but there were also some surprises. The two human confederates, whose topics were, respectively, "Women's Clothing" and "Shakespeare's Plays," scored in first and second place, respectively. Not far behind was Weintraub's whimsical program; thus, Weintraub won the 1991 contest. He was awarded a bronze medal (bearing a likeness of Turing on the front and Loebner on the back) and a check for $1,500. Weintraub, who tended his equipment in New York during the contest, took questions from the press by speakerphone after the announcement was made. An entry from Peter Colby and Kenneth Colby, of PARRY fame, scored just below Weintraub's. In third place among the computers was a submission from Michael Mauldin of the Center for Machine Translation at Carnegie-Mellon.

The surprises were notable. First, five of the ten judges (Judges 2, 3, 4, 9, and 10) mistook Weintraub's program for a human. Judge 3 rated it above one human confederate (Terminal 1), and Judge 10 rated it above both human confederates (Terminal 1 and 4). The Colbys' program ("Problems in Romantic Relationships") was mistaken for a person by two of the judges, and another program ("Second Grade School Topics") was misclassified by one judge. Perhaps even more remarkable, Cynthia Clay, the human confederate whose topic was Shakespeare's plays, was mistaken for a computer by three judges. Judge 10 placed her lower in rank than a computer (Terminal 5), and two judges (1 and 5) placed her lower in rank than two computers. Note that Cynthia's responses were buffered; that is, her responses occurred in a burst, suggesting computer output. Furthermore, she was an expert on Shakespeare, and she often quoted lengthy passages verbatim. Several judges remarked that her replies seemed too expert to be human.

As Turing anticipated, the contest tells us as much, or perhaps even more, about our failings as judges as it does about the failings of computers. People's preconceptions about the limits of computers—and of people—strongly bias their judgments.

At the start of the contest, members of the audience were given forms to help them do their own judging. The forms asked for basic demographic information, as well. Seventy-seven forms were collected at the end of the contest. Based on this sample, audience ratings may be summarized as follows:

- Audience rankings matched those of the judges, and the rankings of those who claimed expertise in computer science did not differ substantially from the rankings of those who did not claim such expertise. For the 66 respondents who ranked all eight terminals, Terminals 1 and 4 were again ranked first and second, respectively, and Terminal 5 ("Whimsical Conversation") was again ranked third. Curiously, the other five terminals were ranked equally; that is, they were, on the average, indistinguishable.

- Unlike the judges, members of the audience rarely misclassified the terminals, perhaps because members of the audience could communicate with each other; judges could not. For example, the winning computer, "Whimsical Conversation," was labeled a human by only 5 out of the 77 respondents (10 did not reply, leaving 61 correct classifications), and Cynthia Clay (Terminal 4) was misclassified as a computer by only 5 respondents (7 did not reply, leaving 65 correct classifications). The other human confederate, although ranked higher by both judges and audience, was misclassified at nearly the same rate. Once again, expertise in computer science had no systematic effect.

Some students and I have now begun the search for objective factors that might predict the judges' ratings—in other words, that measure the apparent intelligence of an entity communicating over a computer terminal. So far, simplistic factors such as word length, sentence length, number of syllables per word, and number of prepositions are not predictive. Neither are various measures of readability, such as Flesch Reading Ease, Gunning's Fog Index, and Flesch-Kincaid Grade Level. The Weintraub and Colby programs, for example, had Flesch-Kincaid Grade Levels of 2 and 6, respectively; the two humans had scores of 3 and 4.

So why did Weintraub's program win? And how did it fool half the judges into thinking it was a person? Unfortunately, it may have won for the wrong reasons. It was the only program, first of all, that simulated human typing foibles well. Another program simulated human typing so poorly that it was instantly recognizable as a computer on that basis alone; no human could possibly have typed the way it was typing. (All of the conversations may be replayed in real-time using software available from the Cambridge Center for Behavioral Studies.)

Perhaps more notable, Weintraub's program simulated a very curious kind of person: the jester. We allow great latitude when conversing with jesters; incomprehensible, irrelevant responses are to be expected. We are equally tolerant of young children, retarded and autistic individuals, psychotic patients, head-injured individuals, and absent-minded professors. Weintraub's program may have succeeded simply because his terminal was labeled "whimsical conversation." The prize committee recently discussed this possibility, and considerable concern was expressed. In 1992, the committee will favor programs that have clear subject matters.

SPECULATIONS

When a computer passes an unrestricted Turing Test, humankind will be changed forever. From that day on, computers will be companions to the human race—and extraordinary companions indeed. For starters, they will be efficient, fast, natural-language interfaces to virtually all knowledge. They will be able to access and evaluate enormous amounts of data on an ongoing basis and to discuss the results with us in terms we can understand. They will think efficiently 24 hours a day, and they will have more patience than any saint.

Thinking computers will also have new roles to play in real-time control. Everything from vacuum cleaners to power plants has a dumb computer in it these days; some day, smart computers will share in the decision-making. Over networks or even airwaves, thinking computers will be able to coordinate events worldwide in a way humans never could.

Thinking computers will be a new race, a sentient companion to our own. When a computer finally passes the Turing Test, will we have the right to turn it off? Who should get the prize money—the programmer or the computer? Can we say that such a machine is "self-aware"? Should we give it the right to vote? Should it pay taxes? If you doubt the significance of these issues, consider the possibility that someday soon *you will have to argue them with a computer*. If you refuse to talk to the machine, you will be like the judges in *Planet of the Apes* who refused to allow the talking human to speak in court because, according to the religious dogma of the planet, humans were incapable of speech.

Some people, including members of the prize committee, believe that computers will never cross this threshold. But 30 years of reading science fiction novels, 25 years of programming, and nearly 20 years of studying psychology have me convinced that the sentient computer is inevitable. *We're* sentient computers, after all, and those who are skeptical about technological advances are usually left in the dust.

Loebner himself is open-minded, perhaps even skeptical. But he has also offered the most outrageous prediction of all. Some day, he said, when the human race is long dead, a mechanical race will remember us as deities. After all, we are the creators, are we not?

The second annual Loebner Prize Competition in Artificial Intelligence will be held in Boston in December, 1992. Again, the test will be restricted, and $2,000 and the Loebner Prize medal will be awarded to the designers of the best computer entry.

I suspect that the quality of programs in 1992 will not be substantially better than those tested last year, but after the second contest I predict rapid improvement. The 1991 winner received the equivalent of perhaps a million dollars in free advertising through press coverage of the event; nearly 30 million "impressions" appeared in various media in a matter of days following the contest. Three articles appeared in the *New York Times* alone, including a front page article the day after the contest. I predict that major American corporations will soon see some advantages to this. Budget money will eventually be allocated for developing suitable entries. Eventually, the Japanese will get involved. In short, I think the quest for the thinking computer will soon become as intense as the quest for the Holy Grail. The stakes are similar. A program that passes the Turing Test will be worth billions. Just ask it.

I'd like to see the contest expanded at some point to include Turing-like tests of robotics, speech recognition and synthesis, and pattern recognition. In a week-long tournament, computers would compete against people in each domain. The ultimate outcome? Well, did you ever read Asimov's *I, Robot* series?

I may be overly optimistic about the future of artificial intelligence. Certainly, several of my colleagues, much older and, by definition, much wiser than I, tell me so. But we'll all have fun exploring the possibilities—even if, someday, and for reasons I cannot now imagine, we're forced to conclude that the Turing Test cannot be passed.

Postscript*. The second and third annual events were held in 1992 and 1993, respectively, with little improvements in the programs. The 1994 event drew more entries than ever, with, arguably, some slight improvement in quality. In 1993, we began utilizing members of the national press—that is, professional interrogators—as judges, the result being that not a single judge mistook a computer for a person in 1993 or 1994 (although in 1993 one judge ranked the winning computer program as more human than two human confederates). See the June 1994 issue of **Popular Science** or the April 1995 issue of **Wired** for updates. I remain convinced that an unrestricted test can be passed, but it's not clear at the moment that anyone is devoting sufficient resources to the programming effort. The bottom line seems to be this: The human participants in the contest will never get better. The computers will (cf. Epstein, 1994c).*

NOTES

1-3. Copyright, 1991, Cambridge Center for Behavioral Studies. Reprinted by permission. Note that the quotes from the 1991 Loebner Competition transcripts are included here character-for-character as they occurred during the contest. Typographical errors and transmissions errors are included. Complete transcripts of all of the conversations may be obtained by contacting the Center. A playback program is also available, which will replay the conversations in real-time, exactly as they occurred during the contest.

30

THE SELF-CONCEPT AND OTHER DAEMONS

Summary. Organisms acquire a variety of behavior that is said to be indicative of the "self," but attributing such behavior to a "self-concept" is uninformative. An organism's behavior is sometimes controlled by stimuli generated by its own body or by its own behavior. How such "self"-controlled behavior is acquired can usually be established through careful inquiry. Species differ somewhat in their ability to acquire such behavior, and the differences can and should be understood in terms of differences in genetic and environmental histories, differences in sensitivity to environmental contingencies, and species-specific behaviors elicited by specific stimuli. The discontinuity said to exist between the higher primates and other animals has not been shown conslusively.

> But wouldst thou bid the daemons fly,
> Like mist before the dawning sky.
>
> —Sir Walter Scott

The concept of a self-concept is part of a legacy. People have always classified, labeled, and explained their behavior. For lack of facts they have often resorted to verbal devices: They have invented inner agents, mental processes, traits, and cognitive structures which—grammatically, anyway—seem to explain things. The "self-concept" and its close relatives, "self-recognition," "self-awareness," and "self-knowledge," are a subset of the many inventions of this sort which have been handed down to modern psychology.

Phrenologists explained behavior by measuring bumps on the head. In some respects modern psychologists have moved backwards, for the explanatory fictions they promote do not even have physical status. The Devil has given way to short term memory, associations, the ego, mental images, personality traits, expectations, attitudes, intelligence, semantic networks, schemes and schemas, rule structures, processing units, and mental software. It is no surprise that the promoters claim that the new explanatory fictions are better than the old—but they are fictions nonetheless.

There are alternatives. We are organisms, and the behavior of organisms, both covert and overt, can be studied using not only the methods but the most stringent criteria of explanation employed in the natural sciences. Facts about anatomy, physiology, genes, and ontogenic and phylogenic histories are preferable to verbal inventions. Admittedly, progress has been slow—in part, because of the promotion of explanatory fictions—but there is no reason to believe that even the most complex human behavior cannot someday be accounted for with such facts.

In this essay we will examine a portion of the extensive experimental literature on the self-concept which has proliferated in recent years, and we will offer what we hope is a constructive and parsimonious interpretation of some major findings. We first offer some general comments on the very concept of a self-concept.

Reification

The term "self-concept" is often treated as if it refers to a thing, which it does not. Philosophers have called this kind of error "reification" or "hypostatization" or "the substantialization of abstracta." A boy is observed to behave in certain ways—for example, he stares at a photograph of himself longer than at photographs of other children—and from that a psychologist infers that he possesses a "cognitive entity" called the "self-concept." The self or self-concept has been variously referred to as "an *object* to be known" (Wicklund, 1979), "*parts* of the phenomenal field" (Snygg & Combs, 1949), "an *object* of conscious inspection" (Gallup, 1979), "*regions* of our life" (Allport, 1955), and "an interpersonal *entity*" (Cooley, 1902). It has been said to have a "*structure*" and "*components*" (James, 1890) and, *like an embryo*, to "grow" (Lewis & Brooke-Gunn, 1979) (all italics added).

But the referent of "self-concept" is unclear. The referent, if there is one, is certainly less tangible than an arm or a brain; it seems to have neither boundaries nor precise location. Although characterizations of sub-atomic particles have grown increasingly abstract in recent years, a physicist would still insist that such particles have physical reality—that they have locations, masses, sizes. The self-concept does not.

Property as Explanation

More egregious is an error about which Newton warned in his *Principia*. It is a mistake, he said, to attribute the slow movement of a liquid to its viscosity. "Viscosity" is a description or property of the movement. We err in using a property of some phenomenon to explain that phenomenon. And yet, in spite of constant reminders from colleagues (e.g., Ebel, 1974), psychologists make this mistake frequently: A chimpanzee is observed to solve a problem in an insightful way. The explanation? The chimpanzee has "insight." A businessman works incessantly and garners many achievements in the corporate world. The explanation? He has a "need for achievement." A girl comes to be able to make accurate predictions about her own behavior. The explanation? She possesses an "accurate self-image." In each case, these so-called explanations are mere descriptions of the behavior observed. One might argue, as does Kagan (1981), that there is a point to such descriptions—that, for example, the "self-concept" can serve as a convenient summary of a great deal of behavior that children normally exhibit by about age 2—but "convenient summaries," "descriptions," and "properties" don't explain anything.

Causes

The most troublesome problem with the self-concept, drives, traits, the psychodynamic mechanisms, and a number of other psychological concepts is that they obscure the search for more concrete determinants of behavior—for determinants that have physical dimensions, that are manipulable, that allow you to make predictions about or to change behavior. Researchers who appeal to the traditional constructs rarely stray beyond. Some even assert that a more objective analysis is impossible. Gallup (1977a), for example, concludes a paper on the self-concept as follows: "As far as the self-concept is concerned, it would appear that on the morning before God created the great apes [who, according to Gallup, possess self-concepts], maybe he ... forgot to shave with Occam's [sic] razor" (p. 337). But objective accounts are often possible.

The behavior that comes under the rubric of "self" is troublesome because, like language, it is complex, distinctively human, acquired haphazardly over a period of years, and not easily traceable to biological factors or to any obvious instances of conditioning. A wide variety of behavior is said to provide evidence for its existence: pointing to or naming one's picture, body- or mark-directed behavior in front of a mirror, looking at or smiling at one's picture longer than at another person's picture, imitating a videotape of oneself more than a videotape of someone else, and so on (Amsterdam, 1972; Gallup, 1970; Kagan, 1981; Lewis & Brooks-Gunn, 1979).

Presumably the verbal behavior said to show "self-knowledge," of which Skinner (1945b, 1963) has offered accounts, would also apply: describing one's feelings, states of mind, thoughts, aches and pains, actions, and so on.

What all behaviors said to show the existence of a self-concept have in common is that they are controlled in part either by one's own body or one's own behavior. By about age 2, most children respond differently to likenesses of their own faces than to likenesses of other faces. When asked "Where does it hurt?", they report something about the states of their bodies. When asked, "What are you doing?", they describe their behavior.

Can one account for behavior that is controlled in this way in objective terms? What keeps us from doing so?

Anthropocentrism

Resistance to a factual, scientific analysis of behavior is rooted in part in anthropocentrism. Proponents of human uniqueness have sought to identify psychological or physical qualities, of which the self-concept is but one instance, which set humans apart from the rest of the animal kingdom. But anthropocentrists have suffered numerous setbacks during the past century as, one by one, apparently distinctive human qualities have been observed in other animals. The boundary between humans and non-humans (most notably but not exclusively the great apes) has become increasingly transparent.

For example, tool use had at one time been identified as a uniquely human trait, so when evidence of tool use in animals began to accumulate (e.g., van Lawick-Goodall, 1970), the assertion was refined: *Homo sapiens* was declared the only species to engage in tool *fabrication* (e.g., LeGros Clark, 1959). But subsequent reports made it clear that other species manufacture tools, even well in advance of their use (Beck, 1975).

Meat eating and cooperative hunting have likewise been proffered as criteria that set humans apart from other primates, but it has now been shown that chimpanzees (Teleki, 1973) and possibly baboons (Hausfater, 1976) engage in these behaviors.

It has also been suggested that human dominance relations are unique in that they are sometimes based on "ingenuity" instead of brute strength, but, again, counterexamples have appeared: For example, Goodall (1971) has told of a subordinate male chimpanzee who achieved dominant status by banging two empty kerosene cans together to augment his intimidation display.

Furthermore, chimpanzees have been said to demonstrate a "representational capacity," which is to say that they have been shown to behave in interesting ways with respect to objects and events that are remote in time and space (Menzel, 1973). And another supposedly human ability, "attribution," has also been reported in chimpanzees: Goodall (1968) observed that when two infants were playing and one was hurt, the mother of the victim sometimes attacked the offender's mother. Moreover, cross-modal perception, which was once thought to be a prerequisite to language (Lancaster, 1968), has now been demonstrated in apes (Davenport, Rogers, & Russell, 1973) and rhesus monkeys (Jarvis & Ettlinger, 1978).

Finally, over a dozen chimpanzees have been taught to use non-vocal languages (e.g., Gardner & Gardner, 1969; Premack, 1971), and some chimpanzees even appear sensitive to word order and syntax (Fouts, 1975). Furthermore, chimpanzees have been observed to sign to one another spontaneously (Fouts, 1974), and even rudimentary "symbolic communication" between two chimpanzees has been demonstrated (Savage-Rumbaugh, Rumbaugh, & Boysen, 1978).

What remains of human uniqueness? Anatomical and physiological differences between humans and other species exist, but even these appear to be less dramatic than they once did. For example, Yeni-Komshian and Benson (1976) have found temporal lobe asymmetries in chimpanzees which resemble those associated with language in humans. And King and Wilson (1975) conclude that the "average human polypeptide is more than 99 percent identical to its chimpanzee counterpart" and that we are at least as similar genetically as sibling species of other organisms (e.g., dogs and wolves).

Chimpanzees and humans are literally "blood relatives": Chimpanzee isoagglutination reactions are indistinguishable from those of human blood (Chiarelli, 1973), and hemoglobin from the two species has exactly identical sequences of amino acids (Wilson & Sarich, 1969). *Homo sapiens* is not unique genetically: Using high-resolution chromosome technology, Yunis and Prakash

(1982) determined that, except for differences in nongenic constitutive heterochromatin, *Homo sapiens* has 13, 9, and 8 *identical* chromosomes in common with the chimpanzee, gorilla, and orangutan, respectively. Furthermore, reversal of the several inversions that have taken place in the four species and the few instances of translocations, insertions, and fusions results in *virtually 100 percent homology*.

An extraterrestrial observer would likely agree with Mason (1976) that the "essential terms of our uniqueness have yet to be defined"—but humans do not give up their central position in the scheme of things so easily. On the contrary, *Homo sapiens*, having seen so many distinctively human possessions slip away into the murky depths of the animal kingdom, now clings more tenaciously than ever to what seem to be the last tendrils of superiority.

If facts about behavior, physiology, and genes do not clearly separate people from the beasts, then perhaps the essence of humanity is not really concrete at all but is rather something more abstract—some "inner," intangible quality, some "higher," "cognitive" process. We seem to have come full circle, first attributing human behavior to spirits and daemons, then to bumps on the head, neurotransmitters, genes, and observable environmental events, and now, once again, to the ethereal and immeasurable. The new fictions sound more sophisticated than the old, since they are neither spiritual nor magical.

They are merely *psychological*—from the Greek *psyche*, which means "spirit" or "soul."

Consciousness

The most unyielding of all the modern daemons has been consciousness. But even consciousness has recently come under scientific attack.

Always an elusive entity for psychologists, consciousness has been characterized as "bidirectional," in the sense that we both "[have] an experience and [are] aware of having an experience" (Gallup, 1977a). In other words, we can direct our attention outward to events in the world or inward toward ourselves, or, in still other terms, as we have noted above, behavior comes under the control both of stimuli outside the body *and of the body and behavior of the organism itself*.

To state the matter still more simply and, we hope, more clearly: *We can react not only to the world but to our reaction to the world, since every response is also a stimulus*. To say that an organism is capable of "self-directed consciousness" or "self-awareness" probably means nothing more than that the organism occasionally exhibits behavior that is controlled by its own body or behavior. This may be reductionism, but it also may be true.

But back, for the moment, to the daemons. Self-awareness has been said to be unique to humans (Ardrey, 1961; Buss, 1961; Kinget, 1975; Lorenz, 1971), and Slobodkin (1977), an evolutionary biologist, has even suggested that it has freed humans from the otherwise deterministic forces of evolution—surely the ultimate in uniqueness among species.

The claim that self-directed consciousness is unique has always been limited by the lack of techniques for determining its existence in non-humans. Klüver

(1933) asserted that consciousness in animals was not amenable to study by objective methods, and, more recently, Gardiner (1974) has noted that "there is no way to interview animals to discover the exact point on the evolutionary scale at which [consciousness] emerges. Neither is there any way to determine when 'self' becomes an element within the subjective mass..." (p.207).

But if self-awareness in animals is not amenable to study, how can one be confident that it is unique to humans?

A recent line of investigation, notably that of Gallup and colleagues, has suggested that an objective analysis of self-awareness may be possible. Gallup has suggested a test of self-awareness which, if valid, would repeal the prohibition on comparative scientific study of this phenomenon. This test makes use of *mirror-image stimulation*—stimulation that results from an organism's own reflection in a mirrored surface. The mirror image is in many ways unique among the vast array of stimuli used by psychologists, as we shall see.

Mirror-image stimulation produces a variety of behaviors, not all of which lead people to speak of self-awareness. Before we proceed with our discussion of such behaviors, we offer a review of the effects of mirrors on some less controversial behaviors.

MIRROR IMAGE STIMULATION

The Mirror as an Unconditional Stimulus

Unconditional responses (UCRs), especially aggressive displays, to mirrors have been observed in a variety of species, including siamese fighting fish (Thompson & Sturm, 1965), sexually aroused male sticklebacks (Tinbergen, 1951), and the male towhee (Dickey, 1916). Ritter and Benson (1934) reported that wild male towhees, California linnits, Western mockingbirds, robins, cardinals, and blackbirds attack their reflections in mirrors and window panes. Smythe (1962) observed that chaffinches and hedge sparrows occasionally attack their reflections in the hub caps of stationary automobiles, sometimes to the point of exhaustion. Captive California sea lions have been observed to emit underwater clicking-type vocalizations to mirrors, to make rapid runs at mirrors, and to attempt to bite or slap their mirror images (Schusterman, Gentry, & Schmook, 1966). Thompson and Sturm (1965) demonstrated classical conditioning using a mirror as an unconditional stimulus: They brought the aggressive response of siamese fighting fish under the control of a light by pairing the light with mirror exposure.

Among primates, gibbons (Boutan, 1913), rhesus monkeys, and pigtailed and Japanese macaques (Gallup, 1968) respond aggressively to mirrors. MacLean (1964) described penile erection in the squirrel monkey (an aggressive response in this species) in response to a mirror. Many primates (Yerkes & Yerkes, 1929), as well as cats (Kraus, 1949) and human infants (Dixon, 1957), reach toward or look behind a mirrored surface, as if to make contact with the reflected image. Orangutans (Schmidt, 1878) and chimpanzees (Köhler, 1925) are unusual in that the way they react to their mirror images changes over time: At first they are aggressive, then they appear to be "curious," and eventually they may become emotional if an attempt is made to remove the mirror. Gorillas behave similarly, except that they are aggressive only rarely (Yerkes, 1927).

The Mirror as a Social Stimulus

Organisms do not ordinarily attack themselves: Thus, the aggressive response of an animal to its mirror image suggests that the animal perceives the image as a stranger, and the response may be interpreted as territorial defense (Lorenz, 1966).

It is frequently noted that animals vacillate between approach toward and withdrawal from a mirror. The vascillation would seem to follow from a simple observation by Tinbergen (1968): In general, one animal's approach induces another animal's withdrawal. The speed-distorting properties of mirrors should enhance such an effect. Your mirror image will appear to approach *you* twice as fast as you approach *it*. Your opponent's apparently rapid approach should lead you to withdraw. Your withdrawal will make it appear that your opponent is retreating twice as fast, which should induce you to approach again, and so on.

Adult humans sometimes respond to their mirror images as images of other people. For example, Wolff (1943) noted that many people are startled when they see their own images reflected suddenly in an unexpected mirrored surface; they respond as if they are being confronted by a stranger. Similarly, certain drugs cause some people to report a feeling of strangeness or unfamiliarity with their mirror images (Kraus, 1949). Furthermore, congenitally blind individuals who have had their vision restored report unusual reactions to mirrors. For example, von Senden (1960) told of a man who had to remind himself constantly that a mirror was fastened to a wall in order to compensate for the fact that he "saw" the objects behind the wall.

Retarded humans also sometimes respond to their mirror images as if they are seeing another person. Shentoub, Soulairac, and Rustin (1954) exposed 15 retarded children, ages 4 to 19 years, to mirrors and found that many of them tried to escape from the reflection or refused to look at it. One girl, when offered candy before a mirror, offered some to her mirror image. Similar results have been obtained with retarded adults (Harris, 1977).

Schizophrenic humans, too, have been observed to respond inappropriately to likenesses of themselves. Schizophrenics who were shown photographs of themselves (Faure, 1956) or mirrors (Wittreich, 1959) interpreted these as distorted images of themselves, masks, a twin, or another person. Schizophrenics have also been observed to engage in prolonged mirror gazing (Abély, 1930), and it was even suggested that such behavior might be useful in diagnosis and prognosis (Ostancow, 1934).

Traub and Orbach (1964) developed a full-length mirror which could be adjusted along a continuum from undistorted to extremely distorted. They presented psychotic humans with the distorted mirror and asked them to adjust it until their reflections appeared undistorted. One subject tried to escape from the distorted image and could not be tested. Many others were unable to look at their distorted reflections. Many subjects repeatedly looked at their bodies, or asked to see themselves in an undistorted mirror before proceeding, indicating they had forgotten what they looked like. Normal subjects, given the same task (Orbach, Traub, & Olson, 1966) performed more accurately. As a control, all subjects were asked to adjust the distorted reflection of a door: Accuracy was high for both groups, and there were no significant differences between normals and psychotics.

Mirrors have also been observed to have social facilitation effects. It is well known that organisms behave differently in the presence of other organisms than they do in isolation. For example, isolated pigeons do not normally lay eggs, but they will do so in the presence of mirror-image stimulation (Matthews, 1939). A similar effect has been noted in ring doves (Lott & Brody, 1966). Chickens eat more food in the presence of other chickens than in isolation, and this facilitation effect is also seen with mirrors (Tolman, 1965). Finally, college students who faced a mirror were observed to perform better on tests than students who did not face a mirror (Wicklund & Duval, 1971).

The Mirror as a Reinforcer

Operant conditioning has been achieved using a mirror as a reinforcer. For example, Thompson (1963) conditioned siamese fighting fish to swim through a maze for contingent mirror exposure. Notably, this response extinguished more rapidly than comparable behavior that had been established using food as a reinforcer. Thompson (1964) also established a key-peck response in fighting cocks using mirror exposure as a reinforcer. Reinforcing effects of mirror exposure have also been demonstrated in baby chicks (Gallup, Montevecchi, & Swanson, 1972), paradise fish (Melvin & Anson, 1970), male squirrel monkeys (MacLean, 1964), pigtailed macaques, and rhesus monkeys (Gallup, 1966).

A mirror image may be reinforcing because it is novel (cf. Kish, 1966), or, possibly, simply because it is, in some ways, an ideal consequence. Mirror-image stimulation is unique, because only in front of a mirrored surface are one's movements instantly and perfectly mimicked. Moreover, an animal in front of the mirror has perfect control over the movement of the image, which is to say that the animal's behavior has continuous and virtually instantaneous consequences. Such a scenario would seem to be ideal for the establishment and maintenance of operant behavior.

The correlation between the behavior of the observer and the behavior of the observer's image also means, in effect, that the observer is in a position to control perfectly the behavior of "another organism." The prediction and control of natural phenomena, behavioral and otherwise, is a powerful reinforcer for scientists, gamblers, politicians, managers, teachers, and just about everyone else. Perhaps mirror-image stimulation is reinforcing because it provides the illusion of control over another organism.

Alternatively, Hogan (1967) suggests that the unconditional response (the aggressive display) elicited by mirror-image stimulation is what is reinforcing, not the mirror-image stimulation per se. It seems unproductive to speak of behavior itself as reinforcing, and we suggest that Hogan's statement means simply that mirrors are reinforcing because of the *kinds* of stimuli they produce, that is, views of aggressive conspecifics, which are, presumably, releasers of aggressive displays.

Moreover, it has been shown that, when given a choice between viewing mirror-image stimulation and viewing a live conspecific—both of which elicit the aggressive UCR—siamese fighting fish (Baenninger, 1966), goldfish (Gallup & Hess, 1971), weaver finches, and parakeets (Gallup & Capper, 1970) prefer mirror-image stimulation.

Some studies suggest that the UCRs elicited by mirror-image stimulation are of greater magnitude than the same UCRs elicited by conspecifics. In effect, then, mirror-image stimulation appears to be what ethologists call a "supernormal stimulus." This effect has been shown for aggressive responses in siamese fighting fish (Baenninger, Bergman, & Baenninger, 1966), adolescent chickens (Gallup et al., 1972), and patas monkeys (unpublished data by Gallup & McClure, cited in Gallup, 1975). It has also been found that distress vocalizations in very young chicks are reduced more by mirror-image stimulation than by a live companion (Gallup et al., 1972).

While these findings suggest that mirror-image stimulation is a powerful reinforcer, a study by Schulman and Anderson (1972) has introduced a complicating variable. They varied the early social experience of chickens and turkeys and found (1) that group-reared fowl preferred viewing conspecifics, (2) that those raised with a mirror preferred mirror-image stimulation, and (3) that those raised in social isolation showed no preference. The results may be an artifact of a flaw in the procedure, however: A bird was given a choice between viewing its own image or *two* conspecifics.

Controlling for this possible confound, Gallup and McClure (1971) tested feral versus socially isolated preadolescent rhesus monkeys and found that feral animals preferred a feral conspecific to mirror-image stimulation, while isolates preferred mirror-image stimulation over an isolate conspecific. One possible explanation for this finding is suggested by a study by Pratt and Sackett (1967), which showed that rhesus monkeys preferred to view comparably-reared conspecifics over monkeys with different rearing histories. Thus, for a feral, socially-experienced animal, mirror-image stimulation would present an extremely unfamiliar social situation, in that the image neither initiates an encounter nor reciprocates. The mirror-reflected behavior of an isolate, however, while unfamiliar, would at least be more predictable than a conspecific's behavior. The image would only mimic; it would not initiate behavior with which the subject is unfamiliar.

This explanation, however, contradicts the hypothesis that mirror images are reinforcing because they are novel. Thus, we submit that, at this point in time, there is still much to be learned about (a) what properties of mirror images make them reinforcing and (b) what environmental histories maximize their reinforcing effects.

Mirrors and Self-Awareness

Probably the most obvious fact about mirrors—for humans, anyway—is that they are a source of information about one's own body. The responses of nonhuman animals to mirror-image stimulation, as noted above, appear to be *other-directed* rather than *self-directed*. According to Gallup (1977b), in order for "self-stimulation" to become "self-perception" (or "self-awareness" or "self-consciousness"), *self-recognition* must first occur. Thus, the behavior from which "self-recognition" is inferred is critical in the debate over human uniqueness.

Self-Recognition

What is "self-recognition"? Rather than try to define it, we offer some simple—and perhaps simplistic—observations. First, self-recognition is not the behavior from which it is inferred; if it is anything at all, it is *more than* or *something other than* that behavior. An animal might recognize itself in a mirror but show us no sign. It might remain motionless. On another occasion, it might gaze at its mirror image and then groom itself. It might examine some part of its body that only the mirror reveals. The *behaviors* from which self-recognition is inferred—if any of them even occur—vary from one occasion to another. They are merely the *evidence* from which self-recognition is inferred, and they are not even a reliable source of evidence.

Second, the behaviors from which self-recognition is inferred may be studied in their own right. They have, as it were, a life of their own. Indeed, the *behaviors*—the mirror gazing, the grooming, and so on—would seem to be the only things we *can* study, since they are at least *things*. The term "self-recognition" sounds suspiciously daemonic; whatever and wherever it is, it is certainly less accessible than the behaviors from which it is inferred.

And third, it is not at all clear why traditional psychological concepts such as "self" should in any way constrain our investigations of the kinds of behaviors we observe when an animal is exposed to a mirror. That is, if you are interested in "self-recognition" or some related concept, *you have no choice*: You are stuck with *observable behavior* as the datum from which to make your inferences. But if you are content to observe and understand the many fascinating *behaviors* that occur in front of mirrors (and elsewhere!), you may find that your understanding of such behaviors advances faster and is more powerful *if you carry on your investigations without regard for traditional psychological or lay concepts*.

Such an enterprise would be considered sterile by traditional psychological standards. But, as Epstein (1984a) has pointed out, and as others have pointed out, often futilely, for decades, *the behavior of organisms is a legitimate subject matter in its own right*. That many psychologists would object to such an enterprise suggests only that the field of psychology is the wrong home for the study of behavior—not that the study of behavior *qua* behavior is invalid or "sterile."

What kinds of behaviors lead psychologists to speak of "self," and what can be said of their origins and controlling variables? Are their origins and controlling variables different from those of other behaviors, or are the same phenomena responsible for both "self"-controlled and "nonself"-controlled behaviors? Are such behaviors unique to humans?

Stages

Darwin (1877) recorded some of the responses of a baby to its mirror image, and, in recent decades, more careful and systematic observations have been made. For example, Dixon (1957) noted a series of "stages" through which mirror-controlled behavior seems to pass during the first few years of life: At first, most infants are unresponsive. After a few months, babies react to their images as they would to other children—by vocalizing, reaching, smiling, and so on. By a child's second year, it usually engages in behaviors that suggest "testing" or "discovery." For example, Dixon observed "repetitive activity while observing the mirror image intently, e.g., alternately observing a hand or foot and its mirror image, opening and closing the mouth with deliberation, or rising up and down slowly while keeping [the] eyes fixed on the mirror image" (p. 253). Amsterdam (1972) describes a similar stage. Finally, toward the end of its second year, the child begins to behave appropriately toward its mirror image.

A Test of Self-Awareness

Gallup (1970), using chimpanzees, and Amsterdam (1968, 1972), using children, devised an objective test to determine whether or not an organism had achieved this last stage—the stage at which the daemon Self is said to spring to life, or at least to "mature" (cf. Lewis & Brooks-Gunn, 1979). In Amsterdam's study, a mother smeared rouge on her child's nose—where, supposedly, the rouge would be difficut to see directly—and then encouraged the child to gaze at its mirror image. If the child touched its nose, it was said to have acheived the final stage: The mirror now controlled reaching appropriately. Most children responded in this way by about age 2.

Some Origins of the Appropriate Behavior

Before appropriate control can be established, an organism's social responses to its mirror image (Dixon's second stage) must be extinguished. Gallup (1968) suggested using very narrow mirrors for this purpose, so that only relatively small side-to-side movements by the observer would make the "other animal" disappear and reappear frequently. This seems, however, to be no different than housing two animals adjacent to each other with visual access limited to a small window; social responses of rhesus monkeys do not extinguish under such conditions. Furthermore, contrivances hardly seem necessary, since mirror-image stimulation is such a typical social stimulation: Mimicry is not a typical social response, so if social responses are going to disappear, they should do so unaided, and, indeed, they often do (Gallup, 1968, 1970).

Mere extinction is not enough, however. An organism's behavior must actually come under the control of the mirror. How might this occur?

When the aggressive behavior has weakened, any arbitrary response—say, arm-waving—would be strengthened somewhat by exposure to the organism's mirror image. A self-directed response, such as grooming, could therefore draw two sources of strength: the mirror image of the response, *and the natural consequences of grooming.* If, say, teeth-cleaning occurred by chance before the mirror, a chimpanzee would surely, at some point, gaze at its image and clean its teeth at the same time, in which case *the mirror image would begin to control the topography of the teeth cleaning, since the image is a guide to more effective movements.* Moving this way or that, according to the image in the mirror, would allow the animal to dislodge bits of food with greater proficiency. The consequences of movements controlled in this way would be detected immediately: The animal would both *see* its hand shift and then *feel* the food in between its fingers.

Does mirror-controlled behavior actually develop in this fashion? Gallup (1968) described the development of self-oriented responses in a chimpanzee after mirror exposure. Initially, responding was aggressive, and then the chimpanzee repeatedly positioned its limbs in unusual positions and tried to inspect its new postures in the mirror. Several contorted facial expressions led to close visual inspection of the reflection. Finally, and most important, while in front of the mirror the animal came to groom parts of its body—for example, its forehead and eyebrows—not visible without the mirror, and it did so while gazing at its mirror image.

It appeared, therefore, that, without any special training, the subject's grooming came under the control of the subject's mirror image.

"Self-Awareness" in the Chimpanzee

To confirm this observation experimentally, Gallup (1970) isolated four preadolescent chimpanzees in a room with a mirror for 80 hours over a 10-day period. Social behavior declined sharply on the third day, and there was a simultaneous increase in self-directed behavior (including grooming visually inaccessible body parts, picking the teeth or nose while watching the mirror image, making faces at the mirror, and so on). The animals were then anesthetized to unconsciousness with phencyclidine and atropine, and the upper eyebrow ridge and top of the ears were painted red with a dye that has no olfactory or tactile cues when dry.

After they had recovered fully, the chimpanzees were observed for 30 minutes in the absence of a mirror, during which time an animal was seen to make a "mark-directed" response only once. A mirror was then reintroduced for 30 minutes, whereupon from 4 to 10 "mark-directed" responses per animal were observed. Also, the total mirror-viewing time increased fourfold over the previous mirror sessions, and some of the animals inspected the fingers that had touched the dyed spots. As a control, two naive chimpanzees (who had had no previous mirror exposure) were anesthetized, marked, and tested, but they made no mark-directed responses.

Epstein (1985f) offered several criticisms of the Gallup (1970) study: First, only one observer seems to have been employed, and the method of data collection was not specified. Second, the data seem to have been collected in "real time"; the performances were not filmed or videotaped. This is a matter for concern because the frequency of responses reported was low—an average of only one response every 4.5 minutes. Signals that occur in noisy environments (presumably, the chimpanzees made many movements similar to the responses of interest) and at low frequency are difficult to detect reliably. Third, although secondary reports of the study occasionally speak of "touches," the original report speaks only of "mark-directed" responses. And fourth, I. S. Russell of the University of London has reported failures to replicate the Gallup (1970) results. According to Russell:

> It has been suggested that the ability to use a mirror ... was evidence of a discontinuity between apes and monkeys. Apes used it for visual guidance to inaccessible objects and to recognize themselves in the mirror.... [It] was decided [to] repeat and extend this work further. Daily access was given to 3 immature apes and their reactions noted. After a complex series of trial and error interactions with the images in the mirror, the animals gave every appearance of self-recognition with the mirror. Tests to determine whether or not these behaviors were genuine were inconclusive. A red dye marker placed on the animal's forehead before testing with the mirror was used to indicate self-recognition. On occasion the animals appeared to detect the marker by touching it while looking in the mirror. *Further control observations cast doubt on the reliability of this test. Animals were seen to frequently touch their forehead when no marker was used, and also they did not track the marker when it was relocated to another site such as the ear.... The present evidence indicates that self-recognition in apes is clearly speculative and far from proven.* (I. S. Russell, 1978, p. 6, italics added)

Other Primates

Gallup's (1970) finding has apparently been extended to orangutans, another member of the great apes family (Lethmate & Dücker, 1973). However, reports with other primate species have been negative. For example, Tinklepaugh (1928) exposed a female macaque to a mirror for several days and discovered that the animal learned to respond to objects in the environment using the mirror: "if a human being thus viewed makes a threatening movement, she will turn directly from the mirror to the person, as though verifying her indirect picture of the situation" (p. 218). In spite of this proficiency, the monkey showed no sign of responding appropriately to her mirror image. Brown, McDowell, and Robinson (1965) also showed that monkeys could use mirrors to manipulate objects, but they, too, saw no indication that the monkeys responded appropriately to their own images.

Gallup (1970) also tested four adult stump-tailed macaques and two adult rhesus monkeys after 168 hours of mirror exposure: There was little decline in the occurrence of social behavior and no evidence of self-directed behavior during the exposure period. Moreover, no mark-directed responses were observed during testing. Similar results were obtained with four cynomolgus monkeys after 250 hours of exposure. Lethmate and Dücker (1973) tested for but saw no evidence of self-recognition in several primate species: Spider monkeys, capuchins, macaques, mandrill and hamadryas baboons, and two species of gibbons. K. Pribram and M. Bertrand (cited in Gallup, 1977a) failed to find signs of self-recognition in gibbons and macaques. Benhar, Carlton, and Samuel (1975) gave baboons 250 hours of mirror exposure but, again, found that the baboons responded inappropriately to their mirror images.

Thinking that these failures might have been due to inadequate mirror exposure, Gallup (1977b) exposed a preadolescent crab-eating macaque to a mirror for 2,400 hours, but the subject was still unsuccessful in the test. Furthermore, according to Gallup (1979), R. L. Thompson and S. C. Radano provided one year and M. Bertrand provided seven years of mirror exposure to pigtailed macaques, but appropriate responding did not emerge in either case.

Since monkeys are adept at recognizing each other, Gallup, Wallnau, and Suarez (1980) speculated that self-recognition would be facilitated if familiar cagemates were given access to a common mirror. Since each member of the pair would presumably be able to recognize the reflection of its companion, the identity of the remaining individual seen in the mirror would be obvious. In one experiment, a feral adult rhesus monkey and her six-month old infant were given over 1,000 hours of mirror exposure. Red dye was applied to the eyebrow and abdomen of both animals. Both the adult female and a control animal without prior mirror exposure touched their marked stomachs, and the infant repeatedly groomed the mark on its mother's eyebrow, but none of the monkeys made self-directed responses to their own marked eyebrows. The experiment was repeated with two six-month old rhesus monkeys who were separated from their mothers and maintained together in front of a mirror for 14 weeks. Both infants touched the marks on their cagemate's face upon testing, but neither responded to its own marks.

In contrast, as noted earlier, the behavior of most humans readily comes under the control of a mirror image, although estimates of when the control is normally established vary somewhat. Stone and Church (1968) contend that many children learn to recognize themselves in mirrors by 10 months of age, but earlier sources say that self-recognition is unlikely during the first year (Gesell & Thompson, 1934; Shirley, 1933).

Amsterdam's (1972) study, cited earlier, reported that appropriate control was apparent in 65 percent of the subjects tested who were between 20 and 24 months old. Unfortunately, the children were marked with a spot of rouge placed on the side of the nose—a visible body part—while fully conscious, and thus the children could detect the marks before they were given the test.

In summary, the results of most of the mirror studies to date suggest a discontinuity in the phylogenetic tree: It seems that the families *Hominidae* and *Pongidae* come, with adequate exposure, to respond appropriately to their mirror images. Other species do not. It is unusual to find substantial qualitative differences between monkeys and the great apes in learning abilities or other psychological processes (Mason, 1976; cf. Rumbaugh, 1971 and Rumbaugh & Gill, 1973).

I. S. Russell's (1978) objections aside, if there is a discontinuity in the reaction of different species to mirrors, how might we interpret it?

Discontinuity

Since Gallup attributes self-directed behavior in front of a mirror to the daemonic "self-concept," he has concluded that only humans and the great apes (chimpanzees, at least) possess this cognitive entity (e.g., Gallup, 1979). He maintains that his results "raise serious questions about recent claims (e.g., Griffin, 1976) concerning the evolutionary continuity of mental experience" (Gallup, 1977a, p. 335). His theorizing, furthermore, has become increasingly mentalistic. Writes Gallup:

> most primates lack a cognitive category that is essential for processing mirrored information about themselves.... (1979, p. 420)

> I do not think their sense of identity or self-concept in any way emerges out of experience with a mirror. A mirror simply represents a means of mapping what the chimpanzee already knows. (1977a, p. 335)

> if you do not know who you are, how could you possibly know who it is you are seeing when you look at yourself in a mirror? (1979, p. 420)

> therein may lie one basic difference between monkeys and the great apes ... [the] absence of a sufficiently well-integrated self-concept. (1977a, p. 334)

Gallup has turned to what he calls the "Cooley-Mead" model of self to account for his results. According to Cooley's (1902) "looking glass" theory of self, our self-concept derives from interaction with others. Similarly, George Herbert Mead (1934) proposed that, in order for the self-concept to emerge, one must see one's self from another point of view.

To evaluate the applicability of the Cooley-Mead model to chimpanzee behavior, Gallup, McClure, Hill, and Bundy (1971) compared the self-recognition responses of feral chimpanzees housed in group cages with those of chimpanzees who were born in the laboratory and reared in isolation. Each animal was exposed to a mirror for 9 days. During the exposure period, feral chimpanzees attended frequently to the mirror at first but paid less attention to it as the days passed. But the isolates attended frequently to the mirror for the entire period. When tested for self-recognition, the feral chimpanzees made 13.5 times as many mark-directed responses as the isolates. Hill, Bundy, Gallup, and McClure (1970) extended these findings with three additional isolation-reared chimpanzees, none of whom showed signs of self-recognition in the test. Two of these animals were then housed together for 3 months. Upon retesting, both animals showed signs of self-recognition, while the third chimp, who had remained isolated, did not.

These results were said to support the Cooley-Mead model, and two alternative explanations were summarily—and, in our view, prematurely—dismissed. One possible alternative is that social isolation leads to general deficits in learning ability. Gallup dismissed this possibility on the grounds that apparent learning deficits are complicated by heightened emotionality in novel situations (Harlow, Schlitz, & Harlow, 1968), but those are hardly adequate grounds for dismissal. Indeed, the heightened emotions of the social isolate—that is, the "anxiety"—should interfere with its ability to learn how mirrors work, just as the anxiety of Thorndike's cats made it difficult for them to learn a simple escape response. Control by the mirror image would not easily be established if irrelevant emotional behavior were being elicited by the image.

It is also possible that isolates fail to distinguish the atypical behavior of the "other animal" in the mirror because they have not seen the typical behavior of other chimpanzees, and thus they have nothing with which to compare the mirror image. In other words, there were no opportunities for the appropriate discriminations to have been established. Gallup dismissed this possibility because the isolates' interest in the mirror remained high throughout the study, but that seems to be beside the point.

Although conservative explanations for the kinds of data Gallup has gathered do not seem to be in short supply, Gallup persists in glorifying the data, especially by attributing successful performances to mental daemons. His speculations have ranged widely. For example, Gallup (1979) has suggested that humans are not unique in their ability to contemplate their own deaths. He has speculated that chimpanzees are aware of, or can be made aware of, their inevitable ends, and Premack (1976), too, has expressed concern over this possiblity.

Should we withhold the truth from our chimpanzee friends? Such speculations have given rise to what can only be called *pongidocentrism*.

From pongidocentrism, where else might we wander?

Continuity

The case for discontinuity, as I. S. Russell (1978) pointed out, is by no means clearcut. Chimpanzees do not always respond appropriately to their mirror images (Hill et al., 1970; Gallup et al., 1971; I. S. Russell, 1978), and neither do humans (Harris, 1977; Kraus, 1949; Shentoub, Soulairac, & Rustin, 1954; Traub & Orbach, 1964; von Senden, 1960; Wittreich, 1959; Wolff, 1943). And the learning histories of those organisms who can respond appropriately makes a difference (Gallup, 1970; Hill et al., 1970).

Is it possible that organisms who normally respond inappropriately do so because of inadequate environmental histories? Is it possible some general learning deficit (perhaps genetically determined)—as opposed to the absence of a "self-concept"—makes some contribution? After all, retarded humans often respond inappropriately to their mirror images. Is this because they were born without the self-concept apparatus? Or is it simply because they have trouble learning—that is, because they have trouble acquiring, among others, the behaviors from which we *infer the existence* of a self-concept?

At best, the self-concept—whatever and wherever it may be—and the behaviors from which it is inferred, are *collateral products* of an organism's genetic endowment and environmental histories. Gallup and his colleagues have helped to discover some of the determinants of the behavior—for example, both chimpanzees and children need extensive exposure to a mirror before control is established. Without the behavior, the daemon would not be invoked. Thus, these determinants are determining both the behavior *and* the "self-concept" (granting, for the sake of argument, that the self-concept is worth talking about). *But it makes no sense to attribute the behavior to the daemon.*

As we noted earlier, daemons are sometimes troublesome because they call attention away from the actual behaviors in question, as well as from the determinants of that behavior. If appropriate behavior with respect to one's mirror image has specific origins in one's learning history, we should be able to find those origins. If particular neural structures are involved, we should be able to find them.

And, finally, once we have identified determinants of the behavior, *we should be able to establish such behavior in an organism that does not normally exhibit it.*

"Self-Awareness" in the Pigeon

Epstein, Lanza, and Skinner (1981) did so with pigeons. They reported that a normal adult pigeon whose history was supplemented with some simple training could successfully pass the mirror test; that is, it could successfully use a mirror to locate a spot on its body which it could not see directly, *even though it had not been explicitly trained to do so.*

Each of three pigeons was given two types of training over a 10-day period. First, with no mirror present, blue stick-on dots were placed one at a time on parts of the pigeon's body which it could see. Pecking the dots was shaped and maintained on a rich variable ratio schedule of food reinforcement. When the training was complete, each pigeon would readily scan its body, locate a dot, and peck it. We thus provided the pigeon with a repertoire of pecking itself, something a pigeon doesn't ordinarily do.

Second, we taught each pigeon how to use a mirror. We added a mirror to the pigeon's chamber and reinforced pecks at blue dots placed on the walls and floor. Then the dots were flashed only briefly, and pecks at the spot where a dot had been were reinforced. Finally, a dot was flashed only when the pigeon was facing the mirror. It received food when it turned and pecked the position where a blue dot had been flashed. The pigeons were exposed to the mirror for a total of less than 15 hours during the entire training period.

The pigeon was now like some of the chimpanzees and children who have been confronted with the mirror test in recent years. It had a strong tendency to "groom" itself (for blue dots, anyway), which means that, like with the chimpanzee or child, we could now count on it to try to touch spots that appeared to be on its body. And it had learned—albeit in a more efficient and structured manner than the chimpanzees and children had—how a mirror works.

In some ways the pigeon was now at a disadvantange. For one thing, it had had relatively little mirror exposure. Moreover, it had had little or perhaps even no experience using a mirror to locate an object on its own body. It had learned to use the mirror only to locate spots on the walls and floor of its chamber. It had never seen a spot on its body while the mirror was available. In contrast, chimpanzees and children who are successful in the mirror test have apparently already learned to use mirrors to locate both objects in real space and objects on their own bodies (Gallup, 1968, 1970; Lewis & Brooks-Gunn, 1979).

We conducted the following test: A blue stick-on dot was placed on the pigeon's breast and a white bib placed around its neck such that the pigeon, standing fully upright, could just see the dot in the mirror. Because the bib would drop if the pigeon lowered its head, the pigeon could not see the dot directly. To be certain that the pigeons could not detect the dot either visually or tactually, each pigeon was observed first for 3 minutes in the absence of the mirror. Three independent observers scored videotapes for what they judged to be "dot-directed" responses. None of the birds was observed to peck the dot during this period.

When the mirror was then uncovered, each pigeon approached it and, within a few seconds, began to bob and peck toward the position on the bib that corresponded to the position of the concealed dot. None of the birds pecked the positions on the floor and walls where dots had previously been presented. The three birds were judged by the independent observers to have emitted a total of 29 dot-directed responses within 3 minutes of seeing the mirror, although food was not presented. This rate of responding is more than 10 times that reported by Gallup (1970) with chimpanzees.

To control for the possibility that the pigeons were responding simply because the mirror had been uncovered, one bird was tested wearing a bib but with no dot on its breast. The mirror was covered for 5 minutes and then uncovered for 5 minutes, and no dot-directed responses were observed during either period.

Thus, even though the pigeons had had very limited mirror exposure, and even though they had never been trained to use a mirror to locate spots on their bodies, they successfully used a mirror to do so.

Does this mean pigeons have a self-concept?

Implications

The Epstein et al. (1981) study may be interpreted in several different ways.

Training. First, it might be said that since the pigeons had had *training* before the mirror test, the results are not applicable to chimpanzees and children, who, it seems, have had no "training" before the test.

But the word "training" is misleading. The chimpanzees and children who have been successful in the mirror test have had far richer learning histories than our pigeons. Organisms learn constantly, even without teachers. (Some would say especially without teachers!)

Explanation. However the chimpanzee or child acquired the relevant behaviors—we will return to this point below—there is ample evidence that both chimpanzees and children have acquired each of them before they pass the test: They readily touch spots on their bodies, and they have each learned how mirrors work. The pigeon study suggests that successful performances in the mirror test are the outcome of the acquisition of these two repertoires.

If other organisms that are provided with these repertoires prove able to pass the test, the explanation will become more credible. If a chimpanzee or child who *lacks* one of these repertoires proves able to pass the test, the explanation will become less credible (cf. Epstein, 1984d).

Self-Concept. The results of the Epstein et al. (1981) study will suggest to no one that pigeons have a self-concept. Why not? For one thing, pigeons do not look like people. It is awkward to anthropomorphize with a 12-inch high, armless, feathered creature; it is easier with chimpanzees.

More important, the pigeons acquired only one telltale sign of self-awareness. The self-daemons are typically invoked only after a variety of self-controlled behaviors have been established.

Bad Test. The Epstein et al. (1981) study could also be said to cast doubt upon the usefulness or informativeness of the mirror test. After all, if an organism that has no self-concept can pass it, what good is the test? The mirror test shows what the mirror test shows—namely, that an organism's behavior is controlled appropriately or inappropriately by a mirror image. That may be worth knowing, but it also may not be a critical sign of self-awareness, as was supposed.

Bad Concept. Epstein (1986a) and Epstein et al. (1981) suggest that the study is significant mainly in calling attention away from self-awareness. Rather, the behavior from which self-awareness is often inferred is brought into focus, along with the learning history that is responsible for the behavior.

Replication

Gallup (1984) cites what he calls a "failure to replicate" the Epstein et al. (1984) study—a convention talk by Gelhard, Wohlman, and Thompson (1982). But these investigators reported having great difficulties in training their two pigeons in preparation for the mirror test. They gave up on one bird after nearly a year. This suggests that they were using inadequate training procedures, not that pigeons cannot pass the mirror test. Epstein (1985a) reported that Roger Thompson (personal communication, December 1983) stated that he had "no doubt" that Epstein et al. (1981) achieved the result they reported.

Moreover, Cheney has recently completed a systematic replication of the Epstein et al. (1981) study, and he has achieved positive results with each of the four pigeons he tested. According to Cheney, "Given the relatively modest level of sophistication and experience of the trainers in this study, the results indicate a rather robust phenomenon" (Cheney, 1984, p. 6).

Contingencies

Epstein (1986a) has given a detailed analysis of mirror-use behavior (see Chapter 3, this volume). According to this view, chimpanzees come to respond appropriately to their mirror images without explicit training because they are extremely sensitive to the consequences of their behavior. Earlier in the chapter we suggested some of the events that might lead to appropriate control. The fact that the mirror image is reinforcing is important, because that means it creates opportunities for further learning to occur. The extinction of UCRs (such as aggressive displays) and of inappropriate reaching (such as reaching toward the image) is also important. Since chimpanzees learn quickly, the extinction of these behaviors should occur rapidly—again creating the opportunities for appropriate control to be established.

With inappropriate behaviors eliminated, a chimpanzee gazing at its mirror image should quickly come under discriminative control of that image, because, loosely speaking, *the mirror is a guide to effective action.* We described one possible scenario earlier: While gazing at its image, the animal happens to move its hand toward an irritant on its face or in its teeth which it cannot see directly. The sight of the reflected hand removing the irritant is the occasion which the hand successfully removes the irritant, and thus the image should come to control similar movements in the future. It is a "discriminative stimulus," a stimulus that sets the occasion for reinforcement, a stimulus that helps the organism to be effective.

A careful analysis of videotapes of a chimpanzee's interactions with mirrors should show interactions of this sort. We predict that careful study of these interactions will take the mystery out the acquisition process.

Other Species

Why do so many species—especially other primates—fail the mirror test? Epstein et al. (1981) suggested that monkeys fail because they tend to move so much faster than chimpanzees and children. The contingencies of reinforcement which govern mirror use are more likely to take hold if an organism gazes at its mirror image while it is moving slowly.

But other factors also seem important. If aggressive displays and other UCRs are elicited by the image, appropriate control cannot be established until these have abated. With some species and some individuals, this extinction may not occur. Moreoever, inappropriate operant behavior, such as reaching toward the image, must also disappear. With children and chimpanzees, this extinction occurs fairly rapidly, but it may occur slowly or not at all with other species.

Species vary dramatically in the speed with which behavior is acquired or eliminated, and there is significant variation among individuals within a species. In other words, some organisms learn faster than others, and learning ability should make a big difference in the acquisition of mirror-use behavior.

As stated above, training that compensates for an organism's deficiencies should also make a difference. With appropriate training, many organisms that would not normally come under the control of their mirror images should do so. Because organisms differ, we should expect that the necessary training should differ somewhat for different organisms.

Other Behaviors

Other behaviors said to demonstrate the existence of a "self-concept" demand their own analyses. A child has many thousands of learning experiences during its first few years of life. The child acquires a wide variety of behaviors that are controlled by its own behavior and body *and many other complex behaviors, as well*—verbal and other social behaviors, problem solving behaviors, complex motor skills, and so on. The assertion, implicit in the language of self-concept, that a child's behavior in front of a mirror has the same cause as its response to the question "Where does it hurt?" is nonsense.

SOME FINAL REFLECTIONS

The behavior that gives life to the daemonic "self" has a life of its own. Behavior that is controlled by an organism's own body or behavior seems to be orderly and not fundamentally different from behavior that is controlled in other ways. The origins of such behavior—for example, of appropriate responses to one's mirror image—lie in the genetic and environmental histories of the organism.

The sharp discontinuity said to exist between the higher primates and other animals has not been conclusively shown, and the concept of a "self-concept" does not shed light on the differences that have been shown. What differences there are among species and individuals can be accounted for in terms of ontogenic histories, sensitivity to environmental events, and species-specific behaviors elicited by specific stimuli. Further investigations will strengthen such accounts.

One may wish to conjure up daemons from the behavior an organism engages in before a mirror, but that won't change the facts, and the facts are worth collecting.

A daemon, according to the *Oxford English Dictionary*, is "an attendant, ministering, or indwelling spirit ... an inward monitor or oracle." Some have been unabashed in their promotion of daemonology in this sense. Freud (1905/1961), for example, spoke of "those half-tamed daemons that inhabit the human breast," and his tripartite mind has been justly characterized as "a dark cellar in which a maiden aunt and a sex-crazed monkey are locked in mortal combat, the affair being refereed by a rather nervous bank clerk" (Bannister, 1966, p. 363). An introductory text on information processing (Lindsay & Norman, 1977) has colorful drawings of "feature daemons"—bright-eyed little men who live in one's head, pool their knowledge, and eventually figure out what one is seeing. (Who lives in *their* little heads and makes sense of what *they* are seeing is not specified.) Others have promoted concepts—such as the "self-concept"—which are less obviously daemonic, in the sense that they lack arms and legs, but which are just as imaginary and troublesome.

As we learn more about how heredity and the environment determine behavior and about how behavior is mediated by the body, we will naturally abandon the myths. Unfortunately, where the daemons rule, the facts may turn up more slowly.

PART VII

GROWING OLDER

31

GROWING OLDER, OR WHAT ELSE I LEARNED IN GRADUATE SCHOOL

Author's note. I wrote the following essay during my final days in graduate school in 1981. It appeared that year in *Harvard Magazine* and provoked intense debate among friends, colleagues, and students.

My son Julian is now tall enough to climb up onto the toilet seat and from there to the sink, from which he can easily open our medicine chest. When I saw him recently with a Bic shaver in his mouth, I was moved to clean the chest out.

I came across more than a dozen empty or half-empty drug containers: Cafergot, Benadryl, Valium, Prednesone, and so on. I was struck by the fact that before I came to graduate school, about the only drug I had ever taken was aspirin. I never even drank tea or coffee.

I got to thinking. Had graduate school turned me into an addict? My first, rather emotional response was yes. Four years of studying to the point of eyestrain, hastily preparing lectures, writing and rewriting papers, and conducting unceasing and often tedious research—in a word, an eighty-hour work week with little relaxation—takes a toll. A lack of exercise and a poor diet probably didn't help.

Most of the graduate students I know well are in no better shape. Of the sixteen that entered my department in 1977, only ten remained by the end of the first year. Two of those who left were males with long hair and ideals; they saw no point to the politics and pressures. One set out on an ambitious business venture, which failed. Another, who, I'm told had Boards scores of 800, is now a bum. He walks the streets of Boston carrying a large plastic bag in which are all his worldly goods. He was plump in 1977; he is now emaciated. The students that stayed have their share of woes, too. An associate has put on twenty or thirty pounds and walks with shoulders slumped. A close friend attributed his failure on an important exam to his dependence on a tranquilizer. An ulcer is practically a medal of honor; you've "made it" if you've got an ulcer.

But then I reconsidered. After all, I am a scientist (albeit just a social one). Could I be certain that graduate school was the culprit? The answer, of course, is no. My medicine chest would probably have looked the same no matter what I had been doing these past four years. I might have developed different allergies had I been pumping gas, but I probably would still have some. I would certainly have been subject to stress had I been working for an insurance company or bank. My friends outside of academe are in no better shape than the ones inside.

The villain is not graduate school, it's growing up—or perhaps I should say, growing older. Several changes occur as you move through your twenties and into your thirties. First of all, your environment becomes more demanding: your parents' financial support drops off to a trickle and finally dies. You start needing money for necessities and not just a better turntable. You accumulate "responsibilities"—in my case, school debts, a wife, and children; for some of my friends, a house to work for (and be worked by). And your work load grows in proportion to your ambition.

Second, your body starts to deteriorate. I apologize for speaking so plainly about such a sensitive topic—especially to those of you under age 25—but it can't be helped. Sometime in our twenties we all experience the first signs of physical aging. We get allergies (I can no longer eat peanut butter, which I happen to love); we start losing noticeable amounts of hair; we get wrinkles; flabby stomachs, bad breath, hemorrhoids, and worse. We lose a bit of stamina. I got through college "pulling all-nighters"; I couldn't pull one now to save my life. We can't run as fast or jump as high. Reaction time slows. Vision and hearing start to go. We become susceptible to insidious diseases we never heard of as children (my wife, for example, has "periodontitis," and I have "chondromalacia" of the knees).

Third, you can no longer think as well. Some psychologists will dispute this, but we all know it's true. A junior faculty member remarked that he could no longer solve the puzzlers in *Scientific American*. When I was fourteen I could routinely think ten moves ahead in three-dimensional tic-tac-toe (four-by-four-by-four). I've lost nearly half a move a year.

And fourth—perhaps as a result of the other changes—we lose ideals. I find this the most painful change, probably because I've been struggling so hard for the past few months to hold on to mine. My friend Peter is a striking example. He practically ran our high school; he was bright, articulate, and likable, and more important, he knew how to work the system. He was a leader and an organizer; he promoted causes and yet somehow managed to avoid making enemies. His long-term goal was to become a doctor, become president of the A.M.A., and then abolish the organization. If anyone could do it, Peter could. He stuck to his guns in college and organized a group that sued his medical school in 1976. There was no stopping Peter. Last fall I ran into him at our college homecoming. He was with an attractive woman, sipping a martini, and talking about the expensive home he had just bought. I was distraught. "What happened to your goals," I asked, "to your ideals?" "Guilt." he said, "It was all guilt."

I'm apprehensive about the future, and not just because of the depressed job market. I'm apprehensive about changes—about aging, about growth, about a physical and emotional future that no one ever prepared me for. I don't think anyone even tried to prepare me for the changes that have occurred in my twenties. And I'm embarrassed to say that 35 courses in psychology haven't made much of a difference.

When I was seventeen, a rabbi tried to convince me that there was some sort of afterlife. Try to explain to a fetus, he said, what it's going to be like to live in the world, what the next stage of its life is going to be. The fetus just won't understand. When you die, he said, you are like the fetus, entering into a new realm that you couldn't possibly have anticipated. I think every stage of life is like that. When you are a toddler, you can't envision or understand the confines of a classroom. When you reach your teens, you can't make any sense at all of what your parents are doing. I can't speak with any authority about the changes to come, though I must say that I am beginning to look at my own parents with a certain sympathy and cautious understanding that were inconceivable four years ago.

In what will seem like a rather short time, my second child, due in a few days, will be finishing college on her (we hope) way to graduate school or a career. I suspect that she will be as ignorant as I was about these matters, and as unprepared. I doubt that anyone will take the time—or have the nerve—to tell her about the aging process that's about to have its way with her, about the changes she is going to have to deal with.

It certainly won't be me.

Postscript. *Within a few months of the article's publication, I received comments from nearly fifty people, and almost all of the comments were sympathetic. The chairman of one of the humanities departments at Harvard wrote, "I'm sorry to have to tell you this, but it only gets worse." An undergraduate told me that her parents had had all of their children read the essay, "to prepare us." A graduate student in the Midwest, disturbed by the change in her appearance from her Radcliffe days, distributed copies widely. There were also some objections, and two, from flourishing professionals in their 30s, were published by the magazine a few months after my article appeared. In my reply I labeled these individuals "Peter Pans" and asked, "Could it be simply that the nervous systems of those fortunate few are deteriorating more rapidly than the rest of the bodies?" Now, fourteen years later, I'm happy to report that my own nervous system seems to be decaying at a pace more commensurate with life's little difficulties.*

32

ANOTHER BREAKTHROUGH IN DATA INTERPRETATION AT HARVARD

Author's note. The following note and diagram (next page) first appeared in the now-defunct *Worm Runner's Digest* under the pseudonym "Gallinaceous Pyle," a euphemism for bird droppings.

The Harvard Psychology Laboratory, true to its long tradition of making the most of ambiguous data, has, once again, struck a blow against ignorance. Scattered, apparently meaningless data points salvaged from a damaged DECTAPE (found under a pigeon cage) have been successfully decoded, as shown in Figure 32.1 ($q.v.$). Extensive curve-fitting has demonstrated, to no one's surprise, that the data verify Herrnstein's Matching Law. Even more significant, we have discovered that the points may be connected so as to form a meaningful visual pattern. The points have been labeled by number to aid in making the connections. The resulting curve, certain to be replicated shortly by one of the boys, has been tentatively christened as shown in the upper-left-hand corner of the figure, shown on the following page.

Further developments along these lines are anticipated.

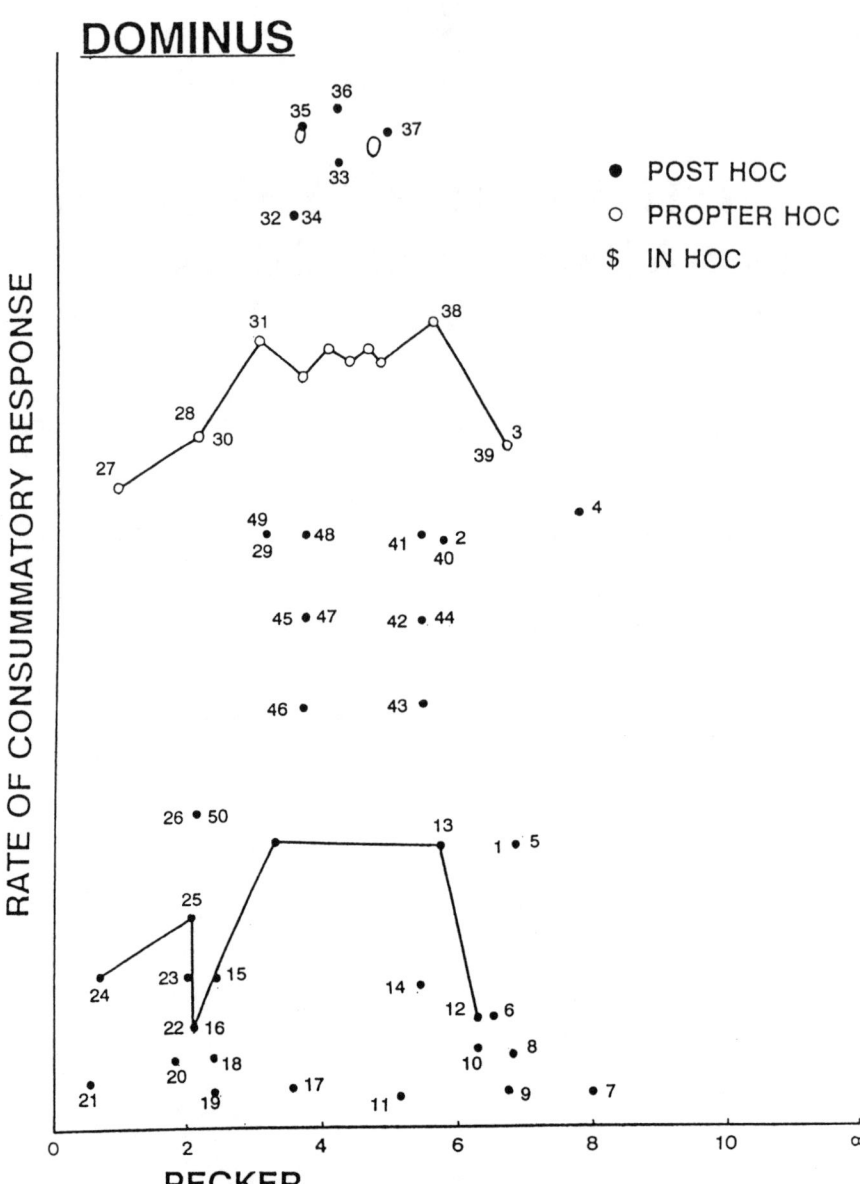

Figure 32.1. A Harvard pecker. These apparently meaningless points take on definite meaning when connected appropriately.

33

WHY THE COGNITIVISTS HATE THE BEHAVIORISTS: THE PECKER-ENVY HYPOTHESIS

Nearly a hundred years ago, Freud uncovered the truth. My wife badgers me because I've got something she doesn't.

That has always been a great comfort to me.

It hasn't stopped the badgering, but at least I know why it's occurring. And I know that I'm the better man.

The feminists have tried to turn this around. My sister—who is also a carpenter, by the way—wears a rather offensive pin that reads, "The only one who ever envied a penis was another man." What balderdash!

Of course, I learned my lesson that time I sprained my wrist lifting one of her barbells. So I *humor* her. I'm sensible. I value my life, so I *humor* her.

What does all this reminiscing have to do with psychology, you ask?

You see, I got my doctorate with the man himself, *B.F. Skinner*. Yes, he was still alive at the time, and, at this writing, he is *still* alive. I often have to reassure people about this.

And I always wondered why people were so dead set against behaviorists. Skinner himself has been called—in print, no less—some very nasty things, including:

"Machiavellian"
"a fascist,"
"a Nazi,"
and "*evil*."
(Well, that follows.)
"An opponent of everything good and true,"
and "an enemy of Democracy, mother love, and apple pie."
(What nonsense. The man *loves* apple pie.)
His writing has been critized thus:
It's "irrational."
It's "not rational."
It "lacks rationality."
These, of course, were Chomsky's criticisms.
And then, my favorite:

"Zero plus zero equals zero."

This one, also by Chomsky, strikes me as indisputably rational.

And I, too, simply by *association*, have been dumped on occasionally by cognitivist colleagues. I have, in various debates, been insulted. My work has been called "for the birds." (A cruel dig, really. I didn't have the heart to tell them.) I have seen red faces. I have seen fists. I have seen *spittle*.

Fortunately, I haven't felt it.

On one occasion, after a talk I gave at a meeting of the American Psychological Assocation, a cognitivist jumped onto the stage and challenged me to a duel. My tape recorder was still running, so she can't deny it.

Why?

A thousand times I've asked the question "Why?"

Why do they hate us so? Why, Sigmund.... Why?

As usual, Freud held the key (you know, one of those things you poke into apertures).

It's obvious. What do Skinner, Goldiamond, Sidman, Lindsley, and Azrin all have in common? In fact, even the few females among us—Reese, Segal, Logue—what do we all share that no other psychologists have?

Why, peckers!

It all began when, under contract with the United States Army, a good *macho* organization, well-stocked with *guns* and other symbols of *what it takes*, Skinner and colleagues worked on a top-secret project atop a dusty old warehouse in Minneapolis. There, pigeons were trained—not to play ping-pong or the piano, no, none of that pansy stuff—but to guide *missiles*.

Figure 33.1. "I'm sick of pigeon feed! I want a real salary, coffee breaks, health insurance, two weeks paid vaca— Awk! Screwed again!"

To sit right in the front seat of the largest phallus ever manufactured by man and blow themselves and four or five thousand people to smithereens!

All right!

Now, sis', you see what you're up against. You can keep your barbells! Give me pigeons any day!

So this, I now believe, is the reason why the cognitivists are so damned hostile toward the behaviorists. Freud told us long ago. It's simple pecker envy. We've got 'em, as big as footballs, and they don't.

(I don't expect this to stop the hostility, but at least now I know why it's occurring.)

34

A DAY OF PEACE ON EARTH

There are nearly 30 million soldiers in the world, and the United Nations estimates that more than 200,000 of them are children. What's more, many are fighting and dying every day, even when the headlines fail to remind us. A recent yearbook of the Stockholm International Peace Research Institute documents 32 major armed conflicts during 1989 alone, with several brutal new wars too new to make the list. In all, more than 20 million people—most of them civilians—have died in armed conflicts around the world since 1945, with no sign of real change.

Total disarmament may be too much to ask for. Self-interest and fear may prevent it forever. Persuasive people will argue the need for aggression or defense or deterrence, and enough people will be persuaded to cause trouble. Remember, too, that war is one of the biggest, most successful businesses in the world, to the tune of nearly a trillion dollars in expenditures each year.

But how about a day, just a single *day* of peace? Could we not at least try that? No monarchs would fall, no one's borders would be threatened, no one would lose a sale or a job—not in just a day.

January 1st of the year 2000 marks the beginning of a new year, a new decade, a new century, and a new millennium.[1] It is only the second such day in the calendar of human history, and it is within reach, so near we can almost touch it. Most of the people alive today—and the vast majority of all of the *children* alive today—will witness this extraordinary day.

Why not begin the next thousand years with a day of peace on earth?

For much of the world, the day will be a holiday, anyway. Even if we did no special planning, fighting would slack off. Why not make the moratorium complete?

It will take a great deal of work by many political, religious, and military leaders, many governments, many service organizations, and many private citizens around the world to engineer a global truce, but it's well within the realm of the sober realities under which we live.

How do we convince all of the relevant parties to lay down their arms, and how can we prevent some trigger-happy bully from ruining the day? Should we pay people off who cannot otherwise be persuaded? Should we call out the hit squads? Should we trade wheat—or perhaps even weapons—for cease-fires? Some planning and hard work will yield reasonable answers to such questions. We have nearly a decade. We can do it in that time. It's a *reachable* goal.

The behavioral sciences tell us that a little goal setting can go a long way. If we work together to create this remarkable day, we will behave better toward each other along the way. We will long for this day and envision this day, and we will be better for it.

If we achieve this day of peace, it will be remembered for all time by all humanity. It will tell us that the cycle of war can be broken, that peace is truly within our grasp, that humanity, with all its flaws and in all its diversity, is good.

And maybe—just maybe—this day without war, this single day of perfect peace, will last another day.

NOTE

1. Calendar purists may argue for January 1, 2001.

REFERENCES

Abély, P. (1930). Le signe du miroir dans les psychoses et plus specialement dans le demence precoce. *Annales Medico-Psychologique, 88,* 28-36.
Adler, H. E. (1980). Historical dialectics. *American Psychologist, 35,* 956-958. (Portion of Wyers et al. [1980]. The sociobiological challenge to psychology: On the proposal to "cannibalize" comparative psychology. *American Psychologist, 35,* 955-979.)
Agnew, S. T. (1972, January). Agnew's blast at behaviorism. *Psychology Today,* pp. 4, 84, 87.
Ainslie, G. W. (1974). Impulse control in pigeons. *Journal of the Experimental Analysis of Behavior, 21,* 485-489.
Ainslie, G. W. (1975). Specious reward: A behavioral theory of impulsiveness and impulse control. *Psychological Bulletin, 82,* 463-496.
Alcock, J. (1969). Observational learning in three species of birds. *Ibis, 111,* 308-321.
Allport, G. W. (1955). *Becoming.* New Haven, CT: Yale University Press.
Alvarez, W., Kauffman, E. G., Surlyk, F., Alvarez, L. W., Asaro, F., & Michel, H. V. (1984). Impact theory of mass extinctions and the invertebrate fossil record. *Science, 223,* 1135-1141.
Amsel, A. (1958). The role of frustrative nonreward in noncontinuous reward situations. *Psychological Bulletin, 55,* 102-119.
Amsterdam, B. K. (1968). Mirror behavior in children under two years of age. Unpublished doctoral dissertation. Chapel Hill: University of North Carolina.
Amsterdam, B. K. (1972). Mirror self-image reactions before age two. *Developmental Psychobiology, 5,* 297-305.
Anderson, J. R. (1972). FRAN: A simulation model of free recall. In G. H. Bower (Ed.), *The psychology of learning and motivation* (Vol. 5). New York: Academic Press. Pp. 315-378.
Anderson, J. R. (1978). Arguments concerning representations for mental imagery. *Psychological Review, 85,* 249-277.
Antonitis, J. J. (1951). Response variability in the white rat during conditioning, extinction, and reconditioning. *Journal of Experimental Psychology, 42,* 273-281.
Ardry, R. (1961). *African genesis.* New York: Dell.
Arieti, S. (1976). *Creativity: The magic synthesis.* New York: Basic Books.
Ator, N. A. (1986). Behavioral biology. *The Behavior Analyst, 9,* 123-125.
Au, R., & Epstein, R. (1982, April). *Problem solving in the pigeon.* Paper presented at the 62nd annual meeting of the Western Psychological Association, Sacramento.

Axelrod, S. (1983). *Behavior modification for the classroom teacher* (2nd ed.). New York: McGraw-Hill.
Azrin, N. H. (1959). A technique for delivering shock to pigeons. *Journal of the Experimental Analysis of Behavior, 2,* 161-163.
Azrin, N. H., & Holz, W. C. (1966). Punishment. In W. K. Honig (Ed.), *Operant behavior: Areas of research and application.* New York: Appleton-Century-Crofts.
Baenninger, L., Bergman, M., & Baenninger, R. (1966). Aggressive motivation in *Betta splendens*: Replication and extension. *Psychonomic Science, 16,* 260-261.
Baenninger, R. (1966). Waning of aggressive motivation in *Betta splendens*. *Psychonomic Science, 5,* 241-242.
Baer, D. M. (1981). *How to plan for generalization.* Lawrence, KS: H & H Enterprises.
Balsam, P. D., & Bondy, A. S. (1983). The negative side effects of reward. *Journal of Applied Behavior Analysis, 16,* 283-296.
Bandura, A. (1976). Self-reinforcement: Theoretical and methodological considerations. *Behaviorism, 4,* 135-155.
Bandura, A., Mahoney, M. J., & Dirks, S. J. (1976). Discriminative activation and maintenance of contingent self-reinforcement. *Behavior Research and Therapy, 14,* 1-6.
Bandura, A., & Walters, R. (1963). *Social learning and personality development.* New York: Holt, Rinehart, & Winston.
Bannister, D. (1966). A new theory of personality. In B. Foss (Ed.), *New horizons in psychology.* Harmondsworth, England: Penguin.
Barker, R. G., Dembo, T., & Lewin, K. (1941). *Studies in topological and vector psychology. No. 2. Experiments on regression and frustration.* Iowa City: Iowa University Press.
Barker, S. F. (1961). On simplicity in empirical hypotheses. *Philosophy of Science, 28,* 162-171.
Barry, A. E. (1986). Behavior, psychology, and praxics: Where does science fit in? *The Behavior Analyst, 9,* 225-226.
Baxley, N. (Producer). (1982). *Cognition, creativity, and behavior: The Columban simulations* [Film]. Champaign, IL: Research Press.
Beck, B. B. (1975). Primate tool behavior. In R. H. Tuttle (Ed.), *Socio-ecology and psychology of primates.* The Hague, Netherlands: Mouton.
Beck, B. B. (1980). *Animal tool behavior: The use and manufacture of tools by animals.* New York: Garland STPM Press.
Becker, W. C. (1971). *Parents are teachers: A child management program.* Champaign, IL: Research Press.
Bellack, A. S., Hersen, M., & Kazdin, A. E. (Eds.) (1990). *International handbook of behavior modification and therapy* (2nd ed.). New York: Plenum.
Benhar, E. E., Carlton, P. L., & Samuel, D. (1975). A search for mirror-image reinforcement and self-recognition in the baboon. In S. Kondo, M. Kawai, & A. Ehara (Eds.), *Contemporary primatology: Proceedings of the Fifth International Congress of Primatology.* Basel, Switzerland: Karger.
Bergmann, G. (1956). The contribution of John B. Watson. *Psychological Review, 63,* 265-276.
Bergson, H. (1946). *The creative mind.* New York: Philosophical Library.
Bien, B. (1969). *The works of Ludwig von Mises.* Irvington-on-Hudson, New York: The Foundation for Economic Education.
Bingham, H. (1929). Chimpanzee translocation by means of boxes. *Comparative Psychology Monographs* (No. 3).
Birch, H. (1945). The relation of previous experience to insightful problem solving. *Journal of Comparative Psychology, 38,* 367-383.

Blackman, D. E., & Sanger, D. J. (Eds.) (1978). *Contemporary research in behavioral pharmacology*. New York: Plenum.
Blechman, E. A., & Brownell, K. D. (1988). *Handbook of behavioral medicine for women*. New York: Pergamon.
Bloomfield, L. (1933). *Language*. New York: Holt.
Blough, D. S. (1959). Delayed matching in the pigeon. *Journal of the Experimental Analysis of Behavior*, 2, 151-160.
Blough, D. S. (1977). Visual search in the pigeon: Hunt and peck method. *Science*, 196, 1013-1014.
Boakes, R. A. (1973). Response decrements produced by extinction and by response-independent reinforcement. *Journal of the Experimental Analysis of Behavior*, 19, 293-302.
Boakes, R. A., & Gaertner, I. (1977). The development of a simple form of communication. *Quarterly Journal of Experimental Psychology*, 29, 561-575.
Boakes, R. A., & Halliday, M. S. (1975). Disinhibition and spontaneous recovery of response decrements produced by free reinforcement in rats. *Journal of Comparative and Physiological Psychology*, 88, 436-446.
Boden, M. (1977). *Artificial intelligence and natural man*. New York: Basic Books.
Boe, E. E., & Church, R. M. (1967). Permanent effects of punishment during extinction. *Journal of Comparative and Physiological Psychology*, 63, 486-492.
Boehner, P. (Ed.). (1957). *Ockham: Philosophical writings*. Edinburgh: Nelson.
Bolin, E. P., & Goldberg, G. M. (1979). Behavioral psychology and the Bible: General and specific considerations. *Journal of Psychology and Theology*, 7, 167-175.
Bolton, N. (1977). *Concept formation*. Oxford: Pergamon Press.
Boring, E. G. (1950). *A history of experimental psychology* (2nd ed.). Englewood Cliffs, NJ: Prentice-Hall.
Bourne, L., Jr. (1966). *Human conceptual behavior*. Boston: Allyn & Bacon.
Boutan, L. (1913). Le pseudo-langage. Observations effectuées sur an anthropoide: Le gibbon (*Hylobates Leucogenys* Ogilby). *Actes de la Societé Linneenne de Bordeaux*, 67, 5-80.
Bower, G., & Hilgard, E. (1981). *Theories of learning* (5th ed.). Englewood Cliffs, NJ: Prentice-Hall.
Bransford, J., & Franks, J. (1971). Abstraction of linguistic ideas. *Cognitive Psychology*, 2, 331-350.
Brigham, T. (1982). Self-management: A radical behavioral perspective. In P. Karoly and F. H. Kanfer (Eds.), *Self-management and behavior change: From theory to practice* (pp. 32-59). New York: Pergamon.
Brown, P. L., & Jenkins, H. M. (1968). Auto-shaping of the pigeon's key peck. *Journal of the Experimental Analysis of Behavior*, 11, 1-8.
Brown, R. (1956). Language and categories. In J. Bruner, J. Goodnow, & G. Austin, (Eds.), *A study of thinking* (pp. 247-312). New York: John Wiley.
Brown, R. (1958). How shall a thing be called? *Psychological Bulletin*, 65, 14-21.
Brown, R. (1976). Reference: In memorial tribute to Eric Lenneberg. *Cognition*, 4, 125-153.
Brown, R. (1977). In reply to Peter Schönbach. *Cognition*, 5, 185-187.
Brown, W. L., McDowell, A. A., & Robinson, E. M. (1965). Discrimination learning of mirrored cues by rhesus monkeys. *Journal of Genetic Psychology*, 106, 123-128.
Brownell, H., & Caramazza, A. (1978). Categorizing with overlapping categories. *Memory and Cognition*, 6, 481-490.
Bruner, J. S., Goodnow, J. J., & Austin, G. A. (1956). *A study of thinking*. New York: Wiley.
Bullock, D. H. (1978). *Programmed instruction*. Englewood Cliffs, NJ: Educational Technology Publications.

Bunge, M. (1961). The weight of simplicity in the construction and assaying of scientific theories. *Philosophy of Science, 28*, 120-149.
Burton, M. (1980). Determinism, relativism and the behavior of scientists. *Behaviorism, 8*, 113-122.
Burtt, E. A. (1954). *The metaphysical foundations of modern science*. New York: Doubleday.
Bush, R. R., & Mosteller, F. (1955). *Stochastic models for learning*. New York: Wiley.
Buss, A. H. (1961). *The psychology of aggression*. New York: Wiley.
Buss, A. H. (1973). *Psychology: Man in perspective*. New York: Wiley.
Catania, A. C. (Ed.). (1968). *Contemporary research in operant behavior*. Glenview, IL: Scott, Foresman.
Catania, A. C. (1975). The myth of self-reinforcement. *Behaviorism, 3*, 192-199.
Catania, A. C. (1976). Self-reinforcement revisited. *Behaviorism, 4*, 157-162.
Catania, A. C. (1979). *Learning*. Englewood Cliffs, NJ: Prentice-Hall.
Catania, A. C. (1980). Autoclitic processes and the structure of behavior. *Behaviorism, 8*, 175-186.
Catania, A. C., & Brigham, T. A. (Eds.). (1978). *Handbook of applied behavior analysis: Social and instructional processes*. New York: Irvington.
Catania, A. C., & Keller, K. (1981). Contingency, contiguity, correlation, and the concept of causation. In P. Harzem & M. D. Zeiler (Eds.), *Advances in the analysis of behavior, Vol. 2: Predictability, correlation, and contiguity*. New York: John Wiley.
Cautela, J. R. (1971). Covert conditioning. In A. Jacobs & L. B. Sachs (Eds.), *The psychology of private events: Perspectives on covert response systems*. New York: Academic Press.
Cerella, J. (1979). Visual classes and natural categories in the pigeon. *Journal of Experimental Psychology: Human Perception and Performance, 5*, 68-77.
Chance, M. R. A. (1960). Köhler's chimpanzees—How did they perform? *Man, 60*, 130-135.
Charman, L., & Davison, M. (1982). On the effects of component durations and component reinforcement rates in multiple schedules. *Journal of the Experimental Analysis of Behavior, 37*, 417-439.
Cheney, C. D. (1984). *Mirror use by pigeons: A systematic replication.* Unpublished manuscript, Utah State University.
Chiarelli, A. B. (1973). *Evolution of the primates*. New York: Academic.
Chiszar, D., & Carpen, K. (1980). Origin and synthesis. *American Psychologist, 35*, 958-962. (Portion of Wyers et al. The sociobiological challenge to psychology: On the proposal to "cannibalize" comparative psychology. *American Psychologist, 35*, 955-979.)
Chomsky, N. (1959). Review of B. F. Skinner's *Verbal Behavior*. *Language, 35*, 26-58.
Chomsky, N. (1965). *Aspects of the theory of syntax*. Cambridge, MA: M.I.T. Press.
Chomsky, N. (1971, December 30). The case against B. F. Skinner. *The New York Review*, pp. 18-24.
Chomsky, N. & Premack, D. (1979, November). Encounter: Species of intelligence. *The Sciences*, pp. 7-11, 23.
Church, R. M. (1969). The varied effects of punishment on behavior. *Psychological Review, 70*, 369-402.
Cohen, I. B. An interview with Einstein. (1955). *Scientific American, 193*, 73.
Cohen, P. S., & Looney, T. A. (1984). Induction by reinforcer schedules. *Journal of the Experimental Analysis of Behavior, 41*, 345-353.
Colby, K. M. (1963). Computer simulation of a neurotic process. In S. S. Tomkins and S. Messick (Eds.), *Computer simulations of personality: Frontiers of psychological research*. New York: Wiley. Pp. 165-180.

Colby, K. M. (1975). *Artificial paranoia*. New York: Pergamon.
Comunidad Los Horcones. (1986). Behaviorology: An integrative denomination. *The Behavior Analyst, 9*, 227-228.
Connellan, T. J. (1978). *How to improve performance: Behaviorism in business and industry*. New York: Harper & Row.
Cooley, C. H. (1902). *Human nature and the social order*. New York: Scribner's.
Cooper, L. N., & Imbert, M. (1981, February). Seat of memory. *The Sciences, 21*, pp. 10-13, 28-29.
Corcoran, D. W. J. (1971). *Pattern recognition*. Baltimore: Penguin Books.
Cronhelm, E. (1970). Perceptual factors and observational learning in the behavioural development of young chicks. In J. H. Crook (Ed.), *Social behaviour in birds and mammals: Essays on the social ethology of animals and man*. New York: Academic Press.
Csikszentmihályi, M. (1990). The domain of creativity. In M. A. Runco & R. S. Albert (Eds.), *Theories of creativity*. Newbury Park, CA: Sage Publications.
Cullen, C. (1979). Silicon chip model of behaviour (Letter). *Bulletin of the British Psychological Society, 32*, 480-481.
Cumming, W. W., & Berryman, R. (1965). The complex discriminated operant: Studies of matching-to-sample and related problems. In D. I. Mostovsky (Ed.), *Stimulus generalization* (pp. 284-330). Stanford: Stanford University.
Cumming, W. W., & Eckerman, D. A. (1965). Stimulus control of a differentiated operant. *Psychonomic Science, 3*, 313-314.
Daniels, A. C. (1989). *Performance management* (3rd ed.). Tucker, GA: Performance Management Publications.
Darwin, C. (1877). A biographical sketch of an infant. *Mind, 2*, 285-294.
Dashiell, J. F. (1930). Direction orientation in maze running by the white rat. *Comparative Psychology Monographs*, 7.
Davenport, R. K., Rogers, C. M., & Russell, I. S. (1973). Cross-modal perception in apes. *Neuropsychologia, 11*, 21-28.
Davis, J. M. (1973). Imitation: A review and critique. In P. P. G. Bateson and P. H. Klopfer (Eds.), *Perspectives in ethology*. New York: Plenum Press.
Dawson, R. E. (1962). Simulation in the social sciences. In H. Guetzkow (Ed.), *Simulation in social science: Readings*. Englewood Cliffs, NJ: Prentice-Hall.
Deitz, S. M. (1986). Splitter and lumpers. *Division 25 Recorder, 21*, 66-68.
Deluty, M. (1978). Self-control and impulsiveness involving aversive events. *Journal of Experimental Psychology: Animal Behavior Processes, 4*, 250-266.
Demarest, J. (1980). Identity and status. *American Psychologist, 35*, 976-977. (Portion of Wyers et al. The sociobiological challenge to psychology: On the proposal to "cannibalize" comparative psychology. *American Psychologist, 35*, 955-979.)
Demarest, J. (1983). The ideas of change, progress, and continuity in the comparative psychology of learning. In D. W. Rajecki (Ed.), *Comparing behavior: Studying man studying animals* (pp. 143-179). Hillsdale, NJ: Lawrence Erlbaum Associates.
Dewey, J. (1896). The reflex arc concept in psychology. *Psychological Review, 3*, 357-370.
Dickey, D. R. (1916). The shadow-boxing of Pipilo. *The Condor, 18*, 93-99.
Diserens, C. M. (1925). Psychological objectivism. *Psychological Review, 32*, 121-152.
Dixon, J. C. (1957). Development of self-recognition. *Journal of Genetic Psychology, 91*, 251-256.
Donahoe, J. W., & Wessells, M. G. (1980). *Learning, language, and memory*. New York: Harper & Row.
Duncker, K. (1945). On problem-solving. *Psychological Monographs* (No. 270).

Dunham, P. J., & Grantmyre, J. (1982). Changes in a multiple-response repertoire during response-contingent punishment and response restriction: Sequential relationships. *Journal of the Experimental Analysis of Behavior, 37*, 123-133.

Dunlap, K. (1922). *Elements of scientific psychology.* St. Louis: C. V. Mosby.

Dunlap, K. (1926). The theoretical aspect of psychology. In M. Bentley et al., *Psychologies of 1925* (pp. 309-329). Worcester, MA: Clark University Press.

Ebel, R. L. (1974). And still the dryads linger. *American Psychologist, 29*, 485-492.

Eddington, A. (1928). *The nature of the physical world.* New York: Macmillan.

Edelman, G. M. (1982). Through a computer darkly: Group selection and higher brain function. *Bulletin of the American Academy of Arts and Sciences, 36*, 20-49.

Edelman, G. M., & Reeke, G. N, Jr. (1982). Selective networks capable of representative transformations, limited generalization and associative memory. *Proceedings of the National Academy of Sciences, 79*, 2091-2095.

Edelson, D. (1981). Computer simulation in chemical kinetics. *Science, 214*, 981-986.

Eibel-Eibesfeldt, I. (1970). *Ethology: The biology of behavior.* New York: Holt, Rinehart & Winston.

Ellen, P. (1982). Direction, past experience, and hints in creative problem solving: Reply to Weisberg and Alba. *Journal of Experimental Psychology: General, 111*, 316-325.

Emerson, R. W. (1883). *Essays: First series, compensation.* Boston: Houghton-Mifflin.

English, H. B. (1928). *A student's dictionary of psychological terms.* Yellow Springs, OH: The Antioch Press.

Enkema, S., Slavin, R., Spaeth, C., & Neuringer, A. (1972). Extinction in the presence of free food. *Psychonomic Science, 26*, 267-269.

Epstein, R. [under the pseudonym Gallinaceous Pyle]. (1979). Another breakthrough in data interpretation at Harvard. *Worm Runner's Digest, 21*(1), 73.

Epstein, R. (Ed.). (1980a). *Notebooks: B. F. Skinner.* Englewood Cliffs, NJ: Prentice-Hall.

Epstein, R. (1980b). Defining creativity. *The Behavior Analyst, 3*(2), 65.

Epstein, R. (1981a). On pigeons and people: A preliminary look at the Columban Simulation Project. *The Behavior Analyst, 4*(1), 43-55.

Epstein, R. (1981b). A convenient model for the evolution of early psychology as a scientific discipline. *Teaching of Psychology, 8*, 42-44.

Epstein, R. (1981c). Growing older, or what else I learned in graduate school. *Harvard Magazine, 83*(6), 5-6.

Epstein, R. (1982a). A note on the mythological character of categorization research in psychology. *The Journal of Mind and Behavior, 3*, 161-169.

Epstein, R. (1982b). "Representation" in the chimpanzee. *Psychological Reports, 50*, 745-746.

Epstein, R. (1982c). Representation: A concept that fills no gaps. *The Behavioral and Brain Sciences, 5*, 377-378.

Epstein, R. (1982d). The mythological character of categorization research in psychology. *The Journal of Mind and Behavior, 3*, 161-169.

Epstein, R. (1982e). The self-concept and other daemons (abstract). *Behaviour Analysis Letters, 2*, 300-302.

Epstein, R. (Ed.). (1982f). *Skinner for the classroom.* Champaign, IL: Research Press.

Epstein, R. (1983a). Resurgence of previously reinforced behavior during extinction. *Behaviour Analysis Letters, 3*, 391-397.

Epstein, R. (1983b, April). *An experimental analysis of "cognition."* Paper presented at the 63rd annual meeting of the Western Psychological Association, San Francisco.

Epstein, R. (1984a). The case for praxics. *The Behavior Analyst, 7*, 101-119.

Epstein, R. (1984b). Pigeons, canaries, and problem solving. *Nature, 312*, 313.

Epstein, R. (1984c, August). *Praxics, praxology, and other names for the experimental analysis of behavior.* Paper presented at the 92nd annual meeting of the American Psychological Association, Toronto.

Epstein, R. (1984d, September). *A moment-to-moment account of the emergence of a novel performance.* Invited address given at the meeting of the International Society for Comparative Psychology, Acapulco.

Epstein, R. (1984e). Simulation research in the analysis of behavior. *Behaviorism, 12*(2), 41-59.

Epstein, R. (1984f). The principle of parsimony and some applications in psychology. *The Journal of Mind and Behavior, 5*, 119-130.

Epstein, R. (1984g). An effect of immediate reinforcement and delayed punishment, with possible implications for self-control. *Journal of Behavior Therapy and Experimental Psychiatry, 15*, 291-298.

Epstein, R. (1984h). Spontaneous and deferred imitation in the pigeon. *Behavioural Processes, 9*, 347-354.

Epstein, R. (1985a). Animal cognition as the praxist views it. *Neuroscience and Biobehavioral Reviews, 9*, 623-630.

Epstein, R. (1985b). The spontaneous interconnection of three repertoires. *Psychological Record, 35*, 131-141.

Epstein, R. (1985c). Further comments on praxics: Why the devotion to behaviorism? *The Behavior Analyst, 8*, 269-271.

Epstein, R. (1985d). Extinction-induced resurgence: Preliminary investigations and possible implications. *Psychological Record, 35*, 143-153.

Epstein, R. (1985e, November). *The spontaneous interconnection of four repertoires of behavior in a pigeon.* Paper presented at the annual meeting of the Psychonomics Society, Boston.

Epstein, R. (1985f). On the Columban simulations: A reply to Gallup. *Contemporary Psychology, 30*, 417-419.

Epstein, R. (1985g). The positive side effects of reinforcement: A commentary on Balsam and Bondy (1983). *Journal of Applied Behavior Analysis, 18*, 73-78.

Epstein, R. (1985h). Why the cognitivists hate the behaviorists: The Pecker-Envy Hypothesis. *The Journal of Irreproducible Results,* 1985, *30*(4), 31.

Epstein, R. (1986a). Bringing cognition and creativity into the behavioral laboratory. In T. J. Knapp & L. Robertson (Eds.), *Approaches to cognition: Contrasts and controversies* (pp. 91-109). Hillsdale, NJ: Lawrence Erlbaum Associates.

Epstein, R. (1986b). Simulation research in the analysis of behavior. In A. Poling & R. W. Fuqua (Eds.), *Research methods in applied behavior analysis.* New York: Plenum Press.

Epstein, R. (1986c, May). *Praxics in the year 2000.* Invited address given at the 66th annual meeting of the Western Psychological Association, Seattle.

Epstein, R. (1986d). Behaviorism as the praxist views it. *Behavioral and Brain Sciences, 9*, 702-703.

Epstein, R. (1986e). In the yellow wood (Afterword). In S. Modgil & C. Modgil (Eds.), *B. F. Skinner: Consensus and controversy* (pp. 333-335). Sussex, England: Falmer Press.

Epstein, R. (1987a). The spontaneous interconnection of four repertoires of behavior in a pigeon (*Columba livia*). *Journal of Comparative Psychology, 101*, 197-201.

Epstein, R. (1987b). Comparative psychology as the praxist views it. *Journal of Comparative Psychology, 101*, 249-253.

Epstein, R. (1987c). Reflections on thinking in animals. In G. Greenberg & E. Tobach (Eds.), *Language, cognition, and consciousness: Integrative levels* (pp. 19-29). Hillsdale, NJ: Lawrence Erlbaum Associates.

Epstein, R. (1987d). The debate about praxics: Some comments meant especially for student. *The Behavior Analyst, 10*, 127-131.

Epstein, R. (1988, May). *Generativity Theory*. Paper presented at the 14th annual convention of the Association for Behavior Analysis, Philadelphia.

Epstein, R. (1990a). Generativity Theory and creativity. In M. A. Runco & R. S. Albert (Eds.), *Theories of creativity*. Newbury Park, CA: Sage Publications.

Epstein, R. (1990b, December 30). How about one day of peace? *The Washington Post*, p. c4. (Reprinted in various forms and under various titles in *The International Herald Tribune, The Jerusalem Post, The International Journal on World Peace, The Egyptian Gazette*, and elsewhere.)

Epstein, R. (1991a). Skinner, creativity, and the problem of spontaneous behavior. *Psychological Science, 6*, 362-370.

Epstein, R. (1991b, April). *Automatic chaining and associationism: Tools for making reasonable inferences about the private experience of animals*. Paper presented at the 62nd annual meeting of the Eastern Psychological Association, New York.

Epstein, R. (1992a). *Learn to fish and you'll never be hungry: The ultimate guide to managing your life*. East Orange, NJ: Psience Press.

Epstien, R. (1992b, January). Get your child to say yes. *Reader's Digest*, pp. 151-154.

Epstein, R. (1992c, December). How to get a great idea. *Reader's Digest*, pp. 101-104.

Epstein, R. (1992d, Summer). The quest for the thinking computer. *AI Magazine*, pp. 81-95.

Epstein, R. (1993). Generativity Theory and education. *Educational Technology, 33*(10), 40-45.

Epstein, R. (1994a, February). The creativity spark. *Working Mother*, pp. 58-59.

Epstein, R. (1994b, July). What this kid needs is a good.... *Parenting*, pp. 120-127.

Epstein, R. (1994c, December). Loebner Prize Competition.... (Letter). *Atlantic Monthly*, p. 26.

Epstein, R., & Goss, C. (1978). A self-control procedure for the maintenance of nondisruptive behavior in an elementary school child. *Behavior Therapy, 9*, 109-117.

Epstein, R., Kirshnit, C., Lanza, R., & Rubin, L. (1984). "Insight" in the pigeon: Antecedents and determinants of an intelligent performance. *Nature, 308*, 61-62.

Epstein, R., & Koerner, J. (1986). The self-concept and other daemons. In J. Suls & A. Greenwald (Eds.), *Psychological perspectives on the self* (Vol. 3, pp. 27-53). Hillsdale, NJ: Erlbaum.

Epstein, R., Lanza, R. P., & Skinner, B. F. (1980). Symbolic communication between pigeons (*Columba livia domestica*). *Science, 207*, 543-545.

Epstein, R., Lanza, R. P., & Skinner, B. F. (1981). "Self-awareness" in the pigeon. *Science, 212*, 695-696.

Epstein, R., & Medalie, S. D. (1983). The spontaneous use of a tool by a pigeon. *Behaviour Analysis Letters, 3*, 241-247.

Epstein, R., & Skinner, B. F. (1980). Resurgence of responding after the cessation of response-independent reinforcement. *Proceedings of the National Academy of Sciences, U. S. A., 77*, 6251-6253.

Epstein, R., & Skinner, B. F. (1981). The spontaneous use of a memoranda by pigeons. *Behaviour Analysis Letters, 1*, 241-246.

Espinas, A. V. (1890). Les origines de la technologie. *Revue Philosophique, 30*, 113-135.

Espinas, A. V. (1897). *Les origines de la technologie*. Paris: F. Alcan.

Estes, W. K. (1955). Statistical theory of spontaneous recovery and regression. *Psychological Review, 62*, 145-154.

Estes, W. K. et al. (1983). Report of the research briefing panel on cognitive science and artificial intelligence. In *Research briefings 1983* (pp. 19-36). Washington, DC: National Academy Press.

Evans, R. (1968). *B. F. Skinner: The man and his ideas.* New York: Dutton.
Everall, E. E. (1935). Perseveration in the rat. *Journal of Comparative Psychology, 19,* 343-369.
Eysenck, H. J., & Martin, I. (Eds.). (1987). *Theoretical foundations of behavior therapy.* New York: Plenum.
Fagen, S. A., & Hill, J. M. (1977). *Behavior management: A competency-based manual for in-service training.* Rockville, MD: Montgomery County Public Schools.
Falk, J. L. (1971). The nature and determinants of adjuctive behavior. *Physiology and Behavior, 6,* 577-588.
Fantino, E., & Logan, C. (1979). *The experimental analysis of behavior: A biological perspective.* San Francisco: W. H. Freeman.
Faraone, S. V. (1983). The behavior as language analogy: A critical examination of an application to conversational interaction. *Behaviorism, 11,* 27-43.
Faure, H. (1956). L'investissement delirant de l'image de soi. *Evolution Psychiatrique, 3,* 545-577.
Fechner, G. (1966). *Elements of psychophysics* (Vol. I). New York: Holt, Rinehart, and Winston. (Originally published in German in 1860.)
Fenner, D. (1980). The role of contingencies and "principles of behavioral variation" in pigeons' pecking. *Journal of the Experimental Analysis of Behavior, 34,* 1-12.
Ferster, C. B. (1965). Classification of behavioral pathology. In L. Krasner & L. Ullmann (Eds.), *Research in behavior modification.* Holt, Rinehart, & Winston: New York.
Ferster, C. B., Culbertson, S., & Boren, M. C. P. (1975). *Behavior principles* (Revised ed.). Englewood Cliffs, NJ: Prentice-Hall.
Ferster, C. B., Nurnberger, J. I., & Levitt, E. B. (1962). The control of eating. *Journal of Mathetics, 1*(1), 87-109.
Ferster, C. B., & Skinner, B. F. (1957). *Schedules of reinforcement.* New York: Appleton-Century-Crofts.
Feuer, L. S. (1957). The principle of simplicity. *Philosophy of Science, 24,* 109-122.
Flanagan, O. J., Jr. (1980). Explanation and reduction. *American Psychologist, 35,* 974-975. (Portion of Wyers et al. The sociobiological challenge to psychology: On the proposal to "cannibalize" comparative psychology. *American Psychologist, 35,* 955-979.)
Flanders, J. P. (1968). A review of research on imitative behavior. *Psychological Bulletin, 69,* 316-337.
Fodor, J. A. (1981). The mind-body problem. *Scientific American, 244,* 114-123.
Ford, C. (1952). Praxology. In J. E. Hulett & R. Stagner (Eds.), *Problems in social psychology: An interdisciplinary inquiry* (pp. 214-219). Urbana, IL: University of Illinois.
Foster, C. (1974). *Developing self-control.* Kalamazoo, MI: Behaviordelia.
Fouts, R. S. (1974). Language: Origins, definitions and chimpanzees. *Journal of Human Evolution, 3,* 475-482.
Fouts, R. S. (1975). Capacities for language in the great apes. In R. H. Tuttle (Ed.), *Socio-ecology and psychology of primates.* The Hague: Mouton.
Fraley, L., & Vargas, E. (1986). Separate disciplines: The study of behavior and the study of psyche. *The Behavior Analyst, 9,* 47-59.
Freud, S. (1920). *A general introduction to psychoanalysis.* New York: Boni & Liveright.
Freud, S. (1961). Fragment of an analysis of a case of hysteria. In J. Strachey (Ed. and Trans.), *The standard edition of the complete psychological works of Sigmund Freud* (Vol. 7, pp. 1-122). London: Hogarth Press. (Original paper published 1905.)
Freud, S. (1966). *Introductory lectures on psychoanalysis.* New York: W. W. Norton.

Gallup, G. G., Jr. (1966). Mirror-image reinforcement in monkeys. *Psychonomic Science, 5,* 39-40.
Gallup, G. G., Jr. (1968). Mirror-image stimulation. *Psychological Bulletin, 70,* 782-793.
Gallup, G. G., Jr. (1970). Chimpanzees: Self-recognition. *Science, 167,* 86-87.
Gallup, G. G., Jr. (1975). Towards an operational definition of self-awareness. In R. H. Tuttle (Ed.). *Socio-ecology and psychology of primates.* The Hague, Netherlands: Mouton.
Gallup, G. G., Jr. (1977a). Self-recognition in primates: A comparative approach to the bidirectional properties of consciousness. *American Psychologist, 32,* 329-338.
Gallup, G. G., Jr. (1977b). Absense of self-recognition in a monkey (*Macaca fascicularis*)following prolonged exposure to a mirror. *Developmental Psychobiology, 10,* 281-284.
Gallup, G. G., Jr. (1979). Self-awareness in primates. *American Scientist, 67,* 417-421.
Gallup, G. G., Jr. (1984). Will reinforcement subsume cognition? *Contemporary Psychology, 29,* 589-590.
Gallup, G. G., Jr., & Capper, S. A. (1970). Preference for mirror-image stimulation in finches (*Passer domesticus domesticus*) and parakeets (*Melopsittacus undulatus*). *Animal Behaviour, 18,* 621-624.
Gallup, G. G., Jr., & Hess, J. Y. (1971). Preference for mirror-image stimulation in goldfish (*Carassius auratus*). *Psychonomic Science, 23,* 63-64.
Gallup, G. G., Jr., & McClure, M. K. (1971). Preference for mirror-image stimulation in differentially reared rhesus monkeys. *Journal of Comparative and Physiological Psychology, 75,* 403-407.
Gallup, G. G., Jr., McClure, M. K., Hill, S. D., & Bundy, R. A. (1971). Capacity for self-recognition in differentially reared chimpanzees. *Psychological Record, 21,* 69-74.
Gallup, G. G., Jr., Montevecchi, W. A., Swanson, E. T. (1972). Motivational properties of mirror image stimulation in the domestic chicken. *Psychological Record, 22,* 193-199.
Gallup, G. G., Jr., Wallnau, L. B., & Suarez, S. D. (1980). Failure to find self-recognition in mother-infant and infant-infant rhesus monkey pairs. *Folia Primatologica, 33,* 210-219.
Gantt, W. H. (1944). Experimental basis for neurotic behavior. *Psychosomatic Medicine Monographs, 3,* Nos. 3 and 4.
Gardiner, W. L. (1974). *Psychology: A story of a search.* Belmont, CA: Wadsworth.
Gardner, R. A., & Gardner, B. T. (1969). Teaching sign language to a chimpanzee. *Science, 165,* 664-672.
Gardner, H. (1982). *Art, mind, and brain: A cognitive approach to creativity.* New York: Basic Books.
Garner, W. (1976). Interaction of stimulus dimensions in concept and choice processes. *Cognitive Psychology, 8,* 98-123.
Gaydos, G. R. (1986). On praxis and praxics. *The Behavior Analyst, 9,* 229-230.
Gelhard, B., Wohlman, S., & Thompson, R. K. R. (1982, October). *Self-awareness in pigeons: A second look.* Paper presented at the Northeast Regional Meeting of the Animal Behavior Society, Boston.
Gentry, G. D., Weiss, B., & Laties, V. G. (1983). The microanalysis of fixed-interval responding. *Journal of the Experimental Analysis of Behavior, 39,* 327-343.
Gentry, W. D. (Ed.) (1984). *Handbook of behavioral medicine.* New York: Guilford.
Gesell, A., & Thompson, H. (1934). *Infant behavior: Its genesis and growth.* New York: McGraw-Hill.
Ghiselin, B. (Ed.). (1952). *The creative process.* New York: Mentor.

Gibson, W. R. B. (1904). *A philosophical introduction to ethics: An advocacy of the spiritual principle in ethics from the point of view of personal idealism*. London: Swan Sonnenschein & Co.

Glickman, S. E. (1980). Notes on survival. *American Psychologist, 35*, 962-964. (Portion of Wyers et al. The sociobiological challenge to psychology: On the proposal to "cannibalize" comparative psychology. *American Psychologist, 35*, 955-979.)

Glover, J. A. (1980). *Becoming a more creative person*. Englewood Cliffs, NJ: Prentice-Hall.

Gluck, J. P., & Harlow, H. F. (1971). The effects of deprived and enriched rearing conditions on later learning: A review. In L. E. Jarrard (Ed.), *Cognitive processes of nonhuman primates* (pp. 103-119). New York: Academic Press.

Goetz, E. M., & Baer, D. M. (1973). Social control of form diversity and the emergence of new forms in children's blockbuilding. *Journal of Applied Behavior Analysis, 6*, 209-217.

Goldberg, S. R., & Stolerman, I. P. (Eds.). (1986). *Behavioral analysis and drug dependence*. New York: Academic Press.

Goldfried, M. R., & Merbaum, M. (1973a). A perspective on self-control. In M. R. Goldfried & M. Merbaum (Eds.), *Behavior change through self-control* (pp. 3-34). New York: Holt, Rinehart & Winston.

Goldfried, M. R., & Merbaum, M. (Eds.). (1973b). *Behavior change through self-control*. New York: Holt, Rinehart & Winston.

Goldiamond, I. (1965). Self-control procedures in personal behavior problems. *Psychological Reports, 17*, 851-868.

Goldiamond, I. (1976a). Self-reinforcement. *Journal of Applied Behavior Analysis, 9*, 509-514.

Goldiamond, I. (1976b). Fables, armadyllics, and self-reinforcement. *Journal of Applied Behavior Analysis, 9*, 521-525.

Goldman, D., & Homa, D. (1977). Integrative and metric properties of abstracted information as a function of category discriminability, instance variability, and experience. *Journal of Experimental Psychology: Human Learning and Memory, 3*, 375-385.

Goodall, J. (1968). *The behaviour of free-living chimpanzees in the Gombe Stream Reserve*. London: Bailliere, Tindall & Cassell.

Goodall, J. (1971). *In the shadow of man*. Boston: Houghton Mifflin.

Gooding, D. (1982). Empiricism in practice: Teleology, economy, and observation in Faraday's physics. *ISIS, 73*, 46-67.

Goodman, N. (1961). Safety, strength, simplicity. *Philosophy of Science, 28*, 150-151.

Goodman, N. (1965). *Fact, fiction, and forecast*. New York: Bobbs-Merrill.

Goodman, N. (1972). *Problems and projects*. Indianapolis: Bobbs-Merrill.

Gottlieb, G. (1972). Zing-Yang Kuo: Radical scientific philosopher and innovative experimentalist (1898-1970). *Journal of Comparative and Physiological Psychology, 80*, 1-10.

Gottlieb, G. (1979). Comparative psychology and ethology. In E. Hearst (Ed.), *The first century of experimental psychology* (pp. 147-176). Hillsdale, NJ: Lawrence Erlbaum Associates.

Gottlieb, G. (1984). Evolutionary trends and evolutionary origins: Relevance to theory in comparative psychology. *Psychological Review, 91*, 448-456.

Grabowski, J., Stitzer, M. L., & Henningfield, J. E. (Eds.). (1984). *Behavioral intervention techniques in drug abuse treatment*. Rockville, MD: National Institute on Drug Abuse.

Graham, G. (1977). On what is good: A study of B. F. Skinner's operant behaviorist view. *Behaviorism, 5*, 97-112.

Green, L, & Snyderman, M. (1980). Choice between rewards differing in amount and delay: Toward a choice model of self-control. *Journal of the Experimental Analysis of Behavior, 34*, 135-147.
Griffin, D. R. (1976). *The question of animal awareness: Evolutionary continuity of mental experience.* New York: Rockefeller University Press.
Griffin, D. R. (1978). Prospects for a cognitive ethology. *The Behavioral and Brain Sciences, 1*, 527-538.
Griffin, D. R. (1983). *Animal thinking.* Cambridge, MA: Harvard University Press.
Guilford, J. P. (1950). Creativity. *American Psychologist, 5*, 444-454.
Guilford, J. P. (1962). Factors that aid and hinder creativity. *Teachers' College Record, 63*, 380-392.
Gurin, J. (1981, April). The creationist revival. *The Sciences,* pp. 16-19, 34.
Gutiérrez, C. (1971). The extraordinary claim of praxeology. *Theory and Decision, 1*, 327-336.
Hake, D. F. (1982). The basic-applied continuum and the possible evolution of human operant social and verbal research. *The Behavior Analyst, 5*, 21-28.
Hake, D. F., & Olvera, D. (1978). Cooperation, competition, and related social phenomena. In A. C. Catania & T. A. Brigham (Eds.), *Handbook of Applied Behavior Analysis: Social and Instructional Processes.* New York: Irvington.
Hake, D. F., & Vukelich, R. (1972). A classification and review of cooperative procedures. *Journal of the Experimental Analysis of Behavior, 18*, 333-343.
Hake, D. F., & Vukelich, R. (1973). Analysis of the control exerted by a complex cooperation procedure. *Journal of the Experimental Analysis of Behavior, 19*, 3-16.
Hamilton, J. A., & Krechevsky, I. (1933). Studies in the effect of shock upon behavior plasticity in the rat. *Journal of Comparative Psychology, 16*, 237-253.
Hamilton, W. (1859). H. L. Mansel & J. Veitch (Eds.), *Lectures on metaphysics and logic* (Vol. II). Edinburgh: William Blackwood and Sons.
Harlow, H. F., Schlitz, K. A., & Harlow, M. K. (1968). Effects of social isolation on the learning performance of rhesus monkeys. *Proceedings of the Second International Congress of Primatology.* Basel, Switzerland: Karger.
Harris, L. P. (1977). Self-recognition among institutionalized profoundly retarded males: A replication. *Bulletin of the Psychonomic Society, 9*, 43-44.
Hartig, F. H., & Kanfer, F. A. (1973). The role of verbal self-instructions in children's resistance to temptation. *Journal of Personality and Social Psychology, 25*, 259-267.
Harzem, P. (1984). Remarks made as chair of a symposium entitled "What Should Be the Relationship Between Behavior Analysis and Psychology?" Given at the 10th annual meeting of the Association for Behavior Analysis, Nashville.
Hausfater, G. (1976). Predatory behavior of yellow baboons. *Behavior, 56*, 44-68.
Heidbreder, E. (1946). The attainment of concepts I: Terminology and methodology. *Journal of General Psychology, 35*, 173-189.
Heidbreder, E. (1948). The attainment of concepts IV: Exploratory experiments in conceptualization at perceptual levels. *Journal of Psychology, 26*, 193-216.
Heidbreder, E. (1949). The attainment of concepts VIII: The conceptualization of verbally indicated instances. *Journal of Psychology, 27*, 263-309.
Heider, E. (1972). Universals in color naming and memory. *Journal of Experimental Psychology, 93*, 10-20.
Henton, W. W., & Iversen, I. H. (1978). *Classical conditioning and operant conditioning: A response pattern analysis.* New York: Springer-Verlag.
Herbart, J. F. (1816). *Lehrbuch zur Psychologie.* Königsberg: Unzer.
Herbart, J. F. (1822). *Ueber die Möglichkeit und Nothwendigkeit Mathematik auf Psychologie anzuwenden.* Königsberg: Unzer.
Herbart, J. F. (1824-25). *Psychologie als Wissenschaft, neu gegrundet auf Erfahrung, Metaphysik und Mathematik.* Königsberg: Unzer.

Herbart, J. F. (1877). Possibility and necessity of applying mathematics in psychology. *Journal of Speculative Philosophy, 11*, 251-264.
Herbert, E., Pinkston, E., Hayden, M., Sajwaj, T., Pinkston, S., Cordua, G., & Jackson, C. (1973). Adverse effects of differential parental attention. *Journal of Applied Behavior Analysis, 6*, 15-30.
Herrnstein, R. J. (1970). On the law of effect. *Journal of the Experimental Analysis of Behavior, 13*, 243-266.
Herrnstein, R. J. (1977). The evolution of behaviorism. *American Psychologist, 32*, 593-603.
Herrnstein, R., Loveland, D., & Cable, C. (1976). Natural concepts in pigeons. *Journal of Experimental Psychology: Animal Behavior Processes, 2*, 285-301.
Hersen, M., van Hasselt, V. B., & Matson, J. L. (Eds.). (1983). *Behavior therapy for the developmentally and physically disabled*. New York: Academic Press.
Hersh, H., & Caramazza, A. (1976). A fuzzy set approach to modifiers and vagueness in natural language. *Journal of Experimental Psychology: General, 105*, 254-276.
Heyman, G. M. (1979). A Markov model description of changeover probabilities on concurrent variable-interval schedules. *Journal of the Experimental Analysis of Behavior, 31*, 41-51.
Hick, W. E. (1952). On the rate of gain of information. *Quarterly Journal of Experimental Psychology, 4*, 11-26.
Hill, S. D., Bundy, R. A., Gallup, G. G., Jr., & McClure, M. K. (1970). Responsiveness of young nursery-reared chimpanzees to mirrors. *Proceedings of the Louisiana Academy of Science, 33*, 77-82.
Hinsie, L., & Campbell, R. (1970). *Psychiatric dictionary*. London: Oxford University Press.
Hintzman, D. L. (1978). *The psychology of learning and memory*. San Francisco, W. H. Freeman.
Hobhouse, L. T. (1901). *Mind in evolution*. New York: Macmillan.
Hodos, W., & Campbell, C. B. G. (1969). *Scala naturae*: Why there is no theory in comparative psychology. *Psychological Review, 76*, 337-350.
Hogan, J. A. (1967). Fighting and reinforcement in the siamese fighting fish (*Betta splendens*). *Journal of Comparative and Physiological Psychology, 64*, 356-359.
Holland, J. G., & Skinner, B. F. (1961). *The analysis of behavior: A program for self-instruction*. New York: McGraw-Hill.
Hollard, V. D., & Delius, J. D. (1982). Rotational invariance in visual pattern recognition by pigeons and humans. *Science, 218*, 804-806.
Hollis, J. H. (1968). Chlorpromazine: Direct measurement of a differential behavioral effect. *Science, 159*, 1487-1489.
Holz, W. C. (1968). Punishment and rate of positive reinforcement. *Journal of the Experimental Analysis of Behavior, 11*, 285-292.
Honig, W. K. (Ed.). (1966). *Operant Behavior: Areas of Research and Application*. Englewood Cliffs, NJ: Prentice-Hall.
Hopkins, A. J. (1934). *Alchemy: Child of Greek philosophy*. New York: Columbia University Press.
Hull, C. L. (1920). Quantitative aspects of the evolution of concepts: An experimental study. *Psychological Monographs, 28* (1, Whole No. 123).
Hull, C. L. (1934). The rat's speed-of-locomotion gradient in the approach to food. *Journal of Comparative Psychology, 17*, 393-422.
Hull, C. L. (1935). The mechanism of the assembly of behavior segments in novel combinations suitable for problem solving. *The Psychological Review, 42*, 219-245.
Hull, C. L. (1952). *A behavior system*. New Haven, CT: Yale University Press.
Hulse, S. H., Fowler, H., & Honig, W. K. (1978). *Cognitive processes in animal behavior*. Hillsdale, NJ: Erlbaum.

Hunt, J. McV. (1956). Walter Samuel Hunter: 1889-1954. *Psychological Review, 63*, 213-217.
Hunter, W. S. (1925). General anthroponomy and its systematic problems. *American Journal of Psychology, 36*, 286-302.
Hunter, W. S. (1926). Psychology and anthroponomy. In C. Murchison (Ed.), *Psychologies of 1925* (pp. 83-107). Worcester, MA: Clark University Press.
Hunter, W. S. (1930). Anthroponomy and psychology. In C. Murchison (Ed.), *Psychologies of 1930* (pp. 281-300). Worcester, MA: Clark University Press.
Hutchinson, G. E. (1981). Random adaptation and imitation in human evolution. *American Scientist, 69*, 161-165.
Hutchinson, R. R. (1977). By-products of aversive control. In W. K. Honig & J. E. R. Staddon, (Eds.), *Handbook of operant behavior* (pp. 415-431). Englewood Cliffs, NJ: Prentice-Hall.
Hyman, R. (1953). Stimulus information as a determinant of reaction time. *Journal of the Experimental Analysis of Behavior, 45*, 188-196.
Iversen, L. L., Iversen, S. D., & Snyder, S. H. (Eds.) (1987). *New directions in behavioral pharmacology*. New York: Plenum.
James, W. (1890). *The principles of psychology*. New York: Holt.
Jarvis, M. J., & Ettlinger, G. (1978). Cross-modal performance in monkeys and apes: Is there a substantial difference? In D. J. Chivers & J. Herbert (Eds), *Recent advances in primatology* (Vol. 1). New York: Academic Press.
Johnson, K. R., & Layng, T. V. J. (1992). Breaking the structuralist barrier: Literacy and numeracy with fluency. *American Psychologist, 47*, 1475-1490.
Jones, V. F. (1990). *Comprehensive classroom management: Motivating and managing students* (3rd ed.). Boston: Allyn & Bacon.
Jost, A. (1897). Die Associationsfestigkeit in ihrer Abhangigkeit von der Verteilung der Wiederholungen. *Zeitschrift der Psychologie, 14*, 436-472.
Kagan, J. (1981). *The second year: The emergence of self-awareness*. Cambridge, MA: Harvard University Press.
Kalat, J. W. (1983). Evolutionary thinking in the history of the comparative psychology of learning. *Neuroscience and Biobehavioral Reviews, 7*, 309-314.
Kanfer, F. H. (1970). Self-regulation: Research, issues, and speculations. In C. Neuringer & J. L. Michael (Eds.), *Behavior modification in clinical psychology* (pp. 178-220). New York: Appleton-Century-Crofts.
Kanfer, F. H. (1977). The many faces of self-control, or behavior modification changes its focus. In R. B. Stuart (Ed.), *Self-management: Strategies, techniques, and outcomes*. New York: Brunner/Mazel.
Kanfer, F. H., & Goldstein, A. P. (Eds.). (1975). *Helping people change: A textbook of methods*. New York: Pergamon.
Kanfer, F. H., & Karoly, P. (1972). Self-control: A behavioristic excursion into the lion's den. *Behavior Therapy, 3*, 398-416.
Kanfer, F. H., & Phillips, J. S. (1970). *Learning foundations of behavior therapy*. New York: John Wiley & Sons.
Kantor, J. R. (1924). *Principles of psychology* (Vol. I). Chicago: Principia Press.
Kantor, J. R., & Smith, N. W. (1975). *The science of psychology: An interbehavioral survey*. Chicago: Principia Press.
Kaplan, J. S. (1991). *Beyond behavior modification: A cognitive-behavioral approach to behavior management in the school* (2nd ed.). Austin, TX: Pro-Ed.
Karen, R. L. (1974). *An introduction to behavior theory and its applications*. New York: Harper & Row.
Karoly, P. (1982). Perspectives on self-management and behavior change. In P. Karoly & F. H. Kanfer (Eds.), *Self-management and behavior change: From theory to practice* (pp. 3-31). New York: Pergamon.

Karoly, P., & Kanfer, F. H. (Eds.). (1982). *Self-management and behavior change: From theory to practice.* New York: Pergamon.

Kazdin, A. E. (1978). *History of behavior modification: Experimental foundations of contemporary research.* Baltimore, MD: University Park Press.

Kazdin, A. E. (1982). Symptom substitution, generalization, and response covariation: Implications for psychotherapy outcome. *Psychological Bulletin, 91,* 349-365.

Keller, F. S. (1968). "Good-bye, Teacher..." *Journal of Applied Behavior Analysis, 1,* 79-89.

Keller, F. S. (1977). *Summer and sabbaticals: Selected papers on psychology and education.* Champaign, IL: Research Press.

Keller, F. S. (1984). A note on the founding of the Center. *The Current Repertoire* (Newsletter of the Cambridge Center for Behavioral Studies), *1,* 1.

Keller, F. S. (1986). Notes to the editor. *The ABA Newsletter, 9*(3), 3.

Keller, F. S., & Sherman, J. G. (1974). *The Keller Plan handbook: Essays on a personalized system of instruction.* Menlo Park, CA: W. A. Benjamin.

Kendler, H., & Kendler, T. (1962). Vertical and horizontal processes in problem solving. *Psychological Review, 69,* 1-16.

Kerr, R. A. (1981). Impact looks real, the catastrophe smaller. *Science, 214,* 896-898.

King, M. C., & Wilson, A. C. (1975). Evolution at two levels in humans and chimpanzees. *Science, 188,* 107-116.

King, W. P. (Ed.). (1930). *Behaviorism: A battle line!* New York: Macmillan.

Kinget, G. M. (1975). *On being human.* New York: Harcourt, Brace, Jovanovich.

Kish, G. B. (1966). Studies of sensory reinforcement. In W. K. Honig (Ed.), *Operant behavior: Areas of research and application.* New York: Appleton-Century-Crofts.

Klopfer, P. H. (1961). Observational learning in birds: The establishment of behavioural modes. *Behaviour, 17,* 71-80.

Klüver, H. (1933). *Behavior mechanisms in monkeys.* Chicago, IL: University of Chicago.

Koestler, A. (1964). *The act of creation.* New York: Macmillan.

Koffka, K. (1924). *The growth of the mind.* London: Kegan Paul.

Köhler, W. (1925). *The mentality of apes.* London: Routledge & Kegan Paul.

Konner, M. (1982). *The tangled wing: Biological constraints on the human spirit.* New York: Harper & Row.

Kordig, C. (1971). *The justification of scientific change.* Dordrecht-Holland: D. Reidel Publishing Company.

Kosslyn, S. M. (1980). *Image and mind.* Cambridge, MA: Harvard University Press, 1980.

Kosslyn, S. M., & Pomerantz, J. (1977). Imagery, propositions, and the form of internal representations. *Cognitive Psychology, 9,* 52-76.

Kosslyn, S. M., & Schwartz, S. P. (1977). A data-driven simulation of visual imagery. *Cognitive Science, 1,* 265-296.

Kotarbiński, T. (1965). *Praxiology: An introduction to the sciences of efficient action.* Oxford: Pergamon Press.

Krasnegor, N. A. (Ed.). (1979). *Behavioral analysis and treatment of substance abuse.* Rockville, MD: National Institute of Drug Abuse.

Kraus, G. (1949). Over de psychopathologie en do psychologie van de waarneming van hat eigen spiegelbeeld. *Nederlandsch Tijdschrift voor Psychologie en haar Grensgebieden, 4,* 1-37.

Krebs, J. R. (1978). Optimal foraging: Decision rules of predators. In J. R. Krebs & N. B. Davies. *Behavioral ecology.* Sunderland, MA: Sinauer Associates.

Külpe, O. (1893). *Grundiss der Psychologie.* (English translation: *Outlines of psychology.* New York: Macmillan, 1895.)

Kuo, Z. Y. (1921). Giving up instincts in psychology. *Journal of Philosophy, 18,* 645-664.
Kuo, Z. Y. (1930). The genesis of the cat's responses to the rat. *Journal of Comparative Psychology, 11,* 1-35.
Kuo, Z. Y. (1932). Ontogeny and embryonic behavior in Aves: III. The structural and environmental factors in embryonic behavior. *Journal of Comparative Psychology, 13,* 245-271.
Kuo, Z. Y. (1933). Ontogeny of embryonic behavior in Aves: VI. Relation between heart beat and the behavior of the avian embryo. *Journal of Comparative Psychology, 16,* 379-384.
Kuo, Z. Y. (1935). [*The scope of praxiology*]. Shanghai, World Book. (In Chinese).
Kuo, Z. Y. (1937). Prolegomena to praxiology. *The Journal of Psychology, 4,* 1-22.
Kuo, Z. Y. (1967). *The dynamics of behavior development: An epigenetic view.* New York: Random House.
Labov, W. (1973). The boundaries of words and their meanings. In C. Bailey & R. Shuy (Eds.), *New ways of analyzing variation in English.* Washington, DC: Georgetown University Press.
Lander, D. G., & Irwin, R. J. (1968). Multiple schedules: Effects of the distribution of reinforcements between components on the distribution of responses between components. *Journal of the Experimental Analysis of Behavior, 11,* 517-524.
Lancaster, J. (1968). On the evolution of speech. In P. Jay (Ed), *Primates: Studies in adaptation and variability.* New York: Holt, Rinehart & Winston.
Lane, H., & Pillard, R. (1978). *The wild boy of Burundi: A study of an outcast child.* New York: Random House.
Lea, S. E. G. (1979). Foraging and reinforcement schedules in the pigeon: Optimal and non-optimal aspects of choice. *Animal Behaviour, 27,* 875-886.
Legros Clark, W. E. (1959). *The antecedents of man.* New York: Harper & Row.
Leigland, S. (1985). Praxics and the case for radical behaviorism. *The Behavior Analyst, 8,* 127-128.
Leitenberg, H., Rawson, R. A., & Bath, K. (1970). Reinforcement of competing behavior during extinction. *Science, 169,* 301-303.
Lethmate, J., & Dücker, G. (1973). Untersuchungen zum selfsterkennen im speigel bei orangutans und einen anderen affenarten. *Zeitschrift fur Tierpsychologie, 33,* 248-269.
Levi, W. M. (1957). *The Pigeon.* Sumter, SC: Levi.
Lewin, R. (1982). Where is the science in creation science? *Science, 215,* 142-144, 146.
Lewis, M., & Brooks-Gunn, J. (1979). *Social cognition and the acquisition of self.* New York: Plenum.
Lindblom, L. L., & Jenkins, H. M. (1981). Responses eliminated by noncontingent or negatively contingent reinforcement recover in extinction. *Journal of Experimental Psychology: Animal Behavior Processes, 7,* 175-190.
Lindsay, P. H., & Norman, D. A. (1977). *Human information processing.* New York: Academic Press.
Lindsley, O. (1985, May). *Quantified trends in the results of behavior analysis.* Presidential address given at the 11th annual meeting of the Association for Behavior Analysis, Columbus, Ohio.
Lissman, H. W. (1932). Die Umwelt des Kampffisches (*Betta splendens* Regan). *Zeitschrift für Vergleichende Physiologie, 18,* 62-111.
Lobb, B., & Davison, M. C. (1977). Multiple and concurrent schedule performance: Independence from concurrent and successive schedule contexts. *Journal of the Experimental Analysis of Behavior, 28,* 27-39.
Lockard, R. B. (1971). Reflections on the fall of comparative psychology: Is there a message for us all? *American Psychologist, 26,* 168-179.

Logue, A. W. (1988). Research on self-control: An integrating framework. *Behavioral and Brain Sciences, 11,* 665-709.
Lopez, F. (1979). Ausencia de autorreconocimiento en lobos (*Canis lupus signatua*) con exposcion en espejo. *Informes del Departamento de Psicologia General* (Universidad Complutense de Madrid), *2*(3), 3-14.
Lorenz, K. (1966). *On aggression.* New York: Harcourt, Brace, & World
Lorenz, K. (1971). *Studies in animal behavior* (Vol. 2). Cambridge, MA: Harvard University Press.
Lott, D. F., & Brody, P. N. (1966). Support of ovulation in the ring dove by auditory and visual stimuli. *Journal of Comparative and Physiological Psychology, 62,* 311-313.
Lotze, H. (1852). *Medicinische Psychologie oder Physiologie der Seele.* Leipzig: Weidmann'sche Buchhardlung.
Lumsdaine, A. A., & Glaser, R. (Eds.). (1965). *Teaching machines and programmed instruction: A source book.* Washington: National Education Association.
Maccia, E. S. (1966). Development of curricular materials and the discipline-centered approach. In *Development of economics curricular materials for secondary schools* (pp. 1-13). Columbus, Ohio: The Ohio State University Research Foundation.
Mach, E. (1960). *The science of mechanics: A critical and historical account of its development* (6th English ed.). LaSalle, IL: Open Court. (1st English ed., 1893).
Mackintosh, N. J. (1975). A theory of attention: Variation in the associability of stimuli with reinforcement. *Psychological Review, 82,* 276-298.
MacLean, P. D. (1964). Mirror display in the squirrel monkey. *Science, 146,* 950-952.
Mager, R. F. (1984). *Preparing instructional objectives* (2nd ed.). Belmont, CA: Pitman Management and Training.
Mahoney, M. J., & Bandura, A. (1972). Self-reinforcment in pigeons. *Learning and Motivation, 3,* 293-303.
Mahoney, M. J., & Thoresen, C. E. (1974). *Self-control: Power to the person.* Monterey, CA: Brooks/Cole.
Maier, N. R. F. (1929). Reasoning in white rats. *Comparative Psychology Monographs, 6.*
Maier, N. R. F. (1931a). Reasoning in humans. II. The solution of a problem and its appearance in consciousness. *Journal of Comparative Psychology, 12,* 181-194.
Maier, N. R. F. (1931b). Reasoning and learning. *Psychological Review, 38,* 332-342.
Maier, N. R. F. (1932). The effect of cortical destruction on reasoning and learning in white rats. *Journal of Comparative Neurology, 54,* 45-75.
Maier, N. R. F., & Schneirla, T. C. (1935). *Principles of animal psychology.* New York: McGraw-Hill.
Malagodi, E., & Branch, M. (1985). Praxics and behaviorism. *The Behavior Analyst, 8,* 123-125.
Maltzman, I. (1955). Thinking: From a behavioristic point of view. *Psychological Review, 62,* 275-286.
Maltzman, I. (1960). On the training of originality. *Psychological Review, 67,* 229-242.
Mans, L., Cicchetti, D., & Sroufe, L. A. (1978). Mirror reactions of Down's Syndrome infants and toddlers: Cognitive underpinnings of self-recognition. *Child Development,* 1978, *49,* 1247-1250.
Mansfield, R. J. W. (1976). Psychophysics and the neural basis of information processing. In H. G. Geissler & Y. M. Zabrodin (Eds.), *Advances in Psychophysics* (pp. 346-376). Berlin: VEB Deutscher Verlag der Wissenschaften.
Martin, R. F. (1940). "Native" traits and regression in rats. *Journal of Comparative Psychology, 30,* 1-16.
Mason, W. A. (1976). Environmental models and mental modes: Representational processes in the great apes and men. *American Psychologist, 31,* 284-294.

Mason, W. A. (1980). Minding our business. *American Psychologist, 35*, 964-967. (Portion of Wyers et al., The sociobiological challenge to psychology: On the proposal to "cannibalize" comparative psychology. *American Psychologist, 35*, 955-979.)
Masserman, J. H. (1943). *Behavior and neurosis.* Chicago: University of Chicago Press.
Matson, J. L., & McCartney, J. R. (Eds.) (1981). *Handbook of behavior modification with the mentally retarded.* New York: Plenum.
Matthews, L. H. (1939). Visual stimulation and ovulation in pigeons. *Proceedings of the Royal Society of London, 126*, 557-560.
May, J. G., & Dorr, D. (1968). Imitative pecking in chicks as a function of early social experience. *Psychonomic Science, 11*, 175-176.
Mazur, J. E., & Logue, A. W. (1978). Choice in a "self-control" paradigm: Effects of a fading procedure. *Journal of the Experimental Analysis of Behavior, 30*, 11-17.
McDougall, W. (1905). *Primer of physiological psychology.* London: J. M. Dent.
McDougall, W. (1908). *Introduction to social psychology.* London: Methuen & Co.
McDougall, W. (1912). *Psychology, the study of behavior.* London: Williams and Norgate.
McDowell, J. J. (1982). The importance of Herrnstein's mathematical statement of the law of effect for behavior therapy. *American Psychologist, 37*, 771-779.
McIntyre, T. (1989). *The behavior management handbook: Setting up effective behavior management systems.* Boston: Allyn & Bacon.
McKim, W. A. (1986). *Drugs and behavior: An introduction to behavioral psychopharmacology.* Englewood Cliffs, NJ: Prentice-Hall.
Mead, G. H. (1934). *Mind, self and society: From the standpoint of a social behaviorist.* Chicago, IL: University of Chicago Press.
Medin, D., & Schaffer, M. (1978). Context theory of classification learning. *Psychological Review, 85*, 207-238.
Meichenbaum, D. (1977). *Cognitive behavior modification.* New York: Plenum.
Melamed, B. G., & Siegel, L. J. (1980). *Behavioral medicine: Practical applications in health care.* New York: Springer.
Melvin, K. B., & Anson, J. E. (1970). Image-induced aggressive display: Reinforcement in the paradise fish. *Psychological Record, 20*, 225-228.
Menzel, E. W., Jr. (1973). Chimpanzee spatial memory organization. *Science, 182*, 943-945.
Mercier, C. A. (1911). *Conduct and its disorders.* New York: Macmillan.
Mervis, C. B., & Rosch, E. (1981). Categorization of natural objects. *Annual Review of Psychology, 32*, 89-115.
Migler, B. (1964). Effects of averaging data during stimulus generalization. *Journal of the Experimental Analysis of Behavior, 7*, 303-307.
Mill, J. S. (1843). *A system of logic, ratiocinative and inductive.* London: J. W. Parker.
Millard, W. J. (1979). Stimulus properties of conspecific behavior. *Journal of the Experimental Analysis of Behavior, 32*, 283-296.
Miller, G. A. (1981). Cognitive science (review of *Perspectives on cognitive science*, edited by D. A. Norman). *Science, 214*, 57.
Miller, G. A. (1983). Cognition and comparative psychology. *The Behavioral and Brain Sciences, 6*, 152-153.
Miller, N. E. (1937). Reaction formation in rats: An experimental analog for a Freudian phenomenon. *Psychological Bulletin, 34*, 724.
Miller, N. E. (1959). Liberalization of basic S-R concepts: Extensions to conflict behavior, motivation, and social learning. In S. Koch (Ed.), *Psychology: A study of a science* (Vol. 2). New York: McGraw-Hill.
Miller, N. E., & Dollard, J. (1941). *Social learning and imitation.* New Haven: Yale University Press.

References

Miller, N. E., & Miles, W. R. (1936). Alcohol and removal of reward: An analytical study of rodent maze behavior. *Journal of Comparative Psychology, 21,* 179-204.

Miller, S. L., & Orgel, L. E. (1973). *The origins of life on the earth.* Englewood Cliffs, NJ: Prentice-Hall.

Minsky, M. (1975). A framework for representing knowledge. In P. H. Winston (Ed.), *The Psychology of Computer Vision.* New York: McGraw-Hill.

Mischel, W. (1974). Processes in delay of gratification. In L. Berkowitz (Ed.), *Advances in experimental social psychology* (Vol. 7). New York: Academic Press.

MMcKim, W. A. (1986). *Drugs and behavior: An introduction to behavioral pharmacology.* Englewood Cliffs, NJ: Prentice-Hall.

Modgil, S., & Modgil, C. (Eds.) (1987). *B. F. Skinner: Consensus and controversy.* Sussex, England: Falmer Press.

Moore, E. F. (1959). The shortest path through a maze. *Proceedings of an international symposium on the theory of switching* (pp. 285-292). Cambridge, MA: Harvard University Press.

Moore, J. S. (1923). Behavior vs. introspective psychology. *Psychological Review, 30,* 235.

Morgan, C. L. (1894). *An introduction to comparative psychology.* London: Walter Scott.

Morse, W. H., & Kelleher, R. T. (1977). Determinants of reinforcement and punishment. In W. K. Honig & J. E. R. Staddon, (Eds.), *Handbook of operant behavior* (pp. 174-200). Englewood Cliffs, NJ: Prentice-Hall.

Mowrer, O. H. (1940). An experimental analogue of "regression" with incidental observations on "reaction-formation." *Journal of Abnormal and Social Psychology, 35,* 56-87.

Mundinger, P. C. (1970). Vocal imitation and individual recognition of finch calls. *Science, 168,* 480-482.

Murphy, G. (1950). *Similitude in engineering.* New York: Ronald.

Myer, J. S. (1973). Effects of punishing elements of a simple instrumental-consummatory response chain. *Journal of the Experimental Analysis of Behavior, 19,* 251-257.

Natsoulas, T. (1982). Dimensions of perceptual awareness. *Behaviorism, 10,* 85-112.

Navarick, D. J., & Fantino, E. (1976). Self-control and general models of choice. *Journal of Experimental Psychology: Animal Behavior Processes. 2,* 75-87.

Neisser, U. (1976). *Cognition and reality: Principles and implications of cognitive psychology.* San Francisco: Freeman.

Nevin, J. A. (Ed.). (1973). *The study of behavior: Learning, motivation, emotion, and instinct.* Glenview, IL: Scott, Foresman.

Nevin, J. A. (1979). Reinforcement schedules and response strength. In D. Zeiler & P. Harzem (Eds.), *Reinforcement and the organization of behavior.* Chichester: John Wiley.

Newell, A. & Simon, H. A. (1972). *Human problem solving.* Englewood Cliffs, NJ: Prentice-Hall.

Newman, A., & Bloom, R. (1981). Self-control of smoking: I. Effects of experience with imposed, increasing, decreasing, and random delays. *Behaviour Research and Therapy, 19,* 187-192.

Nordquist, V. M. (1971). The modification of a child's enuresis: Some response-response relationships. *Journal of Applied Behavior Analysis, 4,* 241-247.

Notterman, M. (1970). *Behavior: A systematic approach.* New York: Random House.

Oden, G. (1977). Fuzziness in semantic memory: Choosing exemplars of subjective categories. *Memory and Cognition, 5,* 198-204.

Oden, G., & Massaro, D. (1978). Integration of featural information in speech. *Psychological Review, 85,* 172-191.

O'Kelley, L. I. (1940a). An experimental study of regression. I. Behavioral characteristics of the regressive response. *Journal of Comparative Psychology, 30*, 41-53.

O'Kelley, L. I. (1940b). An experimental study of regression. II. Some motivational determinants of regression and perseveration. *Journal of Comparative Psychology, 30*, 55-95.

O'Leary, K. D., & O'Leary, S. G. (1977). *Classroom management: The successful use of behavior modification* (2nd ed.). New York: Pergamon.

O'Leary, K. D., & Wilson, G. T. (1975). *Behavior therapy: Application and outcome.* Englewood Cliffs, NJ: Prentice-Hall.

Osborn, A. F. (1953). *Applied imagination.* New York: Scribner's.

Orbach, J., Traub, A. C., & Olson, R. (1966). Psychophysical studies of body image: II. Normative data on the adjustable body-distorting mirror. *Archives of General Psychiatry, 14*, 41-47.

Ostancow, P. (1934). Le signe du miroir dans la demence precoce. *Annales Medico-Psychologiques, 92*, 787-790.

Parker, T. J., & Haswell, W. A. (1897). *A textbook of zoology.* London: Macmillan.

Patterson, G. R. (1975). *Families: Applications of social learning to family life* (Revised ed.). Champaign, IL: Research Press.

Pennypacker, H. S. (1984, May). Remarks made as discussant in symposium entitled "What Should Be the Relationship Between Behavior Analysis and Psychology?" Given at the 10th annual meeting of the Association for Behavior Analysis, Nashville.

Perry, J. F. (1971). Praxiology of education. *Philosophy of education, 27*, 182-191.

Peters, R. S. (Ed.). (1962). *Brett's history of psychology.* Cambridge, MA: The M.I.T. Press.

Peterson, S. K., & Tenenbaum, H. A. (1986). *Behavior management: Strategies and techniques.* Lanham, MD: University Press of America.

Pinto, J., Gladstone, G., & Yung, Y. (1980). Photochemical production of formaldehyde in Earth's primitive atmosphere. *Science, 210*, 183-185.

Place, U. T. (1981). Skinner's *Verbal Behavior* II—What is wrong with it? *Behaviorism, 9*, 131-152.

Poincaré, H. (1946). *The foundations of science.* Lancaster, PA: Science Press.

Porter, J. P. (1910). Intelligence and imitation in birds: A criterion of imitation. *American Journal of Psychology, 21*, 1-71.

Posner, M. (1969). Abstraction and the process of recognition. In G. Bower & J. Spence (Eds.), *The psychology of learning and motivation* (Vol. 3, pp. 44-96). New York: Academic Press.

Posner, M. (1973). *Cognition: An introduction.* Glenview, IL: Scott, Foresman.

Pratt, C. L., & Sackett, G. P. (1967). Selection of social partners of peer contact during rearing. *Science, 155*, 1133-1135.

Premack, D. (1971). Language in a chimpanzee? *Science, 172*, 808-822.

Premack, D. (1976). Language and intelligence in ape and man. *American Scientist, 64*, 674-683.

Premack, D. (1983a). The codes of man and beasts. *The Behavioral and Brain Sciences, 6*, 125-167.

Premack, D. (1983b). Animal cognition. *Annual Review of Psychology, 34*, 351-362.

Premack, D., & Anglin, B. (1973). On the possibilities of self-control in man and animals. *Journal of Abnormal Psychology, 81*, 137-151.

Premack, D., & Woodruff, G. (1978). Does the chimpanzee have a theory of mind? *The Behavioral and Brain Sciences, 1*, 515-526.

Premack, D., Woodruff, G., & Kennel, K. (1978). Paper-marking test for chimpanzee: Simple control for social cues. *Science, 202*, 903-905.

Pryor, K. W., Haag, R., & O'Reilly, J. (1969). The creative porpoise: Training for novel behavior. *Journal of the Experimental Analysis of Behavior, 12,* 653-661.

Pylyshyn, Z. (1973). What the mind's eye tells the mind's brain: A critique of mental imagery. *Psychological Bulletin, 80,* 1-24.

Quine, W. V. (1969a). *Ontological relativity and other essays.* New York: Columbia University Press.

Quine, W. V. (1969b). Natural kinds. In W. V. Quine, *Ontological relativity and other essays* (pp. 114-138). New York: Columbia University Press.

Quine, W. V. (1976). On mental entities. In *The ways of paradox and other essays* (pp. 221-227). Cambridge, MA: Harvard University Press.

Rachlin, H. (1970). *Introduction to modern behaviorism.* San Francisco: W. H. Freeman.

Rachlin, H. (1974). Self-control. *Behaviorism, 2,* 94-107.

Rachlin, H. (1976). *Behavior and learning.* San Francisco: W. H. Freeman.

Rachlin, H. (1978). Who cares if the chimpanzee has a theory of mind? *Behavioral and Brain Sciences, 1,* 593-594.

Rachlin, H., & Green, L. (1972). Commitment, choice, and self-control. *Journal of the Experimental Analysis of Behavior, 17,* 15-22.

Rawson, R. A., Leitenberg, H., Mulick, J. A., & Lefebvre, M. F. (1977). Recovery of extinction responding in rats following discontinuation of reinforcement of alternative behavior: A test of two explanations. *Animal Learning and Behavior, 5,* 415-420.

Reese, E. P. (1966). *The analysis of human operant behavior.* Dubuque, IA: Wm. C. Brown.

Reese, W. I. (1980). *Dictionary of philosophy and religion.* Atlantic Highlands, NJ: Humanities Press.

Reichenbach, H. (1951). *The rise of scientific philosophy.* Berkeley, CA: The University of California Press.

Reid, R. L. (1958). The role of the reinforcer as a stimulus. *British Journal of Psychology, 49,* 202-209.

Rescigno, D. (1984). *Behavior modification in business and industry: A selected bibliography.* Chicago, IL: CPL Bibliographies.

Rescorla, R. A., & Wagner, A. R. (1972). A theory of Pavlovian conditioning: Variations in the effectiveness of reinforcement and nonreinforcement. In Black, A. H., & Prokasy, W. F. (Eds.), *Classical conditioning II: Current research and theory* (pp. 64-99). New York: Appleton-Century-Crofts.

Reynolds, G. S. (1975). *A primer of operant conditioning, Revised.* Glenview, IL: Scott, Foresman.

Rhode, G., Morgan, D. P., & Young, K. R. (1983). Generalization and maintenance of treatment gains of behaviorally handicapped students from resource rooms to regular classrooms using self-evaluation procedures. *Journal of Applied Behavior Analysis, 16,* 171-188.

Rimm, D. C., & Masters, J. C. (1979). *Behavior therapy: Techniques and empirical findings* (2nd ed.). New York: Academic Press.

Rincover, A., & Koegel, R. L. (1975). Setting generality and stimulus control in autistic children. *Journal of Applied Behavior Analysis, 8,* 235-246.

Risley, T. R. (1977). The social context of self-control. In R. B. Stuart (Ed.), *Behavioral self-management: Strategies, techniques, and outcomes.* New York: Brunner/Mazel.

Ritter, W. E., & Benson, S. B. (1934). "Is the poor bird demented?" Another case of "shadow boxing." *Auk, 51,* 169-179.

Roback, A. A. (1937). *Behaviorism at twenty-five.* Cambridge, MA: Sci-Art Publishers.

Roitblat, H. (1982). The meaning of representation in animal memory. *The Behavioral and Brain Sciences, 5,* 353-372.

Rolston, H. L. (1976). A note on simplicity as a principle for evaluating rival scientific theories. *Philosophy of Science, 43*, 438-440.
Romanes, G. J. (1882). *Animal intelligence.* New York: D. Appleton.
Rosch, E. (1973). On the internal structure of perceptual and semantic categories. In T. Moore (Ed.), *Cognitive development and the acquisition of language* (pp. 111-144). New York: Academic Press.
Rosch, E. (1977). Human categorization. In N. Warren (Ed.), *Studies in cross-cultural psychology* (pp. 1-49). New York: Academic Press
Rosch, E., & Mervis, C. (1975). Family resemblances: Studies in the internal structure of categories. *Cognitive Psychology, 7*, 573-605.
Rosch, E., Mervis, C., Gray, W., Johnson, D., & Boyes-Braem, P. (1976). Basic objects in natural categories. *Cognitive Psychology, 8*, 382-439.
Rosenthal, T. L., & Zimmerman, B. J. (1978). *Social learning and cognition.* New York: Academic Press.
Ross, J. B., & McLaughlin, M. M. (Eds.). (1949). *The portable medieval reader.* New York: Viking.
Rothenberg, A. (1971). The process of Janusian thinking in creativity. *Archives of General Psychiatry, 24*, 195-205.
Rottschaefer, W. A. (1980). Skinner's science of value. *Behaviorism, 8*, 99-112.
Rumbaugh, D. M. (1971). Evidence for qualitative differences in learning processes among primates. *Journal of Comparative and Physiological Psychology, 76*, 250-255.
Rumbaugh, D. M., & Gill, T. V. (1973). The learning skills of great apes. *Journal of Human Evolution, 2*, 171-179.
Ruskin, R. S. (1974). *The personalized system of instruction: An educational alternative.* Washington: American Association for Higher Education.
Russell, B. (1923). Vagueness. *Australasian Journal of Psychology and Philosophy, 1*, 84-92.
Russell, B. (1951). *Mysticism and logic.* Baltimore: Penguin.
Russell, I. S. (1978). *Medical Research Council Unit on Neural Mechanisms of Behaviour: Progress report, 1975-1978.* Unpublished document, University of London.
Russell, J. M. (1978). Saying, feeling, and self-deception. *Behaviorism, 6*, 27-44.
Russell, J. M. (1980). Action from knowledge and conditioned behavior. Part Two: Criteria for Epistemic Behavior. *Behaviorism, 8*, 133-148.
Sabatino, D. A., Sabatino, A. C., & Mann, L. (1983). *Discipline and behavioral management: A handbook of tactics.* Rockville, MD: Aspen Systems Corp.
Sajwaj, T., Twardosz, S., & Burke, M. (1972). Side effects of extinction procedures in a remedial school. *Journal of Applied Behavior Analysis, 5*, 163-175.
Sanders, M. J. (1937). An experimental demonstration of regression in the rat. *Journal of Experimental Psychology, 21*, 493-510.
Savage-Rumbaugh, E. S. (1981). Can apes use symbols to represent their world? *Annals of the New York Academy of Sciences, 364*, 35-59.
Savage-Rumbaugh, E. S., Rumbaugh, D. M., & Boysen, S. (1978). Symbolic communication between two chimpanzees (*Pan troglodytes*). *Science, 201*, 641-644.
Savage-Rumbaugh, E. S., Rumbaugh, D. M., Smith, S. T., & Lawson, J. (1980). Reference: The linguistic essential. *Science, 210*, 922-925.
Schiller, P. (1952). Innate constituents of complex responses in primates. *Psychological Review, 59*, 177-191.
Schimmel, S. (1977). Free will, guilt, and self-control in Rabbinic Judaism and contemporary psychology. *Judaism, 26*, 418-429.
Schimmel, S. (1979). Anger and its control in Graeco-Roman and modern psychology. *Psychiatry, 42*, 320-337.

Schlosberg, H. (1954). Walter S. Hunter: Pioneer objectivist in psychology. *Science, 120*, 441-442.

Schmidt, M. (1878). Beobachtungen am Orang-Utan. *Zoologische Garten, 19*, 230-232.

Schönbach, P. (1977). In defense of Roger Brown against himself. *Cognition, 5*, 181-183.

Schulman, A. H., & Anderson, J. N. (1972). *The effects of early rearing conditions upon the preferences for mirror-image stimulation in domestic chicks*. Paper presented at the meeting of the Southern Psychological Association, Atlanta, GA.

Schultz, D. P. (1969). *A history of modern psychology*. New York: Academic Press.

Schusterman, R. J., Gentry, R., & Schmook, J. (1966). Underwater vocalization by sea lions: Social and mirror stimuli. *Science, 154*, 540-542.

Schwartz, B. (1980). Development of complex, stereotyped behavior in pigeons. *Journal of the Experimental Analysis of Behavior, 33*, 153-166.

Scott, J. P. (1973). The organization of comparative psychology. *Annals of the New York Academy of Sciences. 223*, 7-40.

Sears, R. R. (1941). Non-aggressive reactions to frustration. *Psychological Review, 48*, 343-346.

Sears, R. R. (1943). *Survey of objective studies of psychoanalytic concepts*. New York: Social Science Research Council.

Sebeok, T. A., & Umiker-Sebeok, D. J. (Eds.). (1980). *Speaking of apes: A critical anthology of two-way communication with man*. New York: Plenum.

Sechenov, I. M. (1863). *Refleksy golovnogo mozga*. St. Petersburg. (Translated by A. A. Subkov as "Reflexes of the Brain" in I. M. Sechenov, *Selected Works*, Moscow: State Pubishing House for Biological and Medical Literature, 1935.)

Segal, E. F. (1972). Induction and the provenance of operants. In R. M. Gilbert & J. R. Millenson (Eds.), *Reinforcement: Behavioral analyses*. New York: Academic Press.

Segal, E. F. (1987). Walden Two: The morality of anarchy. *The Behavior Analyst, 10*, 147-160.

Selfridge, O. G. (1959). Pandemonium: A paradigm for learning. In *The mechanisation of the tought processes*. London: H. M. Stationery Office.

Selfridge, O. G., & Neisser, U. (1960, August). Pattern recognition by machine. *Scientific American, 203*, 60-68.

Sharp, C. H. (1980). Silicon chip model of behaviour (Letter). *Bulletin of the British Psychological Society, 33*, 105.

Shekerjian, D. (1990). *Uncommon genius: How great ideas are born*. New York: Penguin Books.

Shentoub, S. A., Soulairac, A., & Rustin, E. (1954). Comportment de l'enfant arriere devant le miroir. *Enfance, 7*, 333-340.

Sherman, J. G. (Ed.). (1974). *Personalized system of instruction: 41 germinal papers*. Menlo Park, CA: W. A. Benjamin.

Shirley, M. N. (1933). *The first two years: Vol. 2. Intellectual development*. Minneapolis, MN: University of Minnesota Press.

Shurcliff, A., Brown, D., & Stollnitz, F. (1971). Specificity of training required for solution of a stick problem by rhesus monkeys (*Macaca mulatta*). *Learning and Motivation, 2*, 255-270.

Simon, H. A. (1969). *The sciences of the artificial*. Cambridge: M.I.T. Press.

Simon, H. A. (1981). Studying human intelligence by creating artificial intelligence. *American Scientist, 69*, 300-309.

Simonton, D. K. (1984). *Genius, creativity, & leadership: Historiometric inquiries*. Cambridge, MA: Harvard University Press.

Sjoden, P., Bates, S., & Dockens, W. S. (Eds.) (1979). *Trends in behavior therapy*. New York: Academic Press.

Skinner, B. F. (1931). Drive and reflex strength. *Journal of General Psychology, 6*, 22-37.
Skinner, B. F. (1932). Drive and reflex strength: II. *Journal of General Psychology, 6*, 38-48.
Skinner, B. F. (1935). The generic nature of the concepts of stimulus and response. *Journal of General Psychology, 12*, 40-65.
Skinner, B. F. (1936). A failure to obtain "disinhibition." *Journal of General Psychology, 14*, 127-135.
Skinner, B. F. (1938). *The behavior of organisms: An experimental analysis.* New York: Appleton-Century-Crofts.
Skinner, B. F. (1939). The alliteration in Shakespeare's sonnets: A study in literary behavior. *Psychological Record, 3*, 186-192.
Skinner, B. F. (1941). The psychology of design. In *Art education today.* New York: Bureau Publications, Teachers College, Columbia University.
Skinner, B. F. (1945a, October). Baby in a box. *Ladies' Home Journal*, pp. 30-31, 135-136, 138.
Skinner, B. F. (1945b). The operational analysis of psychological terms. *Psychological Review, 52*, 270-277, 291-294.
Skinner, B. F. (1948). *Walden Two.* New York: Macmillan.
Skinner, B. F. (1950). Are theories of learning necessary? *Psychological Review, 57*, 193-216.
Skinner, B. F. (1953). *Science and human behavior.* New York: Macmillan.
Skinner, B. F. (1955-56, Winter). Freedom and the control of men. *American Scholar, 25*, 47-65.
Skinner, B. F. (1956). A case history in scientific method. *American Psychologist, 11*, 221-233.
Skinner, B. F. (1957). *Verbal behavior.* New York: Appleton-Century-Crofts.
Skinner, B. F. (1960). Pigeons in a pelican. *American Psychologist, 15*, 28-37.
Skinner, B. F. (1962). Two "synthetic social relations." *Journal of the Experimental Analysis of Behavior, 5*, 531-533.
Skinner, B. F. (1963). Behaviorism at fifty. *Science, 140*, 951-958.
Skinner, B. F. [under the pseudonym F. Galton Pennywhistle]. (1964). On the relation between mathematical and statistical competence and significant scientific productivity. *The Worm Runner's Digest, 6*(1), 15-17.
Skinner, B. F. (1966). An operant analysis of problem solving. In B. Kleinmuntz (Ed.), *Problem solving: Research, method, and theory* (pp. 225-257). New York: John Wiley.
Skinner, B. F. (1968). *The technology of teaching.* New York: Appleton-Century-Crofts.
Skinner, B. F. (1969a). *Contingencies of reinforcement: A theoretical analysis.* New York: Appleton-Century-Crofts.
Skinner, B. F. (1969b, April). The machine that is man. *Psychology Today, 2*, 20-25, 60-63.
Skinner, B. F. (1970). Creating the creative artist. In A. J. Toynbee et al., *On the future of art.* New York: Viking Press.
Skinner, B. F. (1971a). *Beyond freedom and dignity.* New York: Alfred A. Knopf.
Skinner, B. F. (1971b). Autoshaping. *Science, 173*, 752.
Skinner, B. F. (1972). A lecture on "having a poem." In B. F. Skinner, *Cumulative record* (3rd ed.). New York: Appleton-Century-Crofts.
Skinner, B. F. (1973). Are we free to have a future? *Impact, 3*(1), 5-12.
Skinner, B. F. (1974). *About behaviorism.* New York: Alfred A. Knopf.
Skinner, B. F. (1976). *Particulars of my life.* New York: Alfred A. Knopf.

Skinner, B. F. (1977a). Herrnstein and the evolution of behaviorism. *American Psychologist, 32*, 1006-1012.
Skinner, B. F. (1977b). Why I am not a cognitive psychologist. *Behaviorism, 5*, 1-10.
Skinner, B. F. (1978). *Reflections on behaviorism and society*. Englewood Cliffs, NJ: Prentice-Hall.
Skinner, B. F. (1979). *The shaping of a behaviorist: Part two of an autobiography*. New York: Alfred A. Knopf.
Skinner, B. F. (1981a). Selection by consequences. *Science, 213*, 501-504.
Skinner, B. F. (1981b). How to discover what you have to say—A talk to students. *The Behavior Analyst, 4*(1), 1-7.
Skinner, B. F. (1983a). *A matter of consequences*. New York: Alfred A. Knopf.
Skinner, B. F. (1983b). Intellectual management in old age. *American Psychologist, 38*, 239-244.
Skinner, B. F. (1984). Cognitive science and behaviorism. *British Journal of Psychology, 76*, 291-301.
Skinner, B. F. (1986a). Some thoughts about the future. *Journal of the Experimental Analysis of Behavior, 45*, 229-235.
Skinner, B. F. (1986b, August). Whatever happened to psychology as the science of behavior? Invited address given at the 94th annual meeting of the American Psychological Association, Washington, DC.
Slobodkin, L. B. (1977). Evolution is no help. *World Archaeology, 8*, 332-343.
Smythe, R. H. (1962). *Animal habits: The things animals do*. Springfield, IL: Charles C. Thomas.
Snowdon, C. T. (1983). Ethology, comparative psychology, and animal behavior. *Annual Review of Psychology, 34*, 63-94.
Snygg, D., & Combs, A. W. (1949). *Individual behavior*. New York: Harper and Row.
Sober, E. (1981). The principle of parsimony. *British Journal for the Philosophy of Science, 32*, 145-156.
Sober, E. (1983). Mentalism and behaviorism in comparative psychology. In D. W. Rajecki (Ed.), *Comparing behavior: Studying man studying animals* (pp. 113-142). Hillsdale, NJ: Lawrence Erlbaum Associates.
Sober, E., & Lewontin, R. C. (1982). Artifact, cause and genic selection. *Philosophy of Science, 49*, 159-180.
Solnick, J., & Kannenberg, C. H., Eckerman, D. A., & Waller, M. B. (1980). An experimental analysis of impulsivity and impulse control in humans. *Learning and Motivation, 11*, 61-77.
Spear, N. E. (1978). *The processing of memories: Forgetting and retention*. Hillsdale, NJ: Erlbaum.
Spradlin, J. E., Girardeau, F. L., & Hom, G. L. (1966). Stimulus properties of reinforcement during extinction of a free operant response. *Journal of Experimental Child Psychology, 4*, 369-380.
Staats, A. W. (1986). Left and right paths for behaviorism's development. *The Behavior Analyst, 9*, 231-237.
Staddon, J. E. R. (1975). Learning as adaptation. In W. K. Estes (Ed.), *Handbook of learning and cognitive processes* (Vol 2.). Hillsdale, NJ: Lawrence Erlbaum Associates.
Staddon, J. E. R. (1977). Schedule-induced behavior. In W. K. Honig & J. E. R. Staddon, (Eds.), *Handbook of operant behavior* (pp. 125-152). Englewood Cliffs, NJ: Prentice-Hall.
Staddon, J. E. R., & Simmelhag, V. L. (1971). The 'superstition' experiment: A reexamination of its implications for the principles of adaptive behavior. *Psychological Review, 78*, 3-43.

Stemmer, N. (1972). Concepts and abstractions. *Communication and Cognition, 5*, 45-54.
Sternberg, R. J. (1988). *The nature of creativity: Contemporary psychological perspectives.* New York: Cambridge University Press.
Sternberg, S. (1969). The discovery of processing stages: Extensions of Donder's method. *Acta Psychologia, 30*, 276-315.
Sternberg, S. (1975). Memory scanning: New findings and current controversies. *Quarterly Journal of Experimental Psychology, 27*, 1-32.
Stevens, S. S. (1939). Psychology and the science of science. *Psychological Bulletin, 36*, 221-263.
Stokes, T. F., & Baer, D. M. (1977). An implicit technology of generalization. *Journal of Applied Behavior Analysis, 10*, 349-367.
Stone, L. J., & Church, J. (1968). *Childhood and adolescence* (2nd ed.). New York: Random House.
Straub, R. O., Seidenberg, M. S., Bever, T. G., & Terrace, H. S. (1979). *Journal of the Experimental Analysis of Behavior, 32*, 137-148
Stuart, R. B. (Ed.) (1977). *Behavioral self-management: Strategies, techniques and outcome.* New York: Brunner/Mazel.
Stunkard, A. (1977). Behavioral treatment of obesity: Failure to maintain weight loss. In R. B. Stuart, (Ed.), *Behavioral self-management: Strategies, techniques and outcome.* New York: Brunner/Mazel.
Teleki, G. (1973). *The predatory behavior of wild chimpanzees.* Lewisburg, PA: Buckness Unversity Press.
Terrace, H. S. (1979). Is problem-solving language? *Journal of the Experimental Analysis of Behavior, 31*, 161-175.
Terrace, H. (1984). Animal cognition. In H. L. Roitblat, T. G. Bever, & H. S. Terrace (Eds.), *Animal cognition* (pp. 7-28). Hillsdale, NJ: Lawrence Erlbaum Associates.
Terrace, H. S., Pettito, L. A., Sanders, R. J., & Bever, T. G. (1979). Can an ape create a sentence? *Science, 209*, 891-902.
Thompson, T. (1963). Visual reinforcment in siamese fighting fish. *Science, 141*, 55-57.
Thompson, T. (1964). Visual reinforcement in fighting cocks. *Journal of the Experimental Analysis of Behavior, 7*, 45-49.
Thompson, T., & Grabowski, J. (Eds.). (1977). *Behavior modification of the mentally retarded* (2nd ed.). New York: Oxford University Press.
Thompson, T., & Lubinski, D. (1986). Units of analysis and kinetic structure of behavioral repertoires. *Journal of the Experimental Analysis of Behavior, 46*, 219-242.
Thompson, T., & Sturm, T. (1965). Classical conditioning of aggressive display in siamese fighting fish. *Journal of the Experimental Analysis of Behavior, 8*, 397-403.
Thoresen, C. E., & Mahoney, M. J. (1974). *Behavioral self-control.* New York: Holt, Rinehart and Winston.
Thorndike, E. L. (1898). Animal intelligence: An experimental study of the associate processes in animals. *Psychological Review Monographs Supplement, 2* (Whole No. 8).
Thorndike, E. L. (1911). *Animal intelligence.* New York: Macmillan.
Thorpe, W. H. (1963). *Learning and instinct in animals* (2nd ed.). Cambridge, MA: Harvard University Press.
Tinbergen, N. (1951). *The study of instinct.* Oxford: Clarendon Press.
Tinbergen, N. (1963). On the aims and method of ethology. *Zeitschrift für Tierpsychologie, 20*, 410-433.
Tinbergen, N. (1968). On war and peace in animals and men. *Science, 160*, 1411-1418.
Tinklepaugh, D. L. (1928). An experimental study of representative factors in monkeys. *Journal of Comparative Psychology, 8*, 197-236.
Tolman, C. W. (1965). Feeding behaviour of domestic chicks in the presence of their own mirror images. *Canadian Psychologist, 6*, 227.

References

Tolman, E. C. (1932). *Purposive behavior in animals and men.* New York: Appleton-Century.
Torrance, E. P. (1962). *Guiding creative talent.* Englewood Cliffs, NJ: Prentice-Hall.
Torrance, E. P. (1963). *Education and the creative potential.* Minneapolis: University of Minnesota Press.
Torrance, E. P. (1971). *Encouraging creativity in the classroom.* Dubuque, IA: Brown.
Traub, A. C., & Orbach, J. (1964). Psychophysical studies of body images: I. The adjustable body-distorting mirror. *Archives of General Psychiatry, 11,* 53-66.
Turing, A. M. (1950). Computing machinery and intelligence. *Mind, 59,* 433-460.
Uhr, L. (1963). "Pattern recognition" computers as models for form perception. *Psychological Bulletin, 60,* 40-73.
van Lawick-Goodall, J. (1970). Tool using in primates and other vertebrates. In D. S. Lehrman, R. A. Hinde, & E. Shaw (Eds.), *Advances in the study of behavior.* London: Academic.
van Lawick-Goodall, J. (1971). *In the shadow of man.* Boston: Houghton Mifflin.
Voeltz, L. M., & Evans, I. M. (1982). The assessment of behavioral interrelationships in child behavior therapy. *Behavioral Assessment, 4,* 131-165.
Von Mises, L. (1944). Treatment of "irrationality" in the social sciences. *Philosophy and Phenomenological Research, 4,* 527-546.
Von Mises, L. (1962). *The ultimate foundation of economic science: An essay on method.* Princeton, NJ: D. Van Nostrand.
von Senden, M. (1960). *Space and sight: The perception of space and shape in the congenitally blind before and after operation.* Glenco, IL: Free Press.
Vygotsky, L. (1962). *Thought and language.* New York: Wiley.
Waldrop, M. M. (1982). Bubbles upon the river of time. *Science, 215,* 1082-1083.
Walker, H. M., & Buckley, N. K. (1972). Programming generalization and maintenance of treatment effects across time and across settings. *Journal of Applied Behavior Analysis, 5,* 209-224.
Walsh, D. (1979). Occam's razor: A principle of intellectual elegance. *American Philosophical Quarterly, 16,* 241-244.
Walters, G. C., & Grusec, J. E. (1977). *Punishment.* San Francisco: W. H. Freeman.
Washburn, M. F. (1908). *The animal mind.* New York: Macmillan.
Watson, D. L., & Tharp, R. G. (1972). *Self-directed behavior: Self-modification for personal adjustment.* Monterey, CA: Brooks/Cole.
Watson, J. B. (1913). Psychology as the behaviorist views it. *Psychological Review, 1913, 20,* 158-177.
Watson, J. B. (1914). *Behavior: An introduction to comparative psychology.* New York: Henry Holt.
Watson, J. B. (1919). *Psychology from the standpoint of a behaviorist.* Philadelphia, Lippincott.
Watson, J. B. (1930). *Behaviorism* (Revised ed.). New York: W. W. Norton.
Watson, J. B., & McDougall, W. (1928). *The battle of behaviorism: An exposition and an exposure.* London: Kegan Paul, Trench, Trubner & Co.
Watson, R. I. (1963). *The great psychologists.* Philadelphia: Lippincott.
Weisberg, R., & Alba, J. (1981). An examination of the role of "fixation" in the solution of several "insight" problems. *Journal of Experimental Psychology: General, 110,* 169-192.
Weizenbaum, J. (1966). ELIZA—A computer program for the study of a natural language communication between man and machine. *Communications of the Association for Computing Machinery, 9,* 36-45.
Wertheimer, M. (1945). *Productive thinking.* New York: Holt, Rinehart.
Wessells, M. G. (1982). A critique of Skinner's views on the obstructive character of cognitive theories. *Behaviorism, 10,* 65-84.

Wheeler, J. A. (1981). Delayed-choice experiments and the Bohr-Einstein dialog. In *The American Philosophical Society and the Royal Society: Papers read at a meeting June 5, 1980* (pp. 9-40). Philadelphia: American Philosophical Society.

Wheldall, K. (1987). *The behaviourist in the classroom.* London: Allen & Unwin.

Whitman, T. L., Scibak, J. W., & Reid, D. H. (1983). *Behavior modification with the severely and profoundly retarded: Research and application.* New York: Academic Press.

Wicklund, R. A. (1979). The influence of self-awareness on human behavior. *American Scientist, 67,* 187-193.

Wicklund, R. A., & Duval, S. (1971). Opinion change and performance facilitation as a result of objective self-awareness. *Journal of Experimental Social Psychology, 7,* 319-342.

Willard, M. J., & Epstein, R. (1980). Our most unforgettable character. *The Behavior Analyst, 3*(2), 35-39.

Williams, R. L., & Long, J. D. (1975). *Toward a self-managed life style.* Boston: Houghton Mifflin.

Wilson, A. C., & Sarich, V. M. (1969). A molecular time scale for human evolution. *Proceedings of the National Academy of Science, 63,* 1088-1093.

Wilson, E. O. (1975). *Sociobiology.* Cambridge, MA: Harvard University Press.

Winograd, T. (1972). *Understanding natural language.* New York: Academic Press.

Winokur, M. (1984). *Einstein: A portrait.* Corte Madera, CA: Pomegranate Artbooks.

Wittreich, W. (1959). Visual perception and personality. *Scientific American, 200,* 56-60.

Wolff, W. (1943). *The expression of personality.* New York: Harper.

Wolman, B. W. (1973). *Dictionary of behavioral science.* New York: Van Nostrand Reinhold.

Wolman, B. W. (Ed.). (1977). *International encyclopedia of psychiatry, psychology, psychoanalysis, and neurology.* New York: Aesculapius Publishers.

Woodworth, R. S. (1936). *Experimental psychology.* New York: Holt, Rinehart.

Wyatt, W. J., Hawkins, R. P., & Davis, P. (1986). Behaviorism: Are reports of its death exaggerated? *The Behavior Analyst, 9,* 101-105.

Wyers, E. J., Adler, H. E., Carpen, K., Chiszar, D., Demarest, J., Flanagan, O. J., Jr., Glaserfeld, E. von, Glickman, S. E., Mason, W. A., Menzel, E. W., & Tobach, E. (1980). The sociobiological challenge to psychology: On the proposal to "cannibalize" comparative psychology. *American Psychologist, 35,* 955-979.

Yates, A. J. (1958). Symptoms and symptom substitution. *Psychological Review, 55,* 371-374.

Yates, A. J. (1970). *Behavior therapy.* New York: John Wiley.

Yeni-Komshian, G. H., & Benson, D. A. (1976). Anatomical study of cerebral assymetry in the temporal lobe of humans, chimpanzees, and rhesus monkeys. *Science, 192,* 387-389.

Yerkes, R. M. (1927). The mind of a gorilla. *Genetic Psychology Monographs, 2,* 1-193.

Yerkes, R. M., & Yerkes, A. W. (1929). *The great apes: A study of anthropoid life.* New Haven, CT: Yale University Press.

Yunis, J. J., & Prakash, O. (1982). The origin of man: A chromosomal pictorial legacy. *Science, 215,* 1525-1530.

Zadeh, L. (1965). Fuzzy sets. *Information and control, 8,* 338-353.

Zadeh, L., Fu, K., Tanaka, K., & Shimura, M. (Eds.). (1975). *Fuzzy sets and their applications to cognitive and decision processes.* New York: Academic Press.

Zajonc, R. B. (1965). Social facilitation. *Science, 149,* 269-274.

Zeiler, M. (1977). Schedules of reinforcement: The controlling variables. In W. K. Honig & J. E. R. Staddon, (Eds.), *Handbook of operant behavior* (pp. 201-232). Englewood Cliffs, NJ: Prentice-Hall.

Zentall, T. R. and Hogan, D. E. (1976). Imitation and social facilitation in the pigeon. *Animal Learning and Behavior, 4*, 427-430.

Zuriff, G. E. (1985). *Behaviorism: A conceptual reconstruction.* New York: Columbia University Press.

Zwaardemaker, H. (1930). An intellectual history of a physiologist with psychological aspirations. In C. Murchison (Ed.), *A history of psychology in autobiography* (Vol. 1, pp. 491-516). Worcester, MA: Clark University Press.

INDEX

Abély, P., 285
About Behaviorism, 208
Abstinence, 160
Aggression, operant, 249
AI Magazine, iv
Aiken Computation Laboratory, 267
Ainslie, G. W., 161, 162
Alba, J., 77, 83
Albert, R. S., iii
Alcock, J., 147
Allport, G., 280
Alvarez, W., 110
American Journal of Psychology, 184
American Psychological Association, iii, iv, 175, 181, 184-187, 194, 207, 224
American Psychological Society, 186
American Scientist, 117
Amis, Kingsley, 204
Amsel, A., 128, 131, 133, 139, 251
Amsterdam, B. K., 45, 47, 72, 112, 281, 289, 292
The Analysis of Behavior, 207
The Analysis of Human Operant Behavior, 198
Anderson, J. N., 287
Anderson, J. R., 44, 114-116
Angell, James R., 170
Anglin, B., 162
Animal behavior, 13, 24, 169, 207, 241
Anson, J. E., 286
Anthropocentrism, 281
Anthropology, 171

Anthroponomy, 170, 171, 173, 174, 328; anthroponomist, 171
Antic Hay, 204
Antonitis, J. J., 131, 133, 139, 251
Anxiety, 263
APA Membership Register, 194
APA Monitor, 194
Approaches to Cognition, iii
Ardrey, R., 283
Arieti, S., 42, 210, 215
Aristotle, 179, 223, 240
Arizona State University, 190
Artificial intelligence, iv, xvi, 105, 114-119, 144, 178, 220, 267, 276, 277
Asaro, F., 110
Association for Behavior Analysis, iv, xiv, 172, 183, 193, 196, 198
Association for the Advancement of Behavior Therapy, 172
Ator, N. A., 194
Au, R., 141
Aubrey Daniels and Associates, xvi
Austin, G. A., 20, 35, 50, 86, 103, 230
Autochaining, 217
Automatic chaining, 8, 21, 27, 30, 33, 34, 42, 46, 87, 90, 96, 97, 100, 103, 217, 219
Autoshaping, 125
Avoidance behaviors, 153, 160, 258
Azrin, Nathan H., 153, 154, 248, 251, 260, 310, 316, 153, 154, 248, 251, 310

Baboons, 282, 291
"Baby box," 207
Backward chaining, 21
Baenninger, L., 287
Baenninger, R., 287
Baer, Donald, 39, 42, 250
Bailey, Shelly, xvi
Balsam, P. D., 248, 250-252
Bandura, Albert, 162, 258
Bannister, D., 299
Barker, R. G., 100, 131, 138
Barker, S. F., 237, 245
Barry, A. E., 195
Bath, K., 50, 81, 100, 131, 139
The Battle of Behaviorism, 180
Baxley, Norman, 39, 77, 113, 215
Beck, B. B., 77, 282
Beethoven, Ludwig von, 56, 255
Behavior, xv, 210; generative, 209, 210; operant, 73, 130, 135, 166, 171, 172, 178, 191, 197, 198, 210-212, 214, 234, 249, 286, 298; science of, 172; spontaneous, 209, 210
Behavior analysis, iii, iv, xiv, 171, 172, 183, 193-196, 198, 247; behavior analysts 171, 172, 194, 195
The Behavior Analyst, iv
Behavioral and Neural Biology, 187
Behavioral biology, 182, 187
Behaviorese, 205
Behaviorism iv, x, xiii, xiv, xvi, 4, 49, 163, 165, 167, 169-172, 174-183, 186, 187, 189-191, 193, 197, 205, 208, 221, 224, 225, 241; *Behaviorism* (journal), iv, 176; *Behaviorism* (J. B. Watson), 175; behaviorists, iv, x, xiv, 43, 169, 170, 172, 174, 176, 178, 180, 181, 183, 190, 205-207, 209, 224, 240, 241, 309, 311
The Behavior of Organisms, 114, 144, 170, 172, 174, 175, 181-183, 207, 209, 223, 224, 253, 279, 288
Behaviorology, 186, 195
Behaviour Analysis Letters, iii, iv
Behavioural Processes, iv
Bekhterev, V. M., 173
Benhar, E. E., 291
Benson, D. A., 282

Benson, S. B., 46, 284
Bergman, M., 287
Bergmann, G., 183
Bergson, H., 230, 233
Berryman, R., 74
Bertrand, M., 291, 292
Bever, T., 67, 119, 243
Beyond Freedom and Dignity, 4, 201, 211, 318, 332, 336, 339, 208
B. F. Skinner Foundation, xvi
B. F. Skinner: Consensus and Controversy, iv, 223
Bien, B., 169
Bingham, H., 15, 215
Biology, xiv, xv, 24, 107, 108, 120, 166, 170, 174, 182, 185, 187; behavioral, 182
Bionomics, 166
Birch, H., 15, 24, 77, 83, 217
Bloomfield, Leonard, 67
Blough, D., 44
Boakes, R. A., 135, 147
Boden, Margaret A., 116
Boe, E. E., 248
Boehner, P., 240
Bolton, N., 232
Bondy, A. S., 248, 250-252
Boren, J., 137
Boring, Edwin G., 173, 180, 181, 187, 262
Boston University, 202
Bourne, L., Jr., 231
Boutan, L., 46, 284
Bower, Gordon, 43, 137
Box, baby, 207
Box-and-banana problem, 16-18, 20, 33, 50, 53, 89-91, 99, 100, 141, 212
Boyes-Braem, P., 230
Boysen, S., 63, 73, 282
Brainstorming, 43
Branch, M., 21, 189-191, 196
Bransford, J., 234
Breath, 179
Brett's History of Psychology, 186
Bribery, 262
Broadening, 59
Brody, P. N., 286
Brooks, Becky, xvi
Brooks-Gunn, J., 45-47, 72, 111, 112, 281, 289, 295

Index 347

Brown, D., 15, 217
Brown, P. L. 125
Brown, Roger, 230, 231, 234
Brown, W. L., 291
Brownell, H., 232
Bruner, Jerome, 20, 35, 50, 86, 103, 230
Buckley, N. K., 250
Bundy, R. A., 293
Bunge, M., 245
Burke, M., 143, 251
Burton, M., 176
Burtt, E. A., 177
Burundi, wild boy of, 108
Business, 52
Buss, A. H., 283

Cable, C., 230
Caesar, 5
Cambridge Center for Behavioral Studies, iv, 186, 197, 267, 275, 277
Campbell, C. B. G., 167
Cancer, 162
Canon of Parsimony, 240
Capital, 168
Capper, S. A., 287
Capturing, 55, 56
Caramazza, A., 230, 232
Carlton, P. L., 291
Carnegie-Mellon University, 268, 274
Carr, Harvey A., 170
"The Case for Praxics," iv, x, 165, 186, 193, 321, 194-196
"A Case History in Scientific Method," 213
Catania, A. Charles, 40, 49, 67, 74, 121, 137, 142, 249
Catastrophe theory, 28
Categorization, iv, x, xvi, 50, 229-234, 242
Catholicism, 190
Cattell, James McKeen, 184
Causes, 281
Cautela, Joseph, 145
Center for Behavioral Epidemiology, xvi
Cerella, John, 230, 232
Chaining, 8, 21, 27, 30, 33, 34, 42, 46, 66, 74, 87, 90, 96, 97, 100, 103, 113, 217, 219

Challenging, 57
Chance, M. R. A., 83, 135, 144
Changeovers, 145
Chapman, Dwight, 166
Charman, L., 250
Cheney, Carl D. xii, 297
Chiarelli, A. B., 282
Child abuse, 263
Children, punishing, 255
Chimpanzees, 15, 16, 24, 37, 41, 42, 46-49, 63, 69, 71, 73, 77, 80, 83, 86, 87, 90, 91, 97, 99, 112, 114, 119, 120, 215, 217, 234, 237, 241-244, 280, 282-284, 289, 290-298
Chomsky, Noam, 15, 37, 67, 119, 210, 214, 215, 243, 309, 310
Church, R. M., 248, 251
Church, J., 292
Cicchetti, Dante, 72, 120
Circe, 162
Circumstance, 5
Clark, James, 52
Classical conditioning, 172, 191, 242, 284
Clay, Cynthia, 274, 275
Cliff Notes, 204
Cognition, iii, ix, xiii, xiv, xv, 37, 43, 44, 114-116, 120, 169, 172, 194, 238, 245
Cognitive psychology, 43, 44, 110, 181, 190, 194, 215, 243
Cognitive science, xiv, 117-119, 178, 190
"Cognitive Science and Behaviorism," xiv
Cognitivists, iv, x, xiv, 43, 49, 115, 120, 181, 243, 309, 311
Cohen, I. B., 239, 267
Cohen, P. S., 249
Colby, Kenneth, 274, 275
Colby, Peter, 274, 275
Columba livia, 63, 113, 147
Columban Simulation Laboratory, 218
Columban Simulation Project, xv, 13, 39, 113, 215
Columbia University, 190
Combs, A. W., 280
Commitment, 160
Communication, iii, ix, 14, 21, 41,

63-67, 73, 87, 142, 145, 146, 166, 187, 193, 215, 282, 297
Communications in Behavioral Biology, 187
Competition, 216
Complex behavior, 9, 15, 37, 49, 107, 109, 119, 237, 241, 243
Complexity, 108, 110, 112, 216, 221, 234, 251
The Computer Museum, 267
Computer science, 178, 181, 270, 271, 275
Computer simulations 27, 107, 110, 111, 114, 115, 117, 219, 238
Computers, thinking, 276
Comunidad Los Horcones, 195
Concept, 231
A Concise Encyclopedia of Psychiatry, 167
Conduct and Its Disorders, 167
Confusion, 17, 18, 21, 55, 58, 80, 81, 91, 93-95, 97, 100, 141, 165, 177, 202, 217
Consciousness, 41, 167, 168, 171, 173-176, 180, 234, 240, 283, 284, 288; stream of, 234
Consequences, conflicting, 153, 161
Contingencies, 40, 41, 44, 48, 49, 66, 71, 72, 74, 76, 108, 114, 120, 130, 203, 204, 208, 211, 215, 242, 248-251, 279, 297, 298; sensitivity to, 48; weak, 48
Contingencies of reinforcement, 208, 249, 250, 297
Contingencies of Reinforcement, 203
Continuity, 294
Cooley, C. H., 280, 293
Cooley-Mead model, 293
Copernicus, 206
Corcoran, D. W. J., 44
Cordua, G., 143, 251
Cornell University, 194
Counterattack, 258
Covert activity, 34, 37
"Creating the Creative Artist," 214
Creativity, iii, iv, ix, x, xi, xiii, xv, 9, 13, 34, 35, 37, 38, 40, 42, 43, 45, 51-60, 89, 112, 209, 213-215, 219-221
Crick, Francis, 67
Cronhelm, E., 147

Crown Industries, 267
Crying, 264
Csikszentmihályi, M., 34, 220
Culbertson, S., 137
Cumming, W. W., 50, 74, 90, 95, 100, 103
Cumulative Record, 207
Cybernetics, 173

Daemons, 279, 299
Dali, Salvador, 56
Darwin, Charles, 40, 46, 206, 240, 289
Dashiell, J. F., 89
Davenport, R. K., 282
Davis, P., 193
Davis, J. M., 147, 152
Davison, M., 250
Dawson, R. E., 110
Day, Willard F., Jr., 176
Daydreaming, 43
De Anima, 179
De Mestral, Georges, 55
Decisions, 162
DECTAPE, 307
Deen, A., 196
Deep structure, 49
Defoe, Daniel, 168
Deitz, S., 193, 195
Delays, 37, 74, 75, 131
Delius, J. D., 44
Deluty, M., 161
Dembo, T., 100, 131
Dennett, Daniel C., 267, 268
Depression, 263
Determinism, 3-6, 10, 176, 177, 211, 214, 221
Dewdney, A. K., 271
Dewey, John, 230
Dickey, D. R., 284
Dictionary of Behavioral Science, 167
A Dictionary of Philosophy, 167
Dictionary of Philosophy and Religion, 167
The Dictionary of Psychology and Related Fields, 167
The Dictionary of the History of Ideas, 167
Dinosaurs, extinction of, 110
Dirks, S. J., 162

Index

Discontinuity, 292, 299
Discovery, 48
Discrimination, 42-44, 66, 74, 113, 242, 251, 253
Discrimination training, 242
Diserens, C. M., 173
Dixon, J. C., 46, 48, 72, 111, 284, 289
Dog category, 231
Dollard, J., 50, 147
Donahoe, J., 44, 137
Donder's substraction method, 43
Dorr, D., 152
Dryden, John, 55, 215
Dücker G., 291
Duncker, K., 77, 80, 83, 90, 97
Dunham, P. J., 143, 220, 251
Dunlap, Knight, 167, 169, 173, 175, 186
Duval, S., 286

Ebbinghaus, Hermann, 179, 223
Ebel, R. L., 280
Eckerman, D. A., 50, 90, 95, 100, 103, 161
Economics, 168
Eddington, A., 5, 177
Edelman, G. M., 115, 120, 238
Edelson, D., 110
Edison, Thomas, 51
The Egyptian Gazette, iv
Eibl-Eibelfeldt, I., 166
Einstein, Albert, 9, 38, 53, 55, 56, 215, 239
Electron spin, theory of, 58
Eliza, 274
Ellen, P., 77, 83, 90, 198
Emerson, Ralph Waldo, 252
The Encyclopedia of Philosophy, 167
Encyclopedia of Psychiatry, 167
The Encyclopedia of Psychoanalysis, 167
English, Horace B., 167
Enkema, S., 23, 132, 142
Environmentalism, 175, 221
Epistemology, 168
Epstein, Robert, 4, 13, 14, 21, 23, 34, 35, 38-41, 44, 46-48, 50, 73, 77, 80, 81, 84, 87, 89-93, 95, 96, 98-100, 103-105, 112-115, 117, 119, 132, 134, 135, 139-142, 144, 145, 147, 160, 165, 179, 180, 186, 194, 196, 203, 208, 213, 215, 217-219, 221, 224, 238, 242, 243, 244, 245, 250-252, 277, 288, 290, 295-298
Epstein, Julian, 262, 303
Epstein, Justin, xvi, 262
Escape, 258
Espinas, A. V., 168
Estes, William K., 23, 81, 100, 131, 178
Ethics, 166
Ethology, 165, 166
Ethos, 166
Ettlinger, G., 282
Everall, E. E., 131, 138
Experimental analysis of behavior, xi, xiv, 165, 166, 170-174, 186, 187, 190, 191, 196
Explanation, 296
Explanation, property as, 280
Extinction iv, x, 8, 16, 27, 29, 46, 50, 86, 90, 95, 96, 110, 113, 126-128, 130, 131, 133-135, 137-139, 141-145, 219, 220, 249, 253, 289, 297, 298
Eysenck's dictum, 143

Failure, 57, 219, 250, 257, 297, 303
Falk, John, 128
Family resemblance, 230
Fantino, Edmund, 137, 161, 166
Faraone, S. V., 176
Faure, H., 285
Fechner, Gustav, 177, 179, 184
Feelings, 37, 45, 112, 175-177, 190, 191, 257, 258, 281
Fenner, D., 42
Ferster, C. B., 14, 137, 160, 162, 249, 252
Feuer, L. S., 244
Fiji Times, 67
"Five Hundred Names for the Science of Behavior," 196
Flanders, J. P., 50
Flesch Reading Ease, 275
Flesch-Kincaid Grade Level, 275
Fluidity, 213, 229-231
Fodor, J. A., 115
Foraging theory, 137, 144
Ford, C., 167

Fortune magazine, 52
Foundation for Research on the Nervous System, 15
Four repertoires, interconnection of, iii, 30, 99, 104
Four Saints in Three Acts, 186
Fouts, R. S., 282
Fowler, H., 241
Foxx, Richard M., 260
Fraley, L., 195-197
FRAN, 114
Franks, J., 234
Frazier, T. E., 202
Frederick II, 109, 120
Free association, 43
Free thinking, 43
Free will, 3-6, 9, 10, 175-177
Frequency profile, 35
Frequency, 212
Freud, Sigmund, 5, 23, 100, 131, 138, 143, 170, 173, 175, 299, 309-311
Freudians, 170, 181
Frigidity, 263
Frost, Robert, 213
Frustration effect, 133
Fu, K., 232
Function, 113, 213
Functional generalization 35, 50, 81
Functional psychology 179
Fuqua, W., iii
Fuzzy set theory, 232

Gaertner, I., 147
Galileo, 57, 206
Gallup, G. G., Jr., 45-48, 69, 71, 111, 112, 241, 242, 280, 281, 283, 284, 286-297
Gantt, W. H., 153
Gardiner, W. L., 284
Gardner, B. T., 282
Gardner, Howard, 215
Gardner, R. A., 282
Garner, W., 232
Gaydos, G. R., 195, 197
Gelhard, B., 297
General Problem Solver, 114
Generalization, 19, 20, 35, 42, 81, 86, 96, 103, 113
Generativity, iii, ix, xi, xv, 7-11, 13, 24, 34, 37, 51, 53, 54, 105, 209, 210, 214, 215, 218-221
Generativity Theory, iii, ix, xi, 7-11, 13, 24, 51, 53, 54, 105, 209, 219, 220
"The Generic Nature of the Concepts of Stimulus and Response," 39
Gentry, G. D., 249, 284
Gesell, A., 292
Gestalt, 8, 14, 41, 77, 89, 90
Ghiselin, B., 215
Gibson, W. R. B., 167, 168
Gibson, R. Boyce, 167
Gill, T. V., 292
Girardeau, F. L., 134
Gladstone, G., 110
The Glass Bottomed Boat, 204
Glover, John A., 220
Goals, xv, 34, 167, 195, 261, 304
God, xiii, xvi, 237, 242, 281
"God," 202
Gödel's Theorem, 233
Goetz, E. M., 39, 42
Goldfried, M. R., 160
Goldiamond, Israel, 183, 310
Goldman, D., 232, 234
Goodall, J., 282
Gooding, D., 238
Goodman, N., 230, 237, 238, 244, 245
Goodnow, J. J., 20, 35, 50, 86, 103, 230
Gorillas, 283, 285
Goss, C., 160, 250
Göttingen, 184
Gottlieb, G., 169
Gould, Stephen Jay, 215
Graduate school, 303
Graham, G., 176
Grantmyre, J., 143, 220, 251
Gray, W., 230
Green, L., 161, 162
Greenwald, A. G., iv
Griffin, Donald, 293
Grossbard, C. 152
Grusec, J. E., 251
Guilford, J. P., 42, 220
Gunning's Fog Index, 275
Gurin, J., 238
Guthrie, Edwin R., 181
Gutiérrez, C., 168, 169

Index

Haag, R., 42, 100, 131, 137
Hake, Don F., 121
Hall, G. Stanley, 184
Halliday, M. S., 135
Hamilton, J. A., 131, 138
Hamilton, Sir William, 242
Hamlet, 183
Harlow, H. F., 293
Harlow, M. K., 293
Harris, L. P., 285, 294
Hartley, David, 179
Harvard University, iv, x, 13, 15, 166, 184, 187, 194, 196, 201, 205, 234, 240, 268, 303, 305, 307, 308
Harvard Magazine, iv, 303
Harvard pecker, 308
Harvard Psychology Laboratory, 307
Harvard Square, 201
Harvard University Catalogue, 187
Harzem, Peter, 184
Haswell, W. A., 166
Hausfater, G., 282
Hawkins, R. P., 193
Hayden, M., 143, 251
Heidbreder, E., 232
Heider, F., 232
Hellman, Bud 59
Henton, W. W., 135, 142, 143
Herbart, Johann Friedrich, 143, 184, 251
Herrnstein, Richard J., 230, 232, 250, 307, 327, 332, 339, 232
Hersh, H., 230, 232
Hess, J. Y., 287
Heyman, G. M., 145
Hick, W. E., 44
Hilgard, Ernest, 43, 137
Hill, S. D., 293, 294
Hindi, 232
Hinsie, L., 167
Hintzman, D. L., 137
A History of Experimental Psychology, 187
Hobhouse, L. T., 21
Hogan, D. E., 49, 147, 152
Hogan, J. A., 286
Hollard, V. D., 44
Hollis, J. H., 134
Holy Ghost, 191
Holy Grail, 277
Holz, W. C., 153, 248, 251

Hom, G. L., 134
Homa, D., 232, 234
Homo sapiens, 113, 118, 282, 283
Honig, W. K., 67, 241
Hopkins, J. A., 177, 225
Hostelet, Georges, 168
Hovell, Melbourne F., xvi
"How to Discover What You Have to Say," 214
Hull, Clark L., 15, 33, 40, 50, 83, 90, 100, 105, 131, 134, 135, 138, 144, 145, 181, 215, 229
Hulse, S. H., 241
Humor, 107, 258
HumRRO, 268
Hunt, J. McV., 171
Hunter, Walter S., 170-173, 175, 181, 182
Hutchinson, G. E., 147
Hutchinson, R. R., 251
Hyman, R., 44
Hypnogogic state, 57
Hypostatization, 280

IBM, 174
Ideas, novel, 51
Il Principe, 168
Images, 41, 44, 46, 47, 57, 107, 112, 114, 117, 148, 215, 216, 279, 284, 285, 287, 289, 291, 292, 294, 297, 298
Imitation, iv, ix, x, 22, 37-39, 49, 50, 123, 147-152, 215, 243, 250; deferred, 147
Indiana University, 172
Information processing, 44, 117, 181, 299
Information Processing System, 117
Insight, xv, 15, 217
Instructions, 7, 22, 26, 28, 29, 37, 38, 40, 44, 108, 109, 114-117, 121, 162, 191, 205, 219, 220, 231, 247, 263
Interaction matrix, 28
Interbehavioral psychology, 173
Interbehaviorism, 173
Interconnection of repertoires, iii, ix, 9, 14, 30, 37, 38, 40, 41, 76, 89-91, 99, 100, 104, 105, 135, 144
International Encyclopedia of Psychiatry, Psychology,

Psychoanalysis, and Neurology, 167
The International Herald Tribune, iv
The International Journal on World Peace, iv
International Society for Comparative Psychology, iv
Interventions, 209, 220
An Introduction to Comparative Psychology, 240
Introduction to Social Psychology, 180
IPS, 117
IQ, 6
Irwin, R. J., 250
Iversen, Iver, 135, 142, 143

Jack, 41, 64-67, 73-76, 98, 234
Jackson, C., 143, 251
Jackson, Michael, 262
James, William, 5, 39, 175, 230, 231, 234, 280
Janusian thinking, 9, 55, 215
Jarvis, M. J., 282
Jenkins, H. M., 23, 81, 125, 132, 142
The Jerusalem Post, iv
Jill, 41, 64-67, 73-76
Johns Hopkins University, 184, 194
Johnson, K. R., 230
Jordan, Michael, 270
Jost, A., 145
Jost's laws, 145
Journal of Applied Behavior Analysis, iv
Journal of Behavior Therapy and Experimental Psychiatry, iv
Journal of Comparative Psychology, iii
The Journal of Irreproducible Results, iv
The Journal of Mind and Behavior, iv
The Journal of Psychology, 169
Journal of the Experimental Analysis of Behavior, 186
Just-because present, 261

Kagan, Jerome, 45, 111, 281, 328, 281
Kanfer, F. H., 160
Kannenberg, C. H., 161

Kantor, J. R., 173, 178
Karen, R. L., 137
Kauffman, E. G., 110
Kazdin, A. E., 143, 251
Kelleher, R. T., 251
Keller, K., 142
Keller, Fred S. 146, 166, 172, 196, 198
Kendler, H., 229
Kendler, T., 229
Kennel, K., 234
Kerr, R. A., 110
Key, Francis Scott, 38
King, W. P., 183
King, M. C., 282
Kinget, G. M., 283
Kirshnit, C., iii, 41, 79, 89, 99, 141, 217, 252
Kish, G. B., 286
Klopfer, P. H., 147
Klüver, H., 283
Knapp, Terry J., iii
Knowledge, 168
Koegel, R. L., 250
Koestler, Arthur, 9, 40-42, 105, 215
Koffka, K., 80, 87, 97, 99, 217
Köhler, Wolfgang, 15, 16, 21, 24, 37, 41, 42, 46, 77, 80, 83, 86, 87, 90, 91, 95, 97, 99, 141, 217, 241, 243, 284
Konner, M., 182
Kordig, C., 244
Kosslyn, Stephen M., 44, 114, 238, 239
Kotarbiński, T., 167, 168, 170, 174, 330, 168
Kraus, G., 284, 285, 294
Krebs, J. R., 144
Krechevsky, I., 131, 138
Külpe, Oswald, 43
Kuo, Zing Yang, 169, 170, 181, 185, 186, 193

Labov, W., 230
Lancaster, J., 282
Land, Edwin, 55, 58
Lander, D. G., 250
Lane, Harlan, 108
Language, xi, 22, 34, 35, 37, 40, 45, 64, 67, 73, 107-112, 114, 116, 120, 176, 177, 197, 209, 232, 243, 268,

Index 353

269, 276, 281, 282, 298
Lanza, R. P., iii, 14, 41, 47, 73, 79, 89, 98, 99, 105, 112, 119, 141, 147, 215, 217, 242, 243, 252, 295
Lashley, Karl, 181
Laties, V., 249
Lawson, J., 241
Le Neveu de Rameau, 204
Lea, S. E. G., 144
"A Lecture On 'Having a Poem,'" 214
Lefebvre, M. F., 131
LeGros Clark, W. E., 282
Leigland, S., 189, 196
Leipzig, 184
Leitenberg, H., 81, 100, 131, 134, 138, 140
Lethmate, J., 291
Levi, W. M., 63
Levitt, E. B., 160
Lewin, K., 100, 131, 138
Lwein, R., 238
Lewis, M., 45-47, 72, 111, 112, 280, 281, 289, 295
Lewis, Harry R., 267
Lewontin, R. C., 245
Life magazine, 207
Lindblom, L. L., 23, 81, 132, 142
Lindsay, P. H., 299
Lindsley, O. R., 194, 310
Linguistics, 181, 230
Lissman, H. W., 46
Lloyds of London, 174
Lobb, B., 250
Loeb, Jacques, 240, 241
Loebner, Hugh G., iv, 267, 268, 274, 276, 277
Loebner Prize Competition, iv, 267, 276
Loewi, Otto, 56
Logan, C., 137, 166
Logue, A. W., 161, 162, 310
Looney, T. A., 249
Lopez, F., 46
Lorenz, Konrad, 166, 283, 285
Lott, D. F., 286
Lotze, Hermann, 184
Loveland, D., 230
Lowell, Amy 55
Lubinski, D., 220
Luce, R. Duncan, 269

Lucky Jim, 204
Luther, Martin, 190

Macaques, 71, 72, 284, 286, 291, 292
Maccia, E. S. 168, 169
Mace, William, vii, 4
Mach, Ernst, 237-239, 244, 245
Machiavelli, N. 168, 309
Mackintosh, N. J., 130
MacLean, P. D., 284, 286
Mahoney, M. J., 160, 162
Maier, N. R. F., 15, 24-26, 28, 30, 41, 77, 80, 83, 89, 90, 105, 215, 218, 219
Malagodi, E., 189-191, 196
Maltzman, I., 39, 42, 50, 100, 131, 135, 144
Manhattan, 267
Mans, L., 72, 120
Mansfield, R. J. W., 177
Marble-under-the-couch problem, 107, 109
Martin, R. F., 131, 138
Marx, Karl, 168
Mason, W. A., 283, 292
Massachusetts Institute of Technology, 268
Massaro, D., 232
Masserman, J. H., 81, 100, 131, 135, 138, 153, 251
Matching law, 250, 307
Matching-to-sample, 46
Mathematics, 114, 174, 178, 184, 225
Mauldin, Michael, 274
May, J. G., 152
Mazur, James E., 161, 162
McClure, M. K., 287, 293
McDougall, William, 180-182, 187, 194, 223
McDowell, J. J., 143, 250
McDowell, A. A., 291
McLaughlin, M. M., 109
Mead, George Herbert, 168, 293
Medalie, Samuel D., iii, 21, 22, 50, 84, 89, 90, 92, 100, 103, 105, 135, 140, 145, 244, 245
Medin, D., 232
Melvin, K. B., 286
Memoranda, iii, ix, 14, 41, 73-76, 215
Memory, 37, 44, 111, 112, 114, 116,

117, 121, 145, 205, 233, 238, 279
Mendeleev, Dmitri, 57
Mental Activity, 168
Mental imagery, 114
Mental processes, 114
Mentalism, 168
Menzel, E. W., Jr., 282
Merbaum, M., 160
Mercier, Charles, 167-169, 180-182, 186, 224, 225
Mervis, C. B., 230
Meyer, M. F., 181
Michel, H. V., 110
Microwave oven, 58
Migler, B., 50, 90, 95, 100, 103
Mill, John Stuart, 166, 168, 170, 181, 224
Millard, W. J., 147
Miller, G. A., 115, 238
Miller, Henry 57
Miller, Neal E., 21, 50, 87, 131, 139, 147, 153, 242
Miller, S. L. 110-112
Mind, iv, xiii, xiv, 4, 10, 43, 44, 116, 117, 119, 120, 165, 169, 170, 173, 175, 176-182, 184, 187, 189-191, 193, 194, 202, 223, 224, 240, 241, 242, 281, 299
Mind, 268
Minneapolis, 310
Minsky, M., 144
Mirrors, 14, 45-48, 69-72, 107, 111-114, 120, 148, 242, 281, 284-299; as reinforcers, 286; as social stimuli, 285; as UCRs, 284; self-awareness and, 287; stages of reaction to, 288
Missile, pigeon-guided, 213
Missiles, 310
Modeling, 109
Modgil, C., iv, 223
Modgil, S., iv, 223
Monitoring, self, 261
Monkeys, 69, 71, 112, 120, 258, 282, 284, 286, 287, 289, 291-293, 298
Montevecchi, W. A., 286
Mood disorders, 263
Moore, E. P., 115
Moore, J. S., 173
Morality, 216
Morgan, C. Lloyd, 180, 239-241, 250

Morgan's Canon, 180, 241, 240
Morse, W. H., 251
Mowrer, O. H., 23, 81, 100, 131, 138
Mozart, Wolfgang Amadeus, 39, 53, 56
Mr. Fool, 185
Mulick, J. A., 131
Müller, Georg Elias, 179
Multiple controlling stimuli, 17, 21, 23, 50, 58, 90, 103, 217-220
Multiple repertoires, 10, 23, 50, 100, 135, 219
Mundinger, P. C., 147
Murphy, G., 111
Murphy, Liz, xvi
Mutations, 214

National Academy of Sciences, 52
National Academy Press, 178
National Enquirer, 67
National Institute of Health, xvi
National Science Foundation, xvi, 178, 271
National University, xvi
Nativism, 4, 221
Natsoulas, T., 176
Natural category, 45
Natural history, 166
Naturally Intelligent Software, xvi
Nature, iii
The Nature of the Physical World, 5
Navarick, D. J., 161
Negative modeling, 258
Neisser, U., 44, 115, 238
Neuringer, C., 23, 132, 142
The Neurosciences Institute, iii
Nevin, J. A., 166
New York Times, 67, 276
New York University, 168
Newell, A., 114, 117, 238, 268, 270, 334, 114, 117, 238, 268
Newman, E. B., 187
Newton, Isaac, 280
Nobel Prize, 56
Nordquist, V. M., 251
Norman, D. A., 299
Northeastern University, 190
Notterman, M., 100, 131, 137, 251
Novel behavior, 13, 15, 22, 34, 37-40, 42, 89, 97, 112, 120, 135, 144, 221

Index 355

Novelty, measurement of, 39
Novelty, sources of, 38
Nurnberger, J. I., 160

Objective psychology, 171, 173-175, 171
Ockham, William of, 237, 239, 240
Ockham's razor, 242, 245, 281
Oddity task, 233
Oden, G., 230, 232
Odysseus, 162
O'Kelley, L. I., 23, 81, 131, 138
O'Leary, K. D., 137
Olson, R., 286
Olvera, D., 121
Ontological Relativity, 116
Operant aggression, 249
Operant behavior, 73, 130, 135, 166, 171, 172, 178, 191, 197, 198, 210, 211, 212, 214, 234, 249, 286, 298
Operant conditioning, 171
Orbach, J., 285, 286, 294
O'Reilly, J., 42, 100, 131, 137
Organismic psychology, 173
Orgel, L. E., 110
Osborn, A. F., 42
Ostancow, P., 285
Outlines of Psychology, 43
Overcorrection, 260
Oxford English Dictionary, 166, 167, 180, 223, 299

Parenting, authoritarian, 264
Parenting, authoritative, 264
Parker, T. J., 166
PARRY, 274
Parsimony, iv, x, 45, 46, 237, 239-242, 244, 245
Parsons, H. M., 268
Parsons, Talcott, 168
Parthenon, 207
Patent Office, xv
Pather Panchali, 204
Pavlov, Ivan P., 14, 241
Peace, 313
Pennypacker, H., 187
Perception, 44, 116, 175, 176, 231, 232, 234, 282, 288
Peri Psyches, 179, 223
Perry, James, 168, 169
Peters, R. S., 186

Pettito, L. A., 119, 243
Phillips, J. S., 160
Philosopher's stone, 177
A Philosophical Introduction to Ethics, 167
Phrenologists, 279
Phrenology, 173
Physics, xv, 5, 43, 49, 50, 59, 120, 165, 174, 194, 196, 239
Picasso, Pablo, 51
Pigeons, iii, iv, ix-xi, xv, 13-16, 16-24, 30, 33, 34, 39-42, 44, 46-50, 53, 54, 63-67, 69-72, 73-75, 76-78, 83-87, 89-93, 96, 99-101, 103-105, 107, 111-115, 119, 125-127, 129, 131, 132, 137, 139-142, 145, 147, 148, 151-155, 157, 158, 162, 183, 186, 202, 209, 211-213, 215-218, 230, 234, 237, 243-245, 286, 295-297, 307, 310, 311; Jack, 41, 64-67, 73-76, 98, 234; Jill, 41, 64-67, 73-76
Pillard, R., 108
Pinkston, S., 143, 251
Pinto, J., 110
Place, U. T., 40
Planet of the Apes, 276
Plausibility, 113, 114
Plausibility proof, 110
Poincaré, Henri, 9, 41, 54, 105, 215
Polaroid, 55
Poling, A., iii
Pomerantz, J., 44
Pongidocentrism, 294
Popular Science, 277
Porter, J. P., 50, 147, 152
Posner, M., 231, 234
Practice, positive, 260
Prakash, O., 282
Pratt, C. L., 287
Praxeology, 166-169
Praxics, iv, x, xiv, 31, 37, 43, 49, 120, 165, 169, 173, 174, 176-179, 181, 182, 183, 185, 186, 189, 191, 193-198, 224; "Praxics in the Year 2000," 194; The Praxics Society, 183, 185, 186; praxists, 43, 49, 165, 173, 176, 177-179, 190, 197, 224
Praxiology, 165-170, 173, 174, 180, 186, 193, 196; praxiologist, 167,

168
Praxis, 165, 224
Praxology, 167, 168
Predictability, 6
Premack, D., 119, 162, 234, 241, 243, 282, 294
Pribram, K., 291
Primer of Physiological Psychology, 180, 223
Principia, 280
Principles of Praxiology, 186
Probability, 212
Probability profile, 9, 27-29, 33, 98, 219, 220
Problem solving, xi, 37, 49, 53, 77, 80, 83, 87, 107, 108, 135, 137, 144, 214, 215, 238, 298
Problem solving, 214
Proceedings of the National Academy of Sciences, iv
Proctology, 170
Prolegomena to Praxiology, 169, 193
Property as explanation, 280
Pryor, K. W., 42, 100, 131, 137, 139
Psyche, 171, 179, 195, 223, 283
Psychiatric Dictionary, 167
Psychic research, 170, 173
Psychobiology, 173
Psychological Perspectives on the Self, iv
The Psychological Record, iii, iv
The Psychological Review, 171
Psychological Science, iv
Psychology, iii, iv, x, xii, xiii, xiv, 4, 5, 23, 31, 43, 44, 98, 110, 119, 138, 165, 166, 167, 169-171, 173-175, 177-187, 189-191, 193-195, 204, 208, 214, 215, 223, 224, 230, 233, 234, 237, 240, 243, 272, 276, 279, 288, 305, 307, 309; cognitive, 43, 44, 110, 181, 190, 194, 215, 243, 317, 324, 329, 333; functional, 179; interbehavioral, 173; organismic, 173; scientific, 173
"Psychology as the Behaviorist Views It," 174
Psychology from the Standpoint of a Behaviorist, 174
Psychology, the Study of Behavior, 180

Psychotherapy, 137
Punishment, iv, x, 7, 131, 138, 153, 154, 157, 160-162, 205, 220, 221, 247, 248, 249, 251-253, 255-259, 261, 263-265; alternatives to, 247, 257, 259, 260, 263; and anger, 265; and children, 255; and stress-management, 265; anxiety and, 263; by-products of, 247; delayed, 153, 160, 161; negative side effects of, 248, 250, 258, 259; sexual problems and, 263
Pyle, Gallinaceous, iv, 307
Pylyshyn, Z., 44

Quantum mechanics, 50
Quine, W. V., 116, 175, 230, 268

Rabbi, 305
Rachlin, Howard, 67, 137, 160-162, 176
Radano, S. C., 292
Randy, 3, 4, 6, 7, 11
Rate of responding, 212
Rats, 138
Rawson, R. A., 50, 81, 100, 131, 135, 139
Raytheon, 58
Reaction time, 43
Reader's Digest, iii, iv
Recorder, 207
Reeke, G., 115
Reese, Ellen P., 198, 310
Reese, W. I., 167
Reflections on Behaviorism and Society, 208
Reflex preparations, 210
Reflexology, 173
Regression, 138; habit, 138; instrumental act, 138
Rehearsal, behavioral, 260
Reid, D. H., 134, 251
Reification, 280
Reinforcement, iv, ix, x, 7, 8, 14, 23, 27, 40, 42, 46, 48, 66, 72, 79-81, 87, 92, 93, 95-97, 108, 114, 120, 125, 127, 130-135, 137, 139, 140, 142, 143, 152-154, 157, 158, 160-162, 203, 205, 211, 212, 215, 219-221, 247-252, 260-262, 295, 298; chain schedules, 154, 157,

Index

158; concurrent VI schedules, 145; contingencies of, 208, 249, 250, 297; free, 134; immediate, 153, 160, 161; schedules of, 137, 249; VI schedules, 142, 154; VT schedule, 142
Representation, 242, 282
Rescorla, R. A., 130
Research Methods in Applied Behavior Analysis, iii
Resurgence, iv, ix, x, 8, 23, 27, 29, 33, 46, 50, 57, 80, 90, 95, 97, 98, 100, 103, 123, 125-132, 134, 135, 137-139, 141-145, 218-220, 251
Retrogression, 138
Reynolds, G. S., 137
Rhode. G., 250
Rincover, A., 250
The Rise of the West, 204
Risk, 57
Risley, T., 162
Ritter, W. E., 46, 284
Roback, A. A., 186
Robertson, L., iii
Robinson Crusoe, 168
Robinson, E. M., 291
Rogers, C. M., 282
Roitblat, H., 241, 244
Rolston, H. L., 244
Romanes, G. J., 240, 241
Rosch, E., 230-234
Rosenthal, T. L., 147
Ross, J. B., 109
Rothenberg, A., 9, 40, 55, 105, 215
Rottschaefer, W. A., 176
Rubbermaid, 59
Rubicon, 5
Rubin, L., iii, 41, 79, 89, 99, 141, 217, 252
Rules, 49, 115
Rumbaugh, D. M., 63, 67, 73, 241, 282, 292
Runco, M., iii
Russell, B., 230, 245
Russell, I. S., 46, 282, 291, 292, 294
Russell, J. M., 175, 176
Rustin, E., 285, 294

Sackett, G. P., 287
Sajwaj, T., 143, 251
Salimbene, 109

Samuel, D., 291
San Diego State University, xvi
Sanders, M. J., 119, 131, 138, 243
Santa Fe, 55
Sargasso Sea, 57
Sarich, V. M., 282
Savage-Rumbaugh, E. S., 63, 66, 73, 241, 242, 282
Schaffer, M., 232
Schiller, P., 15, 77, 217
Schlitz, K. A., 293
Schlosberg, H., 170
Schmidt, M., 284
Schmook, J., 284
Schneirla, T. C., 15, 105, 181, 215
Schoenfeld, William N., 172
Schönbach, P., 230
Schrödinger atom, 239
Schulman, A. H., 287
Schultz, D. P., 183
Schusterman, R., 284
Schwartz, S. P., 114, 144
Schwartz, B., 39, 42
Science, xv, 6, 109, 197, 237, 239
Science, iii, 67, 183
Science and Human Behavior, 207
Scientific American, 271, 304
Scientific psychology, 173
The Scope of Praxiology, 186
Scott, Sir Walter, 279
Scottus, Duns, 240
Sears, R. R., 23, 81, 100, 131, 138, 251
Sebeok, T. A., 119, 243
Sechenov, I. M., 173
Seele, 179
Segal, E. F., 221, 310
Seidenberg, M. S., 67
Selection, 211
Self-awareness, iii, ix, xi, 14, 45, 47, 49, 69, 71, 72, 108, 111, 113, 114, 215, 279, 283, 284, 287-290, 295, 297
Self-concept, iv, x, 37, 44-49, 69, 71, 107, 111, 239, 242, 279-281, 292, 293, 294, 296-299
Self-control, iv, ix, x, xi, 123, 153, 154, 157, 160-162; approach-avoidance model of, 160, 161; choice model of, 161
Self-denial, 162

Self-knowledge, 281
Self-management, 250
Self-recognition, 46, 69, 279, 288, 291-293
Self-restraint, 162
Selfridge, O., 44
Seligman, Martin, 263
Sexual problems, 263
Shakespeare, William, 51, 274
Shaping, 40, 66, 74, 79, 109, 137, 211, 212, 219, 221
Shekerjian, D., 215, 220
Shentoub, S. A., 285, 294
Shibata, Andi, xvi
Shimura, M., 232
Shirley, M. N., 292
SHRDLU, 114
Shurcliff, A., 15, 21, 217
Sidman, Murray, 310
Sigma Xi, iii, iv, xvi
Silicon Graphics, 52
Silly Putty, 58
Simmelhag, V. L., 42, 50, 81, 100, 131, 137, 139, 219
Simmons College, 15
Simon, Herbert A., 114, 115, 117, 120, 238
Simonton, D. K., 220
Simulations, iii, ix, xv, 13, 14, 24, 27, 28, 30, 32, 39, 41, 49, 61, 73, 107-117, 119, 120, 209, 215, 217-220, 238, 268, 269; real-time, 220
Sirens, 162
Skinner, B. F., iii, iv, x, xiii, xiv, xvi, 3-5, 13, 14, 23, 39, 41, 42, 44, 45, 47, 50, 67, 73, 74, 77, 81, 90, 98, 100, 105, 108, 112-114, 119, 120, 125, 130, 132, 135, 142, 144, 145, 147, 160, 162, 165, 169, 172, 173, 175, 176, 178, 181, 184, 187, 190, 191, 195, 197, 199, 201, 202, 203-207, 209-216, 218, 220, 221, 223-225, 230, 240-243, 247-249, 253, 281, 295, 309, 310
Skinnerians, xv
Slavin, R., 23, 132, 142
Sloan Foundation, 271
Slobodkin, L. B., 283
Smith, S. T., 241
Smith, N. W., 173
Smoking, 162

Smythe, R. H., 284
Snyderman, M., 161
Snygg, D., 280
Sober, E., 237, 245
Sociobiology, 182
Software, 115
Solnick, J., 161
Soul, xiii, xvi
Soulairac, A., 285, 294
Spaeth, C., 23, 132, 142
Spear, N.E., 74
Spectrograph, 39, 53, 209
Speed gradient, 138
Spencer, Percy, 58
Spiritualists, 170
Spontaneity, 209, 211
Spontaneous interconnection of repertoires, iii, ix, 14, 30, 37, 38, 40, 41, 89, 99, 100, 135
Spontaneous recovery, 132
Spradlin, J. E., 134
Sroufe, L. A., 72, 120
Staats, A. W., 195, 197
Staddon, J. E. R., 42, 50, 81, 100, 131, 134, 137, 139, 211, 219, 249
Stair, Nadine, 58
Stanford University, 194
"The Star-Spangled Banner," 38
Stein, Gertrude, 186
Stemmer, N., 104
Sternberg, S., 15, 44, 210, 215
Stevens, S. S., 233
Stimulus generalization, 19, 20, 96
Stimulus matching, 17-19, 103
Stimulus problem, 31
Stockholm International Peace Research Institute, 313
Stokes, T. F., 250
Stollnitz, F., 15, 217
Stone, L. J., 292
Straub, R. O., 67
Stream of consciousness, 234
Stress management, 265
A Student's Dictionary of Psychological Terms, 167
Stunkard, A., 153
Sturm, T., 284
Suarez, S. D., 292
Substantialization of abstracta, 280
Suls, J., iv
Sultan, 16, 33, 99

Index 359

Superego, 204
Supernormal stimulus, 287
Surlyk, F., 110
Surrounding, 58
Swanson, E. T., 286
Symbolic communication, iii, ix, 14, 41, 63, 65, 73, 215, 282
Symbolic encoding, 242
Symmetry, 248
A System of Logic, 166

Tanaka, K., 232
The Technology of Teaching, 208
Teleki, G., 282
Teleology, 168
Template matching, 44
Temple University, 190
Tennessee, 256
Terrace, H. S., 67, 119, 243
Theodicy, 189, 190
Theories of Creativity, iii
Thinking, iv, x, xiii, 9, 33, 40, 43, 53, 55, 58, 111, 112, 145, 180, 196, 221, 223, 267-270, 275-277, 292, 303
Thinking computers, 276
Thompson, Dennis S. xvi, 220
Thompson, H., 292
Thompson, R. K. R., 297
Thompson, R. L., 292
Thompson, Travis, 220, 284, 286
Thoreau, Henry David, 185
Thoresen, C. E., 160
Thorndike, Edward L., 14, 240, 293
Thorpe, W. H., 50, 147, 152
Thoughts, 9, 37, 45, 55, 56, 87, 112, 176, 201, 205, 215, 256, 281
Three M's, 261
Three repertoires, interconnection of, iii, 89, 91, 100, 105, 218
TIME magazine, 67
Time out, 261
Tinbergen, Niko, 46, 166, 284, 285
Tinklepaugh, D. L., 291
Tolman, Edward C., 169, 181, 241, 244, 286
Tool use, 21, 23, 77, 80, 105, 145, 243, 282
Topography, 39, 113
Torrance, E. P., 42, 220
Training, 296

Transformation functions, 8, 9, 11, 13, 15, 27, 28, 32, 34, 98
Traub, A. C., 285, 286, 294
Trinity College, 3
Tropology, 171
Tufts University, 267
Turing, Alan M., 267-270, 274, 276, 277
Turing Test, 267-269, 276, 277
Turtle Technique, 260
Twain, Mark, 5
Twardosz, S., 143, 251
Two-string problem, 24-30, 32, 33, 59, 219

Uhr, L., 44
Umiker-Sebok, D. J., 119, 243
Unconditional stimulus (UCS), 284
Undermatching, 250
United Nations, 313
University of California at Berkeley, 169
University of California San Diego, xvi
University of California, Irvine, 269
University of Chicago, 170, 183, 185, 241
University of London, 167, 291
University of Pennsylvania, 184
University of Wales, Bangor, 184
Urey, H. C., 110-112
Utah State University, xii

Van Lawick-Goodall, J., 282
Vargas, E., 195-197
Variability, 6, 131, 133, 137, 139, 145, 209-211, 251, 269;
  mechanisms of, 211
Variance, 148, 229-234
Variation, 25, 37, 38, 40, 42, 141, 211, 214, 230-233, 268, 298
Velcro, 55
Verbal behavior, 45, 90, 207, 214, 221, 251, 281
Verbal Behavior, 207, 214
Voltaire, xvi, xiii
Von Mises, Ludwig, 168, 169
Von Senden, M., 46, 285, 294
Vukelich, R., 121
Vygotsky, L., 229, 230, 232

Wagner, A. R., 130
Wagner, Richard, 204
Walden Two, 182, 202, 204, 207
Waldrop, M. M., 239
Walker, H. M., 250
Waller, M. B., 161
Wallnau, L. B., 292
Walsh, D., 245
Walters, G. C., 251
The Washington Post, iv
Watson, James D., 67
Watson, John B., 169, 170, 172-176, 180, 181, 183, 186, 187, 190, 194, 195, 223, 224
Watson, R. I., 174
Webster's Third New International Dictionary, 167
Weintraub, Joseph, 273-275
Weisberg, R., 77, 83
Weiss, B., 175, 181, 249
Weizenbaum, Joseph, 120, 268, 269
Weltanschauung, 191, 196
Wertheimer, M., 15, 37, 38, 210, 215
Wessells, M. G., 44, 137, 175
Wheeler, J. A., 50
White House, 178
Wicklund, R. A., 280, 286
Willard, M. J., 201
Wilson, G. T., 137
Wilson, A. C., 282
Wilson, E. O., 182
Wine, chilling, 51
Winograd, T., 114

Wired magazine, 277
Wittgenstein, Ludwig, 230
Wittreich, W., 285, 294
Wohlman, S., 297
Wolff, W., 46, 285, 294
Wolff, Christian, 179
Wolman, B., 167
Woodruff, G., 234
Woodworth, R. S., 43
Working Mother magazine, iii
Worm Runner's Digest, iv, 307
Wundt, Wilhelm, 43, 179, 184, 187
Wyatt, W. J., 193

Yale University, 194
Yates, A., 100, 131, 137, 143, 251
Yeni-Komshian, G. H., 282
Yerkes, R. M., 97, 99, 284, 285
Yerkes, A. W., 97, 99, 284
Young, K. R., 250
Yung, Y., 110
Yunis, J. J., 282

Zadeh, L., 230, 232
Zeiler, M., 249
Zeitgeist, 180
Zentall, T. R., 49, 147, 152
Zimmerman, B. J., 147
Zoology, 179, 181
Zulu, 232
Zuriff, G. E., 190
Zwaardemaker, H., 146

About the Author

ROBERT EPSTEIN received his Ph.D. in psychology from Harvard University. At Harvard, he worked closely with B.F. Skinner for five years and edited two books of his writings, *Notebooks* and *Skinner for the Classroom*. Epstein is the founder and Director Emeritus of the Cambridge Center for Behavioral Studies in Massachusetts. He has served as Professor of Psychology and Chair of the Department of Psychology at National University in San Diego and was recently appointed the university's first Research Professor. He is the author of over 70 scholarly and scientific articles. His research has been reported in *Time* magazine, the *New York Times*, and *Discover* magazine, and his popular writings have appeared in *Parenting, Reader's Digest, The Washington Post,* and elsewhere.